THE RITE OF BECOMING

THE
RITE OF BECOMING

Stories and Studies of Adolescence

EDITED BY

ARTHUR WALDHORN

Department of English
The City College of New York

AND

HILDA K. WALDHORN

Division of Psychological Services
Polytechnic Institute of Brooklyn

A MERIDIAN BOOK
NEW AMERICAN LIBRARY
TIMES MIRROR

MERIDIAN TRADEMARK REG: U.S. PAT. OFF. AND FOREIGN COUNTRIES
REGISTERED TRADEMARK— MARCA REGISTRADA
HECHO EN CHICAGO, U.S.A.

SIGNET, SIGNET CLASSICS, MENTOR, PLUME and MERIDIAN BOOKS
are published by The New American Library, Inc.,
1301 Avenue of the Americas, New York, New York 10019

FIRST MERIDIAN PRINTING, 1969

3 4 5 6 7 8 9 10 11

PRINTED IN THE UNITED STATES OF AMERICA

FOR THE YOUTHS

WE KNOW BEST

STEPHEN E., VALERIE M.,

AND

DAVID M.

ACKNOWLEDGMENTS

We wish to thank Leo Hamalian and Edmond Volpe of The City College of New York and Frieda Kurash of The Polytechnic Institute of Brooklyn for advice and suggestions. Our special gratitude is due Arthur Zeiger of The City College for reading and commenting upon our essays, Stephen Waldhorn for conscientious assistance with many technical details in preparing the manuscript, and Richard Congdon, our editor, for his interest and insight. Finally, our thanks go to the persons and publishers listed below for permission to reprint or quote from copyrighted material.

Hermann Hesse. "Youth, Beautiful Youth." Translated by Richard and Clara Winston. From *Diesseits Kleine Welt Fabulierbuch* by permission of Suhrkamp Verlag. Copyright, 1954. Published in the United States by Alfred A. Knopf, Inc., *German Stories and Tales,* ed. R. Pick. Copyright, 1954.

Roy Harvey Pearce. "Robin Molineux on the Analyst's Couch: A Note on the Limits of Psychoanalytic Criticism." Reprinted from *Criticism,* Vol. I (Spring, 1959), 83–90, by permission of the author and The Wayne State University Press. Copyright, 1959.

Jessamyn West. "Sixteen." Reprinted from her volume *Cress Delahanty* by permission of Harcourt, Brace & World, Inc. Copyright, 1946, by Jessamyn West.

Alberto Moravia. "Luca." Reprinted from *Two Adolescents,* by Alberto Moravia, by permission of Farrar, Straus, and Giroux, Inc. Copyright, 1950, by Valentino Bompiani & Co.

Hilda K. Waldhorn. "Two Adolescents." Reprinted (with changes) from *Literature and Psychology,* Vol. XII (Spring, 1962), 49–51, by permission of the author and the editor.

James Joyce. "Araby." Reprinted from *Dubliners,* by James Joyce. Originally published by B. W. Heubsch, Inc., in 1916. All rights reserved. Reprinted by permission of The Viking Press, Inc.

George Gibian. Translation of Anton Chekhov's "After the Theater," by permission of the translator.

Ernest Hemingway. "The Three-Day Blow." Reprinted with the permission of Charles Scribner's Sons from *In Our Time.* Copyright, 1925, by Charles Scribner's Sons; renewal copyright, 1953, Ernest Hemingway.

Joseph DeFalco. Quoted materials from pp. 44–49 of *The Hero in Hemingway's Short Stories* reprinted by permission of the University of Pittsburgh Press. Copyright, 1963.

Sherwood Anderson. "The Man Who Became a Woman." Reprinted from *Horses and Men,* published by B. W. Heubsch, Inc., in 1923. Copyright, 1923, by Eleanor Anderson. Reprinted by permission of Harold Ober Associates.

Denton Welch. "When I Was Thirteen." Reprinted from *Brave and Cruel,* published by Faber & Faber, Ltd. By permission of David Higham Associates and the University of Texas. Copyright, 1949.

Philip Roth. "The Conversion of the Jews." Reprinted from *Goodbye, Columbus* by permission of Houghton Mifflin, Co. Copyright, 1959.

Delmore Schwartz. "In Dreams Begin Responsibilities." Reprinted from *In Dreams Begin Responsibilities.* Copyright, 1938, by New Directions. Reprinted by permission of the publishers, New Directions.

Lionel Trilling. "Of This Time, Of That Place." First appearance in *Partisan Review,* Vol. X (January–February, 1943). Copyright, 1943, by the author and reprinted with his permission.

Phillip Young. "Fallen from Time: The Mythic Rip Van Winkle." Reprinted (in part) from *The Kenyon Review,* Vol. XXII (Fall, 1960), by permission of the author and the editor. Copyright, 1960, by Kenyon College, Gambier, Ohio.

PREFACE

The purpose of this anthology has grown out of the professional concerns of its editors. Sharing an interest in problems of literature and psychology, we have tried for many years—often, admittedly, with less than total success—to avoid the senseless conflict that mars most encounters between literary critic and psychologist. Instead, we have sought a common ground and a common language for mutually profitable discourse. This anthology, we believe, offers students and teachers of English and psychology an opportunity to participate in the dialogue.

We feel but small need to defend our focus on the adolescent. Certainly he is not a newcomer to fiction; three of our stories are by nineteenth-century writers—Irving, Hawthorne, and Chekhov. During the early decades of this century too, writers—represented here by Hesse, Joyce, Anderson, and Hemingway—often wrote about the adolescent. Since the second world war, however, the population of adolescents in literature has exploded, and we have acknowledged their universal presence with stories by six contemporary authors, American, English, and Italian.

For better or worse, the adolescent is one of the emerging heroes (or, some might argue, anti-heroes) of contemporary literature and culture. In his own words, he is "happening," and especially "happening" to writers and psychologists. Within the past fifteen years, for example, full-length novels about adolescence have been written by J. D. Salinger, Carson McCullers, Truman Capote, Vladimir Nabokov, and John Knowles; and, in psychology, extensive studies have been made by Erik Erikson, Peter Blos, Bruno Bettelheim, Edgar Friedenberg, and Selma Fraiberg. For many contemporary writers and psychologists, the adolescent symbolizes the confusion and conflict of the mid-twentieth century. Our intention has been to provide literary and psychological source materials usable in an informed exchange of ideas about adolescence.

Beyond all else, our purpose has been to choose readable stories, whether they are but a few pages long, like Chekhov's "After the Theater," or nearly a hundred, like Moravia's "Luca." For each of the thirteen stories we have demanded that, as Thomas Hardy once wrote, "it must be exceptional enough to justify its telling." We have tried to select stories whose record of "exceptional" experience may induce a shock of recognition in each reader and may jar him to self-discovery.

As the title of our anthology suggests, the subject is adolescence as a dynamic process. In these stories (with a single deliberate exception) an apprentice youth faces some physical, intellectual, or emotional conflict that complicates his *becoming* an adult. What distinguishes an adolescent's experience from an adult's is not the range of problems (they are nearly identical) but their unique intensity. Everything is *new*. In Elizabeth Bowen's novel *The Death of the Heart* the sixteen-year-old heroine protests against her boyfriend's weary cynicism: "But after all, Eddie, anything that happens has never happened before. What I mean is, you and I are the first people who have ever been us." Whether it is the transport of first love discovered or the despair of first love lost, or the early stirrings of rebellion against authority, or the newly awakened consciousness of death, the experience is, for an adolescent, fresh and sudden, and its impact upon his sensibility overpowering.

The emotional disturbance the adolescents in these stories endure, however, should not be regarded as disease. Adolescence, Erik Erikson writes, is "not an affliction but a normative crisis." Trying to formulate identity on several levels—self, sexual, social, and occupational—the adolescent ego commonly vacillates between hope and despair. But more often than not—as these stories suggest—each new conflict strengthens that ego and abets the process of identity formation. Emotional upheaval is, then, a step in an ongoing process. Although the disturbance may settle into a permanent disorder, more often it gives the adolescent a chance to translate a threat into a promise.

Subject matter alone cannot determine literary merit. To help the reader approach the more formal problems of fiction, we preface each story with a brief introduction pointing to those problems of technique and theme most deserving attention. We stress especially the relationship between theme and action, character, setting, style, and point of view.

Also in the introductions we provide biographical data relevant to understanding the story, or, when it may illuminate particular aspects of the story, a broad perspective of the writer's total work. Frequently, too, we suggest by statement or by question areas of theme, technique, or both, in which stories may be compared or contrasted.

Always, however, the intent of the introduction is to guide, not to direct.

Our purpose is to be informative and suggestive, not comprehensive or arbitrary.

Each story is followed by an afterword called "More About This Story." Here we have tried to fuse our knowledge to suggest how critic and psychologist may inform one another to attain the fullest insight into the work of the creative artist. For seven of the stories, we have written our own psychologically oriented analyses, drawing freely and eclectically from the theories of Freud, Sullivan, Jung, Erikson, Horney, Fromm, and others. These analyses make no claim to being either exhaustive or conclusive. Their intention is rather to encourage the student to a more detailed study of his own.

For the other six stories we have used three different methods. Moravia's "Luca" has been treated as if it were a clinical report—an approach hardly likely to win universal acclaim, but one capable of providing more insight than a skeptical reader may at first suspect. To the stories by Hemingway and Irving have been appended commentaries by psychoanalytically oriented literary scholars; to Hawthorne's tale a close analysis by a literary critic hostile to psychoanalytic criticism. For two other stories, we have designed questions to spur the student to apply the literary and psychological insights he has already acquired.

A bibliography of recommended literary and psychological readings appears after each discussion.

Although the teacher may assign any of these stories in any order, we do have a general, though flexible, purpose in our arrangement. For one thing, we have arranged the stories in a more or less ascending order of psychological (though not esthetic) complexity. Moreover, several of the stories cluster about certain themes and have been grouped accordingly: Hesse and Hawthorne about the adolescent and his family; Joyce, Chekhov, and Hemingway about the discovery and loss of love; Anderson and Welch about sexual identity. The stories by Roth, Schwartz, and Trilling—perhaps the most psychologically intricate—treat respectively of religious, dream, and academic experience. Washington Irving's tale has been placed at the close of the anthology deliberately to suggest how loose chronological boundaries of adolescence prove to be when subjected to psychological scrutiny.

AW
HKW
New York City
July, 1965

CONTENTS

Youth, Beautiful Youth

BY HERMANN HESSE (1877–1962)

In the years shortly before the first world war Herman Hesse's plaintive tales of youth—*Peter Camenzind, Unterm Rad, Nachbarn,* and the story reprinted here, "Youth, Beautiful Youth"—captured the romantic imagination of young Germans not yet infected with martial passion. Sharply contrasted with the tortured, involuted fiction he wrote between the two world wars, Hesse's earlier writing celebrates homeland, family, and nature.

Hesse's concern in "Youth, Beautiful Youth" is not to analyze malfunctions of the ego, but to attempt a characteristically German *bildungsroman,* the story of a young man's education and initiation. The narrator thinks of his parents with "feelings of deep gratitude and reverence," and sees about them "an aura of purity and holiness" no other humans have ever since had for him. His relationships with brother and sister, uncle and aunts are all similarly warm, relaxed, and affectionate. Toward his house and its furnishings too, and toward the pastoral valley setting and the tiny village, he manifests unabashed love. In brief, the delineation of youth in this early story (written when Hesse was about thirty-four years old) shows none of the pathology evident in *Demian* or *Narziss and Goldmund,* the psychoanalytic novels he wrote after the first world war about oedipal trauma in adolescence.

Nevertheless, the bright world of "Youth, Beautiful Youth" is not wholly without shadows. During this summer which, the narrator says, "in memory seems to have brought my youth to a close," dark patches lie scattered about. Fragmented memories of earlier moods of rebellion flicker across his consciousness. He recalls when "home life was virtual slavery" and he would slip out after bedtime to drink at the tavern.

1

More significantly, he remembers becoming aware that man is basically a "homeless wanderer," a solitary creature "inescapably alone," more kindred to hawk and wolf than to kinfolk. The narrator projects— faintly but discernibly—the later image of Hesse's tormented Harry Haller, the protagonist of *Steppenwolf* (1927), a novel that has become a *vademecum* for the disenchanted and dislocated youth of our own day.

Far too modestly but not without some justification, Hesse once commented, "I know that I am not a story teller." Some may find the plot of "Youth, Beautiful Youth" thin, the time-shifts often disconcerting and inadequately motivated, and the characterization vague. More than the sum of its parts, however, "Youth, Beautiful Youth" remains a delicate wash drawing—Hesse, incidentally, was a proficient and prolific water-colorist—limning the entry of youth into manhood, an early sketch in Hesse's portrait gallery of lonely men.

THE STORY
TRANSLATED BY RICHARD AND CLARA WINSTON

Even my Uncle Matthäus was pleased, after his fashion, to see me again. When a young man who has been in foreign parts for several years comes back home one day and turns out to have done rather well for himself, even the coolest relations will smile and gladly shake his hand.

The small brown suitcase in which I was carrying my worldly goods was still brand-new, with a sound lock and gleaming straps. It contained two clean suits, plenty of underwear, a new pair of boots, a number of books and photographs, two handsome pipes, and a small pistol. In addition I had with me my violin case and a knapsack full of trifles, two hats, a cane and an umbrella, a light coat, and a pair of overshoes. All these things were stout and new, and moreover, sewed into my breast pocket, I had more than two hundred marks in savings and a letter promising me a good position abroad for the coming autumn. It all made quite a respectable outfit. And now, with my journeyman's years behind me, I was returning with all this equipment. I came back a man of the world to my home town, which I had left as a diffident problem child.

With creeping caution the train descended the hill in great winding curves, and with each turn the houses, streets, river, and gardens of the town below came closer and grew more distinct. Soon I could distinguish the roofs and pick out the familiar ones; soon, too, I could count the windows and recognize the stork nests. And while childhood and boyhood and a thousand precious memories of home were wafted toward me out of the valley, my sense of arrogant triumph at the home-coming slowly melted away. My desire to make a big impression upon all those people down there yielded to a feeling of grateful astonishment. Homesickness, which in the course of the years had ceased to trouble me, assailed me powerfully in this last quarter-hour. Every clump of broom near the station platform and every familiar garden fence became strangely precious to me, and I asked each to forgive me for having been able to forget it and get along without it for so long.

When the train passed above our garden, I saw someone standing at the topmost window of the old house and waving a large towel. That must have been my father. And on the veranda my mother and the maid were standing, also waving, and from the top chimney faint blue smoke from the fire for the coffee flowed up into the warm air and out over the little town. All this now belonged to me again; it had all waited for me and was now welcoming me.

At the station the bearded old platform attendant ran about just as excited as he had always been, herding people away from the tracks, and among the people I saw my sister and my younger brother looking for me expectantly. For my baggage, my brother had brought along the little express wagon that had been our pride all through our boyhood. On it we placed my suitcase and knapsack. Fritz pulled and I followed along behind with my sister. She reproved me for wearing my hair so short now, but thought my mustache handsome and my new suitcase very elegant. We laughed and looked into each other's eyes, and from time to time clasped hands again and nodded to Fritz, who went on ahead with the little cart, but kept turning around to look at me. He was as tall as I and had filled out nicely. As he walked ahead of us, I suddenly remembered that when we had been boys I had sometimes hit him in the course of quarrels. I saw again his child's face and his offended or sorrowful eyes, and I felt something of the same painful penitence I had always felt in those days as soon as my anger had ebbed away. Now Fritz strode along, tall and grown up, and already with blond down around his chin.

We went down the avenue of cherry and rowan trees and passed the upper footbridge, a new store, and many old, unchanged houses. Then came the corner by the bridge, and there as always stood my father's house, with open windows, through which I could hear our parrot chortling, and my heart pounded for joy and for all the memories. I went through the cool, dark stone gateway and down the wide stone walk and hurried up the stairs. My father came down them to meet me. He kissed me, smiled, and patted me on the back. Then he led me silently by the hand to the upper door of the vestibule, where my mother was waiting and took me in her arms.

Then the maid, Christine, came running up and shook hands with me, and I went on into the living-room, where the coffee stood ready, and greeted Polly, the parrot. He recognized me at once, climbed from the edge of his cage roof onto my finger, and lowered his beautiful gray head for me to stroke. The room was freshly papered, but otherwise everything remained the same— from the portraits of grandparents and the china closet to the tall clock with its old-fashioned decorations of lilacs. The cups stood ready on the set table, and in my cup was a small bunch of mignonette, which I took out and stuck in my lapel.

Opposite me sat my mother, looking at me and putting soft rolls on my plate. She admonished me not to talk so much that I should forget to eat, and then she herself asked me one question after another that I had to answer. Father listened in silence, stroked his beard, which had turned gray, and looked at me through his glasses with an air of kind scrutiny. And as I reported my experiences, acts, and successes—without being excessively modest —I could not help feeling that I must thank these two for the best of all.

This first day I wanted to see nothing but my dear old home; there would be time enough tomorrow and later on for everything else. And so after the coffee we went through all the rooms, through kitchen, corridors, and bed-chambers, and almost everything was just as it had been before. The few innovations I discovered already seemed old and obvious to the others, and they disputed over whether these changes had not already been made in my day.

In the small garden that lies on the slope of the hill between ivied walls, the afternoon sun fell upon neat paths and rough limestone edgings, upon the half-filled water barrel and the beautiful, vivid flower beds, so that everything seemed smiling. We sat down on the veranda in comfortable chairs. The sunlight flowed, muted, warm, and pale green, through the large transparent leaves of the syringa. A few bees that had lost their way buzzed about, heavy and intoxicated. In gratitude for my return Father bared his head and said the Lord's Prayer. We stood still with folded hands, and though the unusual solemnity dampened my spirits slightly, I nevertheless heard the old and sacred words with gladness, and I spoke the Amen gratefully.

Then Father went to his study, my brother and sister ran off, and the whole house became quiet. I sat alone at the table with my mother. This was the moment I had long been looking forward to, and also dreading. For though my homecoming was glad and welcome, my life in the past several years had not been entirely pure and innocent.

Now Mother looked at me with her beautiful warm eyes and read my face. Perhaps she was considering what to say and what to ask about. I sat in embarrassed silence, playing with my fingers. I was prepared for an examination that on the whole would not be altogether inglorious, but which in certain of its details was bound to make me feel abashed.

For a while she looked quietly into my eyes. Then she took my hand in her fine, small ones.

"Do you still pray a little sometimes?" she asked softly.

"Not any more of late," I had to say, and she gave me a slightly troubled look.

"You'll learn how again," she said then.

And I said: "Perhaps."

Then she was silent for a while, and at last asked: "But you do want to be an upright man, don't you?"

To that I could say yes. And now, instead of putting awkward questions to me, she stroked my hand and nodded to me in a manner that meant she trusted me, even though I made no confessional. And then she asked me about my clothes and laundry, for in the past two years I had taken care of myself and no longer sent things home to be laundered and repaired.

"Tomorrow we will look through everything together," she said after I made my report, and with that the interrogation was over.

Soon afterward my sister came out to the veranda and asked me to come into the house with her. In the parlor she sat down at the piano and took out the music we'd played long ago, which I had neither sung nor heard for so long, but had not forgotten. We sang songs of Schubert and Schumann, and then we set to singing German and foreign folksongs until it was time for supper. My sister set the table while I talked with the parrot, who was supposed to be a male in spite of his name, Polly. He could say a great many things; he mimicked our voices and our laughter and accorded each of us a special and precisely graduated degree of friendliness. He was most intimate with my father, who could do anything he wanted with him; then came my brother, then Mamma, then myself, and last of all my sister, of whom Polly was a little chary.

Polly was the only pet in our house, and was just like one of the children, having been with us for twenty years. He loved conversation, laughter, and music, but not in his immediate vicinity. When he was alone and heard people talking animatedly in the adjoining room, he listened sharply, joined in the conversation and laughed in his good-natured, ironic fashion. And sometimes when he sat alone and quite unobserved on his climbing bars, when everything was silent and the sun shone warmly into the room, he would begin in deep, contented tones to hail life and praise God. His song sounded like a flute; it was solemn, warm, and heartfelt, like the self-forgetful singing of a child at play.

After supper I spent half an hour watering the garden. When I came in again, wet and dirty, I heard from the walk a half-familiar girl's voice speaking inside the house. Quickly I wiped my hands on my handkerchief and entered. There, in a lavender dress and a big straw hat, sat a tall, beautiful girl. When she stood up, looked at me, and held out her hand, I recognized Helene Kurz, a friend of my sister's, with whom I had once upon a time been in love.

"So you still recognize me?" I said smugly.

"Lotte told me you'd come home," she said pleasantly. But I would have liked it better if she had simply said yes. She had grown tall and very pretty indeed. I could think of nothing else to say and went over to the flowers by the window, while she chatted with Mother and Lotte.

My eyes gazed out on the street and my fingers toyed with the geranium leaves, but my thoughts were elsewhere. I saw a slate-cold winter evening; I was ice-skating on the river between the high alder bushes, sweeping in timorous semicircles as I followed at a distance the figure of a girl who scarcely knew how to skate and was being guided by another girl.

Her voice, grown much fuller and deeper than it had been, now sounded familiar and yet almost unknown to me. She had become a young lady, and I felt not in the least her equal in age and station. Rather, it was as though I were still fifteen years old. When she left, I shook hands with her again, but made a needlessly low and ironic bow and said: "Good night, Miss Kurz."

"So she's back home again?" I asked afterward.

"Where else should she be?" Lotte wondered, and I preferred to drop the subject.

At ten o'clock sharp the house was locked up and my parents went to bed. As he kissed me good-night, my father laid his arm around my shoulders and said softly: "It's good to have you back home again. Are you glad, too?"

Everybody went to bed—the maid, too, had bid us good-night some time before—and after doors had opened and shut a few times, a profound nocturnal silence settled over the entire house.

Beforehand I had got myself a mug of beer and chilled it. I now set it on the table in my room, and as smoking was not permitted in the living-rooms of our house, I filled a pipe now and lit it. My two windows looked out over the dark, quiet courtyard, from which stone steps led uphill to the garden. Up above I saw the pines silhouetted black against the sky, and above them the stars twinkling.

I stayed up for more than an hour, watching the moths flitting around my lamp, and slowly blowing my clouds of smoke toward the open windows. Long, silent processions of images passed through my mind, countless memories of home and boyhood days—a vast, silent host rising and glimmering and vanishing again like waves on the surface of a lake.

Next morning I put on my best suit as a token of respect for my native town and my many old acquaintances, and to make it quite clear that I had done well and not come home a poor devil. Above our narrow valley the summer sky was radiantly blue. A haze of dust rose from the white avenues. In front of the near-by post office stood the mail carriages from the forest villages, and in the street small children played with marbles and soft balls.

My first stroll took me over the old stone bridge, the oldest structure in the town. I contemplated the small Gothic chapel on the bridge, which in former days I had raced past hundreds of times. Then I leaned on the parapet and looked up and down the swift green river. The cozy old mill with the white wheel painted on its gable end had vanished, and in its place stood a large new brick building. But otherwise nothing was changed, and, as of old, innumerable geese and ducks swam about on the water and waddled on the banks.

On the other side of the bridge I encountered my first acquaintance, a schoolmate who had gone into the tanning trade. He was wearing a shiny orange-yellow leather apron. He gave me a groping, uncertain look, but did not quite recognize me. Pleased, I nodded to him and strolled on, while he looked back after me and kept trying to recall.

At the window of his workshop I greeted the coppersmith with the marvelous white beard. Then I looked in on the turner, who let the belt of his lathe hum and offered me a pinch of snuff. Then came the market square with its big fountain and the quaint town-hall arcade. The bookseller's shop was there. And though the old fellow had long ago given me a bad character because of my ordering Heine's works, I dropped in and bought a pencil and a picture postcard. From here it had never been far to the school buildings, and so I took a look at the old barracks as I passed. At the gates I scented the familiar, nervous smell of schoolrooms, and scurried on with a sigh of relief to the church and the parsonage.

By the time I had drifted around a few more of the narrow streets and had been shaved at the barber's, it was ten o'clock, time to pay my visit to Uncle Matthäus. I went through the handsome courtyard into his fine house, dusted off my trousers in the cool passageway, and knocked on the door of the living-quarters. Inside I found my aunt and her two daughters sewing. Uncle was already at his office. Everything in this house breathed a spirit of pure, old-fashioned industry, a bit austere and emphatically utilitarian, but also serene and reliable. It was a house of eternal sweeping, dusting, washing, sewing, knitting, and spinning, and nevertheless the daughters found time to make music, and do it very well. Both played the piano and sang, and if they did not know the more modern composers, they were all the more familiar with Handel, Bach, Haydn, and Mozart.

Aunt jumped up to greet me. Her daughters finished their stitches first and then shook hands with me. To my amazement, I was treated quite like a guest of honor and taken into the visitors' room. Moreover, Aunt Berta could not be dissuaded from offering me a glass of wine and assorted pastries. Then she sat down opposite me in one of the company chairs. The daughters stayed at their work in the other room.

This time I was partly subjected to the examination that my kind mother had spared me yesterday. But here too I was not required to embellish an unsatisfactory state of affairs in the telling. My aunt was passionately interested in the personalities of certain well-known preachers, and she questioned me at length about the churches and ministers in all the towns I had lived in. A few small embarrassments cropped up, but with good will we glossed over these and joined in lamenting the death some ten years before of a famous prelate whose sermons I might have been able to hear in Stuttgart if he had lived.

Then the conversation turned to my fortunes, experiences, and prospects, and we decided that I had had good luck and was well started.

"Who would have thought it six years ago?" she remarked.

"Was I really so badly off then?" I could not help asking.

"No, I wouldn't exactly say that. But still your parents were really worried then."

"So was I," I wanted to say, but on the whole she was right, and I did not want to revive the quarrels of the past.

"I guess that is true," I therefore said, and nodded soberly.

"I gather you have tried quite a number of trades."

"Yes, certainly, Aunt. And I regret none of them. For that matter, I don't intend to keep my present one indefinitely."

"You don't say! Do you mean that? When you've just got yourself such a good position? Almost two hundred marks a month—why, that is splendid for a young man."

"Who knows how long it will last, Aunt?"

"What a way to talk! It will last all right if you stick right to it."

"Well, let us hope so. But now I must go upstairs to see Aunt Lydia, and then drop in on Uncle at the office. So good-by for now, Aunt Berta."

"Yes, adieu. It has been a great pleasure to me. Be sure to come around again."

"Of course."

I bade good-by to the two girls in the living-room and from the doorway called another farewell to Aunt. Then I climbed the bright, wide staircase. And if before I had had the feeling that I was breathing an old-fashioned atmosphere, I now entered one positively antique.

In two tiny rooms upstairs lived an octogenarian great-aunt who received me with the delicacy and gallantry of bygone times. There were water-color portraits of great-great-uncles, antimacassars, purses with bouquets of flowers and landscapes embroidered on them in beads, oval picture frames, and a fragrance of sandalwood and delicate old perfume.

Aunt Lydia was wearing a purple dress cut very plain. Except for her near-sightedness and a faint shaking of her head, she was amazingly youthful and spry. She drew me down on a narrow settee, and instead of talking about the distant past asked me about my life and my ideas. She was interested in everything, attentive to everything I said. Old as she was, and remote and ancestral though her rooms smelled and looked, she had gone on frequent travels up to only two years before. Though she did not wholly approve of it, she had a clear and by no means entirely unfavorable conception of the contemporary world, and she liked to refresh and fill out her view of it. At the same time she possessed a charming and graceful adroitness in conversation. When you sat with her, the talk flowed on without pauses and was somehow always interesting and pleasant.

When I left, she kissed me and dismissed me with a gesture of blessing which I have never seen anyone else employ.

I looked up Uncle Matthäus in his office, where he sat bent over newspapers and catalogues. I had made up my mind not to sit down and to leave shortly, and Uncle made it easy for me.

"So you are back in the country again?" he said.

"Yes, back again. It's been a long time."

"And now you are doing well, so I hear?"

"Quite well, thank you."

"You will drop in and say hello to my wife, won't you?"

"I already have been to see her."

"Oh, you have. Good boy. Well then, that's fine."

Whereupon he lowered his gaze to his catalogue again and held out his hand toward me. As he had picked approximately the right direction, I shook his hand quickly and went out with a contented feeling.

Now the official visits were done with, and I went home to dine. In my honor there were rice and roast veal. After dinner my brother, Fritz, took me aside and led me up to his room, where my butterfly collection hung on the wall under glass. My sister wanted to chat with us and stuck her head in at the door, but Fritz importantly waved her away. "No, we have a secret," he said.

Then he scrutinized my face, and when he saw me looking sufficiently curious, he drew a box out from under the bed. The lid of the box was covered with a sheet of tin and weighed down by several good-sized stones.

"Guess what's inside," he said in a low, crafty voice.

I thought about our former hobbies and experiments and guessed: "Lizards?"

"No."

"Ring snakes?"

"Not a bit."

"Caterpillars?"

"No, nothing alive."

"No? Then why is the box shut so tight?"

"There are things more dangerous than caterpillars."

"Dangerous? Aha—powder?"

Instead of replying he removed the lid and I saw inside the box a good-sized arsenal: packages of powder of varying fineness, charcoal, tinder, fuses, lumps of sulphur, boxes of salt-peter, and iron filings.

"Well, what do you say?"

I knew that my father would have been unable to sleep a wink if he had known that a box of such materials was stored in the boys' room. But Fritz was glowing so with joy and the pleasure of having sprung his surprise that I expressed this thought only by a mild remark and instantly accepted his reassurances. For I myself had a certain responsibility for all this, and I was looking forward to a fireworks display as eagerly as an apprentice to quitting-time.

"Will you go in with me?" Fritz asked.

"Of course. We can set the stuff off at night, in gardens here and there, eh?"

"Sure we can. Recently I set off a grenade with half a pound of powder in it, out on the meadows outside of town. It boomed like an earthquake. But now I'm out of money, and we still need all sorts of stuff."

"I'll contribute three marks."

"That's the boy! Then we'll have rockets and giant crackers."

"But you'll be careful, eh?"

"Careful! Nothing's ever happened to *me!*"

This was a reference to a bad accident I had had with fireworks at the age of fourteen; it had missed by a hair costing me my eyesight and my life.

Now he showed me the supplies and the various pieces he had started, initiated me into the mysteries of some of his new experiments and inventions, and stirred up my curiosity about others that he intended to show me and was keeping a deep dark secret for the present. This took up the whole of his noon hour, and then he had to go back to work. After he left I had no sooner covered up the sinister box and stowed it away under the bed than Lotte came in and asked me to come for a walk with her and Papa.

"How does Fritz strike you?" Father said. "He's grown up, hasn't he?"

"Oh yes."

"And is a good deal more serious, don't you think? He's beginning to outgrow his childish pranks at last. Yes, now all my children are grown up."

Getting there anyway, I thought, and felt a bit ashamed. But it was a glorious afternoon; the poppies flamed in the grainfields, the red corn cockles smiled. We walked along slowly, talking of nothing but enjoyable matters. Well-known paths and orchards, the familiar margins of woods, greeted me and beckoned to me; times past rose up once more, sweet and radiant, as though everything had been good and perfect in those days.

"Now I must ask you something," Lotte said. "I have been thinking of inviting a friend of mine here for a few weeks."

"Have you? Where from?"

"From Ulm. She's two years older than me. What do you think? Now that we have you here, that's the main thing, and you must tell me right out if her visit would bother you."

"What's she like?"

"She's taken the teacher's examination—"

"Oh Lord!"

"Not 'Oh Lord' at all. She's very nice and certainly no blue-stocking—not at all. In fact, she hasn't gone in for teaching."

"Why not?"

"You'll have to ask her that yourself."

"Then she is coming?"

"Stupid! It depends on you. If you think you'd rather have just the family all together, she can come some other time. That's why I'm asking you."

"I'll toss a coin."

"If you feel that way about it, say yes right off."

"All right, yes."

"Good. Then I'll write to her today."

"And send her my regards."

"That will hardly overwhelm her with pleasure."

"Incidentally, what is her name?"

"Anna Amberg."

"Amberg is nice. And Anna is a saint's name, but a dull one, if only because you can't make a nickname out of it."

"Would you like Anastasia better?"

"Yes—that could be shortened to Stasi or Stasel."

Meanwhile we had reached the top of the hill, which from one terrace to the next had seemed almost upon us, but had kept receding. Now from a rock we looked down across the queerly foreshortened, steeply sloping fields through which we had climbed, to the town, far below in the narrow valley. Behind us, on rolling land, the black pine forest ran for mile upon mile, broken here and there by narrow meadows or a strip of grainfield that gleamed in sharp contrast to the dark color of the woods.

"Really, no other place is so beautiful as this," I said pensively.

My father smiled and looked at me. "It is your homeland, son. And it is beautiful; that is true."

"Is your homeland more beautiful, Papa?"

"No, but wherever your childhood was, everything is beautiful and sacred. Haven't you ever been homesick, my boy?"

"Oh yes, now and then I have been."

Near by was a wooded spot where in my boyhood days I had often captured robin redbreasts. And a bit farther on there must be the remains of a stone fort that we children had once built. But Father was tired, and after a short rest we turned back and descended the hill by another road.

I wished I could find out a little more about Helene Kurz, but I dared not bring up her name for fear of exposing myself. In the peacefulness and idleness of being home, and with the happy prospect of several weeks of a lazy holiday before me, my youthful heart was beginning to be stirred by longings and plans for romance. All that was needed was a handy pretext. But that was just what I lacked, and the more I was haunted by the image of that beautiful young lady, the more difficult it became for me to ask without embarrassment about her and her circumstances.

As we walked slowly homeward, we gathered large bunches of flowers from the margins of the fields. This was an art I had not practiced for a long time. In our household Mother had established the custom of keeping not only potted plants, but also fresh flowers on all the tables and chests of drawers. In the course of years a great many simple vases, glasses, and jars had been assembled, and we children scarcely ever returned from a walk without bringing home flowers, ferns, or small branches of trees and shrubs.

It seemed to me that I had not even looked at wildflowers for years. For they look very different when you notice them in passing, with an artistic pleasure, as islands of color in a world of green, and when you kneel or stoop to examine them singly and choose the finest for picking. I discovered tiny hidden plants whose blossoms reminded me of outings in my schooldays, and others that my mother particularly liked or had given special private names. These same flowers were all still to be found, and each of them awakened a memory. Out of every blue or yellow calyx my joyous childhood looked up at me, looked with unwonted dearness and nearness into my eyes.

In what we called the salon of our house stood several tall cases of plain pine. Stuffed into these, standing or lying in confused heaps, was a hoard of books dating back several generations. They were not in any kind of order and were rather neglected. As a small boy I had found and read here *Robinson Crusoe* and *Gulliver's Travels,* in yellowed editions with gay woodcuts. Then I had turned to old stories of seafarers and explorers, and later to a good many more literary works such as *Siegwart, Story of a Monastery, The New Amadis, The Sorrows of Werther,* and Ossian. Later still, I took up the many books by Jean Paul, Stilling, Walter Scott, Platen, Balzac, and Victor Hugo, as well as the small edition of Lavater's *Physiognomy* and numerous sets of pretty little almanacs, pocket-sized booklets, and popular calendars, the older ones illustrated with copper engravings by Chodowiecki, the later ones by Ludwig Richter, and the Swiss ones with woodcuts by Disteli.

Now on evenings when there was no family music-making or when I was not manufacturing firecrackers with Fritz, I could take one or another volume from this treasure store into my room and blow the smoke of my pipe into the yellowed pages over which my grandparents had sighed, raved enthusiastically, and pondered. My brother had gutted and consumed for his fireworks one volume of Jean Paul's *Titan.* When I had read the first two volumes and was hunting for the third, he confessed his crime, but claimed that the volume had been in bad shape anyway.

These evenings were always pleasant and entertaining. We sang; Lotte played the piano and Fritz the fiddle; Mamma told stories of our childhood; Polly fluted away in his cage and refused to go to bed. Father rested at the window or pasted away at a scrapbook for his small nephews.

But I did not at all feel it as a disturbing note when one evening Helene

Kurz dropped in again to chat for half an hour. Again and again I looked at her with a sense of amazement at how beautiful and perfect she had become. When she arrived, the candles on the piano were almost burned down, and she joined in the singing of a two-voiced song. But I sang very low, so that I could hear every note of her rich voice. I stood behind her and looked through her brown hair at the candlelight gleaming golden, saw how her shoulders moved slightly as she sang, and thought how delicious it would be to run my hand just a little over her hair.

Without much logic, I had the feeling that we were linked by certain memories of former days because I had been in love with her around the time of my confirmation. Now her casual friendliness was a mild disappointment to me. For it did not occur to me that the relationship had existed only on my side, and that she had known nothing about it.

Afterward, when she took her leave, I picked up my hat and walked to the glass door with her.

"Good night," she said. But instead of taking her hand, I said: "I'll walk you home."

She laughed.

"Oh, no need of that, thank you. You know it isn't customary here."

"Isn't it?" I said, and let her pass. But then my sister took her blue-ribboned straw hat and called out: "I'll go along too."

And the three of us descended the stairs. I eagerly opened the heavy front gate and we stepped out into the warm dusk and walked slowly through the town, across the bridge and the market square, and up to the steep outlying hill where Helene's parents lived. The two girls chattered away like starlings, and I listened and was glad to be with them and one member of a trio. Sometimes I walked more slowly, pretending I was looking up at the sky for weather signs, and lagged a step behind so that I could see how straight and freely she carried her dark head and how firmly and evenly her slender body stepped forward.

At her house Helene shook hands with us and went in. I saw her hat gleaming for a moment in the dark vestibule before the door clapped shut.

"Yes," Lotte said, "she really is a fine girl, isn't she? And there's something so sweet about her."

"There certainly is. How do things stand with your girlfriend? Is she coming soon?"

"I wrote to her yesterday."

"Hm, I see. Well, shall we go home the same way?"

"Oh, we might go by the way of the gardens, at that."

We walked down the narrow lane between the garden fences. It was already dark, and we had to watch where we were going, for there were many sagging plank steps on the path and loose pickets leaning out from the fences.

We had almost reached our garden and could see the living room lamp burning inside the house. Suddenly a low voice said: "Pst! Pst!" and my sister was frightened. But it was our brother, Fritz, who had hidden in the garden to meet us.

"Stand still and watch!" he called to us. Then he lit a fuse with a sulphur match and came over to us.

"Fireworks again?" Lotte scolded him.

"There won't be much of a bang," Fritz assured her. "Just watch, it's my own invention."

We waited until the fuse had burned down. Then it began to crackle and shoot out small reluctant sparks, like wet gun-powder. Fritz was glowing with pleasure.

"Now it will come, in a second, first white fire, then a small bang and a red flame, then a pretty blue one!"

It did not turn out as he expected. Instead, after some jerking and shooting of sparks the precious invention went up all at once, with a loud boom and blast pressure and a white cloud of smoke.

Lotte laughed, and Fritz was unhappy. As I tried to console him, the dense smoke drifted away with solemn deliberation over the dark gardens.

"We did get just a glimpse of the blue," Fritz began, and I admitted that. Then, almost tearfully, he described in detail the making of his pyrotechnical triumph and how it should have gone off.

"We'll try it again," I said.

"Tomorrow?"

"No, Fritz. Let's make it next week."

I might just as well have said tomorrow. But my mind was full of thoughts of Helene Kurz and was lost in the dream of some wonderful happiness that might dawn for me tomorrow—perhaps that she would visit again in the evening or that she might suddenly take a liking to me. In short, I was now engrossed in things that seemed to me more important and more exciting than all the fireworks in the world.

We crossed the garden to the house and found our parents at the backgammon board in the living-room. It was all so simple and natural and could not be any different. And yet everything has turned out so differently that today it all seems infinitely remote to me. For today my old home no longer exists for me. The old house, the garden, and the veranda, the familiar rooms, furniture and pictures, the parrot in his big cage, the dear old town, and the whole valley have become strange to me and no longer belong to me. Mother and Father are dead, and my childhood home is nothing but memories and homesickness. No road leads me back there any longer.

Around eleven o'clock at night, when I was sitting over a fat volume of

Jean Paul, my small oil lamp began to grow dim. It sputtered and made tiny, anxious noises; the flame became red and sooty, and when I examined it and turned the wick up and down, I saw that it was out of oil. I felt sorry about the fine novel I was reading, but it would not do to go groping around in the dark house now, looking for oil.

And so I blew out the smoking lamp and went to bed in a bad temper. Outside, a warm wind had sprung up and was blowing gently through the pines and the lilac bushes. In the grassy yard down below, a cricket was chirping. I could not fall asleep and again began thinking of Helene. I could hope for no more from this well-bred, beautiful girl than to go on looking at her with vain longing, and that was as painful as it was pleasurable. I felt hot and wretched when I imagined her face, the sound of her rich voice, and her walk, the firm and energetic rhythm of her footsteps as she had walked down the street and across the market square this evening.

Finally I jumped up out of bed. I was much too warm and restive to sleep. I went to the window and looked out. Among wispy strips of cloud the waning moon floated pallidly. The cricket was still singing in the yard. What I would have liked best was to go out walking for an hour or so. But our front door was always locked at ten o'clock, and if it ever had to be opened and used after that hour, this always signified an event, something unusual, disturbing, and adventurous. I did not even know where the door-key hung.

I remembered again bygone years when as an adolescent I had sometimes thought our home life was virtual slavery. And at night, with a guilty conscience and adventurous defiance, I had slipped out of the house to have a mug of beer at a tavern that stayed open late. To get out I had used the back door to the garden, which was fastened only by bolts; then I would clamber over the fence and reach the street by way of the narrow lane between the adjoining gardens.

I put on my trousers—the air was so warm that no more clothing was necessary—took my shoes in my hand, and stole out of the house barefoot. Clambering over the garden fence, I set out on a slow stroll through the sleeping town, walking upstream along the river, which flowed along with muted whispers and played with small quivering reflections of the moonlight.

To be up and about outdoors at night, beneath the silent sky and beside quietly flowing water, is always mysterious and stirs the soul to its very depths. At such times we are closer to our origins; we feel a kinship with animals and plants, feel dim memories of a primeval life before houses and towns were built, when man, the homeless wanderer, could regard the woods, streams, mountains, wolves, and hawks as his equals and could love them as friends or hate them as deadly foes. Night also removes our customary sense of community life; when lights are no longer burning and human voices can no longer be heard, one who is still awake feels solitary and sees himself parted from others and thrown upon his own resources. Then that most terrible of all human feelings, that of being inescapably alone, of having to live alone and to taste and endure alone sorrow, fear, and death, underlies our every thought —to the young and healthy only an intimation and a warning, to the feeble a real dread.

I too felt something of this. At least my ill humor faded and gave way to quiet contemplation. It pained me to think that beautiful, desirable Helene would probably never think of me with emotions like those I felt toward her; but I also knew that the grief of an unrequited love was not going to kill me, and I had a vague premonition that life, mysterious life, held darker abysses and worse vicissitudes than a young man's vacation sorrows.

Nevertheless, my stirred-up blood remained warm and, independently of my will, created out of the sluggish breeze caressing hands and a girl's brown hair, so that this walk late at night made me neither tired nor sleepy. So I walked over the rowen grass of the pale fields on the banks of the river, removed my light clothing, and plunged into the cool water. The swift current instantly forced me to put up a stiff resistance. I swam upstream for a quarter of an hour. Depression and melancholy streamed off me with the refreshing river water. Cooled and somewhat tired, I found my clothes again, slipped into them still wet, and returned home and to bed in a light, tranquil frame of mind.

After the excitement of the first few days I gradually fell in with the quiet normality of life at home. How I had roamed around in the outside world, drifting from city to city, knowing many different sorts of people, sometimes working, sometimes dreaming, sometimes studying, and sometimes spending nights carousing, living for a while on bread and milk and then for a while on books and cigars, a different person every month. And here everything was the same as it had been ten and twenty years before. Here the days and weeks ran on in a serene, even tempo. And I, who had become estranged from all this and accustomed to an unstable life of variegated experiences, fitted into this again as if I had never been away. I took an interest in people and things that I had completely forgotten for years, and missed nothing of all that the outside world had meant to me.

The hours and days ran along for me as easily as summer clouds, without leaving a trace behind; each was a colorful picture and each a floating emotion, rising in a rush of music, sounding forth, and soon fading dreamily away. I watered the garden, sang with Lotte, firecrackered with Fritz, chatted with Mother about foreign places and with Father about the latest events in the world; I read Goethe and Jens Peter Jacobsen, and one thing passed into another and went well with the other, and nothing seriously mattered either way.

At the time what seriously mattered to me was Helene Kurz and my feeling for her. But that too existed like everything else; it moved me for hours at a time, then was submerged again for hours. Constant alone was my pulsating, joyous feeling of being alive, the feeling of a swimmer who moves along in smooth water, unhurried and aimless, without effort and without a care. In the woods the jay shrieked and the bilberries ripened; in the garden, roses bloomed and fiery nasturtiums. I took part in it all, thought the world glorious, and wondered what life would be like when eventually I too would become a real man, old and sensible.

One afternoon a large raft came floating through the town. I jumped aboard it, lay down on a pile of boards, and floated downriver for a few hours, past farms and villages and under bridges, while above me the air quivered and sultry clouds seethed with faint thunder, and under me the cool water of the river slapped and laughed fresh and foamy. I imagined that Helene was along; I had abducted her, and we were sitting hand in hand and showing each other the splendors of the world from here all the way downstream to Holland.

When I left the raft far down in the valley, I jumped short and landed in the water up to my chest. But on the warm walk home my steaming clothes dried on my body. And when I reached the first houses of the town again, dusty and weary after my long tramp, I met Helene Kurz wearing a red blouse. I lifted my hat and she nodded, and I thought again of my daydream, of her traveling down the river with me hand in hand and speaking to me as an intimate, and then for the rest of that evening it all seemed hopeless to me and I thought myself a silly dreamer and stargazer. Nevertheless, before going to sleep I smoked my handsome pipe, with two grazing deer painted on its porcelain bowl, and read *Wilhelm Meister* until after eleven o'clock.

The following evening at about half past eight I went up to the Pinnacle with my brother, Fritz. We had a heavy package with us, which we took turns carrying. It contained a dozen giant crackers, six skyrockets, three large grenades, and a variety of small things.

The air was tepid, blue-tinted, and filled with shreds of cloud in motion, which drifted gently away over the church tower and the peaks of the hills, frequently covering the pallid first stars of evening. At the Pinnacle we first rested for a short while after our climb, and I looked down on our narrow river valley lying below in its pale twilight colors. As I looked at the town and the next village, at the bridges and mill-dam and the narrow, shrub-lined river, the twilight mood and the thought of that beautiful girl stole upon me together. I would have preferred to be dreaming there alone and waiting for the moon. But that could not be, for my brother had already unpacked and startled me by exploding two crackers from behind my back; he had linked them with a string, tied them to a pole, and held them out close to my ears.

I was a little annoyed. But Fritz laughed so uproariously and was so pleased with himself that I was quickly infected and joined in. In quick succession we set off three extra-powerful grenades and listened to the tremendous reports booming up and down the valley and dying away in long, rolling echoes. Then came more firecrackers, squibs, and a large catherine-wheel, and to finish it off we slowly sent one after another of our fine skyrockets mounting into the now black night sky.

"You know, a real good rocket like that is almost like worshipping God," said my brother, who sometimes liked to use figures of speech. "Or like singing a beautiful song, don't you think? It's so solemn."

On the way home we tossed our last firecracker into the shingler's yard, at the nasty yard dog, who howled in terror and went on barking ferociously after us for a quarter of an hour. We came home high-spirited and black-fingered, like two young rascals who have been up to all sorts of tricks. And to our parents we sang the praises of our lovely evening walk, the view of the valley and the star-strewn sky.

One morning while I was at the window cleaning out my pipe, Lotte came running up and called: "Well, my girl-friend is arriving today, at eleven."

"Anna Amberg?"

"Yes. You'll come with me to meet her, won't you?"

"All right."

I was not particularly pleased at the prospect of this guest, to whom I had not given a thought. But there was nothing to do about it, and so toward eleven o'clock I went to the railroad station with my sister. We arrived too early and walked up and down in front of the station.

"Perhaps she will be riding second-class," Lotte said.

I stared incredulously at her.

"She might be. Her family are well to do, and though she hasn't any airs . . ."

I shuddered. I imagined a fashionable lady with mincing manners and a pile of baggage stepping out of the second-class car and finding my father's comfortable home pitiful and myself not at all good enough for her.

"If she's traveling second-class, she may just as well travel right past here, for all I care."

Lotte was annoyed and was going to answer me sharply, but then the train pulled in and stopped, and Lotte ran quickly toward it. I followed her at a leisurely pace and saw her girl-friend getting out of a third-class car, armed with a gray silk umbrella, a traveling-rug, and a modest suitcase.

"Anna, this is my brother."

I said hello, and because in spite of the third class I didn't know what she would think of my taking her suitcase myself, light as it was, I beckoned the porter and handed it to him. Then I walked along into the city beside the two girls, wondering at how much they had to tell each other. But I took a liking to Miss Amberg. Of course, I was a bit disappointed that she was not especially pretty, but to make up for that there was something pleasant about her face and voice that was soothing and awakened confidence.

I can still see the way my mother received the two of them at the glass door. Mother had a knack for reading people's faces, and anyone whom she welcomed with her smile, after a first searching look, could be prepared for a good time in her home. I can still see how she looked into Anna Amberg's eyes and then nodded to her and gave her both hands, taking her into her heart and making her at home without saying a word. My suspicion that the stranger would be an intruder promptly vanished, for she took the proffered hands and friendliness with quiet cordiality, and from the very first hour became part of our household.

With all the acumen of my young years, I decided that first day that this pleasant girl had an innocent, natural serenity. She might not know too much about life, but she was a worthwhile chum. I had a dim suspicion of the existence of a higher and worthier serenity that some can acquire out of trouble and suffering, and some never acquire at all; but this I did not really know from experience. For the time being, I remained unaware that our guest possessed this rare kind of tranquil cheerfulness.

Girls with whom one could chum around and talk about life and literature were not often met within my sphere of life in those days. Up to now I had regarded my sister's girl-friends either as objects to fall in love with or as creatures of no importance at all. To associate with a young lady without constraint, and to be able to chat with her about all sorts of things as if she were one of my own friends, was something new and delightful to me. In spite of being on equal terms with her, I sensed in her voice, language, and way of thinking the feminine tone, and I found this warm and sweet.

Quite incidentally I was rather abashed to notice how quietly and skillfully and with what absence of fuss Anna fitted herself into our life and accustomed herself to our ways. For all of the friends I had ever brought home as vacation guests had always made a bit of a to-do and brought with them an alien atmosphere. Even I myself had been louder and more self-important than was needful in the first days after my homecoming.

At times I was amazed at how little special consideration Anna seemed to require. In conversation I could even be almost rude without seeing any sign that she was offended. How different it was with Helene Kurz, by contrast! Toward her, even in the most animated talk, I would not have dared to use anything but the most careful and respectful phrases.

As it happened, Helene Kurz came to see us quite often during this time, and seemed to be fond of my sister's friend. One day we were all invited to a gathering in the garden at Uncle Matthäus's. Coffee and cake were served, and afterward gooseberry wine; in the intervals we played harmless children's games or strolled decorously along the garden paths, whose neatness and precision of themselves imposed dignified behavior.

It was strange to me to see Helene and Anna together and to talk with both at once. With Helene Kurz, who as always looked wonderful, I could talk only about superficial matters, but I did so in the prissiest tone, while with Anna I could chat about even the most interesting subjects without any agitation or sense of strain. And while I was grateful to her, finding conversation with her relaxing and reassuring, I kept glancing away from her to the other, the far prettier girl whose looks ravished me and yet always left me unsatisfied.

My brother, Fritz, was wretchedly bored. After he had eaten as much cake as he could hold, he suggested several rougher games; some we would not enter into, and others we quickly abandoned. In between he drew me aside and complained that the afternoon was terribly insipid. When I shrugged, he alarmed me by confessing that he had a firecracker in his pocket which he intended to set off later on when the girls would, as usual, take their time about bidding each other good-by. I had to argue hard to dissuade him. He then took himself off to the remotest corner of the big garden and lay down under the gooseberry bushes. But I betrayed him by laughing with the others over his childish bad temper, though I was sorry for him and understood his feelings very well.

My two cousins, Aunt Berta's daughters, were quite easy to handle. They were altogether unspoiled and drank in with grateful eagerness jokes that had long since lost all sheen of newness. Uncle had withdrawn immediately after the coffee. Aunt Berta stayed with Lotte most of the time; she was quite willing to dismiss me after I had a few words with her on the art of putting up berries, which made her very pleased with me. And so I hung around the two girls and in pauses of the conversation wondered why it is so much more difficult to talk with a girl you are in love with. I should have liked very much to pay some kind of homage to Helene, but I could think of nothing. Finally I cut two of the many roses in the garden and gave one to Helene, the other to Anna Amberg.

That was the last entirely unclouded day of my holiday. The following day I heard from a casual acquaintance that Helene Kurz had recently been a frequent visitor to such and such a family, and that an engagement would soon be announced. He mentioned this incidentally, among many other items of news, and I was careful not to let on that it meant anything to me. But even though it was only a rumor, I had in any case scarcely dared to hope for much from Helene, and was now convinced that she was out of reach entirely. I returned home utterly unhinged and fled to my room.

Under the circumstances and with my youthful resiliency, I could not go on sorrowing for very long. But for several days I refused all amusement. I took long, lonely walks in the woods, hung around the house feeling sad and vacant, and spent evenings behind closed windows improvising on the violin.

"Is something the matter, my boy?" Papa said to me, laying his hand on my shoulder.

"I didn't sleep well," I replied quite truthfully. I could not manage to tell him any more. But he said something then that I have often recalled since.

"A sleepless night," he said, "is always a bad business. But it is endurable if we have good thoughts. When we lie still and do not sleep, we easily become vexed and turn our mind to vexatious things. But we can also use our will and think good thoughts."

"Can we?" I wondered. For in recent years I had begun to doubt the existence of free will.

"Yes, we can!" Father said emphatically.

I can still remember distinctly the very hour when, after several days of being bitter and gloomy, I came to myself again, forgot my unhappiness, and began living with others and being gay again. We were all sitting in the living-room over afternoon coffee; only Fritz was not there. The others were merry and talkative, but I kept quiet and did not participate, though secretly I was already feeling once more a need to chat and be lively. As young people will, I had surrounded my sorrow with a wall of silence and defiant obstinacy. After the considerate custom of our household, the others had let me alone and respected my obvious low spirits, and now I could not get up the courage to tear down my wall. A short while before, my feeling had been genuine and necessary to me; now I was pretending it, boring myself with it. Moreover, I was ashamed because my period of penance had lasted so short a time.

Suddenly the tranquility of our afternoon coffee was shattered by a jaunty flourish of trumpets, a bold and challenging run of rapid tones that made us all leap to our feet.

"There's a fire!" my sister cried out in alarm.

"That would be a funny fire alarm."

"Then soldiers are going to be quartered on us."

Meanwhile we had all rushed headlong to the windows. On the street, right in front of our house, we saw a swarm of children, and in the midst of them, seated on a huge white horse, was a trumpeter clad in scarlet, his horn and habit resplendent in the sunlight. This looked-up person looked up at all the windows as he trumpeted; he had a tanned face, with a tremendous Hungarian mustachio. He went on frenziedly blowing his horn, mixing his themes with all sorts of random improvisations, until all the windows in the vicinity were crowded with onlookers. Then he put down his instrument, stroked his mustache, placed his left hand on his hip while with his right hand he reined in the restive horse, and delivered a speech. He was passing through, he said, and only for this one single day would his world-famous troupe be stopping in the town. On the earnest pleas of the citizens he would give a "gala performance" that very evening on the meadow near the marsh. There would be "trained horses, elegant balancing acts and a grand pantomine as well." Admission for adults was twenty pfennigs, children ten. Having given his announcement and made sure that all understood, the rider blew one more blast of his shining horn and rode off, followed by the flock of children and a dense white cloud of dust.

The laughter and the joyous anticipation that the circus rider's appearance had stirred up among us was a great help to me. I took advantage of the opportunity to drop my gloomy airs and join in the excitement of the others. Promptly I invited the two girls to the evening performance. After some demurring Papa gave us his permission, and the three of us at once sauntered down to the meadow to take a look at the show. We found two men busy marking off a round arena and fencing it in with rope. Then they began putting up a high scaffolding. Near by, on the steps of a green van, a frightfully fat old woman sat knitting. A pretty white poodle lay at her feet. While we were looking on, the rider returned from town, tied the white horse behind the van, removed his flashy red garments, and in shirtsleeves helped the others set up the scaffolding.

"Poor fellows!" Anna Amberg said. But I said I couldn't see what there was to pity about them. I took up the defense of the circus performers and praised their free, merry gypsy life to the skies. There was nothing I would like better than to go with them, I said; to walk the tightrope and after the performance take the plate around.

"I'd love to see that," Anna laughed merrily.

Whereupon I took my hat instead of a plate, made the gestures of a man taking up a collection, and humbly asked for a small contribution for the clown. Anna put her hand in her pocket, fumbled for a moment, and then threw a pfennig into my hat. I thanked her and dropped it into my vest pocket.

The gaiety I had been repressing burst out of me with stunning force. I was high-spirited as a child all that day. Perhaps being aware of my own fickleness had something to do with this.

In the evening we took Fritz along and went to the performance. Even before we got there we were akindle with excitement and anticipatory pleasure. At the meadow a crowd was surging aimlessly hither and thither. Children stood about, silent and blissful, their eyes wide with expectancy; young rapscallions teased everybody and knocked one another over in front of people's feet; onlookers settled down in the chestnut trees, and the constable strode around with his helmet on. Around the arena a row of seats had been set up; in the center of the arena stood a four-armed scaffold with cans of oil depending from its arms. These were now lit; the crowd pressed closer; the row of seats slowly filled; and above the arena and the many heads swayed the sooty red flame of the kerosene torches.

We had found places on one of the plank seats. A hand-organ sounded out, and the ringmaster appeared in the arena with a small black pony. The clown came in with him and began a conversation, punctuated by many slaps in the face, which evoked loud applause. It began with the clown's asking some insolent question. Answering with a slap in the face, the ringmaster said: "Do you think I'm a camel?"

To which the clown replied: "Now, sir, I know quite well what the difference is between you and a camel."

"Oh, you do, clown? What is the difference?"

"Why, ringmaster, a camel can work for a week without drinking. But you can drink for a week without working."

Another slap, more applause. And so it went on, and even as I marveled at the crudeness of the jokes and the simplicity of the grateful audience, I myself laughed along with everybody else.

The pony made leaps, jumped over a bench, counted to twelve, and played dead. Then came a poodle that jumped through hoops, danced on two legs, and did military drill. In between, the clown constantly reappeared. Then came a goat, a very pretty little animal that balanced itself on a chair.

Finally the clown was asked whether all he could do was stand around and crack jokes. Whereupon he quickly threw off his bulky clown's costume, appeared in red tights, and climbed up the high rope. He was a handsome fellow and did his act well. But even if he had not, it was a fine sight to see the red figure illuminated by the flames of the torches suspended far up under the dark-blue night sky.

Since the performance had taken longer than planned, the pantomine had to be cut out. We too had stayed out beyond our usual hour, and we set off for home at once.

All during the performance we had kept up a lively chatter. I had been sitting next to Anna Amberg, and though we had made nothing but casual remarks to each other, I had been aware all the time of her warm closeness, and now on the way home I missed it a little.

Because I lay in my bed for a long time without falling asleep, I had time to think about that. And as I did so, I became uncomfortably and shamefully conscious of my faithlessness. How had I been able to give up beautiful Helene Kurz so quickly? But with the help of some sophistical reasoning that night and during the next few days, I settled the matter quite neatly and solved all the apparent contradictions to my own satisfaction.

That night, before finally going to sleep, I lit the lamp again, found in my vest pocket the pfennig coin that Anna had given me in jest, and studied it tenderly. It bore the date 1877—in other words, it was just as old as myself. I wrapped it in white paper, labeled it with the initials A. A. and the day's date, and placed it in the innermost slot of my wallet, as a lucky penny.

Half of my holiday—and the first half of a holiday is always longer than the second—had long since passed, and after a week of violent thunderstorms the summer began to grow gradually older and wiser. But I, as though nothing else in the world was of any importance, steered lovelorn, with fluttering pennons, through the almost imperceptibly shortening days; I charged each day with a golden hope and in gay bravado watched each one coming, shining, and going without wishing to stop it and without regretting its passing.

Certainly this bravado sprang from the amazing insouciance of youth, but my mother was also partly to blame for it. For without saying a word about the matter, she let me see that she was well disposed toward my friendship with Anna. Associating with this intelligent and well-mannered girl had certainly done me good; there was no denying that. And it seemed to me that Mamma would also approve a deeper and closer relationship with Anna. So there was no need for worry and concealment, and I behaved toward Anna as I would have toward a dear sister.

Such a situation, however, was far from what I wanted, and after a while this static chumminess between us at times became almost painful to me. For I wished to emerge from the well-fenced garden of friendship into the broad, unbounded fields of love, and had no idea how I could imperceptibly lure my unsuspecting friend out on the open roads. But out of this very conflict there arose, during the last part of my vacation, a deliciously free state of suspension between contentment and desiring more which remains in my memory as a state of great happiness.

So we passed pleasant summer days in our fortunate household. With Mother I had meanwhile returned to the old relationship of a child, so that I could talk to her about my life without constraint, could confess past faults and discuss plans for the future. I still remember one morning how we sat in the arbor winding yarn. I had told Mother what had happened to my belief in God and had finished by asserting that if I were ever to become a believer again, someone would have to come along and convert me.

At this my mother smiled and looked at me. After meditating for a while she said: "Probably no one will ever come along and convert you. But gradually you yourself will learn that it isn't possible to go on through life without faith. For knowledge is good for nothing, you know. Every day you are apt to see someone whom you thought you knew through and through do something that proves how little you really know people or can be certain about anything. And yet people need something they can rely upon; people need certainty. And then it is always better to turn to the Saviour rather than to some professor or Bismarck or anyone else."

"Why?" I asked. "After all, there isn't so much that we know for certain about the Saviour."

"Oh, we know enough. And then too—in the course of ages there have been individuals here and there who were able to die with self-confidence and without fear. It is said that Socrates was one, and there were some others—but not many. In fact, they were very few, and if they were able to die calmly and composedly, it was not because of their wisdom, but because their hearts and consciences were pure. Very well, let us say that these few people were right—each one right for himself. But how many of us are like them? As against these few, you see on the other side thousands upon thousands of poor, ordinary people who have nevertheless been able to die willingly and with composure because they believed in the Saviour. Your grandfather lay suffering terribly for fourteen months before he was granted relief; yet he did not complain and suffered all that pain and death almost cheerfully because the Saviour was his consolation."

And finally Mother said: "I know quite well that I cannot convince you. Faith does not come through reason, any more than love. But you will some day learn that reason does not cover everything, and when you have come to that point, then in your extremity you will snatch at anything that seems to offer support. Perhaps then you will remember some of the things we have said today."

I helped Father in the garden, and often when I went for walks I would bring back for him a sackful of forest soil for him to use on his potted plants. With Fritz I invented new fireworks and burned my fingers setting them off. With Lotte and Anna Amberg I spent whole mornings or afternoons in the woods, helping to pick berries and look for flowers. I read aloud to them from my favorite books and discovered new places for strolls.

The fine summer days ran into one another. I had become accustomed to being about Anna all the time, and when I thought that this would soon come to an end, dark clouds blackened the bright blue of my vacation sky.

And as all loveliness and sweetness is mortal and has its destined end, day after day of this summer, too, slipped through my fingers—this summer which in memory seems to have brought my youth to a close. The family began to talk of my impending departure. Mother once more went carefully through my stock of clothing, mending a few things, and on the day I packed she presented me with two pairs of substantial gray woolen socks that she had knitted herself; neither of us knew that it was to be her last gift to me.

Long dreaded and yet surprising when it came, the last day finally arrived. It was a fair, blue late summer day, with lacy clouds and a soft southeast breeze that played in the garden among the roses, still blooming in great numbers—a breeze that gathered all the fragrance of the summer until, toward noon, it grew tired and went to sleep. Because I had decided to make the most of the day and not to leave until late evening, we young people decided to spend the afternoon on an outing. That left the morning hours for my parents, and I sat between the two of them on the sofa in Father's study. Father had saved a few farewell presents for me. Now, with a kind of joking tone that concealed his emotion, he gave them to me. There was a small old-fashioned purse with a sum of money in it; a pen to carry in the pocket; and a neatly bound notebook that he had made himself and in which he had written in his austere hand a dozen good maxims. He advised me to be sparing but not stingy with the money; to use the pen to write home frequently; and if I found any more good maxims that my experience had tested, to set them down in the notebook beside those others which in his own life he had found useful and true.

We sat together more than two hours, and my parents told me a good many stories of the past, of our own childhood, of theirs, and of the lives of their parents; stories that were new to me and struck me as important. I have forgotten much of what they said, and as at intervals my thoughts kept wandering away to Anna, I may well have not listened to all of the earnest and weighty things they said. But what has remained with me is a vivid memory of that morning in the study and a feeling of deep gratitude and reverence for both my parents, whom today I see in an aura of purity and holiness which no other human beings have for me.

But at the time the farewell I had to take in the afternoon touched me far more deeply. Soon after lunch I set out with the two girls along the road over the mountain. Our destination was a lovely forest gorge, a steep-walled tributary valley of our river.

At first my solemn mood made the other two silent and thoughtful. But when we reached the peak of the mountain, from where the winding valley and forested hills could be seen through the tall red trunks of the firs, I wrenched myself out of my depression with a loud whoop. The girls laughed and instantly started to sing a hiking song. It was *"O Täler weit, o Höhen,"* an old favorite of Mother's, and as I sang along I recalled many joyous outings in the woods in my childhood and on past vacations. Just as soon as the last notes of the song died away, we began, as though by agreement, to talk about those times and about Mother. We spoke of those times with gratitude and pride, for we had had a glorious youth, and I walked hand in hand with Lotte until Anna, laughing, took my other hand. Then we strode along the whole length of the road that ran on the ridge, the three of us swinging our hands in a kind of dance, and it was a joy to be alive.

Then we climbed down a steep, slanting footpath that led to a brook at the bottom of the deep gorge. From a distance we could hear the brook leaping over stones and ledges. Farther upstream along the brook was a favorite inn of ours, where I had invited the two girls to have coffee, cake, and ice cream with me. Descending the hill and along the brook we had to walk in single file, and I remained behind Anna, looking at her and trying to think of some way to speak alone with her before the day ended.

Finally a pretext occurred to me. We were close to our destination and had arrived at a grassy spot covered with wild pinks. I suggested to Lotte that she go on ahead to order the coffee and have a nice garden table set for us, while Anna and I gathered a big bouquet of ferns and flowers, this being such a fine spot to pick them. Lotte thought this a good idea and went ahead.

Anna sat down on a moss-covered rock and began plucking fronds of fern.

"So this is my last day," I began.

"Yes, it's too bad. But you will surely be coming home again soon, won't you?"

"Who knows? Not next year, at any rate, and even if I do come again, it won't be the same."

"Why not?"

"Well, it would be if you should happen to be here again!"

"You know that's not altogether out of the question. But, after all, your coming home this time had nothing to do with me."

"Because I didn't know you then."

"Yes, of course. But you aren't even helping me. You might hand me a few of those pinks over there."

I pulled myself together.

"I'll pick them by and by. But at the moment something else is more important to me. You see, now I have a few minutes alone with you, and that is what I have been waiting for all day. Because—since I must leave today, you know—well, I wanted to ask you, Anna—"

She looked at me, her intelligent face grave and somewhat troubled.

"Wait!" she interrupted my stumbling speech. "I think I know what you want to say to me. And now I must ask you sincerely not to say it!"

"Not say it?"

"No, Hermann. I cannot tell you now why that cannot be, but I don't mind your knowing. Ask your sister some other time, later on. She knows all about it. We have so little time now, and it's a sad story; let's not be sad today. Let us make our bouquet now, until Lotte comes back. And for the rest, let us stay good friends and be jolly together for the rest of this day. Will you?"

"I would if I could."

"All right, then listen. My case is the same as yours: there's someone I care for and cannot have. But when that's how it is, there's all the more reason to cling to the friendship, kindness, and fun that come your way from other quarters, don't you think? That is why I say let us stay good friends and for this last day at least have fun together. Shan't we?"

I murmured yes, and we shook hands on it. The brook sported in its bed and sprayed drops of water up at us; our bouquet grew huge and vivid; and before long we heard my sister's voice approaching us, singing and calling out. When she reached us, I pretended I wanted to drink. I knelt by the brook's edge and dipped my forehead and eyes into the cold, flowing water for a short while. Then I took up the bouquet and we walked together the short distance to the inn.

There under a maple tree a table was set for us, with ice cream, coffee, and cookies. The innkeeper's wife welcomed us, and to my own surprise I found I could talk and answer people and eat as though all were well. I became almost gay; I made a little after-dinner speech and laughed unforcedly when the others laughed.

I will never forget with what simplicity and kindness and amiability Anna helped me to get over my humiliation and sadness that afternoon. Without betraying the fact that something had occurred between us, she treated me with a wonderful friendliness that helped me to act normal. I was filled with the greatest respect for her older and deeper sorrow and for the serene manner in which she bore it.

The narrow forest gorge was filling with early evening shadows when we started out again. But on the ridge, which we reached after a quick climb, we caught up with the sinking sun and walked for another hour in its warm light before we lost sight of it again as we descended to the town. I looked back at the sun one last time as it hovered, large and pink among the tops of the black pines, and I thought that tomorrow, far from here, I would see it again in foreign places.

In the evening, after I had taken my leave of all in the household, Lotte and Anna walked with me to the station and waved after me as the train slid away into the darkness.

I stood at the window of the car and looked out on the town, where street lamps were already lit and windows glowed brightly. As the train approached our garden, I caught sight of a powerful blood-red flare. There stood my brother, Frtiz, holding a Bengal light in each hand. At the very moment that I waved to him and rode by, he sent a skyrocket shooting straight up into the air. Leaning out, I saw it mount and pause, describe a gentle arc, and vanish in a rain of red sparks.

MORE ABOUT THIS STORY

The complex relationship between Hesse's life and art at once enlightens and puzzles the reader who tries to resolve the paradoxes implicit in them. At first one discovers a romantic esthete, then an earthy realist, and, soon afterwards, a tortured expressionist. Not until Hesse was past fifty could he force into perspective the crises of his childhood, his first marriage, and his world view. Only then could Hesse transcend his self-acknowledged schizophrenic and manic-depressive inclinations and discover what one critic calls "the peace of sincere self-affirmation and life-affirmation." Hesse's sights, however, remained ever fixed on the crucial experience of every man who tries "to find his way to himself."

Significantly, the mood of Hesse's latest work recaptures the serenity found in early stories like "Youth, Beautiful Youth." Eric Peters has written that it is Hesse's "remarkable capacity to pull back into the world of light and air, of lakes, mountains and streams, of browsing cattle and singing children, of men and women going about their daily duties and indulging in simple pleasures, that has prevented him from hurtling into the abyss which must many a time have gaped at his feet." [1] It is, of course, psychologically sound to hypothesize that Hesse's life-long desire for warm, loving relationships had its origin in these early, formative years. Moreover, it is reasonable to suppose that his parents—despite their pietistic, Swabian insistence upon man's innate guilt and their own other-worldliness—transmitted other, more positive values that sustained Hesse through the despair that engulfed him during his middle years.

If, then, we wish to integrate those later years of peace with what Joseph Mileck calls the "years of romantically morbid preoccupation with the sordid and pathetic aspects of his childhood and youth," Hesse's "Youth, Beautiful Youth" affords a valuable link. Something of each mode infuses the story, for though the young man's immediate experience may seem at first glance cloyingly sweet, his memories intrude also sharp images of rebellion and hostility. Unlike most of Hesse's early heroes, however, he is neither pure dreamer nor pure cynic nor pure *isolato*. Rather is he a youth who, vacationing at home and seeking to renew faith in himself, absorbs strength from the comfortable and familiar environment of his childhood and adolescence.

At first, stuffily proud of his self-image as a successful, well-traveled young man of the world, he conceals from himself the fact that he remains in most ways a boy. He cannot, for example, entirely let go his adolescent enthusiasms (like joining his brother Fritz to set off firecrackers) or repress his immature fantasies about Helene Kurz, his early love. With the help of his family and Anna Amberg, however, the youth attains maturity. He suffers in the process, of course, but only mildly, and the result is benign and salutary.

In the quasi-autobiographical portraiture of "Youth, Beautiful Youth," then, Hesse at least temporarily assimilated his resentment toward parental restriction and achieved an integrated, "normal" acceptance of himself, his family, and his society. The young man's lingering nostalgia measures the enduring force and quality of these healthy emotional bonds. Perhaps too strikingly manifest to persuade a modern reader, the abundant love, compassion, and patience are nevertheless undeniably sincere. That they had a lasting and ineradicable effect Hesse's own psychic survival attests. Thirty-four years old when he wrote, "Today it all seems infinitely remote to me . . . and my childhood home is nothing but memories and homesickness. No road leads me back there any longer," Hesse could not have known at that time that such memories were indeed to pave the way back for him. Along that road he was to find respite from shattering years of exposure to an era he felt to be morally depraved and dedicated to the extinction of man's soul.

---

[1] Introduction to *Magister Ludi* (New York: F. Ungar, 1949), p. 11.

FOR FURTHER READING

Hesse, Hermann. "Artist and Psychoanalyst," *Psychoanalytic Review,* L (Fall, 1963), 5–10.

Mileck, Joseph. "Hesse and Youth;" "Hesse and Psychology," in *Hermann Hesse and His Critics: Criticism and Bibliography of Half a Century.* Chapel Hill: University of North Carolina Press, 1962, pp. 148–149, 158–165.

————. Introduction to *Steppenwolf.* New York: Holt, Rinehart, and Winston, 1963, pp. vii–xxv.

Peters, Eric. "Hermann Hesse, The Psychological Implications of His Writings," *German Life and Letters,* I (1948), 209–214.

Seidlin, Oscar. "Hermann Hesse: The Exorcism of the Demon," *Symposium,* IV (1950), 325–348.

My Kinsman, Major Molineux

BY NATHANIEL HAWTHORNE (1804–1864)

Although Nathaniel Hawthorne rejected the intolerance and dogmatic Calvinism of his Puritan ancestors, he was, like them, intensely aware of sin and evil. Enterprising, productive, and successful in his mature years (after a dozen grim years of self-imposed solitude during his youth), Hawthorne nevertheless saw man darkly. Unlike the Transcendental optimists, he feared that "so long as the human heart remains unpurified, all the wrongs and miseries will again issue forth from that foul cavern."

In his novels and tales, Hawthorne sought "the truth of the human heart." Archetypal patterns of struggle—good and evil, man and nature, reason and emotion, pride and humility—filled his thoughts, his notebooks, and his fiction. As a result, his characters occasionally seem more allegorical than real, merely emblematic and bloodless moral abstractions. At his best, however—as in "Young Goodman Brown," "Roger Malvin's Burial," "My Kinsman, Major Molineux," and, of course, *The Scarlet Letter*—Hawthorne transmutes allegory to symbol and fuses character, incident, and moral into art.

Critics have almost unanimously acclaimed "My Kinsman, Major Molineux" as one of Hawthorne's most effective tales, especially because its control of structure, symbol, and theme keeps the boy's experience credible on a literal, realistic level even as it plunges below the surface of the rational toward the tangled depths of the unconscious. Color imagery and a subtly effective interplay of images of light and dark underscore the symbolic initiation rite of the innocent, country-bred Robin into the nightmare world of experience. Hawthorne's tale is about many things, but it is also a celebration of the *rite de passage*, the

31

journey from adolescence to maturity. Note, for example, Robin's emergence from the carefree forest of his boyhood, his Hades-like ferry trip, his meanderings through the dark, labyrinthine streets of the city, his profound loneliness, doubts, fears, and yearning for escape. Always, however, he is inexorably thrust toward the climactic episode of his ritual, the brutal humiliation of the Major, a gruesome scene in which Robin himself participates in the terrible mockery of his kinsman.

On a simpler level, Hawthorne's story is, as Q. D. Leavis has noted, "the prophetic forecast of the rejection of England," with Robin the symbol of Young America, the Major a "representative in New England of the British civil and military rule." Though valid, the historical analysis skims the surface of a tale whose meanings must be dug from within. Each person, place, and object contributes to an awareness of Robin's development, and, without embarking on a wild symbol search, the reader should be alert for important signposts along the way. Above all, he should study the import of Robin's quest and the implications of its resolution. What, in other words, does Robin seek in the image of his kinsman? Is the Major king and country, authority, tradition? Or is he a surrogate father-image, an Oedipal figure who must be destroyed but whose destruction breeds endless guilt in his destroyer?

"My Kinsman, Major Molineux" is a story rich in psychological implications, ambiguous, as is "the truth of the human heart," but never wilfully obscure. In it, as Hyatt Waggoner has observed, "form is significant, technique is revelation, images are functional."

THE STORY[1]

After the kings of Great Britain had assumed the right of appointing the colonial governors, the measures of the latter seldom met with the ready and generous approbation which had been paid to those of their predecessors, under the original charters. The people looked with most jealous scrutiny to the exercise of power which did not emanate from themselves, and they usually rewarded their rulers with slender gratitude for the compliances by which, in softening their instructions from beyond the sea, they had incurred the reprehension of those who gave them. The annals of Massachusetts Bay will inform us, that of six governors in the space of about forty years from the surrender of the old charter, under James II., two imprisoned by a popular insurrection; a third, as Hutchinson inclines to believe, was driven from the province by the whizzing of a musket-ball; a fourth, in the opinion of the same historian, was hastened to his grave by continual bickerings with the House of Representatives; and the remaining two, as well as their successors,

---

[1] First published in *The Token* (1832) and later in *The Snow Image and Other Tales* (1852).

till the Revolution, were favored with few and brief intervals of peaceful sway. The inferior members of the court party, in times of high political excitement, led scarcely a more desirable life. These remarks may serve as a preface to the following adventures, which chanced upon a summer night, not far from a hundred years ago. The reader, in order to avoid a long and dry detail of colonial affairs, is requested to dispense with an account of the train of circumstances that had caused much temporary inflammation of the popular mind.

It was near nine o'clock of a moonlight evening, when a boat crossed the ferry with a single passenger, who had obtained his conveyance at that unusual hour by the promise of an extra fare. While he stood on the landing-place, searching in either pocket for the means of fulfilling his agreement, the ferryman lifted a lantern, by the aid of which, and the newly risen moon, he took a very accurate survey of the stranger's figure. He was a youth of barely eighteen years, evidently country-bred, and now, as it should seem, upon his first visit to town. He was clad in a coarse gray coat, well worn, but in excellent repair; his under garments were durably constructed of leather, and fitted tight to a pair of serviceable and well-shaped limbs; his stockings of blue yarn were the incontrovertible work of a mother or a sister; and on his head was a three-cornered hat, which in its better days had perhaps sheltered the graver brow of the lad's father. Under his left arm was a heavy cudgel formed of an oak sapling, and retaining a part of the hardened root; and his equipment was completed by a wallet, not so abundantly stocked as to incommode the vigorous shoulders on which it hung. Brown, curly hair, well-shaped features, and bright, cheerful eyes were nature's gifts, and worth all that art could have done for his adornment.

The youth, one of whose names was Robin, finally drew from his pocket the half of a little province bill of five shillings, which, in the depreciation in that sort of currency, did but satisfy the ferryman's demand, with the surplus of a sexangular piece of parchment, valued at three pence. He then walked forward into the town, with as light a step as if his day's journey had not already exceeded thirty miles, and with as eager an eye as if he were entering London city, instead of the little metropolis of a New England colony. Before Robin had proceeded far, however, it occurred to him that he knew not whither to direct his steps; so he paused, and looked up and down the narrow street, scrutinizing the small and mean wooden buildings that were scattered on either side.

"This low hovel cannot be my kinsman's dwelling," thought he, "nor yonder old house, where the moonlight enters at the broken casement; and truly I see none hereabouts that might be worthy of him. It would have been wise to inquire my way of the ferryman, and doubtless he would have gone with me, and earned a shilling from the Major for his pains. But the next man I meet will do as well."

He resumed his walk, and was glad to perceive that the street now became wider, and the houses more respectable in their appearance. He soon discerned a figure moving on moderately in advance, and hastened his steps to overtake it. As Robin drew nigh, he saw that the passenger was a man in years, with a full periwig of gray hair, a wide-skirted coat of dark cloth, and silk stockings rolled above his knees. He carried a long and polished cane, which he struck down perpendicularly before him at every step; and at regular intervals he uttered two successive hems, of a peculiarly solemn and sepulchral intonation. Having made these observations, Robin laid hold of the skirt of the old man's coat, just when the light from the open door and windows of a barber's shop fell upon both their figures.

"Good evening to you, honored sir," said he, making a low bow, and still retaining his hold of the skirt. "I pray you tell me whereabouts is the dwelling of my kinsman, Major Molineux."

The youth's question was uttered very loudly; and one of the barbers, whose razor was descending on a well-soaped chin, and another who was dressing a Ramillies wig, left their occupations, and came to the door. The citizen, in the mean time, turned a long-favored countenance upon Robin, and answered him in a tone of excessive anger and annoyance. His two sepulchral hems, however, broke into the very centre of his rebuke, with most singular effect, like a thought of the cold grave obtruding among wrathful passions.

"Let go my garment, fellow! I tell you, I know not the man you speak of. What! I have authority, I have—hem, hem—authority; and if this be the respect you show for your betters, your feet shall be brought acquainted with the stocks by daylight, tomorrow morning!"

Robin released the old man's skirt, and hastened away, pursued by an ill-mannered roar of laughter from the barber's shop. He was at first considerably surprised by the result of his question, but, being a shrewd youth, soon thought himself able to account for the mystery.

"This is some country representative," was his conclusion, "who has never seen the inside of my kinsman's door, and lacks the breeding to answer a stranger civilly. The man is old, or verily—I might be tempted to turn back and smite him on the nose. Ah, Robin, Robin! even the barber's boys laugh at you for choosing such a guide! You will be wiser in time, friend Robin."

He now became entangled in a succession of crooked and narrow streets, which crossed each other, and meandered at no great distance from the waterside. The smell of tar was obvious to his nostrils, the masts of vessels pierced the moonlight above the tops of the buildings, and the numerous signs, which Robin paused to read, informed him that he was near the centre of business. But the streets were empty, the shops were closed, and lights were visible only in the second stories of a few dwelling-houses. At length, on the corner of a narrow lane, through which he was passing, he beheld the broad countenance of a British hero swinging before the door of an inn, whence proceeded the voices of many guests. The casement of one of the lower windows was thrown back, and a very thin curtain permitted Robin to distinguish a party at supper, round a well-furnished table. The fragrance of the good cheer steamed forth into the outer air, and the youth could not fail to recollect that the last remnant of his travelling stock of provision had yielded to his morning appetite, and that noon had found and left him dinnerless.

"Oh, that a parchment three-penny might give me a right to sit down at yonder table!" said Robin, with a sigh. "But the Major will make me welcome to the best of his victuals; so I will even step boldly in, and inquire my way to his dwelling."

He entered the tavern, and was guided by the murmur of voices and the fumes of tobacco to the public-room. It was a long and low apartment, with oaken walls, grown dark in the continual smoke, and a floor which was thickly sanded, but of no immaculate purity. A number of persons—the larger part of whom appeared to be mariners, or in some way connected with the sea—occupied the wooden benches, or leather-bottomed chairs, conversing on various matters, and occasionally lending their attention to some topic of general interest. Three or four little groups were draining as many bowls of punch, which the West India trade had long since made a familiar drink in the colony. Others, who had the appearance of men who lived by regular and laborious handicraft, preferred the insulated bliss of an unshared potation, and became more taciturn under its influence. Nearly all, in short, evinced a predilection for the Good Creature in some of its various shapes, for this is a vice to which, as Fast Day sermons of a hundred years ago will testify, we have a long hereditary claim. The only guests to whom Robin's sympathies inclined him were two or three sheepish countrymen, who were using the inn somewhat after the fashion of a Turkish caravansary; they had gotten themselves into the darkest corner of the room, and heedless of the Nicotian atmosphere, were supping on the bread of their own ovens, and the bacon cured in their own chimney-smoke. But though Robin felt a sort of brotherhood with these strangers, his eyes were attracted from them to a person who stood near the door, holding whispered conversation with a group of ill-dressed associates. His features were separately striking almost to grotesqueness, and the whole face left a deep impression on the memory. The forehead bulged out into a double prominence, with a vale between; the nose came boldly forth in an irregular curve, and its bridge was of more than a finger's breadth; the eyebrows were deep and shaggy, and the eyes glowed beneath them like fire in a cave.

While Robin deliberated of whom to inquire respecting his kinsman's dwelling, he was accosted by the innkeeper, a little man in a stained white apron, who had come to pay his professional welcome to the stranger. Being in the second generation from a French Protestant, he seemed to have inherited the courtesy of his parent nation; but no variety of circumstances was ever known to change his voice from the one shrill note in which he now addressed Robin.

"From the country, I presume, sir?" said he, with a profound bow. "Beg leave to congratulate you on your arrival, and trust you intend a long stay with us. Fine town here, sir, beautiful buildings, and much that may interest a stranger. May I hope for the honor of your commands in respect to supper?"

"The man sees a family likeness! the rogue has guessed that I am related to the Major!" thought Robin, who had hitherto experienced little superfluous civility.

All eyes were now turned on the country lad, standing at the door, in his worn three-cornered hat, gray coat, leather breeches, and blue yarn stockings, leaning on an oaken cudgel, and bearing a wallet on his back.

Robin replied to the courteous innkeeper, with such an assumption of confidence as befitted the Major's relative. "My honest friend," he said, "I shall make it a point to patronize your house on some occasion, when"—here he could not help lowering his voice—"when I may have more than a parchment three-pence in my pocket. My present business," continued he, speaking with lofty confidence, "is merely to inquire my way to the dwelling of my kinsman, Major Molineux."

There was a sudden and general movement in the room, which Robin interpreted as expressing the eagerness of each individual to become his guide. But the innkeeper turned his eyes to a written paper on the wall, which he read, or seemed to read, with occasional recurrences to the young man's figure.

"What have we here?" said he, breaking his speech into little dry fragments. " 'Left the house of the subscriber, bounden servant, Hezekiah Mudge,—had on, when he went away, gray coat, leather breeches, master's third-best hat. One pound currency reward to whosoever shall lodge him in any jail of the providence.' Better trudge, boy; better trudge!"

Robin had begun to draw his hand towards the lighter end of the oak cudgel, but a strange hostility in every countenance induced him to relinquish his purpose of breaking the courteous innkeeper's head. As he turned to leave the room, he encountered a sneering glance from the bold-featured personage whom he had before noticed; and no sooner was he beyond the door, than he heard a general laugh, in which the innkeeper's voice might be distinguished, like the dropping of small stones into a kettle.

"Now, is it not strange," thought Robin, with his usual shrewdness,—"is it not strange that the confession of an empty pocket should outweigh the name of my kinsman, Major Molineux? Oh, if I had one of those grinning rascals in the woods, where I and my oak sapling grew up together, I would teach him that my arm is heavy though my purse be light!"

On turning the corner of the narrow lane, Robin found himself in a spacious street, with an unbroken line of lofty houses on each side, and a steepled building at the upper end, whence the ringing of a bell announced the hour of nine. The light of the moon, and the lamps from the numerous shop-windows, discovered people promenading on the pavement, and amongst them Robin had hoped to recognize his hitherto inscrutable relative. The result of his former inquiries made him unwilling to hazard another, in a scene of such publicity, and he determined to walk slowly and silently up the street, thrusting his face close to that of every elderly gentleman, in search of the Major's lineaments. In his progress, Robin encountered many gay and gallant figures. Embroidered garments of showy colors, enormous periwigs, gold-laced hats, and silver-hilted swords glided past him and dazzled his optics. Travelled youths, imitators of the European fine gentlemen of the period, trod jauntily along, half dancing to the fashionable tunes which they hummed, and making poor Robin ashamed of his quiet and natural gait. At length, after many pauses to examine the gorgeous display of goods in the shop-windows, and after suffering some rebukes for the impertinence of his scrutiny into people's faces, the Major's kinsman found himself near the steepled building, still unsuccessful in his search. As yet, however, he had seen only one side of the thronged street; so Robin crossed, and continued the same sort of inquisition down the opposite pavement, with stronger hopes than the philosopher seeking an honest man, but with no better fortune. He had arrived about midway towards the lower end, from which his course began, when he overheard the approach of some one who struck down a cane on the flag-stones at every step, uttering at regular intervals, two sepulchral hems.

"Mercy on us!" quoth Robin, recognizing the sound.

Turning a corner, which chanced to be close at his right hand, he hastened to pursue his researches in some other part of the town. His patience now was wearing low, and he seemed to feel more fatigue from his rambles since he crossed the ferry, than from his journey of several days on the other side. Hunger also pleaded loudly within him, and Robin began to balance the propriety of demanding, violently, and with lifted cudgel, the necessary guidance from the first solitary passenger whom he should meet. While a resolution to this effect was gaining strength, he entered a street of mean appearance, on either side of which a row of ill-built houses was straggling towards the harbor. The moonlight fell upon no passenger along the whole extent, but in the third domicile which Robin passed there was a half-opened door, and his keen glance detected a woman's garment within.

"My luck may be better here," said he to himself.

Accordingly, he approached the door, and beheld it shut closer as he did so; yet an open space remained, sufficing for the fair occupant to observe the stranger, without a corresponding display on her part. All that Robin could discern was a strip of scarlet petticoat, and the occasional sparkle of an eye, as if the moonbeams were trembling on some bright thing.

"Pretty mistress," for I may call her so with a good conscience, thought the shrewd youth, since I know nothing to the contrary,—"my sweet pretty mistress, will you be kind enough to tell me whereabouts I must seek the dwelling of my kinsman, Major Molineux?"

Robin's voice was plaintive and winning, and the female, seeing nothing to be shunned in the handsome country youth, thrust open the door, and came forth into the moonlight. She was a dainty little figure, with a white neck, round arms, and a slender waist, at the extremity of which her scarlet petticoat jutted out over a hoop, as if she were standing in a balloon. Moreover, her face was oval and pretty, her hair dark beneath the little cap, and her bright eyes possessed a sly freedom, which triumphed over those of Robin.

"Major Molineux dwells here," said this fair woman.

Now, her voice was the sweetest Robin had heard that night, yet he could not help doubting whether that sweet voice spoke Gospel truth. He looked up and down the mean street, and then surveyed the house before which they stood. It was a small, dark edifice of two stories, the second of which projected over the lower floor, and the front apartment had the aspect of a shop for petty commodities.

"Now, truly, I am in luck," replied Robin, cunningly, "and so indeed is my kinsman, the Major, in having so pretty a housekeeper. But I prithee trouble him to step to the door; I will deliver him a message from his friends in the country, and then go back to my lodgings at the inn."

"Nay, the Major has been abed this hour or more," said the lady of the scarlet petticoat; "and it would be to little purpose to disturb him to-night, seeing his evening draught was of the strongest. But he is a kind-hearted man, and it would be as much as my life's worth to let a kinsman of his turn away from the door. You are the good old gentleman's very picture, and I could swear that was his rainy-weather hat. Also he has garments very much resembling those leather small-clothes. But come in, I pray, for I bid you hearty welcome in his name."

So saying, the fair and hospitable dame took our hero by the hand; and the touch was light, and the force was gentleness, and though Robin read in her eyes what he did not hear in her words, yet the slender-waisted woman in the scarlet petticoat proved stronger than the athletic country youth. She had drawn his half-willing footsteps nearly to the threshold, when the opening of a door in the neighborhood startled the Major's housekeeper, and, leaving the Major's kinsman, she vanished speedily into her own domicile. A heavy yawn preceded the appearance of a man, who, like the Moonshine of Pyramus and Thisbe, carried a lantern, needlessly aiding his sister luminary in the heavens. As he walked sleepily up the street, he turned his broad, dull face on Robin, and displayed a long staff, spiked at the end.

"Home, vagabond, home!" said the watchman, in accents that seemed to fall asleep as soon as they were uttered. "Home, or we'll set you in the stocks by peep of day!"

"This is the second hint of the kind," thought Robin. "I wish they would end my difficulties, by setting me there to-night."

Nevertheless, the youth felt an instinctive antipathy towards the guardian of midnight order, which at first prevented him from asking his usual question. But just when the man was about to vanish behind the corner, Robin resolved not to lose the opportunity, and shouted lustily after him,—

"I say, friend! will you guide me to the house of my kinsman, Major Molineux?"

The watchman made no reply, but turned the corner and was gone; yet Robin seemed to hear the sound of drowsy laughter stealing along the solitary street. At that moment, also, a pleasant titter saluted him from the open window above his head; he looked up, and caught the sparkle of a saucy eye; a round arm beckoned to him, and next he heard light footsteps descending the staircase within. But Robin, being of the household of a New England clergyman, was a good youth, as well as a shrewd one; so he resisted temptation, and fled away.

He now roamed desperately, and at random, through the town, almost ready to believe that a spell was on him, like that by which a wizard of his country had once kept three pursuers wandering, a whole winter night, within twenty paces of the cottage which they sought. The streets lay before him, strange and desolate, and the lights were extinguished in almost every house. Twice, however, little parties of men, among whom Robin distinguished individuals in outlandish attire, came hurrying along; but, though on both occasions, they paused to address him, such intercourse did not at all enlighten his perplexity. They did but utter a few words in some language of which Robin knew nothing, and perceiving his inability to answer, bestowed a curse upon him in plain English and hastened away. Finally, the lad determined to knock at the door of every mansion that might appear worthy to be occupied by his kinsman, trusting that perseverance would overcome the fatality that had hitherto thwarted him. Firm in this resolve, he was passing beneath the walls of a church, which formed the corner of two streets, when, as he turned into the shade of its steeple, he encountered a bulky stranger, muffled in a cloak. The man was proceeding with the speed of earnest business, but Robin planted himself full before him, holding the oak cudgel with both hands across his body as a bar to further passage.

"Halt, honest man, and answer me a question," said he, very resolutely. "Tell me, this instant, whereabouts is the dwelling of my kinsman, Major Molineux!"

"Keep your tongue between your teeth, fool, and let me pass!" said a deep, gruff voice, which Robin partly remembered. "Let me pass, or I'll strike you to the earth!"

"No, no neighbor!" cried Robin, flourishing his cudgel, and then thrusting its larger end close to the man's muffled face. "No, no, I'm not the fool you take me for, nor do you pass till I have an answer to my question. Whereabouts is the dwelling of my kinsman, Major Molineux?"

The stranger, instead of attempting to force his passage, stepped back into the moonlight, unmuffled his face, and stared full into that of Robin.

"Watch here an hour, and Major Molineux will pass by," said he.

Robin gazed with dismay and astonishment on the unprecedented physiognomy of the speaker. The forehead with its double prominence, the broad hooked nose, the shaggy eyebrows, and fiery eyes were those which he had noticed at the inn, but the man's complexion had undergone a singular, or, more properly, a twofold change. One side of the face blazed an intense red, while the other was black as midnight, the division line being in the broad bridge of the nose; and a mouth which seemed to extend from ear to ear was black or red, in contrast to the color of the cheek. The effect was as if two individual devils, a fiend of fire and a fiend of darkness, had united themselves to form this infernal visage. The stranger grinned in Robin's face, muffled his party-colored features, and was out of sight in a moment.

"Strange things we travellers see!" ejaculated Robin.

He seated himself, however, upon the steps of the church-door, resolving to wait the appointed time for his kinsman. A few moments were consumed in philosophical speculations upon the species of man who had just left him; but having settled this point shrewdly, rationally, and satisfactory, he was compelled to look elsewhere for his amusement. And first he threw his eyes along the street. It was of more respectable appearance than most of those into which he had wandered; and the moon, creating, like the imaginative power, a beautiful strangeness in familiar objects, gave something of romance to a scene that might not have possessed it in the light of day. The irregular and often quaint architecture of the houses, some of whose roofs were broken into numerous little peaks, while others ascended, steep and narrow, into a single point, and others again were square; the pure snow-white of some of their complexions, the aged darkness of others, and the thousand sparklings, reflected from bright substances in the walls of many; these matters engaged Robin's attention for a while, and then began to grow wearisome. Next he endeavored to define the forms of distant objects, starting away, with almost ghostly indistinctness, just as his eye appeared to grasp them; and finally he took a minute survey of an edifice which stood on the opposite side of the street, directly in front of the church-door, where he was stationed. It was a large, square mansion, distinguished from its neighbors by a balcony, which rested on tall pillars, and by an elaborate Gothic window, communicating therewith.

"Perhaps this is the very house I have been seeking," thought Robin.

Then he strove to speed away the time, by listening to a murmur which swept continually along the street, yet was scarcely audible, except to an unaccustomed ear like his; it was a low, dull, dreamy sound, compounded of many noises, each of which was at too great a distance to be separately heard. Robin marvelled at this snore of a sleeping town, and marvelled more whenever its continuity was broken by now and then a distant shout, apparently loud where it originated. But altogether it was a sleep-inspiring sound, and, to shake off its drowsy influence, Robin arose, and climbed a window-frame, that he might view the interior of the church. There the moonbeams came trembling in, and fell down upon the deserted pews, and extended along the quiet aisles. A fainter yet more awful radiance was hovering around the pulpit, and one solitary ray had dared to rest upon the open page of the great Bible. Had nature, in that deep hour, become a worshipper in the house which man had builded? Or was that heavenly light the visible sanctity of the place,—visible because no earthly and impure feet were within the walls? The scene made Robin's heart shiver with a sensation of loneliness stronger than he had ever felt in the remotest depths of his native woods; so he turned away and sat down again before the door. There were graves around the church, and now an uneasy thought obtruded into Robin's breast. What if the object of his search, which had been so often and so strangely thwarted, were all the time mouldering in his shroud? What if his kinsman should glide through yonder gate, and nod and smile to him in dimly passing by?

"Oh that any breathing thing were here with me!" said Robin.

Recalling his thoughts from this uncomfortable track, he sent them over forest, hill, and stream, and attempted to imagine how that evening of ambiguity and weariness had been spent by his father's household. He pictured them assembled at the door beneath the tree, the great old tree, which had been spared for its huge twisted trunk and venerable shade when a thousand leafy brethren fell. There, at the going down of the summer sun, it was his father's custom to perform domestic worship, that the neighbors might come and join with him like brothers of the family, and that the wayfaring man might pause to drink at that fountain, and keep his heart pure by freshening the memory of home. Robin distinguished the seat of every individual of the little audience; he saw the good man in the midst, holding the Scriptures in the golden light that fell from the western clouds; he beheld him close the book and all rise up to pray. He heard the old thanksgivings for daily mercies, the old supplications for their continuance, to which he had so often listened in weariness, but which were now among his dear rememberances. He perceived the slight inequality of his father's voice when he came to speak of the absent one; he noted how his mother turned her face to the broad and knotted trunk; how his elder brother scorned, because the beard was rough upon his upper lip, to permit his features to be moved; how the younger sister drew down a low hanging branch before her eyes; and how the little one of all, whose sports had hitherto broken the decorum of the scene, understood the prayer for her playmate, and burst into clamorous grief. Then he saw them go in at the door; and when

Robin would have entered also, the latch tinkled into its place, and he was excluded from his home.

"Am I here, or there?" cried Robin, starting; for all at once, when his thoughts had become visible and audible in a dream, the long, wide, solitary street shone out before him.

He aroused himself, and endeavored to fix his attention steadily upon the large edifice which he had surveyed before. But still his mind kept vibrating between fancy and reality; by turns, the pillars of the balcony lengthened into the tall, bare stems of pines, dwindled down to human figures, settled again into their true shape and size, and then commenced a new succession of changes. For a single moment, when he deemed himself awake, he could have sworn that a visage—one which he seemed to remember, yet could not absolutely name as his kinsman's—was looking towards him from the Gothic window. A deeper sleep wrestled with and nearly overcame him, but fled at the sound of footsteps along the opposite pavement. Robin rubbed his eyes, discerned a man passing at the foot of the balcony, and addressed him in a loud, peevish, and lamentable cry.

"Hallo, friend! must I wait here all night for my kinsman, Major Molineux?"

The sleeping echoes awoke, and answered the voice; and the passenger, barely able to discern a figure sitting in the oblique shade of the steeple, traversed the street to obtain a nearer view. He was himself a gentleman in his prime, of open, intelligent, cheerful, and altogether prepossessing countenance. Perceiving a country youth, apparently homeless and without friends, he accosted him in a tone of real kindness, which had become strange to Robin's ears.

"Well, my good lad, why are you sitting here?" inquired he. "Can I be of service to you in any way?"

"I am afraid not, sir," replied Robin, despondingly; "yet I shall take it kindly, if you'll answer me a single question. I've been searching, half the night, for one Major Molineux; now, sir, is there really such a person in these parts, or am I dreaming?"

"Major Molineux! The name is not altogether strange to me," said the gentleman, smiling. "Have you any objection to telling me the nature of your business with him?"

Then Robin briefly related that his father was a clergyman, settled on a small salary, at a long distance back in the country, and that he and Major Molineux were brothers' children. The Major, having inherited riches, and acquired civil and military rank, had visited his cousin, in great pomp, a year or two before; had manifested much interest in Robin and an elder brother, and, being childless himself, had thrown out hints respecting the future establishment of one of them in life. The elder brother was destined to succeed to the farm which his father cultivated in the interval of sacred duties; it was therefore determined that Robin should profit by his kinsman's generous intentions, especially as he seemed to be rather the favorite, and was thought to possess other necessary endowments.

"For I have the name of being a shrewd youth," observed Robin, in this part of his story.

"I doubt not you deserve it," replied his new friend, good-naturedly; "but pray proceed."

"Well, sir, being nearly eighteen years old, and well grown, as you see," continued Robin, drawing himself up to his full height, "I thought it high time to begin in the world. So my mother and sister put me in handsome trim, and my father gave me half the remnant of his last year's salary, and five days ago I started for this place, to pay the Major a visit. But, would you believe it, sir! I crossed the ferry a little after dark, and have yet found nobody that would show me the way to his dwelling; only, an hour or two since, I was told to wait here, and Major Molineux would pass by."

"Can you describe the man who told you this?" inquired the gentleman.

"Oh, he was a very ill-favored fellow, sir," replied Robin, "with two great bumps on his forehead, a hook nose, fiery eyes; and, what struck me as the strangest, his face was of two different colors. Do you happen to know such a man, sir?"

"Not intimately," answered the stranger, "but I chanced to meet him a little time previous to your stopping me. I believe you may trust his word, and that the Major will very shortly pass through this street. In the mean time, as I have a singular curiosity to witness your meeting, I will sit down here upon the steps and bear you company."

He seated himself accordingly, and soon engaged his companion in animated discourse. It was but of brief continuance, however, for a noise of shouting, which had long been remotely audible, drew so much nearer that Robin inquired its cause.

'What may be the meaning of this uproar?" asked he. "Truly, if your town be always as noisy, I shall find little sleep while I am an inhabitant."

"Why, indeed, friend Robin, there do appear to be three or four riotous fellows abroad to-night," replied the gentleman. "You must not expect all the stillness of your native woods here in our streets. But the watch will shortly be at the heels of these lads and"—

"Ay, and set them in the stocks by peep of day," interrupted Robin, recollecting his own encounter with the drowsy lantern-bearer. "But, dear sir, if I may trust my ears, an army of watchmen would never make head against such a multitude of rioters. There were at least a thousand voices went up to make that one shout."

"May not a man have several voices, Robin, as well as two complexions?" said his friend.

"Perhaps a man may; but Heaven forbid that a woman should!" responded the shrewd youth, thinking of the seductive tones of the Major's housekeeper.

The sounds of a trumpet in some neighboring street now became so evident and continual, that Robin's curiosity was strongly excited. In addition to the shouts, he heard frequent bursts from many instruments of discord, and a wild and confused laughter filled up the intervals. Robin rose from the steps, and looked wistfully towards a point whither people seemed to be hastening.

"Surely some prodigious merry-making is going on," exclaimed he. "I have laughed very little since I left home, sir, and should be sorry to lose an opportunity. Shall we step round the corner by that darkish house, and take our share of the fun?"

"Sit down again, sit down, good Robin," replied the gentleman, laying his hand on the skirt of the gray coat. "You forget that we must wait here for your kinsman; and there is reason to believe that he will pass by, in the course of a very few moments."

The near approach of the uproar had now disturbed the neighborhood; windows flew open on all sides; and many heads, in the attire of the pillow, and confused by sleep suddenly broken, were protruded to the gaze of whoever had leisure to observe them. Eager voices hailed each other from house to house, all demanding the explanation, which not a soul could give. Half-dressed men hurried towards the unknown commotion, stumbling as they went over the stone steps that thrust themselves into the narrow footwalk. The shouts, the laughter, and the tuneless bray, the antipodes of music, came onwards with increasing din, till scattered individuals, and then denser bodies, began to appear round a corner at the distance of a hundred yards.

"Will you recognize your kinsman, if he passes in this crowd?" inquired the gentleman.

"Indeed, I can't warrant it, sir; but I'll take my stand here, and keep a bright lookout," answered Robin, descending to the outer edge of the pavement.

A mighty stream of people now emptied into the street, and came rolling slowly towards the church. A single horseman wheeled the corner in the midst of them, and close behind him came a band of fearful wind-instruments, sending forth a fresher discord now that no intervening buildings kept it from the ear. Then a redder light disturbed the moonbeams, and a dense multitude of torches shone along the street, concealing, by their glare, whatever object they illuminated. The single horseman, clad in a military dress, and bearing a drawn sword, rode onward as the leader, and, by his fierce and variegated countenance, appeared like war personified; the red of one cheek was an emblem of fire and sword; the blackness of the other betokened the mourning that attends them. In his train were wild figures in the Indian dress, and many fantastic shapes without a model, giving the whole march a visionary air, as if a dream had broken forth from some feverish brain, and were sweeping visibly through the midnight streets. A mass of people, inactive, except as applauding spectators, hemmed the procession in; and several women ran along the sidewalk, piercing the confusion of heavier sounds with their shrill voices of mirth or terror.

"The double-faced fellow has his eye upon me," muttered Robin, with an indefinite but an uncomfortable idea that he was himself to bear a part in the pageantry.

The leader turned himself in the saddle, and fixed his glance full upon the country youth, as the steed went slowly by. When Robin had freed his eyes from those fiery ones, the musicians were passing before him, and the torches were close at hand; but the unsteady brightness of the latter formed a veil which he could not penetrate. The rattling of wheels over the stones sometimes found its way to his ear, and confused traces of a human form appeared at intervals, and then melted into the vivid light. A moment more, and the leader thundered a command to halt: the trumpets vomited a horrid breath, and then held their peace; the shouts and laughter of the people died away, and there remained only a universal hum, allied to silence. Right before Robin's eyes was an uncovered cart. There the torches blazed the brightest, there the moon shone out like day, and there, in tar-and-feathery dignity, sat his kinsman, Major Molineux!

He was an elderly man, of large and majestic person, and strong, square features, betokening a steady soul; but steady as it was, his enemies had found means to shake it. His face was pale as death, and far more ghastly; the broad forehead was contracted in his agony, so that his eyebrows formed one grizzled line; his eyes were red and wild, and the foam hung white upon his quivering lip. His whole frame was agitated by a quick and continual tremor, which his pride strove to quell, even in those circumstances of overwhelming humiliation. But perhaps the bitterest pang of all was when his eyes met those of Robin; for he evidently knew him on the instant, as the youth stood witnessing the foul disgrace of a head grown gray in honor. They stared at each other in silence, and Robin's knees shook, and his hair bristled, with a mixture of pity and terror. Soon, however, a bewildering excitement began to seize upon his mind; the preceeding adventures of the night, the unexpected appearance of the crowd, the torches, the confused din and the hush that followed, the spectre of his kinsman reviled by that great multiude,—all this, and, more than all, a perception of tremendous ridicule in the whole scene, affected him with a sort of mental inebriety. At that moment a voice of sluggish merriment saluted Robin's ears; he turned instinctively, and just behind the corner of the church stood the lantern-bearer, rubbing his eyes, and drowsily enjoying the lad's amazement. Then he heard a peal of laughter like the ringing of silvery bells; a woman twitched his arm, a saucy eye met his, and he saw the lady of the scarlet petticoat. A sharp, dry cachinnation appealed to his memory, and standing on tiptoe in the crowd, with his white apron over his head, he beheld the courteous little innkeeper. And lastly, there sailed over the heads of the multitude a great, broad laugh, broken in the midst by two sepulchral hems; thus, "Haw, haw, haw,—hem, hem,—haw, haw, haw, haw!"

The sound proceeded from the balcony of the opposite edifice, and thither Robin turned his eyes. In front of the Gothic window stood the old citizen, wrapped in a wide gown, his gray periwig exchanged for a nightcap, which was thrust back from his forehead, and his silk stockings hanging about his legs. He supported himself on his polished cane in a fit of convulsive merriment, which manifested itself on his solemn old features like a funny inscription on a tombstone. Then Robin seemed to hear the voices of the barbers, of the guests of the inn, and of all who had made sport of him that night. The contagion was spreading among the multitude, when all at once, it seized upon Robin, and he sent forth a shout of laughter that echoed through the street,— every man shook his sides, every man emptied his lungs, but Robin's shout was the loudest there. The cloud-spirits peeped from their silvery islands, as the congregated mirth went roaring up the sky! The Man in the Moon heard the far bellow. "Oho," quoth he, "the old earth is frolicsome to-night!"

When there was a momentary calm in that tempestuous sea of sound, the leader gave the sign, the procession resumed its march. On they went, like fiends that throng in mockery around some dead potentate, mighty no more, but majestic still in his agony. On they went, in counterfeited pomp, in senseless uproar, in frenzied merriment, trampling all on an old man's heart. On swept the tumult, and left a silent street behind.

. . . . . .

"Well, Robin, are you dreaming?" inquired the gentleman, laying his hand on the youth's shoulder.

Robin started, and withdrew his arm from the stone post to which he had instinctively clung, as the living stream rolled by him. His cheek was somewhat pale, and his eye not quite as lively as in the earlier part of the evening.

"Will you be kind enough to show me the way to the ferry?" said he, after a moment's pause.

"You have, then, adopted a new subject of inquiry?" observed his companion, with a smile.

"Why, yes, sir," replied Robin, rather dryly. "Thanks to you, and to my other friends, I have at last met my kinsman, and he will scarce desire to see my face again. I begin to grow weary of a town life, sir. Will you show me the way to the ferry?"

"No, my good friend Robin,—not to-night, at least," said the gentleman. "Some few days hence, if you wish it, I will speed you on your journey. Or, if you prefer to remain with us, perhaps, as you are a shrewd youth, you may rise in the world without the help of your kinsman, Major Molineux."

MORE ABOUT THIS STORY

The essay that follows undertakes to answer a psychoanalytic interpretation of
Hawthorne's story advanced by Simon Lesser. Professor Roy Harvey Pearce,
who teaches at the University of California, San Diego, fairly summarizes
Lesser's argument, then proceeds to his attack.[1]

ROBIN MOLINEUX ON THE ANALYST'S COUCH:
A NOTE ON THE LIMITS OF PSYCHOANALYTIC CRITICISM

In our recent discovery that "My Kinsman, Major Molineux" must be given a
major place in the Hawthorne canon, we have inevitably come to look at the
tale through the eyes of psychoanalytic criticism. Inevitably, because not only is
the critic in our time armed, willy-nilly, with at least some of the forms of psychoanalytic understanding, but also because the tale itself seems to be explicitly a
version of what is for psychoanalysis the crucial segment of man's struggle for
adulthood, the Oedipal situation. Even the merest amateur of psychoanalysis (and
who among us is not forced to be at least this?), armed with the latest paperback
manual, cannot but discover (although he may strive mightily to resist it) the
fact that Robin Molineux (he *is* Molineux, for in Major Molineux he seeks his
paternal uncle) is searching for a father figure; that he has a difficult and confusing time finding him; that his search is charged with a sense of dream work; that
he finds him under deeply traumatic conditions; and that—without quite meaning
to—he helps destroy him even as he finds him. Major Molineux is many things: as
many things as we can fit into that primary psychocultural category in which the
father is at once the loved and the hated, a teacher of the ways toward independence
and a lord who denies the very goal he reveals—an Old Priest in a Grove, a Laius, a
Hamlet Senior, a manifestation of the Old Order, and so on, and so on. This is,
of course, because Hawthorne makes him who seeks Major Molineux first of all a
richly human being in a richly human situation; and as in other magisterial works
of art, that very humanity serves to define our understanding of the category in
which we would place both the sought and the seeker, both teacher and pupil,
both master and slave. If the polysemantic possibilities of all this astonish us,
we have only to recall that it was the richly human Oedipus, in *his* richly human
situation, who gave Freud a name for this primary category and so helped him
finally define it. So it is only right that the critic who moves beyond the psychoanalytic amateurism of most of us should come to devote his study of "My Kinsman, Major Molineux" to what he claims to be an "interpretation" of the actual
texture of the "poet's vision."

The words I have placed in quotation marks come from the epigraph to a

---

[1] For an account of the "historicity" of the Molineux figure see Prof. Pearce's
"Hawthorne and the Sense of the Past; or The Immortality of Major Molineux," *English
Literary History*, XXI (1954), 327–349.

chapter in Mr. Simon Lesser's recent *Fiction and the Unconscious*. The chapter called "Conscious and Unconscious Perception" is, I take it, a crucial one for Mr. Lesser's conception of the critic's job of work. It centers on analyses of two works of short fiction, "My Kinsman, Major Molineaux" and Sherwood Anderson's "I Want to Know Why." (The chapter was printed before its inclusion in the book, pretty much as it stands presently, in *Partisan Review*, XXII [1950], 370-390.) Mr. Lesser finds the two pieces to be variations on a single theme, the search for a father; and I think that I can make my point adequately by dealing only with his treatment of the Hawthorne tale. Mr. Lesser hopes, as he tells us at the end, that his discussion "will suggest not only how much may be unconsciously understood when we read fiction but the close bearing of what is unconsciously perceived upon our deepest and most tenacious concerns." In short, he would reveal to us the unconscious motivations in "My Kinsman, Major Molineux," so as to relate those motivations to our own private, secret ones—to make us conscious of the meaning of the tale and of a segment of our own experience, of each as it interpenetrates the other. The tale, that is to say, in its very artistic structure, in its very artistic integrity, would be a means for our further and deeper defining and articulating our own sense of our selves. Such an intention is, I take it, a properly traditional one for the literary critic. But the usual problems arise. To what degree is the critic's analysis of the unconsciously motivated and motivating psychic structure of the tale valid in terms of the structure as a whole, as objectively, totally given? The one criterion for all criticism, psychoanalytic and otherwise, would be just this: the degree to which the critic has accounted for all that goes on in the tale, all that is there; and then, and only then, the degree to which he has related his total analysis to his sense of the tale's humanistic import.

Mr. Lesser's view of "My Kinsman, Major Molineux," is boldly and simply stated:

> To the conscious mind "My Kinsman, Major Molineux" is a story of an ambitious youth's thwarted search for an influential relative he wants to find. To the unconscious, it is a story of the youth's hostile and rebellious feelings for the relative—and for the father—and his wish to be free of adult domination. To the conscious mind it is a story of a search which was unsuccessful because of external difficulties. To the unconscious . . . it is a story of a young man caught up in an enterprise for which he has no stomach and debarred from succeeding in it by internal inhibitions.

To reach this conclusion he emphasizes matters which, to my knowledge, have heretofore been inadequately attended to: the fact that the difficulties which Robin has are clearly made out to be difficulties of his own unconscious creating—that perhaps he does not want to find his kinsman, perhaps he is afraid to; the fact that he "does not pursue his [search] with any ardor"; the fact that there is something more or less ambiguously sexual about the search—particularly in the episode of the whore who assures him that his kinsman is inside her dwelling, asleep. All these facts are made to point to the now obvious conclusion: that if Robin does find his kinsman, he will have to submit to a kind of authority from which he seems to have wanted to escape when he left home. No wonder, Mr.

Lesser would have us conclude, he is hesitant and confused. And no wonder that when he sits on the steps of the church, waiting to see his kinsman, "he has a fantasy in which he imagines that his kinsman is already dead." In his confusion, in his ambiguity over what he really (unconsciously, as the details of the narrative let us know it) wants. And then when the crowd comes by, with Major Molineux a tormented loyalist prisoner in their midst, Robin (unconsciously) senses that the crowd also wants to free itself of the authority which this old man manifests:

> Without a voice being raised in protest, the crowd is acting out the youth's repressed impulses [to assert his freedom of his father] and in effect urging him to act on them also. The joy the crowd takes in asserting its strength and the reappearance of the lady of the scarlet petticoat [the whore who had earlier invited Robin in to see his kinsman] provide him with incentives for letting himself go. . . . The relief he feels that he can vent his hostility for his kinsman and abandon his search for him is the ultimate source of his "riotous mirth." It is fueled by energy which until then was being expended in repression and inner conflict.

Mr. Lesser's Robin, then, is a youth who is finally freed to become an adult. The question remains: Is this Robin, however unconsciously, also Hawthorne's. The answer is a curious one, I think—and the point of this note. It is: No. But not because this Robin is an untrue or distorted representation of Hawthorne's Robin; for so far as it goes, it is true to our sense of him. Rather, it is an incomplete representation of Hawthorne's Robin. Hawthorne's Robin is Mr. Lesser's and a good deal more. For Hawthorne's Robin is not merely freed to become (perhaps he will, perhaps he won't; we aren't told at the end) an adult. As Hawthorne creates him for us, his freedom is not mere freedom, but rather freedom earned at the expense of guilt. And the guilt is explicitly the fundamental aspect of Robin's relation to his world, the world to which Mr. Lesser, in his psychoanalytic earnestness, pays little or no attention.

The kinsman whom Robin seeks out, tries to avoid finding, but finds only in the destroying—this kinsman, it should be remembered, is pictured as a noble, tragic figure, a loyalist caught up in Revolutionary anti-loyalist violence. And those who destroy him—or torment him—are pictured as a crazy mob. Here the very pseudhistoricity of the tale must be taken into account. And whether or not Mr. Lesser knew that the name Molineux, being that of a famous radical leader in Revolutionary Boston, had a bitterly ambiguous meaning for Hawthorne, or that the disguised leader of the mob is a deliberate evocation of the figure well known as a wild and cowardly leader of the Revolutionary Boston mobs—whether or not Mr. Lesser knew these facts, he should (and indeed does, casually) recognize that the story is ironically introduced by a paragraph rationalizing in a progressivist way the behavior of mobs (as we are told, one of the incidental prices for progress) and that the story recalls at the very least, as every red-blooded American should recognize, something like the Boston Tea Party. Hence, Robin in achieving his maturity is, unconsciously, an agent of progress; his coming to maturity, his struggles toward it, is that of the people for whom, as he helplessly identifies with them, he is a kind of surrogate, or icon. The concern of the story is not just Robin's struggles to free himself from authority, but also the implications of that struggle—with all its ambiguous, fearful, nightmarish quality and its hesitating doubt—for his future as a member of the society for whom he is surrogate and/or icon, and thus of the future of that society itself. The energy he takes from the crowd surely fuels Robin's mirth and enables him to free himself of kinsman-like, paternal authority by pushing him to participate in the tormenting of the old major. But it is also—and we are not allowed to forget it, nor is Robin (witness his mood at the end of the tale)—an energy produced in good part by the destruction of another man: a man who, for all that we and Robin know, is totally innocent of the things for which he is tormented and destroyed. The crowd thus is guilty. Robin shares their guilt. Guilt is the price which Hawthorne makes Robin pay for his freedom.

Mr. Lesser will have nothing to do with such guilt. I think that this is because he is concerned only with Robin and not with the tale as a whole, because in effect he has treated Robin as though he were a patient visiting an analyst and Hawthorne as though he were doing the work of an analyst by creating a situation in which Robin's unconscious will work so as to free him from what an analyst would take to be neurotic (or at least, exacerbatedly normal) dependence. To a degree—and Mr. Lesser shows this with remarkable precision—Hawthorne is that analyst. But his responsibility is not simply to "cure" his protagonist (as patient) and leave him to his own (now refurbished, potentially more or less autonomous) ego-centered devices. Rather it is the responsibility of a creator, who must see to it that one of his creations, his Robin, has an adequate and meaningful relationship with the world which, in the tale, is also his creation. The tale, then, projects a created world—not just a single figure, analyzed evocatively and so remarked as being freed by means of a psychic discharge arising out of his involved relations with his world. That he is freed through that world does not mean that he is freed from it; he is rather freed for and with it. And his freedom—and, for Hawthorne I daresay, all freedom—is dreadful. Its goal is a tragic assertion of the inextricable relation of human freedom and unfreedom in the world.

The imaginative writer makes whole worlds. Analyzable protagonist-patients are only part of them—significantly and integrally part of them, but only part of them. And they have their fullest (which is to say, their ultimate) meaning as they wend their unconscious way through the world which they, as it were, have been created into. Robin is taken off the couch and put into his world; he works through his nightmare and is left with the hard world of reality, in which he discovers (or will discover) that he has been all the time. Then, and only then, does (or will) he become what he really is. Mr. Lesser cannot go this far with him. He can only say:

> From one point of view the unacknowledged forces playing upon the apparently simple and candid central character of "My Kinsman, Major Molineux" are deeply abhorrent. Our sympathy for the character should tell us, however, that there is another side to the matter. The tendencies which assert themselves in Robin exist in all men. What he is doing, unwittingly but flamboyantly, is something which every young man does and must do, however gradually, prudently, and inconspicuously: he is destroying an image of paternal authority so that, freed from its restraining influence, he can begin life as an adult.

But an adult, Mr. Lesser in his hyperclinical role fails to say, for and in a world of other adults.

The danger of Mr. Lesser's approach is surely self-evident: It is one of inadequacy and partiality. But it is that kind of inadequacy and partiality which are so not by virtue of what they would forbid, forego, or supplant. Quite the contrary; for Mr. Lesser's approach takes us deeply into the heart of the tale. But he forgets that the heart has meaning only as it activates and is activated by a body. And psychoanalytic criticism would not seem necessarily to have to forget this fact and to stop where Mr. Lesser has stopped. The artist, we now grant, is gifted with a tendency to a kind of controlled regression. He can move deeply into the psyche and is able to evoke something quite close to those primary processes which man, in order to be man living with man, must resist, repress, or sublimate. But to a significant degree the artist *controls* his probing movement; and controlling it, he returns to the world, creates another world, an imaginative world, in which he reveals to us, with all the devices at his command, the forces, directions, and articulations, the meanings, of those unconscious processes —those instinctive powers which we must control and express so that we can live with them: which is to say, with ourselves. The element of control is managed through the creation of a world of men (akin to the world of the reader to whom Hawthorne addresses himself) in which the psyche lives and has its adventures. This element of control makes, *a fortiori,* for import, meaning, and significance. For it is the element whereby relationships are established and maintained. The artist's responsibility is, if not to the world for which he creates, at least to the world he does create. And he does not create his characters merely to be free to be themselves, as the analyst would free his patients. He creates them so that the selves which they may (or may not) freely become can be meaningful in relation to the world which he must create with, for, and through them.

The analyst, as I understand it, above all fights the temptation (one of the difficulties in countertransference) to be a creator, a God. The artist cultivates it; it is his primary illusion, and that he knows it to be so makes it all the more available to him as a crucial factor in his motivation toward creativity. Hawthorne surely cultivated it. And no account of Robin Molineux which declares that his freedom was such as to give him that euphoria which marks the sense of release from neurotic pain and guilt—no such account is a just account of his tale. Mr. Lesser may well think (he implies it certainly) that Robin Molineux's initial disturbance and guilt, since they are like those of all men, are "normally" neurotic. But such traits are part of the objective, literary reality of Robin's character; and Hawthorne doesn't release him from them, as Mr. Lesser would have it that he does. It is within the power of psychoanalytic criticism to account for Robin's behavior. But that criticism cannot—if it will merely "analyze" protagonists like Robin—account for the meaning which Hawthorne imputes to it. Robin cannot be abstracted from the meaning of his guilt-laden world by being shown to be all too human in his neurotic confusion. That confusion, which Mr. Lesser expounds so well, is finally real only in so far as it gives us perspective on Robin's total situation, his total world, as Hawthorne would have us know and judge it.

It may be well that Hawthorne felt that what we call Oedipal guilt was inevitably an element of the growth toward adulthood; yet that nothing—not even the magic of a psychoanalysis of which he dreamed a wild dream in a sketch like "The Haunted Mind"—could free man from it, and that it was integrally part of an all too human reality principle. Then, on this score—*pace* Mr. Lesser—Hawthorne would have to be said not to have been a latently complete Freudian. But I gather that, on this score, Freud himself was, in his later life, not always a manifestly complete Freudian. Reading "My Kinsman, Major Molineux," translating it into Freudian terms, translating those terms back into the context of Robin Molineux's world (a step which Mr. Lesser will not take)—perhaps we could even say that Freud was a latent Puritan. We could settle the matter by looking only at the whole of Freud's text. And the psychonanalytic critic could settle corresponding matters likewise only by looking at the whole of Hawthorne's text—by taking Robin off the couch and putting him back into the tale.

FOR FURTHER READING

Freud, Sigmund. *Totem and Taboo.* New York: Macmillan, 1952.

Gross, Seymour. "Hawthorne's 'My Kinsman, Major Molineux': History as Moral Adventure," *Nineteenth-Century Fiction,* XII (September, 1957), 97–109.

Hoffman, Daniel G. *Form and Fable in American Fiction.* New York: Oxford University Press, 1961, pp. 113–125.

Jung, C. G. *Psychological Reflections.* New York: Harper Torchbooks, 1953, pp. 36–45.

Waggoner, Hyatt H. *Hawthorne, A Critical Study.* Cambridge: Harvard University Press, 1955, pp. 47–53.

Sixteen

BY JESSAMYN WEST (1907–   )

Most of Jessamyn West's stories about Cress Delahanty—first published in *The New Yorker*—capture with affectionate but sharp wit the growing pains of a warm, sprightly, bright, and sensitive California girl. In "Sixteen," however, Miss West explores a darker region of experience, illuminating it with lambent clarity. Above all, this is a story about an adolescent girl's first encounter with death, but it is also a revealing study of the relations between parent and child and of the wide-reaching effects of adolescent love.

Each of the four sections of the story affords some insight into one of these areas of interest, but always the reader's attention awaits the climactic visit to the grandfather's deathbed. Along the way, Miss West foreshadows through image and allusion the girl's impending moment of awareness: at home, the frosty air hints at death; at school, the world is green and moist and Cress buoyantly discovers in a suspended raindrop the mystery of life. But Edwin's allusion to William Blake's "Auguries of Innocence" ironically hints at a more profound insight yet beyond the girl's grasp:

> To see a world in a grain of sand
> And a Heaven in a wild flower,
> Hold Infinity in the palm of your hand,
> And Eternity in an hour.

Only hours later the prophecy comes true when Cress—instead of dining at the *Poinsettia*—places *violets* in her grandfather's hand and he lets them spread across his cheek "like a pulled-up sheet of flowering earth." When image, allusion, structure, and insight mesh, the reader will understand what Cress's parents miss when she says to her grandfather, "It's just the same."

THE STORY

The steam from the kettle had condensed on the cold window and was running down the glass in tear-like trickles. Outside in the orchard the man from the smudge company was refilling the pots with oil. The greasy smell from last night's burning was still in the air. Mr. Delahanty gazed out at the bleak darkening orange grove; Mrs. Delahanty watched her husband eat, nibbling up to the edges of the toast, then stacking the crusts about his tea cup in a neat fence-like arrangement.

"We'll have to call Cress," Mr. Delahanty said, finally. "Your father's likely not to last out the night. She's his only grandchild. She ought to be here."

Mrs. Delahanty pressed her hands to the bones above her eyes. "Cress isn't going to like being called away from college," she said.

"We'll have to call her anyway. It's the only thing to do." Mr. Delahanty swirled the last of his tea around in his cup so as not to miss any sugar.

"Father's liable to lapse into unconsciousness any time," Mrs. Delahanty argued. "Cress'll hate coming and Father won't know whether she's here or not. Why not let her stay at Woolman?"

Neither wanted, in the midst of their sorrow for the good man whose life was ending, to enter into any discussion of Cress. What was the matter with Cress? What had happened to her since she went away to college? She, who had been open and loving? And who now lived inside a world so absolutely fitted to her own size and shape that she felt any intrusion, even that of the death of her own grandfather, to be an unmerited invasion of her privacy. Black magic could not have changed her more quickly and unpleasantly and nothing except magic, it seemed, would give them back their lost daughter.

Mr. Delahanty pushed back his cup and saucer. "Her place is here, Gertrude. I'm going to call her long distance now. She's a bright girl and it's not going to hurt her to miss a few days from classes. What's the dormitory number?"

"I know it as well as our number," Mrs. Delahanty said. "But at the minute it's gone. It's a sign of my reluctance, I suppose. Wait a minute and I'll look it up."

Mr. Delahanty squeezed out from behind the table. "Don't bother. I can get it."

Mrs. Delahanty watched her husband, his usually square shoulders sagging with weariness, wipe a clear place on the steamy windowpane with his napkin.

Some of the green twilight appeared to seep into the warm dingy little kitchen. "I can't ever remember having to smudge before in February. I expect you're right," he added as he went toward the phone. "Cress isn't going to like it."

Cress didn't like it. It was February, the rains had been late and the world was burning with a green fire; a green smoke rolled down the hills and burst shoulder-high in the cover crops that filled the spaces between the trees in the orange orchards. There had been rain earlier in the day and drops still hung from the grass blades, sickle-shaped with their weight. Cress, walking across the campus with Edwin, squatted to look into one of these crystal globes.

"Green from the grass and red from the sun," she told him. "The whole world right there in one raindrop."

"As Blake observed earlier about a grain of sand," said Edwin.

"O.K., show off," Cress told him. "You know it—but I saw it." She took his hand and he pulled her up, swinging her in a semicircle in front of him. "Down there in the grass the world winked at me."

"Don't be precious, Cress," Edwin said.

"I will," Cress said, "just to tease you. I love to tease you, Edwin."

"Why?" Edwin asked.

"Because you love to have me," Cress said confidently, taking his hand. Being older suited Edwin. She remembered when she had liked him in spite of his looks; but now spindly had become spare, and the dark shadow of his beard—Edwin had to shave every day while other boys were still just fuzzy—lay under his pale skin; and the opinions, which had once been so embarrassingly unlike anyone else's, were now celebrated at Woolman as being "Edwinian." Yes, Edwin had changed since that day when she had knocked his tooth out trying to rescue him from the mush pot. And had she changed? Did she also look better to Edwin, almost slender now and the freckles not noticeable except at the height of summer? And with her new-found ability for light talk? They were passing beneath the eucalyptus trees and the silver drops, falling as the wind shook the leaves, stung her face, feeling at once both cool and burning. Meadow larks in the fields which edged the campus sang in the quiet way they have after the rain has stopped.

"Oh, Edwin," Cress said, "no one in the world loves the meadow lark's song the way I do!"

"It's not a competition," Edwin said, "you against the world in an 'I-love-meadow-larks' contest. Take it easy, kid. Love 'em as much as in you lieth, and let it go at that."

"No," she said. "I'm determined to overdo it. Listen," she exclaimed, as two birds sang together. "Not grieving, nor amorous, nor lost. Nothing to read into it. Simply music. Like Mozart. Complete. Finished. Oh, it is rain to listening ears." She glanced at Edwin to see how he took this rhetoric. He took it calmly. She let go his hand and capered amidst the fallen eucalyptus leaves.

"The gardener thinks you've got St. Vitus' dance," Edwin said.

Old Boat Swain, the college gardener whose name was really Swain, was leaning on his hoe, watching her hopping and strutting. She didn't give a hoot about him or what he thought.

"He's old," she told Edwin. "He doesn't exist." She felt less akin to him than to a bird or toad.

There were lights already burning in the dorm windows. Cress could see Ardis and Nina still at their tables, finishing their *Ovid* or looking up a final logarithm. But between five and six most of the girls stopped trying to remember which form of the sonnet Milton had used or when the Congress of Vienna had met, and dressed for dinner. They got out of their sweaters and jackets and into their soft bright dresses. She knew just what she was going to wear when she came downstairs at six to meet Edwin—green silk like the merman's wife. They were going to the Poinsettia for dinner, escaping salmon-wiggle night in the college dining room.

"At six," she told him, "I'll fly down the stairs to meet you like a green wave."

"See you in thirty minutes," Edwin said, leaving her at the dorm steps.

The minute she opened the door, she began to hear the dorm sounds and smell the dorm smells—the hiss and rush of the showers, the thud of the iron, a voice singing, "Dear old Woolman we love so well," the slap of bare feet down the hall, the telephone ringing.

And the smells! Elizabeth Arden and Cashmere Bouquet frothing in the showers; talcum powder falling like snow; *Intoxication* and *Love Me* and *Devon Violet;* rubber-soled sneakers, too, and gym T-shirts still wet with sweat after basketball practice, and the smell of the hot iron on damp wool.

But while she was still listening and smelling, Edith shouted from the top of the stairs, "Long distance for you, Cress. Make it snappy."

Cress took the stairs three at a time, picked up the dangling receiver, pressed it to her ear.

"Tenant calling Crescent Delahanty," the operator said. It was her father: "Grandfather is dying, Cress. Catch the 7:30 home. I'll meet you at the depot."

"What's the matter—Cressie?" Edith asked.

"I have to catch the 7:30 Pacific Electric. Grandfather's dying."

"Oh, poor Cress," Edith cried and pressed her arm about her.

Cress scarcely heard her. Why were they calling her home to watch Grandpa die, she thought, angrily and rebelliously. An old man, past eighty. He'd never been truly alive for her, never more than a rough, hot hand, a scraggly mustache that repelled her when he kissed her, an old fellow who gathered what he called "likely-looking" stones and kept them washed and polished, to turn over and admire. It was silly and unfair to make so much of his dying.

But before she could say a word, Edith was telling the girls. They were crowding about her. "Don't cry," they said. "We'll pack for you. Be brave, darling Cress. Remember your grandfather has had a long happy life. He wouldn't want you to cry."

"Brave Cress—brave Cress," they said. "Just frozen."

She wasn't frozen. She was determined. She was not going to go. It did not make sense. She went downstairs to meet Edwin as she had planned, in her green silk, ready for dinner at the Poinsettia. The girls had told him.

"Are you wearing that home?" he asked.

"I'm not going home," she said. "It's silly and useless. I can't help Grandfather. It's just a convention. What *good* can I do him, sitting there at home?"

"He might do you some good," Edwin said. "Had you thought about that?"

"Why, Edwin!" Cress said. "Why, Edwin!" She had the girls tamed, eating out of her hand, and here was Edwin who loved her—he said so, anyway—cold and disapproving. Looking at herself through Edwin's eyes, she hesitated.

"Go on," Edwin said. "Get what you need and I'll drive you to the station."

She packed her overnight bag and went with him; there didn't seem—once she'd had Edwin's view of herself—anything else to do. But once on the train her resentment returned. The Pacific Electric was hot and smelled of metal and dusty plush. It clicked past a rickety Mexican settlement, through La Habra and Brea, where the pool hall signs swung in the night wind off the ocean. An old man in a spotted corduroy jacket, and his wife, with her hair straggling through the holes in her broken net, sat in front of her.

Neat, thought Cress, anyone can be neat, if he wants to.

Her father, bareheaded, but in his big sheepskin jacket, met her at the depot. It was after nine, cold and raw.

"This is a sorry time, Cress," he said. He put her suitcase in the back of the car and climbed into the driver's seat without opening the door for her.

Cress got in, wrapped her coat tightly about herself. The sky was clear, the wind had died down.

"I don't see any sense in my having to come home," she said at last. "What good can I do Grandpa? If he's dying, how can I help?"

"I was afraid that was the way you might feel about it. So was your mother."

"Oh, Mother," Cress burst out. "Recently she's always trying to put me . . .."

Her father cut her off. "That'll be about enough, Cress. Your place is at home and you're coming home and keeping your mouth shut, whatever you think. I don't know what's happened to you recently. If college does this to you, you'd better stay home permanently."

There was nothing more said until they turned up the palm-lined driveway that led to the house. "Here we are," Mr. Delahanty told her.

Mrs. Delahanty met them at the door, tired and haggard in her Indian design bathrobe.

"Cress," she said, "Grandfather's conscious now. I told him you were coming and he's anxious to see you. You'd better go in right away—this might be the last time he'd know you."

Cress was standing by the fireplace holding first one foot then the other toward the fire. "Oh, Mother, what am I to say?" she asked. "What can I say? Or does Grandfather just want to see me?"

Her father shook his head as if with pain. "Aren't you sorry your grandfather's dying, Cress? Haven't you any pity in your heart? Don't you understand what death means?"

"He's an old man," Cress said obstinately. "It's what we must expect when we grow old," though she, of course, would never grow old.

"Warm your hands, Cress," her mother said. "Grandfather's throat bothers him and it eases him to have it rubbed. I'll give you the ointment and you can rub it in. You won't need to say anything."

Cress slid out of her coat and went across the hall with her mother to visit her grandfather's room. His thin old body was hardly visible beneath the covers; his head, with its gray skin and sunken eyes, lay upon the pillow as if bodiless. The night light frosted his white hair but made black caverns of his closed eyes.

"Father," Mrs. Delahanty said. "Father." But the old man didn't move. There was nothing except the occasional hoarse rasp of an indrawn breath to show that he was alive.

Mrs. Delahanty pulled the cane-bottomed chair a little closer to the bed. "Sit here," she said to Cress, "and rub this into his throat and chest." She opened her father's nightshirt so that an inch or two of bony grizzled chest was bared. "He says that this rubbing relieves him, even if he's asleep or too tired to speak. Rub it in with a slow steady movement." She went out to the living room leaving the door a little ajar.

Cress sat down on the chair and put two squeamish fingers into the jar of gray ointment; but she could see far more sense to this than to any talking or being talked to. If they had brought her home from school because she was needed in helping to care for Grandpa, that she could understand—but not simply to be present at his death. What had death to do with her?

She leaned over him, rubbing, but with eyes shut, dipping her fingers often into the gray grease. The rhythm of the rubbing, the warmth and closeness of the room, after the cold drive, had almost put her to sleep when the old man startled her by lifting a shaking hand to the bunch of yellow violets Edith had pinned to the shoulder of her dress before she left Woolman. She opened her eyes suddenly at his touch, but the old man said nothing, only stroked the violets awkwardly with a trembling forefinger.

Cress unpinned the violets and put them in his hand. "There, Grandpa," she said, "there. They're for you."

The old man's voice was a harsh and faltering whisper and to hear what he said Cress had to lean very close.

"I used to—pick them—on Reservoir Hill. I was always sorry to—plow them up. Still—so sweet. Thanks," he said, "to bring them. To remember. You're like her. Your grandmother," he added after a pause. He closed his eyes, holding the bouquet against his face, letting the wilting blossoms spray across one cheek like a pulled-up sheet of flowering earth. He said one more word, not her name but her grandmother's.

The dikes about Cress's heart broke. "Oh, Grandpa, I love you," she said. He heard her. He knew what she said, his fingers returned the pressure of her hand. "You were always so good to me. You were young and you loved flowers." Then she said what was her great discovery. "And you still do. You still love yellow violets, Grandpa, just like me."

At the sound of her uncontrolled crying, Mr. and Mrs. Delahanty came to the door. "What's the matter, Cress?"

Cress turned, lifted a hand toward them. "Why didn't you tell me?" she demanded. And when they didn't answer, she said, "Edwin knew."

Then she dropped her head on to her grandfather's outstretched hand and said something, evidently to him, which neither her father nor her mother understood.

"It's just the same."

MORE ABOUT THIS STORY

As Cress reluctantly enters her grandfather's bedroom, she cannot understand why she has been called home "simply to be present at his death." Death, she believes, has nothing to do with her. Yet only moments later the rebellious, rather callous girl slips almost imperceptibly into compassionate young womanhood. Through what miracle?

No miracle has been wrought, of course. What has occurred may best be described as a normal growth process (contrast, for example, Luca's prolonged neurotic ordeal in Moravia's story) that has brought the girl to her first stunning awareness of death and its boundless—as well as binding—implications. For one thing, Cress can never more believe that the old gardener simply doesn't exist or that her grandfather has never been truly alive. Now she shares their awareness of mortality: the gap between her youth and their age has suddenly shrunk. Along with this sobering awareness, however, comes a redemptive insight as well, one Peter Blos describes in his psychoanalytic study of adolescence: "Alone and surrounded by man's eternal fear of abandonment and panic, the familiar and life-old need for human closeness awakens; love and understanding are expected to rekindle the trust in life, to blow away the fears of isolation and death. The limitless future of childhood shrinks to realistic proportions, to one of limited chances and goals; but, by the same token, the mastery of time and space and the conquest of helplessness afford a hitherto unknown promise of self-realization. This is the human condition of adolescence which the poet has laid bare." [1]

Cress's rare and touching moment of awareness has been psychologically forecast by a secure relationship with parents who obviously have cared and tried to understand. And her love for Edwin—who has already experienced and profited from such a crisis—helps inestimably to draw Cress toward her new affirmation of life.

FOR FURTHER READING

Kiell, Norman. *The Adolescent Through Fiction: A Psychological Approach.* New York: International Universities Press, 1959, pp. 164–182.

Kunitz, Stanley, ed. *Twentieth-Century Authors.* First Supplement. New York: H. W. Wilson, 1955, p. 1067.

---

[1] *On Adolescence: A Psychoanalytic Interpretation* (New York: Free Press of Glencoe, 1962), p. 13.

Luca

BY ALBERTO MORAVIA (1907–   )

In the prologue to Alberto Moravia's most recent novel, *The Empty Canvas* (1961), the protagonist, a young, well-to-do painter who no longer practices or enjoys his art, recalls "having suffered always from boredom." What he means by "boredom" (whose Italian equivalent, *la noia*, is the original title of the novel) is not merely a failure to be amused; rather is it "a kind of insufficiency, or inadequacy . . . a sense of the absurdity of a reality which is insufficient, or anyhow unable, to convince me of its own effective existence." At times, as bored with sexual passion and violence as with art, he has felt the attraction of death as a form of release, and half intentionally, he nearly kills himself in an automobile accident. At last he accepts life, without hope but with a sure sense that life is better than death, and that reality, however absurd, cannot be ignored. As the novel ends, the artist says—pointedly without assurance—"Once I was well, I would go back to the studio and try to start painting again."

In "Luca" (published in 1948 as "La Disubbidienza," "The Disobedient") Moravia shows a similar preoccupation with the sterility of the human lot. Luca's torpidity and passivity veil a "vindictive complacency," a destructive hostility toward the middle-class world he dwells in. His determination to disobey encompasses not only parental authority and school officials but "the actual fact of living." Images of winter, of "dark and opaque" or "heavy and gray" rain from a "pitch-black sky," and of black trees and dead leaves in the wood where he buries the money—all reflect the boy's conscious, willed drift toward oblivion: "it would be pleasant to curl up and go to sleep for good." Again, however, as in *The Empty Canvas* and several other of Moravia's stories and

61

novels, the protagonist escapes the final, deathly embrace of dissolution. In the love grip of the nurse he recognizes that "that womb was nothing else than the womb of life," the life he has determined to repudiate but at last accepts.

Although Moravia's existential orientation approximates that of Sartre and Camus, it lacks Sartre's engagement with life through political commitment or Camus' through human compassion and love of nature. Implacably critical of the money-oriented middle class of which he is himself a product, Moravia draws with brutal, naturalistic detail the materialism of our age, harshly depicting how it dries up the roots of affection, rots the tree of the family, stunts humanity, and infects the fruit of love. Thus, even though Luca does return to life, many readers will share R. W. B. Lewis' belief that "his recovery is isolated and private, almost metaphysical; it relates him to existing things *qua* existing, but in no sense does it relate him to humanity." [1]

Alberto Moravia (born Pincherle) has been one of Italy's most distinguished and productive authors since, at the age of twenty-two, he gained fame with his first novel, *The Time of Indifference*. Since then, he has published ten novels, more than a half dozen volumes of short stories, and, recently, a collection of critical essays. Moravia's own preference—in his case a wise one—is for the short-story form. In this medium, his rather colorless style and conventional structural form obtrude less conspicuously than they do in his longer fiction. As a result, his concentration on emotional conflict and the attendant psychological process commands attention.

In all of Moravia's writing a searing, moral condemnation of man's inhumanity mingles with a nostalgic yearning for a better world. Despite his seemingly lavish descriptions of sexual passion, he has never pandered to sensationalism. Sex as lust rather than love, like money, symbolizes for Moravia the desecration of the human spirit. What he intends, Moravia writes in his volume of essays *Man as End* (1964), is "a defense of humanism when anti-humanism is the fashion."

THE STORY
TRANSLATED BY ANGUS DAVIDSON

Luca had spent the summer holidays at the usual seaside resort. Now he went back home feeling unwell, feeling, indeed, that he would soon really be sick. He had recently grown with abnormal speed, and at fifteen was already as tall as an adult, but his shoulders were still narrow and thin, and in his white face his eyes, with their too-great intensity, seemed to be consuming the thin cheeks and forehead. If he had realized the delicate state of his health and the dangers that attended it, he might have asked permission of his parents to break off

---

[1] *The Picaresque Saint* (New York: J. B. Lippincott, 1959), p. 50.

his studies; but at his age, when sensitiveness is awake and consciousness still sleeping, he did not relate his weakened physical condition to the deep repugnance which his studies aroused in him. He had always gone to school and it seemed natural to go on doing so—even if the things he had to learn did not present themselves in orderly fashion according to the days and months of the scholastic year but heaped in front of him in a steep, insurmountable mass, like a mountain whose smooth sides offer the climber no hold for hand or foot. His will was not lacking, but rather some physical impulse; some fortitude of the body which he could not identify. Sometimes his body seemed to give way beneath him, as an exhausted horse, dull-eyed with fatigue, gives way beneath the rider who vainly spurs it on.

Often, however, this body of his rebelled when Luca least expected it—not so much before heavy tasks as for reasons of no importance. And then Luca was subject to sudden, furious rages during which his body, already so exhausted, seemed to burn up the little strength it still retained in paroxysms of hatred and revolt. More than anything it was the dumb, inert resistance of inanimate objects, or rather, his own incapacity to make use of such objects without fatigue or injury that threw him into these devastating rages. A tight or badly laced shoe into which he could not easily fit his foot; a school-bound streetcar, barely missed after a long chase; a bottle of ink upset on his exercise book, forcing him to recopy an entire page; the unforeseen, painful impact of his head against the sharp corner of his desk as he raised himself after picking up a fallen book; these and other absurdities were enough to put him beside himself with rage. He would either curse and grind his teeth, sometimes going so far as to childishly bang the corner of the desk with his fist or hurl the inkpot on the floor, or he would burst into violent weeping in which some vast and ancient grief seemed to be pouring itself out. He felt that the world was hostile to him, and he to the world; he felt he was waging continuous, nerve-racking warfare against everything around him.

This revolt of inanimate objects, this incapacity on his part to love and to dominate them, had reached a climax during the summer at the seaside. One particular incident had proved once and for all the state of reciprocal enmity between himself and the world of reality. Luca was a clever mechanic, and when anything went wrong with the electricity in the house he was asked to help. One evening there was a short circuit and the lights went out. Luca, at the sound of his mother's voice calling to him through the dark rooms, was quickly on the scene with his tools. But, whether he had failed to take the precaution of not touching the ground or whether by the dim light of the candle he had not noticed that the wires were touching, the electric current suddenly sprayed and crackled between his fingers and ran through his body. Luca started shouting, and at the same time involuntarily tightened his grip on the wiring, thus intensifying the shock, which in turn made him powerless to loosen his hold on the wire. His mother, terrified and not knowing what to do, hovered around him, while Luca yelled and the electric current continued to vibrate through his body with a malignant power which seemed to come, not from the wires, but from the whole mysterious, hostile world which—although he had no knowledge of it—he hated. At last, after a long interval of confusion, somebody turned off the current at the main switch, and Luca, his hands released, threw himself sobbing into his mother's arms. She did not understand why he was crying in such despair and hugged him mechanically, stroking his head. For a long time Luca continued to weep, his whole body trembling, at the same time feeling bitterly that his mother's caresses no longer protected and comforted him as they had once done. Later, when the lights were on again, it was discovered that the electric shock had caused deep burns in the tips of three of his fingers. The imprint of the wires and, so to speak, of the electricity itself, was clearly visible in a mark which had the jagged shape of a minute flash of lightning.

Another storm of rage came upon him in the train, shortly before he arrived home from his summer holiday. They had risen early and eaten a hasty breakfast in the dismantled house, among trunks and suitcases. As he was swallowing a cup of cheap milk colored with coffee substitute, his mother had said: "Have a good breakfast, because lunch in the dining car is always so late." The idea of lunch in a dining car had immediately delighted him, for he had never been in one. It would be a real pleasure to sit and eat at one of those tiny tables he had sometimes glimpsed from the window of another train. He imagined that the bread and soup and meat would have a quite different taste when eaten at a real little table, with real knives and forks and plates handed by waiters, the landscape meanwhile slipping past one's eyes as the train proceeded on its way. Besides, Luca was extremely sensitive about the opinion of other people and about the formalities of decorous behaviour. He had a whole-hearted loathing of meals eaten on one's knee in a railway carriage, among dirty pieces of paper and fruit peelings and leftovers, with cold, greasy food squashed between the two halves of a gaping roll of bread. During such meals there was always somebody waiting to go to the dining car who would look on with an air of self-satisfaction and disgust at the family crouching over paper bags. On their journey to the seaside there had been such a witness, a scornful, well-dressed old lady. Luca had found himself ashamed to eat, and at the same time ashamed of being ashamed. Overcome by these humiliating feelings, he had scarcely touched his food.

The idea of not having to unwrap greasy bits of paper and devour sandwiches had comforted him, and for a large part of the journey he sat quietly looking out at the countryside. At last the waiter came to make reservations for the dining car, and his father failed to take any tickets. Luca thought he was waiting for the second service, and went on gazing out of the window. Then he heard his father say: "After all, we can buy lunch baskets at Orvieto . . . they're much cheaper and they have much better things in them than what they give you in the dining car." His father, as he pronounced these words, showed no particular feeling; Luca felt that he made this decision, not out of meanness, but simply from good sense. Nor did it seem odd to him that his mother, always pliable in the face of any argument that favored an economy, should answer indifferently: "As you like . . . I should really have preferred to go to the dining car, even if only so as not to get my fingers sticky. . . ." It was, in fact, a case of two people coming to an agreement over a matter of no importance. And in truth the discussion went on for another two minutes, in a calm and affable manner, ending in victory for his father—a victory so gentle, in any case, as to seem more like the meeting of two kindred minds. Luca nevertheless, though he realized that the decision had not been made out of spite, flew into a violent rage.

What offended him most was that neither of them asked his opinion and that they treated him as an inanimate object, which, being a mere object, had neither preferences nor ideas, neither tastes nor wishes. At the same time he felt a profound disappointment; all the more heart-rending and catastrophic because he had been so elated at the idea of having lunch in the dining car. But to all these resentments there was added a further one which did not seem to have any precise origin, nor to arise from this particular trouble—the usual fury that assailed him every time he became aware of revolt and insubordination on the part of things and people in opposition to his own will. This fury seemed to come from some far-off place, and it flared like a fierce fire, scorching him and shaking him from head to foot. He went white in the face, clenched his teeth tightly and shut his eyes. He felt himself grow stiff all over with the violent rage that tautened his body; for a moment he felt impelled to open the door and throw himself out of the train. This suicidal temptation did not frighten him, nor did it seem to him absurd; it was, as he realized, the natural outlet of the furious feeling of impotence that overwhelmed him. He opened his eyes and looked at his parents. As though his rage, like a fierce harsh light, had carved out their features in an altogether new manner, he seemed to be observing them for the first time—his mother fair, thin, with an angular face to which the large nose and tight mouth gave an air of authority and wisdom; his father also fair, but soft and rounded, with indefinite, good-natured features. For the first time he felt the hardness and power of his mother and the good sense and kindheartedness of his father as things that were not only external to himself but actually hostile. Things with which he could not come to any sort of an understanding; and which came from remote centers of origin over which he could exercise no kind of control. He understood, it is true, that if he had made his desire clear they would have at once welcomed it; perhaps his mother, who did not like to go back on a decision, might have opposed it, but not for long. But he realized also that he did not want at any cost to compel them to do a thing that they did not seem to have thought of; all the more because that desire of his now filled him, in turn, with a sort of rage, as being a ridiculous impulse and not worth consideration. In any case, the important thing was not so much the question of whether he had lunch in the dining car or in the compartment as the feeling that his parents were made of the same hostile, defiant matter he was aware of in other things. And like the other things, they could not, with all the love that they felt for him, be tolerated.

In spite of these reflections, his feeling of rage did not leave him, and when they stopped at Orvieto station it was with extreme repugnance that he watched his father get out of the train, buy the lunch baskets and come back, panting, to the compartment. His father carefully closed the door, pulled up the little folding table that was fixed under the window and put the three baskets upon it. Then, with the superficial and slightly mournful solicitude that was habitual with him, he asked the boy: "Luca, are you hungry? Would you like to have lunch at once or would you rather we waited a little?" Luca answered without turning his head: "I'm ready whenever you are."

The train started again; and it seemed to Luca that the sight of the countryside, as it rolled past beneath his eyes, soothed, for a moment, his resentment. But suddenly, from whence he knew not, a new wave of rage assailed him, and unable to contain himself, he got up and left the compartment. He went straight to the lavatory, banging the door furiously behind him. There was a mirror above the washbowl, and he thrust his face close to it, opening his mouth wide as though he were screaming, though in reality no sound came out of his throat. He felt he was screaming, nevertheless, noiselessly, with the whole of his quivering body. The train was rocking and swaying violently, clattering across one switch after another. Everything rattled and creaked in the narrow enclosure, the connecting framework of the carriage, the glass in the window frame, the brass rim around the glass, the tumbler in its holder, the floor where moving iron plates danced and clashed together; Luca stood there, his mouth open, with the feeling that he was screaming louder than the din of the train, while his raging fury seemed to him to be the very train itself which sooner or later must inevitably run off the rails, hurtle down an embankment and smash itself to pieces against the side of a hill. He stayed like that for a short time, strained and rigid; then opened the door and went back to the compartment. His father had opened the lunch baskets and was putting the rolls on a newspaper spread on his knees. "There's one for you," he said, offering the first roll to Luca. He turned to his wife and added: "Would you like some wine at once? But perhaps it would be best to eat first and drink afterwards, when we have our hands free." His father spoke always in a drawling voice, as though he were making feeble proposals which he expected, resignedly, to see rejected. Luca took the roll stuffed with cold meat and bit it angrily. He had no appetite and he ate with an effort, keeping his face obstinately turned toward the window. From the compartment behind him came the rustling of paper bags being unfolded, muttered words of offering or of comment from his father, speaking with his mouth full, or from his mother, answering in monosyllables. As soon as he had finished eating he felt as if the food had stuck in his throat. His rage had not subsided, it persisted at the same level in a state of tension that was perhaps less harsh, but no less painful in its continuance.

It was as though his whole body had remained numb and his mind permanently confused. He gazed unseeing at the landscape, now the countryside of his own native city. And upon his stomach he felt the weight of the food he had eaten, like a big, tightly closed package done up in greaseproof paper, full of partly chewed bits and pieces, exactly like the paper bags full of odds and ends that housewives throw out of their windows into the alleys for the cats of the neighborhood. His mother asked him what was the matter, moving her hand across his forehead to smooth back the hair that had been blown about by the wind. And, from the relief afforded him by the contact of that cool, light hand, accompanied as it was by a feeling of nausea that filled his mouth with saliva, he realized that he was feeling sick.

When they arrived, his parents, busy getting the luggage off the train, took no notice of him. But as they were walking with the crowd along the platform, he knew suddenly that before he had gone much farther he would inevitably be sick. His feeling of nausea, very strong now, was felt in an acid taste and in an uncontrollable urge to open his mouth. They passed one carriage, then another, then a third. From each carriage people were getting out, gay and brisk, leaving behind them in the empty compartments crusts and pieces of paper, cigarette butts and bottles. Here was a fourth carriage, already empty, with all the doors wide open. And then they reached the engine with its cab full of handles and tubes and the mouth of its firebox showing red against the background of black iron. The engineer, his face smoke-stained and greasy, was looking at the people and devouring, with a hearty appetite, half a small loaf filled with what looked to Luca like a kind of green and yellow slush—a spinach omelette. At the sight of the omelette, he was conscious of an even more violent feeling of nausea, as though a current of sympathetic attraction like that between a magnet and a piece of steel had come into being between the slush that the engineer was so eagerly devouring and that other slush that was fermenting in his own stomach. Now they had reached the buffers of the engine; he leaned on one of the headlamps and vomited against the great fuming machine. He heard his mother say in a voice that seemed to him very calm: "I knew he wasn't well"; and at the same time he was conscious of a hand holding his head up. His father kept repeating, in a good-natured tone: "It's nothing . . . it's nothing." And he himself, filled with rage and with a profound grief that he did not understand, started sobbing loudly. But as they led him away, downcast and sobbing, his mother saying to him in a voice of irritation: "Why are you crying? . . . you're almost a man and yet you're crying," it seemed to him that having vomited upon the engine had been, in a way, an act of revenge against the train which had brought him back so ruthlessly to the town, to school, to his lessons; in just the same way that his parents, ruthlessly, had refused him the dining car.

Once he was back home, in the house where so many of his former acts of rebellion had melted away in force of habit or in boredom, his rage took on a different form, one new to him. As though it had realized the futility of violence, it transformed itself suddenly into a desire for renunciation, for resignation. It was still the same old rebellious impulse, but made expert by the defeats it had suffered, its nature changed into something secret and negative. Luca was not acquainted with the terms applicable to social warfare; if he had been, he would not have been slow to recognize, in the new form that his revolt against the world had taken, the characteristics of a strike. His body no longer grew taut in outbursts of furious destructiveness but let itself go slack, like a relaxed violin-string that looks as if it could never be tight again. Frequently, during the long afternoons that he spent at the table in his own room, he would fall asleep, for no reason, since he had slept well the night before. These were dreamless naps, black, empty, more like absences than naps. They would come upon him halfway through a printed phrase or a written page, and it was of no use for him to say: "I'll finish this piece of reading or writing, and then I'll sleep." It was all he could do to rise from the table and drag himself to his bed. No sooner had he lain down than he was asleep. When he abandoned himself to these sudden, heavy attacks of torpor, he experienced the same feeling of vindictive complacency that he had been aware of while vomiting against the engine on his return from his summer holiday. He realized that this complacency had a destructive character and that it expressed his hostility toward the world. His sleep was like a crossing of the arms, a sign of renunciation, since he had not the strength to reject it. Formerly he would have made a desperate effort to resist these attacks of torpor; and finally, alarmed, would have told his parents about them, as he was accustomed to do whenever he thought he was sick. But now, at the back of this complacency, he seemed to detect the presence of a purpose where in the past he would have seen only a weakness. And carried along by this purpose it pleased him to shake off his former pride as a scholar, now useless and a mere encumbrance, and uncaring, to allow time to flow ruinously over a head now finally submerged. But his physical surrender was still, after all, only the vague indication of a path that he had the power either to follow or to abandon. It seemed to him that having once accepted the principle of inertia, he might as well encourage it—if only to demonstrate to himself that he was acting freely and not under compulsion. He not only refused to resist those fits of torpor and forego telling his mother and father about them, but he actually started provoking them in various ways, by deliberately reading long, dull passages or by concentrating his attention on writing exercises devoid of interest. As soon as he felt his eyes beginning to close and warning shudders running down his back, he would get up and throw himself on the bed. With his head low and his feet high, he would feel as though sleep had seized him by the hair and was sucking him down like a clinging, delicious mud, pulling him ever lower and lower. In this sinking sensation, his head seemed to be filled with an opaque, heavy substance while his feet swayed high above, light and empty. Gradually, repeating to himself: "I should be working . . . I should be translating . . . I should be reading," and thinking at the same time, complacently, that the use of the conditional implied that he would neither read, nor translate, nor do any work at all, he would fall asleep.

But sleep was merely a means to an end; he could not always be asleep and since the ultimate object continued to be a revolt against doing any lessons, Luca sought new ways of putting it into effect. This search excited him, like an unsuspected vocation. After the afternoon classes he used to go home with extreme unwillingness, thinking with profound disgust of the hours of home-work that awaited him. Now that it was a question of divesting his work of its obligatory character and of taking away from it all its importance, he found himself watching for the approach of those hours with a lively and pugnacious feeling of impatience—like a man going to accomplish a task that is in accord-ance with his strongest inclinations. He would come out of school, say good-bye to his companions and go slowly home, all alone, at that melancholy hour when day is dying and night is still far off. It seemed to him that everybody went out at that time, driven from indoors by the dreariness of the twilight; and it gave him pleasure to think that he, on the contrary, was headed home-ward. The sky grew dark above his head as he passed through the deserted streets of the quarter in which he lived. He would enter the elevator and go up to the apartment. At that hour it was empty except for the quiet presence of the old servant in the kitchen; his father was still at the office, his mother out paying visits. Luca would go in almost secretly and, without turning on any lights, would steal through the semi-darkness of the other rooms to his own bedroom. He was conscious as he did this of a mournful feeling that he was some kind of animal, ill-adapted for life, slinking back to its lair to die in peace. In his room he would turn on the light, shut the doors and windows and sit down at the small table. He was fully conscious of what he was preparing to do, and he sat down at the table with an almost ritual solemnity; both feeling and attitude were very different from his former boredom and repulsion. He had thought out another method of avoiding his work, besides going to sleep, and in his private language he called it the "distraction exercise." This exercise consisted in reading or writing mechanically, trying at the same time, with all his might, to put himself entirely outside the things he was writing or reading.

Here, for instance, was his history book with the sentence: "Conditions in

France and in Europe were now such as to permit the French government to give attention to the King of Spain's request . . ." As he read these words, Luca would force his attention away from them, isolating them in an empty absurdity. And indeed it seemed to him that the words, as he spelled them out, receded in a kind of flat, vertiginous perspective, growing progressively smaller, like the cards of letters used by oculists to test people's sight; and then, when they had almost disappeared over the horizon of that vast space to whose farthest limit they had retreated, they would leap suddenly forward in block letters, terrifying in their sound and enormous in size: "CONDITIONS IN FRANCE AND IN EUROPE WERE NOW . . ." It pleased him to discover that in these forward and backward movements the words, though they echoed in his mind syllable by syllable, remained incomprehensible, detached from all meaning, destitute of any logical framework, more dead than the words of any dead language. Sometimes, in order to make quite certain of this feeling, he would read aloud and would notice with satisfaction that the sound did not explain the words but rather added a quality of absurdity. Knowing that it needed but a slight effort of the muscles of his ears to make his voice sound detached and strange—as though issuing from some other mouth—he amused himself by repeating the same phrase in flute-like tones like a woman, or in a cavernous voice like an ogre: "Conditions in France and in Europe were now . . ." Usually this exercise ended with the customary falling asleep. He felt sleep coming to him from the feet upward, in the form of a welcome numbness in the legs; he would get up and stagger over to the bed and throw himself upon it. His eyes fixed on the table, where he could see the lamplight falling uselessly upon his abandoned books, he would allow himself to be submerged in the dark waves of sleep. He would sleep for an hour or two, then wake up and discover joyfully that there was no time that day for any more work, and that the next day, at school, he would not know his lesson.

At school these experiments were even easier, for classes and professor had always been foreign to him and had been, even from the first, enveloped in an empty atmosphere of absurd and quite unacceptable reality. Seated at his desk in front of an open book, it was easy for him to fill his eyes and ears with a kind of soft mist through which the voice of the professor explaining the lesson was transmuted into the abstract, magical muttering of a black witch doctor echoing unintelligibly through the savage solitude of an African forest. That, thought Luca, was how the speech of the living must sound in the ears of the dead. He imagined himself to be dead, to have lost the meaning of the spoken word, to be hearing sounds that were disconnected and absurd. He knew that this process of detachment went through three phases—a first phase during which he heard and saw with normal clarity but without understanding; a second in which sounds and shapes dissolved and became confused though they still remained perceptible; and a third in which he no longer either saw or heard and in which everything was swallowed up in that silent mist. It was during one of these experiments that he suddenly heard the professor's voice asking him: "Mansi, may one know what you are thinking about?" He would have liked to answer: "I'm learning how not to think." However, all he said was: "Me? . . . about nothing." "That is obvious," remarked the professor.

Luca, in the past, had had a great deal of self-respect; and he had been among the best pupils. Now, ever since the beginning of the new term, he was among the worst. Under the rain of reprimands and bad reports he experienced a feeling of particular satisfaction, since these reprimands were really eulogies and these bad reports good reports according to the conduct he had now decided to maintain. At the same time, he could not help feeling a profound bitterness at the thought that his status at school was deteriorating every day and would soon become irretrievable. He often asked himself why he behaved this way; and he admitted that he could find no other motive than an obscure point of honor, arid, unpleasant, entirely negative and therefore almost insupportable. "Why do I do this?" he wondered. And meanwhile, amid all these conflicts, time was passing.

The answer to the question: "Why do I do this?" came to Luca quite by chance at this time from an incident of small importance.

One morning, because of the illness of a professor, lessons finished two hours before the usual time. As Luca came out to the street in front of the school, a boy with a football in his arms detached himself from a group and came up to him. This boy had an unusual name, Virginio, and Luca disliked him, chiefly because of his physical appearance. He was very fat, always out of breath and always busy. A soft black down shadowed his upper lip and his cheeks; beneath this his features, lost in fat, were almost embryonic, like those of some monstrous baby, and there was something indefinably feminine about him which had earned him the nickname of Teresina, after a celebrated Fat Woman. He said, panting, and with an air of importance: "We've made up two sides . . . we're going to have a game at the Villa Borghese . . . but we need a goalkeeper . . . would you like to come?"

Luca was a less than mediocre football player, although he liked the game very much; and he realized at once that this invitation from the fat boy, the recognized organizer of the class sporting activities, was an unaccustomed honor for which he ought to show his appreciation. They hardly ever invited him, so that this was an opportunity to be seized for putting his inadequate athletic qualities to the test. His first impulse was to accept, but some mysterious resistance changed the words in his mouth and he said: "I'm sorry . . . but I've got to get home . . . another time, perhaps."

The fat boy wasted no time in discussing the matter; perhaps he already

regretted having asked him. "Hey, Mario . . . d'you want to be goalkeeper?"
he shouted, turning his back on Luca and going off toward another boy.

Luca saw this boy stop and speak to the fat boy. The group of players
walked across and surrounded them. Then, after a short discussion, they
moved off toward the gardens. The football had passed from the fat one's
arms to those of a small, dark boy. The latter swayed as he walked along on
his short legs; then he threw the ball up in front of himself and gave it a
resounding kick which sent it high into the air. The boys scattered over the
roadway and the sidewalks as they ran after the ball. One of them stopped it
with his foot and started dribbling it carefully in front of him.

The street in which the school was situated was long, straight and deserted,
flanked by severe looking factories, convents and offices. Between those rows
of windows, on the clean asphalt, in the clear light of that early November
day, went the group of boys, kicking the ball from one to the other with little
leaps and bounds. Luca stood by the corner of the school building, watching
them as they receded with a bitter satisfaction that did not seem new to him,
though he found it difficult to recall when he had felt it before. Then he
remembered: it was the same satisfaction that the ruin of his school career
aroused in him. This discovery produced a swarm of swift, burning thoughts
and held him entranced as he watched the footballers. It was as if not his
companions but his own boyhood had departed, finally and forever. They
would go on playing forever in the gardens of the villa and he would be
excluded forever from their games. But he had at last understood the reason
that underlay his refusal. Meanwhile the boys went farther and farther away,
growing smaller and smaller in the perspective of the long empty street. At
last they threw the ball into a cross street and disappeared. Only then did
Luca shake off his stupefied meditations and start toward home.

During the following days he observed that the sense of discovery he had
experienced when comparing his refusal to play football with his refusal to
work was confirmed and deepened. It was not so much a precise thought as
a direction that had at last been given to his disordered feelings of disgust
and rebellion. He had believed that he hated only his lessons; now he realized,
when he thought again of the feeling of aversion that the fat boy's invitation
had aroused in him, that he hated other things as well. What things? A rapid
survey brought him to the astonishing discovery that his hostility embraced
not merely one or a few aspects of his life, but all. At Luca's age it is easy
to leap from the obscurest feelings to a strenuous abstract logic, disdainful of
all compromise and of any possible exception. Luca reflected that the world,
in the persons of his mother, his father, his teachers, his schoolfellows, wanted
him to be a good son, a good pupil, a good friend, a good fellow; but he himself had no love for the world, nor for those roles that they wished to impose
upon him, and therefore he must disobey. Not, however, with obscure acts
of violence, with the sterile rages of an exhausted body, as in the past; but

observing an order, a plan, with calmness and detachment, as though applying the rules of a game. The word "disobey" pleased him because it was
familiar. Throughout his childhood and a great part of his boyhood he had
heard his mother say that he must be obedient, that he was disobedient, and
that if he didn't obey she would punish him, and other similar phrases. Perhaps by starting to be disobedient again on a more logical, higher plane, he
was merely rediscovering an attitude of mind which was native to him but
which he had lost. So far he had been disobedient only in the sphere of his
school life, which was the dullest and most absurd part of his existence. But
since the incident of the football game, he was discovering that this disobedience could be extended to other spheres as well; it could embrace other
things which, because they were normal and obvious, had hitherto escaped
him—the affections, for instance; and—an extreme case which immediately
fascinated him—the actual fact of living.

There came to him, at this thought, the feeling that it was truly a kind of
game; it was like a composition complete in itself, an end in itself, with its own
rhythm, its own design, its own meaning. Disobedience was the theme of the
composition, and all the acts that accompanied it and that involved him ever
more deeply were the variations. The game, furthermore, resembled one of those
drawing exercises for beginners, wherein the drawing is already indicated by a
series of dots so that all the inexperienced child has to do is to follow the line of
dots with a pencil. It was a cruel, destructive sort of game, but a game none
the less, because it was carried out on a disinterested, experimental plane. It
was in fact chiefly a question of following that mysterious movement which
grew steadily more rapid and more coherent and which seemed to be carrying him toward utter annihilation; and of discovering, each time, the con-
juncture of circumstances in which to live meant doing certain things, to die,
doing the opposite things, and of regularly choosing the latter. Like all boys,
Luca had a strong sporting sense. He decided that from now on he would
hunt out all the things that bound him to this life for which he felt such a
calm and satiated disgust. All this might have frightened him if he had seen
it as it really was, a kind of suicide. But dressed in the familiar, innocuous
guise of a game it attracted and pleased him.

Oddly enough he did not think of his affection for his parents as a bond
that held him to life and that must be destroyed. As a matter of fact he did
not feel himself bound to them to any greater extent than to the furniture in
his home, or to his schoolfellows. He no longer remembered how or when it
had happened, but in some now fabulous past some irreparable thing certainly had occurred which made him cease to love them. This decay of his
filial love was brought home to him by the comparison of his former feelings
with those of the present. There had been a period when he had had a feeling
of almost religious reverence for his parents, when it had seemed to him that
they were perfect and that they derived from this perfection an authority

that was both lovable and unquestionable. This perfection, he remembered, had seemed to him to be founded upon an almost unbelievable goodness, a goodness that, just because it was unbelievable, was moving in the highest degree. It was not the kind of goodness that later on had been prescribed to him by schoolmistresses and governesses and by his parents themselves, a goodness made up of rules and precepts, of regulations and duties; it was a much wider sort of goodness, indescribable, without beginning and without end, a goodness of which he felt the effects without investigating the causes. To this goodness, furthermore, he had never made any appeal; it was enough for him to be conscious of its omnipotent presence all around him and above him, the source of his life and its ultimate justification. During those years this goodness had been what he thought the sun must be for the grass and for the flowers of the fields—a flood of light, everlasting, indifferent perhaps, but though blind, infinitely generous, impregnating every one of his acts, even the smallest, every moment of his life, even the most fleeting, and imbuing them with warmth and energy. At that time he had really been, without recogniz- ing it, grateful to his parents for having brought him into the world and for being themselves alive; and in that, fundamentally, lay their goodness.

He could not have said whether the certainty of this perfection, made up as it was exclusively of goodness, had declined on account of one precise, detached incident, or through a series of minute facts difficult to remember. The only thing he was sure of was that now nothing at all remained of that perfection and of the veneration he had accorded it. Like the sun, which you cannot look at full in the face and which is all light and nothing but light and whose contours you cannot exactly define, so at one time the countenances of his parents had been unknown to him. He would look at them without dis- tinguishing them, observing nothing but the light of that blinding, beneficent goodness. But today—just as if the brilliant morning had been followed by a dreary evening and those two suns and been transmuted into two dead, cold moons—today he could see their faces clearly, and in those faces the smallest and most disheartening details. He saw them, in fact, with complete precision, in the pitiless light of reality, just as he saw the faces of his school- fellows or his teachers. And because he saw them so well, it seemed to him that they had been degraded to a lower rank. And with this degradation to objects of insignificance there had disappeared from his life the warmth that gave it energy. He did not recognize this with absolute clarity, but he had an obscure intuition that his revolt against the world must have begun just at the time this warmth had diminished.

One incident contributed to the final fixing of his parents' new character and of his new feeling about them. His father, when he came home in the evening, usually took out of his pocket the afternoon papers and gave them to Luca to read; later, at bedtime, he would take them back again because, as Luca knew, he liked to read them in bed before he went to sleep. It was one of those familiar habits that make up the smooth, unbroken surface of everyday life. One evening Luca, perhaps out of absent-mindedness, left the dining-room and went to bed taking the newspapers with him. In bed, after having looked at the pictures and run through some of the articles, he began to think that his father had been left without the papers and would certainly be very sorry not to have them. This mental picture was colored by pathetic reflections of the former paternal goodness, fallen now to the level of mere human goodness, but still moving and lovable. He imagined that his father did not come to ask him for the papers because he did not want to awaken him; and this sacrifice appeared to him to be one more proof of his father's tender affection. Furthermore, he knew that his parents, even after they were in bed, stayed awake until late, chatting or reading. For a long time he weighed the pros and cons, and finally decided to take the newspapers straight to his father in his room. He jumped out of bed, went barefooted into the passage and along to the door of his parents' room. He stood listening for a moment. He thought he could hear them talking and he went in without knocking, with a haste that came from affection and from a desire to repair the wrong done to his father.

The lights were on, as he had expected. The bed took up a large part of the wall opposite the door, so that the first thing Luca saw was the empty pillow and the sheets turned back on both sides of the bed. The empty bed did not hold his attention for more than a moment. To the right of the bed in the farthest corner of the room stood his father and mother in unusual attitudes. His father was wearing wide-striped pyjamas which were crumpled over his fat body; his mother was standing close beside his father, her bony limbs visible through the transparency of her nightgown. His father was clasping to his chest with both arms a bundle which Luca immediately recognized as banknotes and industrial bonds. His mother, standing in front with her arms raised, was fumbling at a picture hanging on the wall.

Luca knew that picture extremely well: it was a copy of a Raphael Madonna, and beneath it was a medieval *prie-dieu* made of dark-colored wood, with a red brocade cushion upon it. As a child, Luca had for a long time been made by his mother to kneel on that cushion when he said his evening prayers. He used to kneel down, join his hands, and turning his eyes up to the picture, repeat in a docile manner the words of the prayer which his mother, sitting beside him, would recite to him, little by little, in a patient voice. This prayer was not at that time distasteful to him; first because it was a thing easily endurable though boring, with that mild, pleasing boredom which is the staple nourishment of infancy, and also because the picture of the Madonna, so gentle, with her Child in her arms, she herself clothed in red and blue, with a pure, luminous landscape behind her, attracted him and gave rein to his imagination. Once, with sleep coming upon him, he had even thought that the picture had nodded and smiled at him. More often, as he repeated mechanically the words of the prayer, he had speculated upon the expression of the Virgin's countenance, or upon the details of the hilly, springlike landscape that opened out behind the shoulders of the figure. Then, in the way these things happen, one day or another—perhaps on their return after the holidays—this habit of saying his prayers there had been interrupted. For a time he had gone on saying his prayers by himself; finally he had given up saying his prayers altogether.

Perhaps he had opened the door without making a noise; perhaps the door had been ajar and he had only to push it; perhaps his parents were so completely absorbed in what they were doing they had not heard him. However that may be, he stood for a long time, motionless at the door, watching them without their noticing his presence. He saw his mother open her arms, take hold of the picture by its frame, detach it from the wall and put it down carefully on the floor, leaning it against the wall. He realized then that the picture had concealed the square, slightly shiny gray surface of the steel door of a safe. "Two b's and one s," his father said, standing close behind his mother. Following her husband's instruction, his mother turned certain discs in the metal door and swung it noiselessly open. It was a small safe, as Luca could see, and contained on its two shelves several other bundles of banknotes and rolls of bonds. "Push them well back," said his father in his usual melting voice; "otherwise we'll never get these in too." His mother obeyed, and Luca saw her pushing far into the safe, with her thin arms, the money and the bonds already there so as to make room for the new ones. Then, acting on a sudden impulse, he went into the room and threw the newspapers down on the bed saying: "There are the papers." He saw his father give a violent start, like a thief caught in the act, and his mother turn her head in astonishment, with a look already severe; then he hurriedly left the room. In his own bedroom, the confused feeling of having done a good deed was mixed with a bitter taste of disappointment and guilt. But he was drowsy, and after turning over in his mind, from various angles, the new, disturbing picture of the safe hidden behind the holy picture and of his parents, in a state of semi-nudity, their arms laden with money, he fell asleep.

Next day he had already almost forgotten the incident, or rather he tried not to think of it. But in the evening, at table, at a moment when his father was not there, his mother observed dryly: "Remember, another time, that one doesn't go into bedrooms without knocking." Luca blushed and felt inclined to answer: "And why did you for so many years make me say my prayers kneeling in front of your money?" The remark came into his mind just as though it had taken shape by itself, during sleep, by a sort of spontaneous coagulation, like ice on a winter night. He realized at once that it was an extremely apposite remark, and felt that it contained much more than he himself meant by it. But he restrained himself and hung his head, pretending to be mortified. Later, thinking over the incident again, he came to the conclusion that it had been, if not the primary cause, at any rate the principal occasion for the progressive decline of his parents to the status of things that were alien and unloved.

But, if affection for his parents no longer held him to life, and if there was now no need for him to take the trouble of destroying it, since it had, so to speak, burnt itself out and destroyed itself, there were still other things that seemed to him too much alive and too obtrusive, which were therefore fitted by natural right to become a part of the game of destruction that he was consistently evolving day by day. Property, for instance. Luca, ever since he had been a baby, had looked upon all objects in his own possession with a feeling of jealousy and exclusiveness which—as generally happens—had been encouraged and stimulated by his parents in every possible way. Ever since his earliest days, toys had always been given him with an accompanying significant exclamation which contained both an opinion and an appeal to his possessive instinct: "Isn't it lovely? . . . Try not to break it."

Later came other toys more ingenious and less simple, such as Meccano and a marionette theatre and with them the first books of fables and children's stories. More than anything else, Luca had been crazy about his little theatre, and his father, noticing this passion, had cultivated it by bringing his son, at least once a week, a present of one or two marionettes. He used to say, in a deliberately careless manner, without raising his eyes from the paper he was reading: "Luca, why don't you go into the hall and have a look in my overcoat pocket? I believe there might be something there for you." Luca, filled with delight and, at the same time, with a strange sort of humiliating feeling that he was succumbing to an almost illicit passion, would run into the hall; and there in fact, sticking out from the pocket of his father's overcoat as it hung on the coatrack, would be a long package with bits of wire projecting from it. When he had undone the paper with impatient fingers, there would appear a couple of warriors with breastplates of shining tin foil, or a grand lady dressed in sky-blue velvet, or a black and red devil armed with a fork, and a white-garbed cook. Luca would embrace his father and then run to his room and place the marionettes beside the others that he already possessed, in a big wooden box with compartments. In this way he had come to own more than a hundred dolls. At first he had tried to make them perform improvised acts on the stage of the tiny theatre, against a background of scenery representing a palace, a forest, or a prison. But then the collector's passion had prevailed over the disinterested taste for playing, and he had been content to lay his marionettes in rows in the big box, as a miser hoards coins at the bottom of a chest. He would count them over and over, kiss them, stroke them, gaze at them for a long time as he knelt on the floor, then put them back in the box—and that was all. He was conscious, as he did this, of an immense satisfaction which, however, he always felt to be mingled with a kind of obscure remorse. This passion for the marionette theatre had lasted longer than any of the others. But in the end the remorse had overcome the passion, he had felt satiety and disgust with his collection of dolls and had abandoned them to the dust at the bottom of a cupboard. His father had noticed this neglect and had ceased to give him any more presents of marionettes.

After the theatre it had been Meccano, the use of which his father had taught him, himself crawling about on the floor and putting together the first simple machines. Finally, at a later age, had come the first adventure stories, the stamp collection, the sporting goods. Every time, the same progression had occurred in his mind, from disinterested amusement to the jealous, inert sense of possession, from attachment to disgust. But this disgust had never been strong enough to induce him to rid himself completely of the objects which no longer interested him. So violent a possessive passion created, between him and the things that had been once so beloved and were now neglected, an obscure bond of jealousy and fear, on account of which—though he completely ceased to make use of them or to enjoy them, though he even sometimes went so far as to forget their very existence—he could never bring himself to give them away or to destroy them. He kept them even if they were spoiled or mutilated, and the drawers in his cupboard were full of odd, crumpled albums of stories, headless or legless marionettes, half-empty boxes of Meccano. The books he was constantly acquiring and reading were an exception; and the stamp collection too, which—though with lessened interest —he continued to enrich with new specimens.

Later on, as the last act in this lengthy initiation into the ownership of property, Luca's father, when he considered him to be old enough, allowed him a small monthly sum as pocket money. Luca drew his allowance on the first day of each month and his father, as he handed him the money, expected in return a kiss of gratitude on the cheek. Money, as Luca soon discovered, aroused in his mind a sense of possession that was more mysterious and more absolute than that aroused by the dolls and other objects, a feeling that was remote from all idea of play or amusement, that was in fact quite incomprehensible. At first he spent it on sweets and books, but on finding that he could get his parents to give him sweets and books without his having to break into his treasure, he took to hoarding it and not spending it. He thought vaguely of saving a sufficient sum for the acquirement of some particularly expensive object—what, he did not know; he was, in reality, succumbing to the same instinct that had made him collect marionettes. Only then it had been a question of objects in which certain characteristics of quality and variety had been more important than mere quantity. Now, on the other hand, in the case of money, which consisted of ugly crumpled notes and coins that all looked alike, only quantity, with its stark numerical increases, counted as a stimulus to his collector's enthusiasm. And so, almost without noticing it, he slipped from the joy of possession—harsh though its taste may have been—into avarice. It was an innocent, ignorant avarice, like the shamelessness of a child that is allowed by its mother to run naked on the beach. So ignorant was it that he announced one day triumphantly to his father that he wanted to save up his monthly allowance until he reached the sum of a thousand *lire*. "Well done," answered his father, kissing him, "but in that case you ought to put your money in the savings bank." And he explained to him that not only would the money be safer than in a box, but also it would increase regularly, without any trouble on his part, just as a plant increases and bears fruit. Only then, in the midst of his father's praises and explanations, did Luca, become aware of an unexplained feeling of shame. And with the excuse that he had not enough money to open a banking account he refused the offer of a savings book. The feeling of shame, however, vanished almost at once; it was but the premature glimmer of a conscience not yet awakened. And the coins and the notes of his monthly pocket money continued to pile up in his desk.

The sacrifice of his possessions and his money, in spite of those former now forgotten emotions of satiety, disgust and shame of which only now did he think he understood the full importance and meaning, was even more difficult than the sacrifice of his pride as a scholar. It was the reluctance of an exhausted body which had led him to shirk his lessons, but he felt he would never have reached the point of repudiating his property had it not been for grief and bewilderment such as are inspired by a cruel and apparently unjustified privation. It was true that, from the moment he discovered that they bound him to the world and forced him to accept it, he had felt a kind of raging hatred for these objects and for his savings, but he knew that he hated them precisely because he loved them and not because they were odious in themselves, like his lessons. He felt himself divided as never before, pulled in one direction by the "game" and the dark, mysterious longing to play it out right to the end, in the other by the painful feeling that he was blowing up his bridges behind him, making impossible any turning back from the unknown, perilous land into which he was venturing. After all, he had passionately loved his books, his stamp albums, his sports equipment; after all, every penny put away in the box had represented, for him, the sacrifice of something that he could have bought and the hope of some other thing that some day he would buy. Those objects and that money were not merely objects and money, but living, tenacious strands in the woof of which his existence was woven. But it was just because of this that he wished to break those threads; for they were also a sign of obedience to the destiny which had been imposed upon him without his being consulted, and to the world against which he had attempted so often, and always in vain, to rebel. Had they been things already dead, abandoned by the love which had in the past made them alive—as in a sense his parents were—their destruction would have been useless. But the contrary was true; and the rules of this bitter game of disobedience admitted no exceptions.

Several times he postponed the act; then finally, one day, made up his mind. Among his schoolfellows there was a certain, quiet, pedantic boy who was convinced of his own perfection both as a scholar and as a boy just as though the conditions of school and boyhood were going to last the whole of his life. He was called Poli and he had a big, close-cropped head very like a pumpkin upon which somebody, with the point of a small knife, had roughly carved the features of a human face. Poli's thin, pinched body also bore out this idea of a pumpkin, for it made one think of the thin, fragile stalks at the end of which, among the furrows of the field or on the roof tiles, these enormous yellow fruits swell to their full size. He was the best boy in the class, and his superiority was always at the same high level and could never be surpassed, whether it was a case of algebra or Latin or Italian or history. This easy and apparently effortless superiority seemed to Luca mysterious, as though it were the product of some kind of witchcraft rather than of a mind subject to forgetfulness and error, like his own. He invited Poli to spend an afternoon at his home, and Poli immediately remarked: "I warn you that if it's a matter of helping you with your homework, nothing doing." Luca slyly assured him that it had nothing at all to do with homework.

Poli arrived, rather diffident, and Luca, after a few words of welcome, announced his intention of making him a present of his stamp collection. As he said this he brought out the collection, four large albums bound in red and gold cloth, and showed them to Poli. The latter, incredulous, suspected a trap or an obligation of some kind. "But why to *me*?" he asked finally; "we're not friends . . . we hardly know each other."

"I think I shall soon be going abroad," Luca answered calmly, "and as I was very fond of this collection, I thought you would be the only person who would keep it in order."

Tempted and at the same time visibly anxious not to show it, Poli, with hesitating fingers, turned the leaves of the albums. Then he said: "I'll give you something in exchange . . . not so valuable as the collection of course . . . but something . . . what would you like?"

"I don't want anything," replied Luca.

Then, to change the subject, he too started turning the leaves, pretending that he wanted to show Poli the best items in the collection. What he really wanted was to test whether he was sorry to be getting rid of it. The stamps, neatly stuck on the thick, gilt-edged pages with their headings in four languages, passed before his eyes. Here were the stamps of various European countries since the war, with republican superscriptions on top of the heads of kings—these had given him a dramatic sense of the political upheavals in those lands. Here were the older and more valuable stamps, the Papal stamps, those of the Italian States, of the German Confederation, simple, small, but beautiful with their faded, delicate colors. Here were the colonial stamps with tropical landscapes and figures of natives; they had not cost much but had made him dream of those far-off countries. Here were the stamps issued to commemorate some great man or some great event—these too had stirred his imagination. He had taken pleasure in acquiring them separately or in small sets at stationers' shops, in sticking them into the albums, examining their price and history in the French catalogue. He had taken pleasure in the figures that indicated their value, followed by the names of exotic coinages he had never seen. He had taken pleasure in the round postmarks canceling them, with the date and the place they came from; but above all in those that had wavy lines, which had made him think of the waves of the sea that the letters must have crossed to arrive at their destinations. He realized, as he turned the pages of the albums, that he was suffering a quite different pain from what he had expected. He had expected to suffer through avarice; he found he was suffering, instead, from self-pity. He was truly furious with himself; he could not help thinking it was as if he were divided into two parts, one of which lay abandoned and wretched on the ground, feebly defending itself, while the other stood over it, striking it without mercy. Closing the album sharply, he said: "Well then, d'you want them or not?"

"Of course I want them."

"Wait while I wrap them up in a newspaper."

Leaving the room, he got a newspaper from a cupboard. While he was looking for it, he thought for a moment that he would go back to Poli and announce that the whole thing had been a joke. But the act of getting rid of the collection appeared to him so much more real and genuine a thing than the keeping of it would have been that he hesitated no longer. He took the newspaper and went back into the room. Poli, who was looking admiringly at the stamps, hastily closed the album as he entered, as though he feared that Luca might change his mind if he showed his delight. Luca asked: "You've got a stamp collection already, haven't you?"

"Yes," replied Poli with an air of wisdom, "but much less complete than this. I shall sell the duplicates and buy other stamps with the money."

When Poli had gone Luca started thinking about how he could best get rid of his books. He had a good number of them, and he loved them even more than the stamps. They were, for the most part, adventure stories, detective novels and historical novels. Luca had had two different feelings about these books. He had had an affection for each individual book, for the sake of what it contained, and at the same time he had conceived a tenacious passion for books as pieces of property. This passion had in it a good deal of avarice, springing as it did rather from the joy of possession than from the character of the thing possessed. At one time he had been seized by a restless desire to fill up the three shelves of his bookcase, and since he had not enough novels, he had put in with them some old birthday presents and school primers. All included, this mixed collection of books amounted to the round figure of three hundred, checked over again and again by Luca, who often threw himself down on the floor to count the books and arrange them in order of size. Now while it had been easy to get rid of the stamp albums, which took up little space, with the books there was the problem of emptying the bookcase without his parents noticing. After thinking it over for a long time he decided to make a lie, a suitable lie that would allow him to destroy his library without arousing any suspicions. One day he went to his mother and said: "Mummy, I want to sell all my books."

"Sell all your books?" she said. "Why?"

"I've read them over and over again," replied Luca; "I want to sell them and buy a phonograph and some records."

It was exactly the right kind of lie. His father and mother would never have allowed such a sale unless it had been for the sake of some new acquisition. For them the only use of property was to create more property. Besides, Luca knew that his mother loved music and could not but be pleased at this new wish on his part. After a pause she said: "But the money from the books won't be enough."

For a moment Luca feared that his mother, touched by his love of music, might offer to buy him the phonograph without his sacrificing his books— though he knew that such generosity, of any kind, was not included among her educational theories; so he hastened to reply: "I'll add my savings to it . . . the whole lot together will make it possible for me to pay the first installments on a phonograph and to buy a few records as well."

Having obtained his mother's approval, Luca asked a second-hand bookseller whom he knew to come to the house. The bookseller, a short young man with a greedy expression and long, curly, greasy hair, came into the room with his overcoat on and his hat in his hand and began to examine the books that Luca handed to him one by one. During this examination Luca wondered again, as before when he had given Poli the stamp collection, whether he was suffering at being separated from his beloved books. He realized his pain was considerably less and that his amused feeling that it was a game, and his consciousness of his own duplicity, partly counterbalanced it. The bookseller, no less interested than Poli had been, tried to depreciate the value of the books, twisting his mouth and repeating that the volumes were too badly damaged and too ordinary; Luca, on his side, pretending to be very angry, contradicted the bookseller's remarks. Finally the latter said, "It's all common stuff . . . I might give you something . . . for the whole lot."

"How much?" asked Luca.

The bookseller twisted his mouth, casting a glance of contempt over the velvet collar of his coat toward the pile of books; then mentioned a figure. "That's not much," said Luca; "let's make it double."

"It's not even worth discussing," answered the bookseller. And he took up his hat which he had placed on the table.

Luca hesitated, then had an idea. He would propose to the bookseller to make one lot of the books together with the puppets and the sports gear. In that way, with one stroke, he would get rid of everything he possessed. "Wait a moment," he said; "I'll throw in some other things and then you can give me the amount I asked for."

"What things?"

Luca went to the far end of the room and opened a cupboard in the wall. In it were a football and some boxing gloves, quite new. There was a sailboat with all its sails spread. There was the marionette theatre, with the marionettes. "I don't keep a junk-shop," said the bookseller. But in his little deepset eyes there was a sudden look of greed.

"This football alone," said Luca, "cost me more than what you are offering me for all my books."

In the end the bookseller accepted Luca's figure and paid the amount. The same day a carrier came and took away the books and the other things in a packing case. When he was alone Luca looked with satisfaction at his empty shelves. It was just as he had said to Poli, he couldn't help thinking, just as if he was getting ready to leave on a long journey. But the joy that he felt in face of the emptiness of his room was not the joy of departure; it was, rather, the mournful, frigid joy of arrival in a bare and uninhabited land where he knew that nothing awaited him. That day he did even less work than usual. Every moment his mind reverted to his books, to his stamp collection, to his sports gear and, at the thought that he had had the strength to get rid of them, he felt an inexhaustible, mysterious, almost sensual satisfaction. He pictured to himself how Poli must be thinking that he was a fool, how the bookseller must be congratulating himself on his excellent deal, and he was pleased that those two should be convinced that they had taken him in. At the same time he was aware of a certain lightness and sense of relief, like someone who has carried a heavy burden a long way and suddenly feels himself free of it.

There remained, however, the money. He had to get rid of it and at the same time somehow or other justify his failure to buy a phonograph. Luca seized the opportunity at supper of announcing in a quiet but sorrowful manner: "There's something I must tell you . . . but you must both promise me you won't be angry . . ."

His parents looked at him in alarm. Luca went on: "This morning in the street car my wallet was stolen—or possibly it fell out of my pocket . . . anyhow I haven't been able to find it since . . . and in it was all my money . . . the money I was going to use to buy the phonograph . . ."

After the usual questions—"How on earth did it happen?—and why weren't you more careful?—and where, exactly, *was* your wallet?—and why did you have *all* your money in it?"—there followed a discussion during which Luca was several times on the point of giving up all hope that his plan would succeed. For his father, filled with pity at so cruel a misfortune, seemed inclined to give him back the amount he had lost; while his mother, irritated at the loss and at her son's carelessness, opposed the plan of compensating him, arguing that the disaster "would serve him as a lesson for the future." Luca saw that, if his father's argument prevailed, he would not only have twice the sum of money that he already possessed, but he would also be forced to buy the phonograph, with the risk of becoming attached to an object so new and so pleasing. He followed the discussion anxiously, trusting only the soft, yielding strain in his father's character. And in the end his mother succeeded in winning her point; with this reservation, however, that if Luca brought home a good report at the end of the term, his parents would make him a present of the phonograph and of an adequate number of records. Luca, knowing that his report would be extremely bad, smiled cheerfully.

It was the beginning of December. One afternoon Luca went out carrying in the pockets of his overcoat all the money he possessed, in silver coins and small notes. It was a day of respite after long rains. The sky was washed clean but was still dark with a smoky, even color, as though its customary blue had been replaced, not by the confused gray of cloud that dissolves in rain or is chased away by the wind, but by a different hue, more settled, more gloomy, forever unchangeable. In the cool, windless air there was the feeling of exhaustion that succeeds the raging of a storm; but a flock of crows, hovering low, seemed to give warning with their watery cries that there would be more rain. Looking up at the sky and turning the money in his pocket, Luca made his way toward the public gardens not far from his home. He knew that at that hour of the day there was no one there and that he could act with the certainty of not being observed. He passed through the big gates and penetrated deep into the gardens. He knew just where he was going—to a place that was bound up in his memory with a sort of fixation of his child-hood years. This was an open space bounded on three sides by large, leafy ilexes and on the fourth by a decorative wall adorned with niches, columns and Roman inscriptions. On the other side of the wall lay the zoological gardens, and you could often hear the roaring of the hungry beasts. As a child, Luca had often been brought for a walk by his governesses to this melancholy, deserted place, whose white gravel was darkly framed by the bronze foliage of the ilexes. While his governess, sitting on a fallen capital, would read a book, Luca would climb up to the gratings of the empty windows in the wall and try to look into the zoo beyond. Or he would wander through the ilex grove at the edge of the open space. It was shady in there, and the ground was covered with several layers of dead leaves, dry at the surface, shiny and damp underneath. Here and there grew clumps of nettles whose bright green seemed to feed on all this decay and which filled Luca with repulsion.

One day at home the governess and the maid had been talking about murder. A young man had been killed; the body had not been found, but some bloodstained garments and the place where these had been discovered had made it seem probable that the corpse had been buried in one of the many public gardens of the town. Luca, without saying a word, pretending to play, had listened for a long time to the comments of the two women; finally he had asked the maid: "Why did they kill him?" She had answered, in a bitter, sharp tone: "Because he was handsome and good, that's why . . . because he was not made for this world"; and he, struck by this phrase, had asked no more questions. But later, he could not have said why, it had become fixed in his mind that the corpse of the young man had been buried in the same open space where he so often went for a walk with his governess. This supposition had no foundation in fact, not even a mistaken or a very slight one; but perhaps for that very reason it had seemed to him irrefutable. His mind full of this terrible and at the same time fascinating secret, it pleased him to be able, as he wandered about the open space, to look with certainty at the precise spot where, beneath the ground, the corpse was crumbling to pieces. It was a corner between the wall and the grove at the foot of a great ilex; and Luca would often stop at the place, fumbling with his foot among the dead leaves or piercing the soft earth all about him with a stick. He knew that the dead man lay below, and not for anything in the world would he have renounced his conviction. Besides, by dint of thinking about it, he had reconstructed the crime in his own way, and had even formed a picture in his mind of what the murdered man and his murderers looked like. The former had evidently been a handsome, good young man, as the maid had said; but with a special sort of beauty and goodness, in no way conspicuous, invisible to most people, secret. As for the others, Luca saw them as being in every way similar to anyone that he met in the street, ordinary, nameless passers-by. They had perhaps killed him in order to rob him, as the papers said; but in truth, as the maid had said, it had been out of hatred for his beauty and his goodness, to remove him from this world for which he was not made. As he thought of the young man and of his death he felt a horrible attraction and at the same time a great compassion. And then as time went on, almost without realizing it he imagined that the murdered man was himself and that the body buried under the ilex was his own. This duplication of himself, brought about by some kind of imaginative fondness both for the appearance and for the fate of the murdered man, seemed to him perfectly natural, nor was it the first time such a thing had happened. On other occasions, when reading books of adventure, he had dreamed of being this or that heroic, successful character. But it was the first time he had happened to fall in love with so gloomy a destiny, and he had an obscure feeling that unlike his other duplications, this one was due to profound causes, to an obsession in which the whole vocation of his life expressed itself. Such an obsession, as generally happens, had gradually through the years dwindled away like a mist that vanishes in the sunshine; it had become transformed into a sad memory and had finally disappeared into oblivion.

But now, on his way to the open space in the gardens, the obsession came back to him in a different form. He knew by this time that no one had ever been buried in the open space, but that space, consecrated once and for all by his imagination, still remained the place where a corpse *ought* to be buried. He would bury the money in the same spot where he once had thought the murdered man lay; and in burying the money he would in a certain sense be burying himself also—or at any rate that part of himself that was attached to the money. And in a vague way mixed up with these more serious matters were memories of buried treasure in circumstances of adventure, echoes of the reading of his early youth.

It was Poe's *The Gold Bug* that he had particularly in mind. But this was a kind of alibi, with the object of removing all quality of the tragic from his sacrifice, of keeping it within the bounds of a game. Apart from the money, he had brought with him a blue glass medicine bottle in which he had enclosed a card explaining eactly where he was going to bury his little treasure. Knowing nothing of ciphers, Luca had contented himself with writing the explanation in schoolboy slang, adding an "f" to each syllable. As in the story he intended to hide this bottle in the hollow of one of the ilexes that surrounded the open space.

He walked across a big square lawn, looking straight in front of him. At the far side of the lawn, the black trunks of the ilex grove swayed back and forth like a crowd seized with panic that rocks to and fro before it breaks and flees. Through the ilexes, the pale whiteness of the gravel catching the light, he had a glimpse of the open space with the wall behind it. He went into the grove, walking with conscious pleasure on the sloping carpet of dead leaves. In the silence under the trees he heard the thin whistle of a bird, and turning he saw the bird itself, big and black, hopping along the ground and then taking flight and hiding among the leaves. He noticed also that as he made his way through the wood he felt a sensation of freedom, and he thought how fine a thing action was, even if it was for the destruction of one's own life, and that action consisted in this—performing acts according to one's own ideas and not merely from necessity.

There was no one in the open space. He walked about for a while, thinking of the time when he had been convinced the corpse was buried there, and he seemed to rediscover intact the lonely, rather sinister feeling of the place which had enthralled him as a child. He looked at the wall with its empty niches, its fragmentary inscriptions, its crumbling cornices. He looked at the windows with the seats beneath them and the big gratings. He climbed up to one of these windows and looked through to the other side, into the zoological garden.

He could see the thick foliage of a laurel hedge, and among the leaves he thought he caught a glimpse of the green and gold feathers of some large exotic bird. A distant roaring made him start: the wild beasts, as in the old days, as always, were hungry. He came down again from the window and walked over to the place he was seeking. There will still the same ilex, ancient, with a great black rift in its trunk, its main branch projecting toward the open space and leaning on a brick support like the arm of a cripple on a crutch. Beneath the ilex was the corpse. There came back to him in all its cruelty and pathos the feeling that it was he himself who was buried there, he himself who had been pitilessly murdered.

He knelt down under the tree and started to dig a hole with his penknife. Beneath the dead leaves, the soil was moist and light, full of decayed fragments of bark. He loosened the earth and then scooped it out with his hand and put it to one side in a small heap. When he had finished making the hole, he slowly took from his pocket the banknotes and started tearing them up one after another, letting the pieces drop down into the hole. He discovered that he felt a profound hatred for this money, the sort of hatred one might feel for a tyrant against whom one has rebelled. The idea, too, that money was held in such high esteem by his parents and that he himself without knowing it had for so many years said his prayers in front of a safe full of money contributed to his resentment. As he tore up the notes he felt he was avenging his prayers, was accomplishing an act of reparation. But money, too, was sacred—though in quite a different way from the sacred picture that had concealed it while he was praying. It was sacred because of the royal effigies and symbols that guaranteed its value; and it was sacred because it might have meant happiness to so many people. To the poor man, for instance, who, every morning as he was going to school, stretched out his hand toward him at the corner of the street. But to give it to a poor man would have been, fundamentally, to respect it, to acknowledge its value. And Luca wanted, instead, truly to destroy it, not merely by his own desire to do so but in actual fact. Detested idol as he felt it to be, nothing less than this blasphemous tearing to pieces could serve utterly to desecrate it.

When he had finished tearing up the notes, he mixed the pieces together, and then pulling an envelope full of silver coins from his pocket, he thrust it into the bottom of the hole on top of the notes. He performed these actions with a sense of austerity that was grave and conscious, yet mingled with a mortal sadness. The thought of the dead man murdered and buried there came back to his mind, and again he was assailed by that strange feeling of pity for himself. Meanwhile he was filling the hole with earth. When he had finished, he leveled the soil and covered the whole thing over with a carpet of dead leaves.

He rose, brushing the knees of his trousers which were damp and dirty with earth, and then he remembered the blue glass bottle and Edgar Allan Poe's story. By now he lacked the courage to carry out this part of his plan. He had a feeling of gloomy, dazed depression and realized that after all it had not been a game. *He* was not the bloodstained, callous pirate at the end of a life of adventure and freedom; this open space was not the deserted shore of some savage land; and in fact no one would ever make the joyful discovery of his poor little treasure of torn banknotes and small silver coins. The unrelieved mediocrity of himself, of the place and of his treasure all at once seemed to him the best proof of the dogged seriousness of what he was doing and of the impossibility of deceiving himself by attributing to it the importance of a mere game. He took the bottle out of his pocket, opened it, pulled out the little scroll and tore it into tiny pieces. He crushed the bottle under his heel. As he went away, he felt he had acted like a madman. All the same there must be some sense in this madness, only he was not yet in a position to discover it.

After that day Luca seemed to fall into a deathly torpor, as though his body, exhausted by the proofs of willpower that it had given, were recovering itself for a last, decisive effort. More and more often he fell asleep halfway through his homework; more and more often at school he fell into fits of abstraction allowing the voices of the professors to spin round him in an empty, sustained silence, like the sound of a broken record endlessly repeating the same phrase. After a few fine days winter had resumed its course and it rained most of the time. The rain descending from a pitch-black sky seemed to be dark and opaque, as though it were mixed with mud, and it spread everywhere a darkness which made Luca feel it would be pleasant to curl up and go to sleep for good. Sometimes, as he did his lessons, he would raise his eyes toward the window and feel convinced that the sky was clearing. He would become absorbed in his work; half an hour later he would look up again and be astonished at the sight of the heavy, gray rain flowing in silent waves down the windowpanes. The sky was like a person weeping in some profound sorrow, who seems every now and then to grow calmer and more serene but who is soon caught up again by grief and starts once more to shed tears, more abundantly and more violently than ever. He liked, above all, the hour between day and night. He liked to linger at his table in front of the rain-streaked windowpanes, forcing himself to read or write in the growing darkness, until the moment when the early winter twilight fell upon his page like an impalpable dust. Then he would rise and throw himself on the bed, falling asleep almost at once. His task remained unfinished.

He had now embarked upon the last part of his plan—physical death. He proceeded, however, indirectly, without understanding what he was doing, by observing his own greediness and forming, in consequence, a determination to suppress it, just as he had suppressed his pride in his work at school and his attachment to property. He had always enjoyed eating, especially at lunch time on his return from school, when in the voracity with which he threw himself upon his food he seemed to recognize the acceptance, by his whole body, of all that he had been and had done before he sat down to table. Besides, there were certain kinds of food which, apart from any question of appetite, he particularly liked—sweets and cakes, for example. And so setting in motion his usual "game" mechanism, he took care to eat only a small amount of the ordinary kinds of food and nothing at all of the things he liked best. At first he cut down the amount he ate by a quarter, then by a half. He left the table hungry, but the sensation was short-lived and soon disappeared. It came back again toward evening, but then he would try to sleep, and by sleeping he succeeded in quelling his hunger. He felt that the less he ate the more easily he would fall asleep.

It seemed, then, that there were rules for death as there were for life. If living meant being enthusiastic about one's lessons, loving one's parents, saving up money, becoming attached to objects, eating, it followed that dying must mean not eating, ridding oneself of all affection both for things and for people, and, above all, sleeping.

His parents did not appear to notice this strange loss of appetite on his part; or rather, he thought probably they did notice it but did not attach importance to it, being used to his frequent caprices in the matter of food. His mother, however, remarked one day, in a severe tone of voice: "Why don't you eat? At your age you need nourishment . . . Even if you're not hungry you ought to force yourself to eat . . . if you don't eat how can you do your lessons?" "Yes, how can I do my lessons?" thought Luca, amused. It pleased him to think that his parents were so far from suspecting that he was deliberately not eating, notwithstanding his appetite which urged him to take nourishment. Not eating. He realized that of all forms of disobedience this was the most serious, the most fundamental, the one that most thoroughly undermined familial authority. His father and mother were there for the special purpose of making him eat. His mother had fed him with the milk of her own breast; his father, like the primitive hunter leaving the cave at dawn armed with bow and arrow to slay some animal on which to feed his family, left home every morning to seek in the town the money that would serve to support him. He felt he had reached the extreme limit of disobedience, that he had arrived in a rarefied atmosphere in which his game was becoming difficult and dangerous. His parents wished him to eat so that he should create strength for himself, and should live; and he, possessed by a feeling of unqualified revolt, wished not to eat, and to die. The game was still on, but he was totally unable to see how far he would have the strength to pursue it. For death had not yet appeared to him as a definite aim, although his every act was a provocation of it.

One day his father placed him in an embarrassing position by making an appeal, not to his appetite, but to a deeper feeling which he did not know he had retained. It was some time since he had reduced his eating, but his parents apparently did not attribute much importance to his loss of appetite. One day he noticed a white package lying beside his father's plate. And at the end of lunch he saw his father take up the package and solemnly undo the string.

It was a cake, the kind that Luca had once liked best. His father put aside the paper and string, placed the cake on a plate and said in his drawling, good-natured voice: "I bought a cake . . . I was passing a confectioner's and I went in and bought it . . . it should be a good one."

"If you bought it for me," said his mother, "you know quite well that I don't like cakes."

"Really I bought it for Luca," said his father; "he used to like them . . . but perhaps"—and he gave a knowing wink—"it may be that, now he's grown big, he's changed his ideas." As he spoke, he pushed the plate toward Luca.

"I'm not hungry any more," said Luca, lowering his eyes.

"Come on," said his father, "there must be a little room left."

He spoke as usual in a mournful, supplicating tone; but it seemed to Luca, that day, that there was a kind of awareness in that eternally beseeching voice of his father. "No, really, I'm not hungry," he repeated.

"Come on, come on," repeated his father, "come on, Luca . . . eat a little bit of it." And he added facetiously: "Anyhow, eat just enough to please Daddy . . . d'you remember," he concluded, turning to his wife, "when he was little that was all you had to say to make him eat?"

"Let him alone," said his mother, "if he's not hungry now, he'll eat it this evening or tomorrow . . . cake keeps well."

But to Luca it had seemed that his father, when he implored him in that way, had said to him "Live!" not "Eat!" And he felt affection for his father, and pity for himself, at one and the same time. He thought his father must have guessed his secret, not through his intelligence, which was not suited to such matters, but through his goodness—that same goodness which once upon a time had made him appear perfect, adorable, and of which in Luca's eyes, in spite of disillusionments, he still seemed to preserve some traces. And he was assailed by a strong temptation to accept the cake and eat it, and with it to accept life. But he realized that to accept life in the form of a slice of cake, even though it was offered by his father's goodness, would be a wretched comedown after he had ruined his school career and got rid of all the things he loved; so clenching his teeth, he hung his head over the plate. "Well?" he heard his father's voice insisting, "don't you really want any?" "I'm not hungry," he repeated. And he sat quite still, his head bowed.

There was a moment's silence. "Well, well, it's a pity," said his father, without showing whether he was really grieved by Luca's refusal. "I bought it specially for you . . . so I'll put it on the sideboard . . . and when you feel like it and are sure no one's watching, you'll eat it, won't you?" And Luca felt a flip on his cheek from the father's hand. He shuddered.

This incident left him with a feeling of deep anguish. He was still tied, and not only by the things he had not yet got rid of, but also by those he thought he had destroyed once and for all, such as his filial love. From that day, there grew in him more strongly than before, the desire to relinquish his existence.

Now one of his mother's sisters was taken sick, and in order to spare her all the noise the two families agreed that her children, twin girls and a little boy of eight, should go to their aunt's house. They were accompanied by their governess, an unmarried woman of good family who had formerly been a French teacher. She was a woman of about thirty-five whose shortness was accentuated by the disparity between her narrow shoulders and her big head with its bulging hair. She was not beautiful, with her dull, inexpressive eyes set level with her face and always dark and bruised looking, her overpale, rather flabby cheeks and her bulging loose mouth, shaded with dark down. But this lack of attractiveness, this appearance of ill health were to a certain extent made up for by the extraordinary vivacity and gaiety of her character. Not merely did she perform quite willingly her humble, tedious duty as a governess, but she brought to it a certain whimsical enthusiasm of her own, playing with her three pupils as though she herself were a child, putting herself on equal terms with them, sometimes wrangling with them or actually bursting into tears if one of them was rude to her. This childishness was in strong contrast with a look of ill-repressed sensuality—more suitable, certainly, to a mature woman than to a child—visible in the tiredness of her eyes, in the slightly suggestive beauty of her hands, and in the softness of her hips. She chattered continually, and her voice was clear and shrill with a mischievous sharpness in it; her talk was interspersed with frequent bursts of silvery laughter. The sitting room next door to Luca's bedroom was assigned to her and the three children for their special use. Therefore, to his own drowsiness and idle fancies there was now added, as further distraction from his work, the noise of his three cousins playing with their governess.

In the morning the governess took the children for a walk in the public gardens; but in the early hours of the afternoon she shut herself up with them in the little sitting room and from then on the noise went on, uninterrupted, till the evening. Sitting at his table, his head heavy with the usual drowsiness, Luca could hear the shouts of the children as they ran about the whole afternoon, the woman shouting and running with them in an unending, untiring agitation and liveliness and gaiety which made his own immobility seem, by contrast, even duller and heavier. Every now and then mysterious bumps, as of overturned furniture or falling bodies, made him jump; these were followed by stifled, joyous laughter. Or he would hear the governess's voice raised loudly and clearly in playful authority, bidding the children not to make a noise, but after a short pause the din would break out again, louder and more concentrated than ever. The children were boisterous by nature and the young woman stimulated this boisterousness of theirs by the facility of her imagination and the vivacity of her own temperament. Sometimes when the noise was at its loudest the governess would open his door and poke her head in, asking, in a manner half knowing and half hypocritical, whether they were disturbing him. It was an idle question, and seemed merely to be part of a general plan for preventing him from working. Luca would answer, without turning round, that it did not matter, that they could make as much noise as they liked. He was not in the least anxious to work and this childish liveliness was yet another excuse for avoiding it.

But sometimes he felt a desire to join in these amusements, so varied and so different from his own solitary, mournful game, and getting up from his table he would open the door of the sitting room and look in. He would see a scene of disorder and of childish gaiety—chairs overturned, tables pushed aside, the governess on all fours on the carpet with a child riding on her back; and he would stand transfixed in the doorway, watching them while they went on playing just as though he were not there. Then, turning around on the floor on hands and knees with her rider on her back, the governess would look up at him with a laughing face from under the disheveled hair hanging down over her nose, asking him in her usual way whether by any chance they were disturbing him. "No . . . no . . . go ahead," Luca would answer, embarrassed: "I just looked in because I wanted a rest." But the governess had already ceased listening to him. With a vigorous shake she would free herself of her rider, who would roll laughing on the floor; then she would get up, ruffled and untidy, and proclaim in a voice of authority: "Now listen everybody . . . we'll play a completely different game . . . but listen, because I shan't explain it twice."

Luca liked the governess because she seemed to him kind and simple and gay, so unlike his mother who, filled as she was with rigid educational theories, would never have dreamed of playing with children in that manner. But a day came when this liking of his was suddenly complicated by a feeling of a different kind. One afternoon, watching her as she caracoled across the room with the little boy on her back, Luca could not help noticing the provoking roundness of her hips as she raised them in the air in an animal-like attitude, and at a movement she made as she turned round toward him his eyes, almost against his will, were attracted to her bosom which through the opening of her blouse was completely visible, including the whole contour of her very white, soft breasts. These breasts hung down like those of an animal and swayed with every movement, and Luca, though he said to himself that it was highly indiscreet to fix his eyes upon them, was quite unable to look away. At that moment she raised her face toward him, frankly intercepted his look and lifted her hand with an instinctive movement toward her breast. But her first modest impulse was arrested by some reflection, and all she did was to smooth back her hair; then, shouting and laughing, she resumed her parade across the room. Luca, noticing the movement, was sure that she had changed and modified it out of coquettishness, and at once he felt deeply disturbed. Still on all fours and with her little rider on her back, she headed for a distant corner of the room. Luca watched her and for the first time could not help thinking it unbecoming that the little boy, as he rode on her back, should beat her on the buttocks with his hands as he might have beaten the crupper of a horse. Perhaps she noticed this look of his, for she gave a sudden shake of her hips in a manner that seemed to him provoking. But this movement caused the child to roll off on to the floor; he hit his head against the corner of a cabinet and burst into tears. At once, transformed instantaneously from animal to woman, she got up, took him by the hand and led him under the lamp, asking him where he was hurt. Luca went back to his room.

During the days that followed he noticed that he rose more and more often from his table and, under one pretext or another, or without any pretext at all, went and looked in at the sitting room door. He would have liked to produce some sort of a lie to conceal the true nature of his attraction—more for his own benefit than for that of the woman, whom he guessed to be pleased by his curiosity, but unaccustomed to lying to himself, he could not find one. He recognized quite frankly that he looked in at the sitting room door in order to see the governess. And that when he looked in he hoped to see her again in that same animal-like attitude, on all fours, her hips sticking up in the air, her breasts dangling. By this time, however, to be conscious of a pleasure meant, for Luca, to hate it. Therefore with the same passion with which he had undertaken the sacrifice of his books and his money and the ruin of his school career, he devoted himself to the destruction of this new tie.

At first he tried to gain control of himself and thrust desire from him. But he soon saw that after resisting nine times out of ten he canceled out all the success he had obtained by going the tenth time, and looking in at the door of the sitting room, in an even more awkward and transparent manner than usual. Instinctively, he tried a different method. He looked in as often as he wanted to, but sought to change the nature of the pleasure by observing the woman minutely. It had been at first a genuine though furtive pleasure, gay and thoughtless as the person who inspired it. Now his object was to introduce a new flavor, that of physical and moral disgust. He made use, unconsciously, of the same cunning that had served him in the case of the money and the books; having loved them and loved them too much he had managed to discover, in the sweet depths of that love, the bitterness of a nauseating satiety, of an injurious servitude; and this bitterness had been a powerful aid to him in getting rid of them. By looking without restraint at the woman, he sought, with a cruelty which he felt to be unjustified and more desperate than ever, to find the defect in this new pleasure of his. But this time, contrary to what had happened in the case of the books and the money, he discovered to his surprise that the tie, far from being severed, had actually become stronger.

The defect lay chiefly in the forbidden, illicit, furtive nature of his contemplation, of which he had been aware from the very beginning without attaching much importance to it. But perhaps the very quality of the pleasure he derived from his contemplation was still the strongest justification of his determination to renounce it. She was not beautiful, as he had at once realized; and this absence of a beauty which might in some way counterbalance the secrecy of desire by the openness of disinterested admiration, might also liberate him from his new bonds. How could he possibly care for those stumpy legs which, when she played at galloping round the room, were visible above the baggy stockings, right up to the luminous, cold whiteness of the thighs? And those breasts, so soft and dangling? And the buttocks, large out of all proportion, giving her a bunched-up look when she was standing, as though in that place her garments concealed not a part of her body but a cumbrous shapeless bundle? These reflections brought him a sort of relief; she was really clumsy looking, no longer young, already going flabby, and he hoped that this clumsiness, this maturity, this flabbiness introducing as they undoubtedly did an element of displeasure into his pleasure, would in the end restrain and deflect its progress. But this did not last long. As a second examination, when he thought he could now look at the governess without feeling disturbed, Luca discovered that she now attracted him just because she was flabby and clumsy and not very young. It was true that there still remained that bitter flavor of disgust that he had wanted deliberately to introduce, but it was no longer a matter for disgust, it was, rather, a new and more exciting cause of attraction. All this, he could not help thinking, had happened without his noticing it, by a sort of alchemy in the darkest depths of his instinct. He understood, too, that if he had been able by some miracle to transform her and make her young and beautiful, he would not have desired her so much. And so the desire of his senses had proved stronger than his desire for death, and by making ugliness attractive had brought him back in spite of himself into the life that he had wished, at all cost, to leave.

This discovery reduced him to despair, for he also realized that, if these longing glances at her hips and bosom sufficed to bring down the laborious edifice of his sacrifices, they certainly did not suffice to make him live in a positive sense. It was too late now, he thought, he had broken the threads that bound him to life and it was impossible to start over again. What sort of a life would it have been, without affections, without obligations, sustained merely by a few moments of furtive lust?

And then, as though she had guessed his thoughts, the woman herself took the initiative. She would burst into Luca's room, pulling one of the children after her, and let herself fall backward on to the bed, legs in the air, in one of their usual merry wrestling-matches; she would come and look in at his door, when the noise reached its height, in order to apologize. She did these things with boisterous assurance, laughing and joking, but it seemed to Luca that she was not as spontaneous as before. She invented a game in which it was necessary for one of the players to absent himself from the sitting room for a short time, and instead of going into the corridor she went into Luca's room, making the excuse that the corridor was cold. She left the door ajar and went close to Luca without making any noise; suddenly she leant over his shoulder, brushing his cheek with her own. "What are you working at? Latin?" "No, French." "Why, I used to teach French . . . let me see what it is . . . *Corneille?*" Her voice, cheerful as it was, seemed to Luca strangely expressionless. And when he turned slightly to answer her, he found her face almost against his own and her big, flat-set eyes gazing intently and smiling at him. Luca noticed her cheeks sagged a little, they were dusted over with pink powder and shiny under the powder grains; he noticed that this detail pleased him just because it displeased him. Perhaps she felt that his look was cruelly penetrating; for she said, laughing: "Go on with your work!" and with a pirouette went to the door. "Can I come in now?" he heard her shout. The children cried to her to come in and she disappeared.

Next day Luca had just dozed off on the bed, when in the confusion of slumber he suddenly felt three or four gesticulating, clinging bodies fall with disagreeable violence on top of him. It was the governess and her three pupils who, chasing each other, had intentionally thrown themselves upon him. The children and the woman struggled together, laughing and shouting, and in order to free himself, Luca too started struggling. And in this scuffle he discovered that his hands, against his will, instinctively sought the woman's body; and while the children were struggling with all the impulsiveness and violence they were capable of she was apparently seeking him out—anxious to prolong the battle instead of trying to free herself. When she made a movement to shake off the children Luca found one of her legs lying across his face, and this time he was sure she had done it on purpose. It was the calf of her leg, and it bounced against his mouth like a well-turned club of light, soft flesh so that his lips, at every rebound, could feel the vibration of the muscles as she tightened them in order not to hurt him. At last she jumped up from the bed, shouting: "That's enough, everybody! . . . And now I've thought of a new game."

The children calmed down instantly, and the governess said: "Now this is the game: we'll put out all the lights and then we'll draw lots. . . . All except one person will hide, and that person must look for the others in the dark and recognize them . . . but he must guess who the other person is in the dark, without speaking, just by feeling. . . . Of course," she added, turning to Luca, "we must put out the light in your room too . . . and, if it doesn't bore you to play with children, do come and play with us, just this once."

Luca, smoothing back his disheveled hair, said: "All right," and the governess concluded: "No locking yourselves in . . . and no hiding in wardrobes." "Can we hide under the beds?" asked the little boy. "Under the beds—yes, that's all right."

They left Luca's room and went back into the sitting room. The governess wrote down their names on bits of paper, mixed them all up and made one of the twins draw lots. "Luca," she announced, as she unfolded the paper. Luca saw his cousins looking at him with envy. "You must stay here in this room," said the governess, "while we go and hide." Luca nodded and sat down in an armchair near the fireplace.

She went out with the children, turning off the sitting-room light as she went, and then the corridor light. Sitting in the darkness Luca listened carefully, he could hear footsteps coming and going, doors opening, whispers, stifled laughter, creakings and bumps. He was completely absorbed in the game now and was trying to make out where the others were hiding. Every now and then a motorcar passing in the street outside threw on the wall a rectangle of bars of light that turned slowly toward the ceiling and then disappeared; and for a moment, in a twilight striped with vivid light, he had a glimpse of the whole room. During one of these illuminations he caught sight of a black figure standing erect in a corner, in the space between the bookshelf and the china cabinet. It was the governess; and Luca thought how cunning of her to hide in the sitting room, which because it was the most obvious place was also the last place he would have thought of. After a moment's reflection, he decided to pretend he was making a careful search in the corridor, whereas he would not really be searching at all; then he would go straight to the corner where she was hiding and shout out her name in a loud voice. He was pleased with this decision; in that way he would show her that he was more cunning than she. Meanwhile from the darkness came the silvery voice of one of the twins, announcing: "We're ready . . . you can begin."

Feeling his way carefully but swiftly he crossed the sitting room and went into the hall. There he stopped, listening. He did not want to run the risk of finding one of his cousins, and in thus preferring the governess he was conscious for the first time of an intention which had nothing to do with the game. He went over to the umbrella stand and pretended to feel about among the sticks and umbrellas. From a long way came a piping, childish voice repeating: "You're cold . . . you're cold." Luca moved a few steps further, knocking his foot purposely against the leg of a chair, then went back into the sitting room, moving with outstretched arms for the corner where the governess stood.

He had intended to leap upon her, seize her, and immediately shout: "The signorina!" But at the last moment, and not without hypocrisy, it seemed to him that this would be finishing the game too quickly, for not the least important part of it consisted in running your hands carefully over the face of the person you had caught before you recognized him. He had reached the corner now, he stretched out his hands into the void and his fingers came into contact with the outline of a cheek. She neither moved nor breathed—a sign that she was playing her part in the game. His fingers wandered round her cheek, down along her chin towards her neck.

But then, as he touched the dimple in her chin, he suddenly realized that a second game had taken the place of the first; and this second game was not really a game at all, but the usual hankering that impelled him every day to leave his table and look into the sitting room. At this thought, a feeling of strong excitement took his breath away and made his face burn. In the meantime, with a now fully conscious hypocrisy, he continued to run his fingers over her face, as though he had difficulty in recognizing her.

He enjoyed stroking her cheeks, even though he was aware of a flabby softness; in fact, he enjoyed it particularly for that reason just as he enjoyed the complicity that joined them together, even though he felt it to be slightly ignoble. And so, he thought once again, the repugnance he felt served only to make his desire stronger and more complicated, like a fire that is fed even by the water that ought to put it out. He followed the outline of her mouth and felt under his finger tips the gentle resistance of the down that shadowed her lips and the stickiness of the greasy make-up. This contact too was both agreeable and disagreeable. From her face his fingers moved down to her neck, and Luca was reminded that she had three little folds there, like three necklaces, which made her neck feel wasted. She did not move, and Luca passed from her neck to the upper part of her breast. At this point the governess became impatient at a caress so hesitating, in which the ambiguous nature of the game was too carefully respected in spite of the darkness and of her own encouraging silence: she took hold of his hand and placed it on her bosom. Luca felt the soft, round breast that seemed under his pressure to change shape and seek to escape his hand that she pressed so frenziedly to her; and then, with the sudden eagerness of a long-restrained protest, he shouted: "The signorina!" She at once dropped his hand; there was a great hubbub, lights went on, the lamp in the sitting room was lit and the little cousins came back. "Well done, Luca!" said the governess, coming out of her corner. "He found me almost at once." The children, disappointed, started a boasting competition about the remarkable places they had hidden in, in order to comfort themselves for not having been found. The youngest said: "I hid in the cupboard where the brooms are kept . . . but there was a smell of wax there and it almost made me sneeze." The governess warned them in a severe tone: "Now don't tell us the places where you hid, or the game will be all over at once."

For a time they talked about the surprises of the game, then the governess announced: "Now it's my turn . . . but look out, hide yourselves well . . . because I know you and I'll find you in no time." She seemed very gay and thoughtless, entirely absorbed in the game. And Luca, as he looked at her, could not help marveling at her duplicity. For this seemed to be not only in her attitude toward him but to extend even to her clothes, to the white silk blouse through which she had made him feel her breast but showed not the slightest sign of crumpling as a result of that violent embrace. Going across to the electric light switch, she added: "Now I'm going to put the light out. . . . Now, quickly, run and hide yourselves."

It was dark again; and Luca hesitated between the two games. He might hide seriously, like his cousins—this was the first game; or he might wait in the corner between the bookshelf and the china cabinet until she found him— and this was the second game, so much more attractive since it was entirely made up of disagreeable things. The first game fitted in with his own permanent game and implied the rejection of this last tie of fleshly attraction and repulsion that bound him to life; the second implied its acceptance. Almost automatically, he started on tiptoe toward the corner by the bookshelf. Another car passed along the street, streaking the walls and ceiling with moving bands of light. Surely the governess, who had not yet left the room, must have seen him.

She behaved exactly as he had behaved. She went out into the corridor, pretended to bustle round and search everywhere, then came back into the sitting room. Luca knew that she was coming toward him by the glowing point of the cigarette between her lips. This red speck, like the planet Mars in a black winter sky, came closer and closer, swaying as it hung suspended at the level of her face. When it was quite near, the little blood-red star moved to the left with a sudden displacement as she took the cigarette out of her mouth. Luca followed it with his eyes and saw it descend a considerable distance; the governess was letting her arm fall to her side. But at the same time a hand slipped in behind his neck with a slow, firm movement like a snake uncoiling. Then, with a mixed smell of tobacco and lipstick, he was conscious of a warm breath on his face, followed immediately by the sensation of two lips crushing themselves against his.

Even in this kiss—the first of his life—he recognized an ambiguous quality, at once agreeable and disagreeable. The woman's lips, thick and soft, spread themselves over his lips, as though to master them, with an enfolding, circular motion which involved not only the mouth but also the chin and the base of the nostrils. Like the edges of a deep wound, these lips seemed inert and lifeless, forced to spread themselves more by the pressure of the two faces against each other than by any voluntary movement. But from the depths behind the lips came a thing full of energy, muscular, pointed, thrusting itself between

Luca's teeth, unclenching them, penetrating violently into his mouth. She curled and uncurled her tongue as though she wished to explore all the intricacies not only of Luca's mouth but of his whole body and was prevented from doing so merely by the shortness of the implement she used; and its wet roughness made him think of the body of a large snail emerging from its shell. Yes, he decided on further reflection, yes, a snail, but a snail gone crazy, indefatigable even though blind, with a vibrant, self-willed vitality such as only an animal can possess. And meanwhile, as the kiss still continued, saliva issued from their confused mouths and trickled down his chin.

Luca had been expecting that she would call out his name, just as he had called hers, thus putting an end both to the game and the kiss. But without taking her mouth from his, she came closer to him with a lively movement of her whole body, and he realized that though he had reached the point where, more disconcerted than attracted, he would willingly have stopped, she intended to continue. Then from the other end of the flat he heard the squeaky voice of his little cousin calling out: "You're not looking . . . You've made an agreement with Luca . . . it's not fair, it's not fair"; and in that cry he seemed to hear the voice of his own innocence at the very moment of its destruction by the fires of sensuality. The governess suddenly left him and stumbled across the room, saying in a gay voice: "Why isn't it fair? I'm still looking." Still panting, Luca took his handkerchief out of his pocket and wiped his wet chin.

The governess' search did not last long. There was a cheerful clatter and Luca knew that she had found one of his cousins. As before, the lights went on and the woman and the three children came back into the sitting room. Luca was quite bewildered by his own discordant sensations. During the kiss, the feeling of repulsion had been stronger than usual, so much so that it almost completely swamped the feeling of pleasure. And yet it was that very repulsion that kindled a burning, impure flame of desire in his blood. He felt that he wanted to kiss her again, and in exactly the same way, with those same sensations. But when the lights went off again, he walked firmly out of the sitting room with a spontaneity that surprised him, and hid in the kitchen, behind the stove.

From there he could hear more than one person walking about in the corridor; besides one of the little girls who was seeking those who had hidden, there must also be the governess seeking for *him*. He was conscious of a sharp pain, as though at the destruction of some beloved living thing which he held more precious than life itself. Time passed, and the confusion in the corridor continued; she was searching for him, and he, behind the stove, felt a strong desire to go to her and take her in his arms. The kitchen door opened, and Luca, filled with joy, seemed already to feel her hand against his cheek. But at the same moment there broke out the usual delighted clatter; the little girl had found her brother. "Ah, you were there," said the governess, as she turned on the light and looked at him from the doorway with an expression at the same time both sly and disappointed.

This time, however, the game came to an unexpected end as children's games generally do, in sudden boredom and confusion. The little boy was complaining that he had hit his head against a cupboard, and a quarrel broke out between the twins, one of whom burst into tears. For a short time Luca stood watching the governess who, taking no notice of him, but gay and lively all the time, was calling her pupils to order; then, seeing that the game was really over, he went to his room and threw himself, in the dark, on his bed.

For some time he could hear the four of them laughing, chasing each other and moving furniture in the sitting room. Finally he dropped off to sleep; but at a sudden silence woke up and saw the door opening and the governess, in a streak of light, coming into the room. In the sitting room the children were talking quietly, a sign that they were getting dressed to go away. She came up to the bed and bent over him, saying: "Were you asleep?"

"Yes," answered Luca, half rising.

"Why don't you come and see me at my place?" she went on, in a low voice. "I don't go to your aunt's on Sundays . . . come and see me next Sunday."

"Where is it?" Luca asked mechanically.

Softly she told him the address, in a confidential voice in which nothing of her accustomed gaiety remained. Then she bent down and for one moment, in a very swift contact between their two mouths, Luca felt again all the sensations of the former, longer kiss. "I'm coming, I'm coming," she shouted as she flung herself toward the door. Luca let himself fall back upon the bed.

That had been on Thursday. More than once during the following three days Luca decided to go and not to go, to yield to love and to reject it. There were a number of reasons—all the reasons, in fact—in favor of accepting; for rejecting there was no reason except that desperate desire to destroy the things that bound him to life—and that was not so much a reason as a point of honor which had an obscure origin and growth in the most secret depths of his spirit. He perceived that the governess with her love desired him to live neither more nor less than his parents with their gifts, or his teacher, with his tasks. This love was pleasing to his senses, just as his parents' gifts were pleasing to his covetousness and his teacher's tasks to his ambition. They were all on the same level—his mother, his father, his teacher, the governess—all trying to drag him into the midst of life, to impose life upon him, to compromise him with life; and it mattered little if the methods were different and if his father and mother and the teacher would have disapproved of the methods adopted by the governess.

The thing that irritated him most was that the hunger of his senses should so easily overthrow his desire for liberation and death. At that time the two cats that belonged to the house, a male and a female, had entered upon their love period. This had happened before, but Luca, apart from watching them with amusement, had paid little attention. Now, after what had happened between him and the governess, he seemed to recognize himself in the male and her in the female. Just like these two animals, which at one moment following each other round, sniffing, then faced each other, staring and miaowing, then jumped on each other, the tomcat seizing the other by the neck with his teeth, the female prostrating herself under the male in the same way he himself, unconsciously obedient to the commands of instinct, had behaved toward the woman. All those comings and goings between his own room and the sitting room, those contacts, that invention of pretexts that would lead to contacts—what else were they but the mutual pursuit of two animals mysteriously troubled by desire? With this difference, however, that the two cats could not rebel against nature because they consisted of nothing but nature; whereas he resented this obedience as an act of humiliating passivity, and the force which imposed it as a tyranny. Furthermore, if he yielded to his senses what reason would he have for neglecting his lessons, for rejecting the joys of possession and vanity, for repudiating affection, for not, in fact, deciding once and for all to play a part in that ready-made world into which his mother, in giving him birth, had introduced him?

He was still hesitating when Sunday arrived. In the morning Luca had decided not to visit the governess; by the time lunch was over he had changed his mind. Conscious at heart of a vague feeling of self-contempt, he announced to his mother that he was going to the movies, and went out. But after a few steps he realized his legs were carrying him in the wrong direction. At the top of the street, against a background of trees, rose the baroque gateway of the public gardens toward which, idly, in the bland light of that early winter afternoon, the first Sunday strollers were making their way. Allowing himself to be drawn along by the sight of the gateway, he went into the garden.

He had not been there since the day he buried the money, almost a month ago, and the nakedness and silence of winter had taken full possession. Only the ilexes had kept their foliage, foliage of an opaque green that gave the impression of ancient metal, cold to the touch; all the other trees raised toward the sky gray, broomlike tufts of straight branches upon which could be seen, here and there, a few tiny yellow leaves which had stuck to the tree by mere inertia. The lawns were bare and parched with not a blade of grass upon them, the seats were deserted, the white marble statues had absorbed the rainwater and revealed, in their dark dampness, the jointures between the many fragments of which they were composed. A green scum, no longer cleft by the toy boats of the children, covered the water in the basins of the fountains. Luca walked along an avenue on earthy gravel that no longer crunched beneath his feet, crossed the big lawn, partly flooded now with wide pools reflecting the sky, and through the grove of trees, reaching the open space. There was the decorative wall with its niches and columns and inscriptions. There was the shady spot, glossy with dead leaves, where he had buried the money. He sat down on an upturned stone capital and looked around.

He felt himself to be in the grip of an uneasy anxiety, but he was not sorry to feel this because it seemed to keep him from thinking about the governess and from the temptation of going to see her. It was the fantastic uneasiness of irresolution, which enormously exaggerates the alternatives of a dilemma but at the same time makes them appear indistinct and unattainable and which contents itself with merely formulating them, appearing to take satisfaction in an inertia which is not concerned with making a choice. Certainly he wanted to go and see the governess, and equally certain he did not want to; but he felt what pleased him most was neither the one nor the other but what lay in the middle between them—this immobility, this apathy, this dim and muffled peace. He knew that if he faced the temptation actively and frankly, it would utilize the very strength of his opposition and turn it to its own advantage. And so the only thing to do was to quell any possible conflict, to remain quiescent.

But he knew why he had come back to this open space in the gardens. Just as a believer comes back to the temple of his religion in order to strengthen himself in his faith, so by visiting again the place of his most solemn sacrifice, he had wanted to convince himself of the impossibility of turning back from that sacrifice. Consecrated by his sacrifice, the natural temple of a religion in which he alone believed and about which he was totally ignorant, this open space exercised an influence upon his mind. And after a long and mysterious pause, it seemed to him he could see, far away, the figure of the governess, as though she had been a halting-place, now left far behind, on a visible path. How could he ever, for the sake of one or two kisses, have placed in jeopardy all that had constituted the desperate principle of this last period of his life? He thought of his money, and thought with extreme repugnance of the possibility of going, avariciously, and digging it up, and putting it in his pocket again and buying sweets or cigarettes with it. But he would have performed the same act of self-betrayal if he had gone to see the woman. She was expecting him at her own home, just as his parents expected him at mealtime and his schoolfellows and teachers at school. They all conspired to favor his weakness. What was there left for him to do, if he were to retain his honesty, but to disappoint them?

Meanwhile time was passing. He noticed the light had become perceptibly less. Through the windows in the wall behind him two or three distant roars reached his ears, and he remembered that it was the lions' feeding time. At the sound of that roaring he imagined he could see the gray cement cages, clean but strangely fetid, with their close black bars and behind the bars the huge, shaggy masses of the crouching lions. He seemed to see the small door open at the end of the long corridor beside the cages, and the keeper, in his gray-striped uniform, come through it, pushing by its bars a small cart full of bleeding joints of meat. He hooks one of them on the end of a long pole and throws it from above to the beast which has risen, roaring, to its feet. The red carrion falls with a wet plop on the floor of the cage and the lion is instantly upon it, seizing it with its claws and tearing it to pieces. He crunches the bones in his teeth, pausing every now and then in his meal to lick the carcass amorously with its rasping tongue, as though kissing it. Luca shuddered at the thought of that piece of flesh, once part of a living animal and now a mere dead, shapeless lump, and, remembering how he had once been told that death in the jaws of a wild beast was almost painless owing to that strange, unconscious pity on the part of the beast itself which takes special care to break the victim's spine, he thought he would like to die in that way— to be seized, killed, devoured. The idea attracted him because in such a death there was a fascinating ruthlessness, more complete than in any death at the hands of a man because unconscious and innocent. It was a death in which man became something other than man, in which he was transformed into food for a starving beast. And this blind and nameless hunger was a worthy sepulchre for a rejected body which could have nothing to do with the world and with mankind, not even through the pity of a tear-stained grave.

But above all he was pleased at the idea of the humiliation inflicted upon human dignity by this use of the human body as food. He remembered that the feeding of the lions in the zoo had always been connected, in his own imagination, with the confused feelings inspired in him by the reading of certain novels concerned with martyrdom, particularly *Fabiola* and *Quo Vadis*. This human dignity, composed entirely of petty honors and repulsive duties, that he hated so much, could not be more completely denied than by placing the human body on the level of butcher's meat. He was reminded of the young virgin, beautiful and of noble birth, who, in one of these books, had been exposed naked to the wild beasts: after she had remained for a long time miraculously unharmed, a lion attacked her and with one blow of its claws tore off her arm; then, still living, she was devoured by the hungry beasts; and there came back to him the feeling of pity he had experienced on reading this episode. But this time the feeling of pity was for himself, as he saw himself thrown down and torn to pieces in place of the young woman. It was the same feeling of pity that had moved him when he had imagined himself murdered and buried in the public gardens; and, in suggesting to him a new picture of his own death, it clarified and confirmed its significance—as of a ritual sacrifice, holy, necessary, inevitable.

He started up as he saw that night had already fallen. He felt frozen from head to foot and he was aware, suddenly, that in truth he was nothing more than a boy who had stayed out later than usual. As he went off down the darkening avenues, in the twilight beneath the trees, he heard the cry of the park keeper, "Closing time . . . closing time"—coming thin and mournful to his ears like a summons back to the world of home and school that he so much hated; and for a moment he thought of staying in the gardens and spending the night in the open space, in company with himself and the shadows of the trees. But his courage failed him, and he went out through the gateway. Now, however, he was afraid of being unable to resist the governess next day, when he saw her again and she provoked him afresh with her tricks.

But next day the governess did not come, because, as he learned from his mother that same evening, his aunt was well again and there was no need for the children to be sent away from the house. Luca was aware of a feeling of disappointment, which he attributed at first to surprise—the surprise of a man who has prepared himself for a fight and then finds, at the last moment, that the fight is not going to take place after all. But later he understood that the disappointment was of a different nature; what he really wanted was to see her again. This desire, simple and direct as a natural appetite, frightened him because it proved that he still clung to life and its doubtful gifts.

After his mother had given him the news, five days went by and Luca hoped that he had forgotten the governess. But on the Sunday morning, as he walked past the telephone, he stopped and almost mechanically dialed her number. She answered him at once, as thought she had been waiting all those days at the other end of the wire. "You didn't come last Sunday," she said.

"I couldn't," Luca answered; "did you wait for me?"

"Yes, I waited for you . . . but not for long." It seemed to him that her voice was not so gay as usual. And now there could be no further question of resisting the temptation. He asked in a low voice: "Can I come today?"

She seemed to be reflecting for a moment; and then she replied: "No, not today . . . I really don't feel at all well."

"I understand," said Luca, in an incredulous, angry tone.

She went on immediately, as though frightened: "It's quite true . . . I don't feel well . . . but come next Sunday—can you manage next Sunday?"

"Yes," said Luca.

"All right—till next Sunday, then."

During the whole week Luca, putting aside completely all inclination toward resistance and sacrifice, did nothing but think of the governess. He thought of her with a profound agitation in which were mixed the sharp desire of the senses and the raging bewilderment of defeat. There was certainly no more question of dying—nor yet of living, unless living meant this state of vexation and anguish. Like a swirling, muddy torrent that allows a man neither to swim nor to rest his foot on dry land, passion dragged him far away from his former resolutions. Everything appeared to him to have lost its substance and importance except the woman whom imagination never ceased to exhibit to him in an inexhaustible variety of flattering and disturbing manifestations. The thing that he had so much feared was now happening—that he would find an interest in life again; but after the destruction of so much, it was a life that was reduced to a mere sting of lust, with no hope of expanding into a wider, more positive feeling. For he realized that he did not love, and would never love, this woman, knowing himself to be drawn to desire her by a narrow, purely animal, instinct. How far removed now was he from the clarity of vision he had attained during his last visit to the open space in the gardens! Neglecting his work, eating and sleeping little, his senses perpetually in a ferment and mind filled with nausea, he waited impatiently for those seven days to pass. On the Sunday, after telling his mother the usual lie about going to the cinema, he left home early.

The governess lived in an old quarter of the town, between the station and the barracks. At the ends of the long streets could be seen black and white sentry boxes and the iron gates of barrack enclosures, and beyond the gates the wide barrack squares surrounded with dusty eucalyptus trees, and above, the white sky. Distant, mournful bugles sounded the call to mess, without any visible response; an air of utter boredom spread outward from the iron gates and rose like a fog over the deserted streets. As he walked hastily through those streets, beside the tall buildings that lined them, he felt his legs giving way beneath him and loathed the impulse that drove him on to make this visit. This quarter of employees' dwellings seemed to him all at once hypocritical; how many other women were hiding behind these ornate, dusty façades as they waited for their lovers or clutched them in their arms? He felt that in spite of his agitation he was doing a perfectly normal thing in going to see the governess, precisely, in fact, the thing that the falsely dignified appearance of the quarter seemed to suggest; and that in the acceptance of this contemptible normality lay the whole of his defeat. It was the normal thing, he reflected, to do one's lessons, to save some money, to have a stamp collection, and finally, at the appropriate age, to go and visit one's mistress in a quarter such as this. He found the house he was looking for not far from the barrack gates. The main door was open, and at the far end of the entrance hall there was an old-fashioned stained-glass window with big lozenges of red and blue. His heart swelling with disgust, his legs trembling, he started up the staircase.

He went up two, three, four floors, stopping at each landing to examine the name-plates. All the time he was thinking of the governess' home and, remembering that her father, who had been dead for years, had been a state official of some distinction, he pictured a series of small, narrow rooms, crammed with all sorts of knickknacks. She would entice him to a shabby sofa in the far corner of one of these little rooms, and from the moment of their first kiss, would remind him, with her indefatigable tongue, of an infuriated snail. Then there would be sweets and cigarettes, languishing looks and jokes; and finally he would be lying on top of her, at once reluctant and awkward, in a confusion of garments tossed aside like the surf that marks a shipwreck. She would send him away with a last kiss in the darkness of a narrow hall filled with overcoats. He would go home again, both the betrayer and the betrayed. All this filled him with profound repugnance; but, as usual, because it was repugnant it attracted him.

When the maid opened the door he was astonished at the pungent, stuffy smell from the hall that smote his face like a hot breath. The maid ushered him in and left him standing there. At the far end of the hall a reddish light came from a lamp apparently wrapped in a cloth of that color. On the other hand the passage leading off the hall was plunged in darkness, and it seemed to him he could hear muffled sobs coming from that direction. The whole house seemed to be permeated by some inexplicable, sorrowful agitation— light, hurried footsteps, moans, rustling garments, creaking doors. He could even distinguish, in the distance, a monotonous voice in prayer. And the smell, the smell that was so pungent in his nostrils, was the smell of disinfectants, of sleep, of sweat; he remembered the same smell in his mother's room years ago during an illness. A tearful voice close beside him made him start. "Who is it? What do you want?" it said.

In front of him in the darkness, her face and breast catching a blood-red glint from the lamp, stood a fat old woman in black. A big tuft of white hair rose up from her forehead, like a plume of feathers, with an almost comic effect. Luca looked into her face and saw, even beneath the red glint of the lamp, that her eyes and her whole face appeared to be inflamed with another, a different, a more fiery red. She repeated her question again and took a step forward, placing herself outside the halo of the lamp. Then, in that uncertain half-light, Luca saw that the redness of her face had remained, and realized that it was the redness of tears shed in despair and spread all over her face by a soaking, inadequate handkerchief.

Mortified, he spoke his own name, adding hurriedly the lie that he had come to ask for news. The old woman muttered some reply that Luca did not understand, ending with: "She's sick—she's terribly sick"; then she shook her head and disappeared into the darkness from which she had come. Behind the old woman Luca noticed for the first time a white figure that seemed to support her—a nurse. Half closing the door, he went out on to the landing.

He hurried home, ran into his room and threw himself upon the bed. It was not so much pity for the governess, whom he did not love and who had been simply the occasion of his desire, that he felt now, but rather hatred against himself, or at least against that part of himself which had inflicted upon him the humiliation of that indecent chase across the town; ending in so mortifying a manner by his finding a death agony where he had expected a lovers' meeting. And so, he could not help thinking, this was what it meant to live, to go on living—doing, with passion and determination, absurd, senseless things for which it was impossible to find any justification and which continually placed the person who did them in a state of slavery, of remorse, of hypocrisy. He recognized now the wisdom of his reflections of two Sundays ago, in the open space at the gardens, a wisdom which was perhaps desperate, but was the only one possible. With the exception of this wisdom which demanded the sacrifice of his life, all else was contradiction and obscurity.

He felt that the actual facts had taught him, mutely, a kind of lesson and had pointed again to the right road, from which he had been led astray by his desires. It was like a piece of music, that scene of confusion and death in the governess' home, like a motif interrupted for a short time by other, contrasting sounds and then taken up again with greater intensity, on a higher, firmer note. It was the motif that had been sounding in his ears for a long time, and that he had done wrong to forget. A motif that was profound, deep-toned, funereal, full of sadness, but at the same time bewitching and peculiarly his own.

"And supposing the governess doesn't die?" he asked himself, with an experimental curiosity. Then, observing that, at the mere mention of such a hope, his senses were reawakened, he was seized, all over again and more strongly than ever, with hatred against himself. He was not even capable of wanting the governess to live for her own sake; she must live and die only for him. This too was what living meant, he reflected; and it was in that way his parents understood life, and his teachers and everyone else. Immediately he felt that he wanted her to die; and that he was able to feel this only at the cost of wanting, even more urgently, to die himself.

His parents, speaking of it casually at table with expressions of conventional pity, gave Luca the news of the governess' death two days after his visit to her home. "She was a good creature," said his mother; "so gay . . . who would have thought it?" His father affirmed, too, that he would never have imagined that a person so full of life could have met such an early death. And the conversation, after a few more comments of the same kind, passed to another subject.

Luca had hoped that her death would inspire him with a feeling, if not of pity, at least of liberation. He discovered, instead, that he continued to think of her with desire and longing, just as when she was alive. As far as he could understand the matter, the sensations awakened in him by this woman seemed to have been hoarded greedily by his sensual memory so they might be doled out, day by day, in the small change of recollection—anyhow until some other woman occupied the dead woman's place in his heart. He was reminded of how, as a child, he had once shut up a live lizard in a box; but the creature had died, and he had insisted on keeping the corpse for several days, until his mother, sickened by the smell, had taken it from him and thrown it away, to his great disgust, for he thought he possessed some remarkable treasure. In the same way, with the same jealous, miserly care, did his memory preserve those two or three amorous sensations which the governess had bequeathed to him and which now smelled of death. And so, to the funereal color that tinged his whole life there was now added the dark shadow of an irresistible necrophilia. And what made it worse than other similar loves for the dead was the fact that he had no idealized love for the complete figure of the governess, but merely, in a sensual manner, for one particular part of her, the only part that had been, for him, alive and effectual—that mouth which now, as he sometimes found himself thinking, must be filled with earth, and which could no longer retain any resemblance to a mouth. In fact he neither remembered nor knew anything of her beyond the kiss that he had received from her; and that kiss, like a smell or a taste which is revived at even the slightest call of memory, came back to him at every moment not so much in the manner of an obsession as of something that has already become habitual, with the vicious regularity of the most mechanical type of thought. It was a wretched, dismal treasure, but he was preparing to live for years upon its revenue. Sometimes at night he would wake up suddenly with the sensation that her mouth was emerging slowly but surely from his pillow, as a flower emerges from the earth, the linen turning into flesh and the flesh, nevertheless, preserving the quality of linen. He would bite hard into his pillow and, until he was quite wide awake, would, with his teeth on edge, grip the cold, saliva-soaked stuff, clinging with all his strength to this hopelessly improbable, but at the same time violently concrete, illusion. So the old mixture of disgust and pleasure continued. This time, however, the disgust was no longer that of a love furtive and impure but partly justified by the woman's eager participation; it was that of a macabre attachment to ragged scraps of a memory cut short by death. It filled all his thoughts with a dreary listlessness. And it brought at the same time, as he realized, a gradual perversion to his senses that were continually oscillating between desire and repulsion. The sensation of the kiss and the idea of death became mingled and fused in a single, obscure excitement which seemed to draw its strength from the deep, overshadowing darkness of impossibility and profanation.

So continued the struggle against the things which bound him to life; and chance had willed that those things were now reduced to the mutilated, shapeless memory of a person who was dead. It was a memory, he sometimes reflected, that with time would undergo the some process of disintegration as the flesh which had produced it; and, like that flesh in the earth in which it was buried, so, with extreme slowness, would decompose in the blackest mud deposit of his mind, but not before he had nourished his life upon it for many years, evoking it and relishing it again and again as long as it was possible. In order to sever this bond and place himself, once and for all, outside the orbit of this memory, he took the streetcar one morning to the cemetery instead of going to school.

He thought vaguely of buying some flowers and scattering them upon the governess' grave—with the idea of propitiating her and of asking her to leave him finally in peace. But, on that cold, misty morning, the cypresses rising above the grey wall of the cemetery at once gave him the feeling that it was a place of convention and show in which any mystery was already discounted in advance. The open iron gates led into the cemetery from a space surrounded by flower stalls. Beyond the gates could be seen the burial ground, like a public garden which, ridiculously, had been planted with crosses instead of flowers. These crosses, as he looked dreamily at them from the open space outside the gates, seemed to be moving confusedly in a whirling geometrical pattern from which all idea of death was excluded. Around him, people were getting off of crowded streetcars, swarming over the open space, buying flowers, moving gently, with unhurried steps, toward the gates. The mortuary chapel, standing conveniently beside the cemetery, with its portico and pediment in colored mosaics, seemed to invite gestures of prearranged, unmysterious piety. This, he could not help thinking, this was a place for the living to perform their ceremonies with perfunctory decorum and smoothness, not a place for the dead. He noticed that below the wall the ground, cracked and tawny in color, sloped steeply away; and that at the top of this slope three tramps were warming themselves around a bonfire—which he at once imagined, for some reason, to have been kindled with refuse from the cemetery, fragments of bone, rags from rotting garments, splinters from coffins. Tongues of flame flickered red in the cold and misty air, and from the flames a column of smoke rose in yellow spirals up the wall, reaching as far as the inclined, motionless tops of the cypresses. At the sight of these flames there came back to his mind the idea of a death shorn of ceremony and pity —like the deaths he had once pictured at the hands of a murderer or in the jaws of a wild beast—a death which served to warm the hands of three ragged beggars, standing in sight of suburban houses, standing beside the streetcar lines. He realized it was useless to go into the cemetery; the woman was in his memory, in his senses, not beneath the marble slab which bore her name. In face of that slab of stone he, like the others, would have performed empty, senseless gestures; or, on the other hand, in order to bring her to mind, would have had to summon up those very memories that he wished to drive away. Out of the corner of his eye he saw a streetcar appear at the corner of the avenue, and ran, at full speed, to the platform. A few minutes later he was home.

In his room he dropped off to sleep, as usual; and then woke with a violent start which recalled to his mind another similar shock given him by the governess when she had deliberately fallen on top of him in her pretended game with her pupils. It was she, there could be no doubt of it; and the sensation of that kiss seemed to be emerging, more intense than ever, from the stuff of his pillow. It seemed that the whole of the night that enveloped him was expressive of that mouth of hers, that the darkness itself formed lips and a tongue in a sultry, crackling silence that was filled with an inescapable presence. There was a kind of malicious scorn in this return of the governess after the failure of his expedition to the cemetery; it was as though she wished to inform him, with all the gaiety and boisterousness that had been hers in life, of the vanity of his attempts to set himself free. As though she wished to say to him in her cheerful manner, falling on top of him and kissing him: "You thought I was dead . . . far from it . . . I'm more alive than ever . . . and *you've* got to live—for *me!*" He raised himself on his elbow enjoying the flavor of the sensation and thinking deeply. It was clear to him that henceforward he would sink, more and more deeply every day, into a darkness from which there was no escape. He was aware that this was not in the least displeasing to him; each step would in fact carry him farther forward toward that ritual sacrifice of himself he had had a presentiment of on that far-off Sunday in the open spaces among the ilexes. From that sacrifice, expressing the obscure but spontaneous religion of his life, would come his liberation— not from a few flowers and a genuflection and the prayer of a hackneyed rite.

One morning, as he hurried out of the house on his way to school, he detected in his mind a presentiment that some conclusion was imminent. It took the form of a suspension of the thought-process and its lucid workings, of an anxious apprehension of some event which, though it had not yet happened, was already facing him, settled and inevitable. He was conscious of a slight, pleasing excitement; it was as though he felt himself to be no longer united and indivisible, but separated into a number of parts which floated about and bobbed up and down beside each other, clustered all together in a becalmed stillness, like broken fragments from a shipwreck in the quiet that follows a storm. He noticed he saw things through different eyes than usual; or rather, he did not see them but made himself master of them by means of an altogether new sense which he could not locate and which seemed to be distributed all over his body. Simultaneously, he was aware of a bitter, unreasonable sadness, a sadness of resignation that made his acts wearisome and conscious, as though each act was an irrevocable step upon a fatal path.

The weather was bad but still undecided, with a low, dark sky which had not yet resolved to shed the rain which burdened it. Occasionally a gust of damp wind stirred the mild, motionless air; then Luca would see all the leaves of the trees in the gardens turn over with a flash of silver, while coils of gray dust rose hissing at the street corners from the dry stones of the pavements. But the wind would fall again at once, and the paving stones remained dry. It was a kind of weather that resembled his own state of mind, and it seemed to him they were like each other in the way they both waited for something to happen. In the end, possibly, it would rain; in the end, possibly, he would come to a decision. He felt that it was for him that the sky had clouded over so threateningly; and that he must keep his eye on it in the way that one actor keeps his eye on another so as not to miss the moment when he has to make his appearance on the stage.

The thing that struck him most forcibly was the new feeling that the most ordinary actions gave him—such as walking through the streets, paying for his trolley ticket, getting out of the streetcar. They were the same actions he had performed for so many years on his way to school, except that whereas in the past he had performed them without noticing, being carried along while he was performing them by an unceasing current of different pre-occupations and thoughts, today, in the utter bareness of his life, the whole of his consciousness, for lack of any other object, was centered upon them; and he felt their ordinariness as an absurd, tyrannical strangeness. This con-sciousness was concerned not so much with the ultimate object of these actions —such as going to school, which had already seemed absurd to him for a long time—as with the actions themselves taken separately; it was this that was new. Why did he move his legs, why did he avoid being run over by a bus, why did he stop and rearrange the pack of books under his arm, why did he pull his hat down on to his forehead? It was as though ordinary life, reduced by now to a thin envelope of habits which had become automatic and were for that precise reason all the more tedious, were about to slip away from him once and for all, as a snake casts its skin in springtime. And with this sense of the total absurdity of all that up till then had never been absurd, he recognized that the long course of his crisis was coming to an end. There was nothing more to be done but give a slight shake and the irksome mem-brane would drop away. He guessed that this shake, and nothing else, was the object of his presentiment.

In front of the school building a black crowd of schoolboys was growing visibly smaller each moment as it was quickly sucked in through the ancient gray jaws of the big gateway. He was only just in time, he could not help thinking; and this thought too seemed to him perfectly ordinary—or, in other words, tyrannical and objectionable. Inside the school it was almost dark and the torrent of boys which swiftly flooded the hall, dividing into so many smaller streams, one for each corridor, seemed to Luca to be imbued with a crazy, nervous gaiety, as though his companions were nursing the same presentiment as himself. He reached the door of his own classroom, then he was in the classroom itself, with the professorial chair standing at the far end between two large maps and the three close rows of desks which—just as the chair brought to mind the image of the professor in the act of teaching—

themselves suggested the rows of schoolboys intent on listening to him. All was preordained: he was already sitting at his desk although the desk was vacant, and his companions were already seated too, though they were crowding round him, and the teacher had already mounted the platform although he had not yet arrived. The lights were on because the bad weather made it so dark, and the dirty panes in the big windows reflected their thin yellow filaments. Luca went to his desk and around him the other boys arranged themselves in their own places. And now the absurd automatism of his own actions came back to him, and he felt a conscientious desire to give that slight shake in order to see what would happen. The professor of Italian, a small, well-groomed man with a plump, white face, entered and walked across the room, scattering silence and attention as he went to his desk. He mounted the platform and turned to face his class, who had risen to their feet. "Sit down," said the professor. And then, with that sensation of taking the plunge that initiates a game, Luca remained standing.

The professor, meanwhile, had sat down; he rubbed his hands together, took a clean handkerchief from his pocket, unfolded it, blew his nose, replaced the handkerchief and arranged himself more comfortably in his chair —all without taking his eyes off the school register that lay open on his desk. Luca could not help thinking that if he had been in the place of the professor he would have regarded it as an intolerable tyranny to perform those gestures which were repeated every morning, themselves the prelude to other gestures which, again, were always the same. In the meantime he still remained on his feet. The professor, having examined the register, looked up at the classroom, saw Luca and asked quietly: "What is it, Mansi?"

"Shall I, shall I not, answer?" Luca wondered. Then he said in a clear voice: "Nothing."

"If it's nothing, then sit down." The professor had an ugly voice, cold and precise; it was obvious, nevertheless, that he liked to hear himself speak.

This time Luca did not open his mouth, and he remained standing. The professor, slightly surprised, looked at him and then repeated: "Did you hear? Sit down."

Again there was silence. The whole class was now looking at Luca with breathless astonishment. The professor stared at him, and added, in a softened voice: "Is there anything you want to say?"

"I've nothing to say," answered Luca, and suddenly sat down. A sigh of relief passed over the class. The professor eyed Luca closely for a moment and then without saying a word, turned back to his register. The lesson was on the *Purgatorio* of Dante, and the professor's usual custom was to choose one of the boys who had good diction and make him read a *canto*, or part of a *canto*, aloud. Then his commentary would follow. The professor's finger ran down the list of names in the register, and Luca was almost sure that it would be himself who would be chosen as reader on this occasion. There were three reasons for this: first, because he read extremely well; second, because it was some time since he had been called upon to read; third—and this was the chief reason—the little incident that he had caused by remaining on his feet had, so to speak, marked him out among the crowd of his fellows and drawn the professor's attention to him.

The professor's finger could be seen running down the first column of names; then it stopped at the beginning of the second. "Mansi," he said.

Another professor, thought Luca, would have perhaps added some joke or witty remark connecting the incident with the summons to read aloud—some such phrase as: "Seeing that you're so fond of standing on your feet, you'd better come up here and read." But this professor was serious and never made jokes. He was one of those teachers who despise their profession and teach in a condescending, detached manner, though with scrupulous care, as if they wished it to be understood that they could do better if they chose. Now, however, for Luca it was a question of deciding whether he was going to obey the summons.

His desk-neighbor was anxiously handing him the volume of the *Divina Commedia,* already open at the right place, while the professor was quietly turning over the pages of his own copy. Teachers and schoolfellows, thought Luca, they all wanted him to live, to go on living. The thought of the governess came into his mind and he felt himself strengthened in his own decision. For the moment he would obey; but as soon as the feeling of the ordinariness of his own actions came over him again, then he would disobey. He realized that it was only by giving this disobedience the mechanical, punctilious character of a game that he would have the strength to carry it through. He took the book, left his desk which was one of the last at the back of the room, and walked toward the platform.

He noticed that the light had grown visibly dimmer. The first drops of rain were flying against the window-panes, flattening themselves into broad liquid patches from which other smaller drops trickled down in brilliant lines. Suddenly he saw himself walking calmly toward the platform, book in hand. And at the same moment he stopped.

He stood still, the raindrops streaked the windowpanes, the professor and the class looked at him. At last the professor asked: "Well, what are you doing, standing there like a post?"

Luca was now wondering how long he would be able to stand there like that without incurring a punishment. But even a punishment seemed to him preferable to the usual automatic obedience. With a punishment, at least, the profoundly coercive nature of life was fully revealed, with no more hypocritical pretences. Then he heard the professor repeat, in the silence: "I'm speaking to you . . . answer me . . . do you feel ill?"

A confused murmur ran through the room, cut short immediately by the professor tapping with his ruler on the desk and shouting: "Silence!" But it was time now. With an effort Luca said, "It's nothing"; and felt that his legs were carrying him forward toward the platform. Again there was a whisper of low voices, and for the second time the professor commanded silence, but without tapping the ruler and in a less imperious tone of voice. Then he turned toward Luca and said shortly: "Read from line 85 of Canto V." Luca lowered his eyes to his book and began:

> Then said another: "Prithee, and so be that desire
> Satisfied which draws thee up the lofty mount
> With kindly pity help my desire.
> I was of Montefeltro, I am Buonconte . . ."

Luca had always been an excellent reader; and the professor, at the sound of his voice reading calmly and with expression, seemed to become calm again himself. And a breath of relief passed through the class, too, in the darkening air. Luca went on reading in a strong, clear voice. In the meantime, however, his mind, as though endowed with a new sense of ubiquity, jumped, so to speak, out of his head and went to the other end of the schoolroom, where, along the wall, hung hats and coats; and from there it looked at him. And thus began again that feeling, at the same time both painful and pleasant, of ordinariness seen under an aspect of strangeness and oppression. Yet he seemed to be reading with vigor, following the meaning of the words which was curiously in harmony with his own feeling. He remembered those many times that he had desired and wooed a death that should be secret, unknown, solitary, obscure. And at the lines:

> There where its name is lost,
> Did I arrive, pierced in the throat,
> Flying on foot, and bloodying the plain.
> There lost I vision, and ended my words
> Upon the name of Mary; and there fell I,
> And my flesh alone was left . . .

a sudden feeling of obscure, distorted pity clutched at his throat. It was the pity toward himself that had moved him the first time he had thought of being killed and buried in the public gardens; and it rose to the surface of his consciousness like a summons to a grave and melancholy, but inevitable, duty. He went on reading in a voice that was less firm, but deep and full of feeling. The idea that it was a game persisted in the form of a desire to be obstinate and disobedient; but it was strangely mixed now with that sharp, surprising sense of pity. He read a few lines more and then wondered whether he should continue, knowing well that the putting of that question to himself meant that he was going to stop. And, in fact, at the line "Then when day was spent, he covered the valley with mist . . ." he broke off.

There was a moment's silence. "Well?" asked the professor. Throughout the room there had fallen the breathless quiet that awaits some unusual event. Everyone was looking at him and the professor. But Luca no longer either saw or heard anything. He was thinking that he was Buonconte, lying dead at the joining of two rivers. He seemed to see rain-burdened clouds driven by the breath of an icy wind, coming in gray drifts from the invisible top of the mountain down to where he lay, wrapping his body in silence and mist. Then, through the mist, it began to rain upon him and all around him; and the rain riddled the soaked ground and spread, in boiling whirlpools, into a lake of swollen, rioting water which joined the swell of a flooded river, and rising, lifted his half-submerged body and carried it away. And as the dense rain continued, he slipped down through the raging water, flat on his back, his arms outspread. He felt a sudden sharp pain; and hearing his name spoken, raised his eyes; two tears slid down his cheeks.

The professor was looking at him with contemptuous surprise: "May we be allowed to know what is happening?" he asked. "Are you going to read, or are you not?"

It was clear then, thought Luca, he must go on being a schoolboy right up to the end; even if he wanted to die. He waited a moment and then asked: "Am I to go on?"

An intense chatter of criticism ran through the darkened classroom. The professor made a sign for the class to be silent, then turned to Luca and said: "Where d'you think you are? Of course you're to go on."

His emotion persisted; the tears had stopped halfway down his cheeks and were tickling him disagreeably. "I shall read down to the end of the Buonconte episode," thought Luca, "because it's *my* episode . . . Then I shall stop." He pulled himself together and started to read again, in a voice made stronger and clearer by the intimate certainty that he was describing the death, not of a character from Dante, but of himself. It seemed to him that the professor was not so much listening to him as looking at him with curiosity. The other boys, too, looked as though they expected some new strangeness on his part. He read two more stanzas without stumbling, and then, as he had foreseen, at the line ". . . then covered and wrapped me with its spoils," he stopped again.

This time the whole class burst out in a confused clatter of voices that were almost exultant though at the same time alarmed. The professor made no attempt to calm the tumult; but, turning toward Luca, said, in his normal voice: "You're not well . . . get your things on and go home . . . we'll talk about it later, in a few days."

"I'm all right," Luca would have liked to answer; but he felt a shiver run all over his body, followed by a wave of damp, feverish heat, and he saw that perhaps the professor was right. And so, he reflected, if you don't agree to be what other people want or believe you to be, you either get punished or you're thought to be ill. This reflection absorbed him while he gathered the books that his neighbor, with pitying, alarmed solicitude, took from under the desk and handed to him one by one. Everyone was looking at him in silence. The rain was streaming down the windowpanes now; and Luca could not help saying to himself that it was the same rain which he had seen, in imagination, enveloping and carrying away his own lifeless body. He took the books under his arm and went toward the back of the classroom. Thirty heads turned to watch him as he went. "Loiacono," said the professor, calling on another of the class. Luca took his overcoat, opened the door and went out.

He hurried through the deserted corridors. Through the open doors of the other schoolrooms he could see rows of desks with attentive students sitting at them; he could hear, lonely in the surrounding silence, the voices of the teachers as they lectured. They were voices like those of priests praying mechanically in some chapel, and the echo from the big rooms made it impossible to distinguish the meaning of the words. He went down the stairs and stood looking out into the street, in a sudden, drenching freshness. It was raining heavily, the pavements were gurgling with water, there was a rain-streaked whiteness in the air; and through that whiteness and those streaks of rain there quivered the intense brilliance of a flash of lightning. He heard thunder in the distance, then nearer, a rumbling uproar like a landslide of loose rocks, ending in a sharp burst which seemed to be the signal for a renewed downpour of rain. Then he stepped out from the doorway and started walking bareheaded through the deluge.

The rain seemed to have transformed the whole town into water. The houses were made of upright, gray water, the pavements of yellowish, gurgling water, the dim, shadowy forms of passers-by running to take shelter under doorways seemed also to be made of water, as were the lamp-posts that undulated like thin, black snakes and the greenish masses of the streetcars that swelled out as they approached from the far end of the street. The rain poured down in one direction and then, as the wind changed, in another—methodically, it might have been said. Luca felt the water running from his hair down the back of his neck, and inside his shirt, down his back. The books under his arm were soaked. He stepped in a puddle up to his ankle. After that he had, at every step, the disagreeable feeling of his foot squeezing out water inside the swollen, slippery confinement of his shoe. And so, walking slowly in water and through water, he reached home.

Once in his own room, he threw himself on the bed and started trembling all over. The trembling shook his body uncontrollably, from head to foot; inside his mouth his teeth made a loud, rattling noise, as though he had two rows of dice in his head. His whole body was aching; and at moments an intense heat, which seemed as if it were lined with ice, ran through him and took possession of his face.

He heard the door open but did not move; he was lying flat on his back, his head at the bottom of the bed and his feet on the pillow. "What are you doing? Whatever's the matter? Why aren't you at school?" he heard his mother asking. "I think I'm sick," he answered unwillingly. He felt a hand on his forehead and then heard his mother exclaim: "Why, you're burning hot . . . You must get into bed at once." At that moment the bells of the church near by began to strike midday.

Luca's illness lasted for almost three months. During the first month, although he had a very high temperature all the time, he remained perfectly lucid, even though—as he sometimes seemed to realize—this lucidity, for the very reason that it concerned itself with a condition that was unhealthy and feverish, was of an abnormal intensity and not infrequently deviated into violent excitement and wild talk. He no longer wished to die; he was certain that he *would* die and that certainty satisfied him. Convinced that death was imminent, all he had to do was to watch its progress and take a secret pleasure in it. He no longer hated himself, as at the time when he had despaired of his own ability to pursue the policy of revolt to its utmost conclusion; instead, he had a feeling of victorious contempt for these forces in himself which still resisted and still wished to bind him to life. They were the forces which had made him love his studies, his parents, the governess; and which now, deprived of their former props, clutched, before they sank, finally, in death's black flood, at the last straws—the broth which the servant made him swallow, spoonful by spoonful, the ray of winter sunshine that reached him where he lay, his mother's distressed eyes, his father's perturbed, anxious expression. He wished to die and he was sure that he was going to die; but when his mother said to him in an unhappy but encouraging voice: "Come along, eat a little more . . . it'll help you get well," those despicable forces prevented him from answering as he would have wished: "But I don't want to get well; I want to die"; and they compelled him, in spite of himself, to smile and to open his mouth. Then he would console himself with the thought, that, after all, these were concessions to other people's lives, not to his own, which by now had cast anchor and departed once and for all from those wretched shores beside which it had dallied for so long.

Under these conditions, the duplicity which had entered into his life from the day when death had appeared to him as the only solution to the problem of his relations with the world—that duplicity now became intensified till it attained the kind of shrill coherence of a comedy of errors. With his parents he played, in a docile manner, the now entirely detached role of the invalid who is going to get well, of the scholar who is going to return to his studies, of the boy who is going to grow up and become a man; but, the moment he was alone, he became merely the dying man, fully conscious and contented, who watches for the approach of his end with a mind filled with hope. He enjoyed taking his own temperature early in the morning, and seeing the shining column inside the thermometer leap rapidly up to the highest degrees; he enjoyed, during the long afternoons, the feeling that his sickness was getting the better of his consciousness, as he lay in a feverish torpor; he enjoyed, during the night, the idea that one of those brief snatches of sleep, full of sweat and fever, to which now and then he abandoned himself, might, without his knowing it, transform itself into death. His longing for death had by this time acquired a peculiar intensity and concreteness; it almost seemed that he longed for death with the sensuality with which, once upon a time, he had longed for the embraces of the governess. To die, it sometimes occurred to him, was perhaps the one true pleasure that life reserved for mankind.

Sometimes his mother would make plans for his future. "After you leave school," she said one day, "you must take your degree. . . . If you go in for law, you can work with your father and inherit his clientele and his chambers. . . . And then, when the right moment comes, you must marry a girl of good family. . . . But before you get married it would be a good thing for you to travel a bit so as to see something of the world. Your father and I agree about this. . . . You must go to France and England; in that way you'll familiarize yourself with the languages, too, by speaking them on the spot . . ."

"But it costs a lot of money to travel like that," said Luca, pretending to take these programs of his mother's seriously.

"Well, we'll give it to you," answered his mother proudly; "we're comfortably off . . . You shall never lack money, provided it's for useful purposes."

"But I shall not merely *not* take a degree, *not* travel, *not* get married," Luca would have liked to shout; "I shall not even, ever again, put my feet on the ground." However, though his mother's obtuseness and assurance aroused in him an access of fury, so that he was conscious of his heart beating twice as fast and his teeth grinding together in spite of himself, he succeeded in controlling himself and answered, in a voice of childish covetousness: "But I should like to go to Germany too."

Certain details of everyday life which had once appeared to concern him closely and to be, in themselves, commendable, now seemed to him to have been thrust away into a remote distance—for example, the newspaper which his father came and read in his room directly after meals. As he looked at his father's figure outlined against the background of the window, and at the newspaper which he held open in his hands, he was filled with disgust for the world in which that newspaper was published, bought and read. This was not so much on account of the futility (which, by now, he discounted) of the things that the newspaper contained, as of the absurdity of the object itself and of its use—that sheet of light, stretched material, covered with black marks, over which his father silently ran his eyes. That was the world in which an infinite number of such things, both unjustified and unjustifiable, were accomplished, the world in which everything went on without any purpose, automatically, through force of inertia; and it was pleasant to think that he would soon be leaving that world. Only once did he allow his thought to be seen—and for one moment it became single instead of double—when his mother, thinking to amuse him, started looking for his stamp collection. He allowed her to rummage about for a little, to no purpose, and then said: "It's not there any more. I gave it away."

"What? You gave it away?" his mother could not help exclaiming, in a sudden, indignant outburst. Then she seemed to recollect that Luca was ill and added, in a gentler voice: "But why did you give it away? Whatever came into your head?"

"I gave it away because I knew I was going to die," Luca answered, in a barely audible voice.

It was only partly true; actually he had got rid of his stamp collection not because he knew he was going to die, but because he wanted to die. But his mother was alarmed and, after a quick, brief glance at him, said, with almost her old hardness: "Now don't talk nonsense . . . What d'you mean, you're going to die? You're going to get well."

Luca seemed to recognize in those words the whole of the tyranny against which he had struggled for so long; and, when his mother had gone out of the room, he said aloud, in a tone of defiance: "Who says I'm going to get well? I'm going to die and I *shall* die."

During the whole time, however—as, indeed, before he fell ill—the longing for death never appeared to him in the guise of a suicidal impulse. If anyone had spoken to him of suicide he would certainly have been surprised, since not even the word, still less the deed, had ever entered his mind. Even in the languor of illness, his longing for death appeared to him in much the same way as it had appeared whenever he had thought about it with clarity and determination—as a necessary sacrifice, the inevitable conclusion of a series of other, minor sacrifices. This sacrifice struck him as a bitter one; but its bitterness was not of the kind that is inspired by an unjust fate, rather it was the bitterness felt by someone who is aware of his own weakness and loneliness in face of an overwhelming task and who knows that he can perform that task only at a high cost to himself—an unutterable bitterness, mingled with an indescribable joy, as though he knew that he was attaining in death an aim that he had pursued all his life. What that aim was, he could not have said; but he knew for certain it was an act of love, if only the other things appeared to be fraught with meaning and because it compelled him to hate so fiercely.

One night he thought he was really dying, or, to be more exact, that he understood the real meaning of his own longing for death. He was asleep; then suddenly he woke up with a painful shock, feeling his whole body—light, now, in its thinness—start violently up, just as a withered shrub starts up out of the ground when pulled by the hand that comes to uproot it. He looked around and then, by the light of the nightlamp on the little table by his bed, he discerned a new and painful intensity in the general look of the room. It was as though a dense and growing vibration had forced all the objects in the room outside their usual limits, and the air seemed rarefied and filled with flashes of light. Although they still retained their own likenesses, the furniture and the other things appeared to be fraught with meaning and to have assumed a hostile, threatening expression. They did not speak, but it was as though they were whispering among themselves in low, malevolent voices. Such an intensity—as of people who, without moving or uttering a word, allow the threatening feelings that fill them to ooze out unmistakably—had the effect of shifting reality to a painful remoteness, and for the first time suggested to him the idea of death as a magical operation allowing him to create a world less absurd, more lovable, more intimate, in which all things would be justified by love. He understood that he owed it, not so much to himself as to the reality outside himself, to die, in order to give that reality a harmony and bring it to life. That cupboard, that chest of drawers, that bookshelf, the whole of this room—and in the same way his parents, his school, his teachers and his school fellows, he himself lying there in bed—all these were something that he had experienced in a dream during all the years of his life, as one experiences an obscure and horrible nightmare into which, whatever efforts one may make, one cannot succeed in introducing any order or sense. At his birth he had not, in reality, begun to live, but rather to dream fearful and absurd dreams. Yes, it was essential for him to die, he thought, to take advantage of the nightmare's greatest intensity to cry out once and then awake.

He remembered having experienced the same sensation of nightmare on that far-off night when, standing in the doorway of his parents' bedroom, he had seen them in their night clothes, their arms full of money, taking down the picture of the Virgin from the wall and uncovering the steel safe. And he understood that it was for them he wanted to die, and for the world of which they formed a part, so as to free himself from that feeling of hatred and absurdity with which they inspired him and which prevented him from loving them as he would have liked. He felt that the act of dying really depended only on himself and was a thing very easily undertaken, now that he knew he was dying not for himself but for others; and a faint, contented smile came to his lips. As he lay beneath his pile of well tucked-in blankets, he could feel the high fever wrapping his limbs in a burning veil of sweat. With the sensation of yielding himself up to death he closed his eyes and fell asleep, the smile still on his lips.

But instead of death came delirium. An assembly of corpulent animals with long snouts sat gravely round his bed, like so many doctors at the bedside of a dying man. They swayed their heads backward and forward, then, like dogs around a bone, threw themselves down on their knees around the bed, stretching out their snouts on top of the bedding. Luca was terrified by these snouts, which were long and flexible, gray and dry and cracked, with occasional bristles here and there standing straight up like pins. At the end of each bristle there was a kind of sucker with quivering eyelashes all around it, and, in the middle of the eyelashes, an eye, sparkling like a diamond, staring at him. The largest and most important of these great animals was at the foot of the bed and stretched out its snout between his legs. Twisting and undulating, the snout grew longer and longer and reached up toward his stomach; and he, weeping and shouting, seized it with both hands and tried to turn it aside. But the snout, though flexible, was hard, and increased in size as he held it in his hands, and reached up toward his face. In the meantime there appeared, on the wall near the door, a number of green excrescences shaped like crooked fingers, which multiplied rapidly and finally formed a cascade of those plants known as "witches' claws," which have upturned, clawlike tendrils. The plant hung down in the place where the coat stand usually was; it looked as if it had grown out of a wide, black crack, in the shape of an ear, which had opened in the wall. Now a wide-brimmed black hat flew about in the air and hung itself up on one of the clawlike excrescences of the plant. Other hats followed it through the pallid air, as though thrown by a skillful hand—men's hats, large and dark and round, women's hats, small, sparkling with sequins, adorned with feathers of different colors, hats of strange fashions such as had never been seen. All these hats fell on the plant, covering it, hiding it completely. And then the whole hat-laden plant detached itself from the crack in the wall and, like an enormous lizard covered with armor from head to tail, started moving about rapidly, here and there, running up and down the wall.

It looked as if it were trying to get down on to the floor in order to hurl itself against Luca's bed, but luckily the room was half full of black, motionless water, and every time the creature reached this water it drew back with obvious disgust, and ran up to the ceiling again. Long black snakes, thin and graceful, were emerging from the water, swaying their flattened heads this way and that; while a great purple bird flew heavily above them, starting from one corner of the ceiling, swooping down to the surface of the water and then rising again toward the opposite corner. Several times the bird skimmed over the bed, and Luca could see its head, with a round white eye which looked as though it were made of glass and a massive curved beak. The bird dived down, seized one of the snakes in the point of its beak and pulled it out of the water, then flew upward again. The snake twisted and turned in the air like a fluttering ribbon as the bird pulled it back and forth over the room. But from the crack in which the coat-stand plant had grown there now opened a deep cleft which zigzagged upward across the wall and continued across the ceiling. Inside this cleft there soon appeared an intensely thick swarm of brown, shiny insects; one of these insects dropped from the ceiling on to the bed, between Luca's legs, and then another and another, then a whole cluster of them, and then hundreds and thousands of them, until the air was darkened. The entire bed was now covered by a wriggling carpet and he was shouting for someone to take them away and pushing back the carpet of insects with both hands as it seemed to be rising up toward his stomach. At his cries, the carpet rolled itself up at the bottom of the bed and remained there, motionless, like a great swarming cylinder.

His attention was attracted by a new peril. Inside the medicine bottles that crowded the little table by his bed were enclosed a number of horrible little bald, hunch-backed dwarfs that stuck out their discolored heads or, more often, their thin arms and long, clawlike hands. Another of these little dwarfs appeared out of an egg that lay on a dish, breaking one end of the egg and poking its head out like a disgusting chicken; its thin legs stuck out at the other end and the dwarf started staggering about, wearing the eggshell like a shirt. Yet another of them was sitting astride the rubber bulb of a glass dropper, and as the bulb was pressed down, Luca could see some blackish substance running up and down inside the glass tube. At a stronger pressure, a third dwarf popped out and at once began putting out its tongue at Luca, dancing about and sniggering and holding with both hands its swollen, whitish paunch which looked like that of a fly when it is carrying eggs. More of these manikins were chasing each other among the medicine bottles, brandishing weapons which turned out to be the forks and spoons that Luca used. They did not really disgust Luca, indeed they almost amused him—except that they seemed to him dirty, and after seeing them come out of the bottles and handle the spoons and forks he thought that both medicines and food would be infected. So he pushed away the medicines and the food with signs of disgust, shouting and weeping; and found comfort in the gestures of approval which were made to him from the wall by a holy old monk with a beard. It was true that, from the wall in front of him, there projected, in contrast, the naked belly of a woman, white and swelling, taut as a drum, with big red ears at each side and a small triangular black beard in the groin beneath it; but he took no notice of it, and had eyes only for the face of the monk, so benign and reassuring. But suddenly a smile came over the old man's face, he opened his mouth, and with an unexpected grimace, stuck out his tongue. It was the governess' tongue, black and rough and moist, and at the end of it trembled the thin horns of a snail; and this snail, projecting from his mouth to an extraordinary length, waved about in the air for a little, extending its horns, then curled back upon itself and started gently stroking the monk's face, reaching up to his nose and forehead. It was a truly enormous snail and it went on and on coming out of his mouth and never stopped stroking the venerable brow framed in white hair, reaching up between the eyes which still gazed at Luca in a serene, benevolent manner. At the same time, on the other wall, the woman's belly split open at the navel and from the gash appeared a knee, as though someone shut up inside the belly was struggling to get out, without success. Then the knee disappeared and a complete naked leg protruded itself cautiously from the gash, the foot stretching down toward the floor . . .

He was continually imploring his parents to deliver him from these unbearable presences; but his parents were not there and he could hear, instead, hissing, intense voices, as of numbers of frantic theatrical prompters, whispering meaningless words hurriedly into his ear. Or there would be sudden loud bursts of tolling bells, their hollow vibrations clashing in the trembling air. A shrill whistle, dry as the sound of compressed steam escaping through a valve, never ceased to make itself heard in a distant corner of the room. And he was shouting for them to turn off the gas, otherwise they would all be asphyxiated.

But all the time, even as he lay helpless beneath the nightmares of delirium, he had the sensation that he was making some progress among his hallucinations, like a traveler among the tree trunks and shadows of a forest, toward an opening that he could not fail to find. And then one day, sitting beside him, in the act of supporting his forehead with one hand and feeding him with the other, he saw a woman whom he did not know but who, manifestly, was not one of those imaginary figures of delirium but a person of flesh and blood. Her head was wrapped, it seemed to him, in a kind of white turban, beneath which her face looked brown and somewhat wasted but well-preserved, like that of a middle-aged woman meticulously made up. This face was held erect, with a bird-like vanity, upon a long, rounded neck; and when he stammered out some confused words of thanks, the carefully made-up eyes, drowned in their paint and their wrinkles, held a spark of sympathy, while the mouth widened in a brilliant, pathetic smile, showing teeth of a doubtful whiteness, of which two were gold. It was the nurse, as he learned later, whom his parents, frightened by his delirium, had engaged to watch beside him night and day. And what he had at first sight mistaken for a turban was a nurse's cap. A white light, which he realized must be that of noonday, streamed through the window; and beside his head a screen, usually to be found in the drawing-room, appeared to be concealing another bed. He made a movement as though to show that the light tired his eyes; and the woman at once rose and went to the window. She was all in white and Luca saw that that small, well-preserved head of hers, like the head of some Oriental bird, was set upon a massive body whose ungainly shapes were broadly displayed by the extreme neatness of her dress. She lowered the blind, plunging the room into a pleasant semidarkness, then came back and sat by the bed, putting out her hand again to support Luca's forehead while with the other she held out the spoon. Luca saw that her hands were long and brown and dry, with painted fingernails. On the little finger of one hand she wore a small ring with a red stone in it.

Then, as the fog of delirium gradually cleared away, although he was in a state of utter prostration following the fall of temperature, he noticed a strange thing which to him was entirely new. The nurse, in spite of being middle-aged and having lost her looks, the room which he had once hated, every single object, in fact, appeared to him in a new light—serene, clean, familiar, lovable, and, so to speak, appetizing. He noted with surprise that he did not so much look at things as cast his eyes greedily upon them, just as a hungry animal throws itself upon a piece of food after a long fast. There beside him, for instance, was the little table covered with phials and bottles among which he had seen those filthy little dwarfs chasing each other. Now he saw honest, simple bottles of different-colored or clear glass, with corks or metal tops, and adorned with labels upon which even the flowing, hurried handwriting of the druggists who had written the prescriptions had a reassuring and affectionate look. Those neatly arranged bottles, the powders and liquids that they contained, the writing on each bottle indicating how such powders and liquids were to be used—he felt that all these things wished him well; and he seemed to be repaying their goodwill with a corresponding feeling of sympathy. When he moved his eyes from the little table to the nurse, whose face he could see in profile behind the bottles, he was conscious of the same feeling of contentment and affection. She was middle-aged; but Luca's eyes, though they could see the wrinkles under the make-up which reddened her cheeks and darkened her eyes, could not help loving those wrinkles, desiring them, even, as details that were richly significant, in the same way that one desires a modest-looking but renowned fruit for the delicious juice it contains. He was almost impelled to put out his hand and stroke those cheeks and those eyes. The thoughts, too, that her face inspired in him, dictated as they were by this new feeling of sympathy, were affectionate and penetrating. He reflected that she must have been very beautiful when she was young and that it must be a very bitter thing for her now to be no longer beautiful; also that, judging by appearance, she must in the past have been wealthy and free and that she was working as a nurse in order to earn her living. But his feeling for her had not an erotic origin—like the feeling, mixed up with repulsion, that he had once had for the governess. In fact, the feeling he now had for the woman he had had, shortly before, for the bottles; and when he turned his eyes away from her to look around the room, he had the same feeling for the various pieces of furniture—no longer haunting and fantastically absurd but calm and familiar, standing quietly round like affectionate old friends. He turned his eyes to the coat stand which he had seen changed into a snail running up and down the walls, and saw now that it was just an ordinary coat stand with three arms; and he was pleased to see that a petticoat and a chemise belonging to the nurse were hanging on it, and was also pleased to notice that they were unpretentious garments, like those of a poor person. Everything, in fact, to these new eyes of his, seemed to have significance—a very humble and homely significance, it is true, but a positive one. To the benevolence that colored all reality with fellow feeling there was added, besides, the sense of an established order, modest but necessary, in which nothing now appeared absurd and devoid of usefulness. Those bottles were just bottles, that coat stand was just a coat stand; nor was there any danger now of seeing the dwarfs' heads sticking out of the former, or of seeing that latter run up the wall.

But his surprise reached its height when the nurse, having fed him, started to wash his face. She took away the tray with the plates and spoons and carried it over to the table by the window; then she spread a bath towel across the bed, disappeared and came back in a moment with an aluminum bowl full of warm water, a piece of soap and a comb. She placed the bowl on the bed, sat down beside it and dipped the soap in the water. As she lightly soaped his face and very gently wiped the soap off again with a little sponge full of delicious warm water, he seemed already to be conscious of a kind of grace and delicacy in his own cheeks. But when, after that, she handed him the mirror and asked him to hold it up while she parted his hair, and he saw his own white, thin face, the feeling that the sight of it inspired in him astonished him profoundly. His face, refined by illness, seemed to have emerged purified from fever and delirium, as a landscape long buffeted and ravaged emerges from the mists of a violent storm. He was conscious of a feeling of love for that adolescent face which looked back at him, dreamy eyed. It was true that this was the same love that he felt for the nurse and for all the other things; but when he remembered the hatred that he had once felt for himself he saw that it was the most important feature of this new change.

The nurse finished combing his hair—in a way in which he himself never used to do it, that is, with the parting at one side. But Luca had no desire to protest. This, too, was a new and pleasing thing, and he felt almost grateful to her for her mistake. She removed the towel from the bed, took the bowl and went out. In a moment she was back, and she sat down in what was apparently her usual place, behind the little bed table, with a book in her hand. The whole room seemed to concentrate itself round this quiet, familiar movement of hers as if by enchantment, so that it, too, became quiet and familiar. Luca lay silent for some time, and then said: "I should like to sit up in bed, with a pillow or two behind my back."

"Well, you must be careful not to catch cold," she answered. She went out and came back with two pillows. She bent over Luca and, putting her arm round his waist, helped him to pull himself up and fitted in the pillows behind him. This effort was enough to make Luca feel the blood leave his face and his sight darken, as though he were about to faint. She helped him to put on a sweater and sat down again. After a moment Luca asked: "I've been very sick, haven't I?"

Resting her book on her knees and looking at him, the nurse answered: "Yes, very."

"I wanted to die," said Luca, with sincerity.

The nurse got up and passed her hand over his hair, gazing at him in an affectionate manner. Then she said: "But you'll get well now."

Luca looked up at her and did not say anything. A sudden emotion brought tears to his eyes. The nurse went on: "You'll get well if you're obedient and do all the things you ought to do." Without saying a word Luca took her hand and began kissing it gently, reflectively. Meanwhile the tears gushed from his wide-open eyes.

One evening toward the end of his convalescence Luca, tired of reading, was dozing with his head lying back on the pillow, when the nurse, with the solemn air of one who announces a piece of good news, appeared in the doorway and said: "Now you must get ready . . . the water's running, and in a moment you're going to have your first bath."

· "A bath . . . won't it make me feel giddy?" asked Luca.

"Don't worry, I'll be there to help you," she answered. She began preparations, coming and going about the room, precise and busy in her movements— movements which were those of a trained nurse and contrasted strongly with her appearance of a decayed gentlewoman. It looked to Luca as though she were joyful at this new step of his along the road to health; and he was grateful to her because, as he knew, he was to her only one sick person among many and she had no reason to be happy at his recovery; rather—since her salary came to an end with the end of his illness—she had reason to be sorry for it. She went out and came back in a short time with a big bath towel which she spread out to warm on the radiator. Then she went to the wardrobe and took out a camel's-hair dressing gown his mother had recently bought for the time when Luca would be getting up. She arranged the bathrobe on the armchair at the foot of the bed and placed a new pair of slippers on the floor. "A nice hot bath," she said as she turned the slippers with their heels toward the bed. "You'll see how well you feel after it." She pronounced these words in an inviting tone, but almost as if speaking to herself, with an abstraction which made them seem all the more natural and affectionate—as though they came truly from her heart and were not said merely to please Luca. Then she went out again, leaving the door open. The bathroom was on the other side of the passage, at no great distance, and the gay, rushing sound of the water could be distinctly heard. The nurse dallied for some time, waiting, perhaps, for the bath to fill; then she rushed in breathlessly, took the dressing gown and held it out, open, to Luca, saying: "Come on, quick . . . the bath's ready . . . up you get."

Formerly Luca would have been ashamed to show himself in pyjamas. But the game was altered, and everything which in the past would have repelled him he now accepted, not without satisfaction. The nurse pulled away the coverings and Luca sat up. All at once he felt his head going round and the blood draining away from his face. The nurse was standing in front of him, holding the bathrobe open, but he could not think of standing up and remained there, in distress, sitting on the bed, his legs hanging down and his face, gone very white, bent over to one side. She understood, and threw down the dressing gown. "You feel weak . . . of course . . . wait a moment, I'll help you." She placed a robust arm around his waist and helped him to his feet. For a moment Luca had the sensation that his feet were not resting on the floor. The weakness showed itself in a kind of hiatus which had the shape of his legs without having either their substance or their strength. "Now put on the dressing gown . . . come along," he heard the nurse saying. Obediently he turned, allowing her to insert first one of his arms and then the other into the wide sleeves, and then stood still, while she swiftly closed the dressing gown around him. "Now walk," she said, holding him round the waist; "don't be afraid . . . I'm here."

Luca took his first steps, leaning heavily against the nurse, while she supported him around the waist. Her expression was one of carefulness and devotion; and, as if the strength he needed came to him from the sight of her face and the contact of her arm across his back, Luca felt that at every step his feet were regaining confidence and were communicating a new and pleasant sense of solidity and safety to his legs and to the whole of his body. Just as, when he had awoken from the nightmares of delirium and had imagined, looking at the furniture in his room, that he had a positive appetite for it, so now he felt that he was hungry for the floor upon which he was walking, and that he was receiving more and more nourishment from it with each step that he took. "Perhaps I'm not as weak as I thought," he said, reinvigorated. The nurse nodded her assent as she continued to support him. Closely enlaced, they left the room; the house seemed deserted, as Luca guessed from the darkness and silence in the passage. They went into the bathroom, and the nurse, having made Luca sit down on a stool, closed the door. It was hot as an oven in the bathroom. The bath was full of bluish water that looked as if it were boiling, and the nurse turned off the taps and placed a new piece of soap in the dish. A little embarrassed, Luca slipped off his dressing gown, which she took and hung up on a hook near the door. Left with nothing on but his pyjamas, Luca thought for a moment of asking the nurse to leave the room. But she did not appear to attach any importance to his embarrassment, nor even to have noticed it; and Luca decided that he would do exactly what she told him to do. "Now take off your pyjamas," she said, "and get into the bath . . . then I'll soap you."

Obediently Luca rose to his feet and slipped off his pyjama jacket. Then the nurse bent down and lightly untied his trousers and pulled them down to his feet, raising herself again at once, a little flushed in the face; but Luca thought that this was because of the effort of stooping. Naked, he stood there hesitating, but felt the nurse put her arm round his waist again and guide him gently toward the bath. Slowly he got into the scalding water, first with one foot, then with the other, and finally, very gradually, he lay down. "How d'you feel?" asked the nurse, sitting down on a stool and looking fixedly at him. "Very weak," replied Luca. And this was true. In the hot water there came back to him an indescribable feeling of emptiness at the back of the neck, accompanied by a slight nausea. The nurse said: "You must stand up, and I'll soap you well . . . You can rinse yourself, and then you must come out of the water at once. It's very weakening if you stay in long." Luca looked at her and then looked at himself in the bath: indistinct, gently undulating, tinged with a faint bluish light, his own body inspired in him, as his face had done the first time he had seen it in the mirror, a feeling of affection. And the sight of his pubic region, where the brown hairs, dusted over with bright little air bubbles, seemed to fluctuate hither and thither round his sexual organ like seaweed round an anemone in the depths of a clear sea-water pool, did not appear to him in any way indecent but in perfect harmony with the rest of his body, which was chaste, thin and white. "Well, are you going to stand up?" asked the nurse. He gave a start, raised his eyes and realized that she too, from her stool, had, like him, been looking at his body lying in the bottom of the bath. "All right," he said; and rose to his feet.

The water came halfway up his legs. A mirror on the wall in front of him showed him himself, quite naked, and the nurse, red in the face, bending down toward him as she soaped his body. She soaped first his back, then his chest and finally his belly. Luca realized then that, whereas the working of his mind was still languid and slow, his sensibility refined, perhaps, by illness, caused him to notice many things which at another time would have escaped him. There was, for example, an excess of zeal and professional skillfullness in the alacrity of the nurse which in some way excited him, though his weakened mind was quite unable to define it. The nurse, her hands white with soap, straightened herself up and said: "Now sit down again." Obediently Luca let himself slip down again into the water.

She went out and after a moment came back again, holding the towel with outstretched arms and crying: "Quick—quick, while it's hot." Luca stood up, hesitated a moment with his foot on the edge of the bath, then climbed out. At once the nurse was upon him, wrapped him up tightly, with a sort of affection, in the burning towel. "Isn't it nice and warm?" Luca, all muffled up, could not but be conscious of a glow of well-being—the first for a very long time. "Now you must dry yourself—quickly," she said. Luca sat down on the stool, and the nurse, on her knees, vigorously rubbed his legs. She put so much energy into it that her face was soon scarlet, and in her kneeling attitude there was a quality of vague but passionate adoration that embarrassed Luca. Then, as her hands moved upward over his legs, she lightly touched his groin, and Luca, instinctively quivering, suddenly realized what till that moment he had merely —and almost in spite of himself—suspected: that chance had willed that he and the nurse should find themselves alone in the flat that evening; and that there was going to be a repetition of what had happened between himself and the governess, months before. But with this difference, that his whole spirit was changed and would now accept what at that time he had thought it his duty to refuse.

After that first light, perhaps involuntary touch, the nurse appeared to lose all her energy; and Luca felt that her hands had become hesitant, as though, instead of massaging him, they wished—and yet at the same time did not wish —to caress him. Her hands moved over his body, but seemed anxious at any cost to avoid his groin; and yet it was straight toward his groin that they would slide, every now and then, from the most distant places, in a swift incursion that was rendered rough and clumsy by haste and remorse. These incursions had a particular character of their own; they were like the pecking of a bird or the bite of an animal, at once furtive and eager. In other respects too, the nurse—flushed in the face, her head bent so that her eyes were concealed— now showed plainly the nature of the feeling that was agitating her. Luca looked at her, and it seemed to him that her flush deepened more and more as the circling strokes of the massage closed in more narrowly about his belly. The whole of that big body of hers, bent forward from the knees, seemed to be straining with the desire, at once encouraged and opposed, to escape from the limits of mere massage into a kind of contact that was freer and of a different nature. But, in contrast to what had once happened with the governess, he did not feel any desire to draw back, any repugnance. He felt himself to be no more than an object in her hands, entirely without any will of his own apart from the wish to be docile and obedient. These reflections almost made him forget the woman and her passion. Finally, after one more positive, more satisfied touch, she rose to her feet, saying: "There, now you can get dressed."

Luca got up and the towel fell to the floor. The massage had produced in him a visible erection; but he noticed with surprise that he felt no shame. This, too, was something new; and it seemed another sign of his new confidence in himself and in the world. Once it would have been impossible for him to accept a physical excitement of this kind simply, without disgust, as without vanity. He would have resented it in every case as a revolt, and his first impulse would have been to oppose and destroy it. But now these manifestations of instinct—whether it was a question of himself or of the nurse, of his desire or hers, and even when they occurred in a manner unforeseen and entirely beyond his control—all these manifestions, it seemed to him, should be welcomed, as so many aspects of a completely lovable, completely understandable reality. There he stood, naked, in front of this woman, with the signs of the excitement of his senses visible in his own body; yet, in spite of it, he felt no desire to be elsewhere or to be other than what he was. Lost in astonishment, he started violently at the nurse's voice saying again: "Well, are you going to get dressed?"

In silence he allowed her to slip on his pyjamas and wrap him again in the dressing gown. As she opened the door she asked him: "How do you feel?"

"Fine."

They left the bathroom and started along the carpeted floor of the passage. The nurse was supporting him, and had now reassumed her usual attitude toward him, professional but solicitous. But in the passage Luca was assailed again by a feeling of extreme weakness; his sight was dimmed; a great coldness chilled his forehead and his temples; and, with a murmur of: "I'm feeling ill," he abandoned himself to the nurse's supporting arm. He realized he must be coming out of a faint when he found he was sitting on his bed with the nurse applying a damp cloth to his forehead, "It's nothing," she said. "It's the bath that has weakened you." Luca did not answer, and the nurse, having removed his dressing gown, turned back the bedclothes and, hoisting up his legs, helped him into bed. He noticed the freshness of the clean sheets as a pleasure which he owed to her. "Now you must try and rest," he heard her say. The door closed and he was left alone.

During the days that followed the nurse never once alluded to the incident in the bathroom. On his side, Luca did not think of reminding her of it, not so much because he would not have liked to follow up those first approaches as because he felt more inclined to submit passively to her will, whatever it might be, rather than exercise his own. It was enough for him, in any case, to understand the meaning of that experience; it mattered little if the experience itself stopped at its very beginning. But he realized that she was thinking about him and about what had happened in the bathroom, and he awaited the result of these reflections with some curiosity. If he went on to attempt, in his own mind, an exact definition of his feeling, he observed that—apart from a strong but generic attraction such as he might have felt for any other woman in similar circumstances—he continued to cherish that affectionate, comprehensive, disinterested feeling that now marked his constant attitude toward everybody and everything. This attitude manifested itself in a polite but sincere curiosity about her character and past. She was now not so much nursing him as keeping him company; and as confidence grew she reached the point of telling him many stories about her life—which were all, or almost all, concerned with her love affairs with a large number of men, of the most diverse ages and conditions. As Luca had imagined, she had been in easy circumstances in her younger days; then her husband had died and in order to make a living she had been compelled to take various jobs, the last of which had been nursing. At first hesitating and reticent, when she saw that Luca showed no surprise she became more and more frank, and finally, in her own rather pathetic way, positively immodest. Hers had been a perfectly ordinary life, full of errors and vanities; and she, in turn, was a perfectly ordinary person with all the prejudices of those who have come down in the world—as, for example, that her job was unworthy of her. But these errors and vanities seemed to Luca, thanks to his new in-dulgent attitude, to be not merely excusable but lovable as well. He was pleased, above all, with her illusion that she was still young and beautiful, an illusion that once upon a time he would have found ridiculous but which was now a vigorous feature of her character. One day when they were speaking of feminine beauty, she rose to her feet and strutted about the room, pulling her dress tightly over her hips and belly and saying: "Look at me and tell me honestly how many women younger than me can boast of a figure like mine." Her eyes sparkled, she smoothed down her buttocks with both her hands, up-lifted her bosom and turned her head this way and that. Luca could not help smiling. But he was pleased when he realized that it was a sympathetic smile.

During this time his strength was returning to him, and now he could take a bath by himself. The first few times the nurse still helped him, but without any recurrence of the disturbances and excitements of the first evening. She seemed really to have given up hope of Luca, but not without a certain sort of affectionate, melancholy regret on her part, as though in the sacrifice of desire she had found a new, albeit sad, love-motif. Luca came to understand this one day when, lying with his eyes half-closed and pretending to be asleep, he had seen her gazing at him for a long time, with a singular expression on her face which he had not at once been able to define. It was a look of perplexity and almost of scorn. It was as though instead of searching in her own consciousness she had been seeking, in his face, the reasons for her own sacrifice; and as though, not finding them there, she had become angry with herself for not having the courage to throw scruples aside and take her pleasure of him as she longed to do.

One evening, having brought him his supper tray, she sat down on the bed and said: "I think this is the last day I shall be staying with you."

Luca raised his eyes from his plate and with a candor not entirely devoid of malice said: "I'm sorry . . . and when are you going?"

"Tomorrow evening," she answered. And then she added, looking straight at him: "I'm sorry too."

Luca looked at her. She was sitting on the bed in an uncomfortable position, her bust and her face twisted round toward him and one hand pressing heavily on the coverlet for support. He noticed, beneath the redness of the rouge on her cheeks, the flush of another, warmer redness, a redness of a stirring and excitement of the blood. As on that day in the bathroom, her eyes, like sparkling stones in old, dull settings, shone through their make-up, pathetically. She added: "I had got quite accustomed to you."

Luca said nothing. She went on, lowering her voice: "Perhaps I was a little in love with you too."

Luca had expected anything rather than this declaration of love. The only amorous experience of his life had been that of his brief relationship with the governess. And he had imagined that, like her, the nurse would herself take the initiative without any words, imposing her own desire upon his passivity. Taken unawares by the sentimental character of a passion that he had hitherto imagined to be imperative and sensual, he was lost for a moment in a cold, surprised embarrassment. He said, in a colorless voice: "Really?"

"Yes," replied the nurse, "but it doesn't matter." She shook her head and lowered her eyes, with a movement of her mouth as if repressing a sob. Then Luca said, with sincerity: "I think I was rather fond of you too . . . but it depended on you . . ."

He left his sentence unfinished and looked at her. It was the truth, he thought, nothing but the truth. But from whence came this self-assurance, not devoid of malice, this self-assurance like that of an accomplished seducer? He was pleased with it, as a new endowment, both as an aid to action and to entering into relations with other people. She raised sparkling eyes toward him and asked: "And so, if I had wanted to. . . ?" Luca nodded. He was thinking now that she would leap upon him, rather as she had done in the bathroom, but with a more open violence and without any hypocrisy; and he was wondering how he ought to behave. At that moment his parents were at table and would not come for at least half an hour. Would that time—so short—be long enough? And might not his mother, for some reason or other, come in before the time? He was conscious that despite these doubts and fears he was not afraid of love nor of its consequences; and he merely added, judiciously: "I thought you wanted to, that day in the bathroom . . . there was no one in the house and it would have been easy . . ."

Contrary to what he had expected, the nurse did not throw herself upon him but rose to her feet and, looking at him from a little way off, put out her arm and slowly stroked his face. Then she said: "You were too weak that day . . . besides, you're just a boy . . ."

Luca reflected that this, too, was an undeniable truth and said nothing, merely lowering his eyes. The nurse took his chin in her hand—just as you do with children when you ask them what they want—and said: "So, if I came tonight . . . would you like me to come?"

Raising his eyes toward her, Luca answered, quite simply: "I would certainly like you to come." Erect and motionless, she brooded over him with her brilliant eyes, so young, so different from the old, dead, painted eyelids between which they shone. Then, in a voice full of promise, generous, maternal, she announced: "Well then . . . if you'd really like me to . . . I'll come."

Luca nodded, as if to say that it was a good plan. The nurse went on: "I'll come . . . but we must be careful . . . we musn't make any noise." For some time she had no longer been sleeping in Luca's room behind the screen; and Luca reflected that she was giving this piece of advice to herself rather than to him. "In a couple of hours, then," she concluded. She looked at him a moment longer, as if to observe the effect of her promise upon him; then took the tray and went out.

Left alone, Luca took up a novel from the little table by the bed and began reading. He soon realized that he was not following the meaning of the words. He felt his cheeks burning fiercely, as though the woman's glances, so laden with desire, had scorched him where they had touched him, from brow to neck. This burning sensation was pleasant and exciting and gave him a feeling of urgent vitality such as he had never known. In order to distract his mind from it, and from the excitement that accompanied it, he began thinking over what had happened. He examined his attitude toward this woman and told himself that it could not have been more honest nor more sincere. She had told him she loved him; but he had limited his reply to saying that he would be pleased if she came; and this was the exact truth. He thought that he would derive pleasure from her coming as he derived pleasure, ever since he had awoken from his delirium, from everything that happened, from every presence, every relationship; and he was glad that he did not experience, toward the nurse, any feeling that was more intense than or different from the feeling inspired in him by other people and by all inanimate things. He was, in reality, hungry for this woman, and this hunger made her desirable to him; but the same way he was hungry for the peaceful light shed by the lamp at his bedside, for the pieces of furniture standing in the shadows, for the night, for the silence that he imagined outside the house, and even for the tiny creaking of the worm that bored its tunnel in the wood of the table. These things, and many others besides, because of this hunger that made them appetizing to him, were all equally lovable and together composed a world which was new to him and, at last, acceptable.

As these thoughts passed through his mind he began to feel sleepy. While he was in this drowsy state his father and mother came in, as they always did, and after the customary recommendations and questions, which he answered vaguely, kissed him and went away. It seemed to him also that the nurse was busy round his bed, tucking in those same blankets which in two hours' time she would be throwing aside so as to lie down beside him; but he was not quite certain that this was not a kind of hallucination. For he was really very sleepy; and as soon as his parents left him, he dropped into un-consciousness.

He slept for some time, with a good, solid sleep that was an expression of that same hunger which, while he was awake, gave him an appetite for everything and everybody. And he had a curious dream—suggested, perhaps, by this hunger—in which he thought he was a tree. Shaped like a tree—black, leafless, rain-soaked, numb with cold—he was standing on the top of a bare, frost-bound hill, stretching out his arms which were branches and his open fingers which were twigs. An immense landscape extended all round, with hills and woods and rivers and fields, and the whole of this landscape was streaked with snow and darkened by winter mists. The sky, heavy with black, unmoving clouds, was mirrored in the flooded fields, and over all there was a profound silence, as of a dead, timeless world. But far away the sun was rising on the horizon. At first it was only a cold, red globe; then, as it rose gradually into the sky, putting the clouds to flight, it became more and more clear and radiant, and he could feel its heat even through the ice-cold bark. Beneath the rays of the sun a vast movement took place over the whole land-scape, as though the woods, and every single tree in them, had shaken off their winter stillness, as though the rivers were swollen with flood-water, the fields fermenting with life, the hills softened and filled with nourishment, like a woman's breasts. All of a sudden a harsh sound—exultant, prolonged, amorous, like the call of a hunting horn—filled the air, breaking that cold silence. And to him it seemed that, starting from his roots deep-sunk in the earth, a wave of joyous hunger spread upward through his trunk; and this, overflowing the casing of bark, burst out through his branches in a thousand green and shining buds. These buds, in their turn, swiftly opened, became leaves, tendrils, boughs. And he felt himself growing, multiplying, pullulating endlessly, in an irresistible, fabulous rush of abundance, in every direction and from every part. All at once he was no longer a tree, but a man, standing upright with his arms raised toward the sun. And, with this sensation of rush and thrusting in his limbs, he awoke. The room was plunged in shadow, except for a small circle of light round the little red-shaded lamp on the bed table. The clock pointed to a quarter past midnight. In a few minutes the nurse would be coming.

Then, as he looked round the darkened room and thought about the nurse, it seemed to him that this hunger of his, in an impulse of impatience and voracity, was passing, at one step, beyond the limits of the present time and of the place where he now was, and was rushing forward into the future, both in time and in space. There, in the darkness, he seemed to see, rising to the surface, the life that remained for him to live—the places, the human faces, the movements, the meetings. He had an overwhelming sensation of aggressive freedom, of unlimited exploration, of lightning flashes of vision; as though the future, catching alight and burning in the fire of imagination, had been consumed and discounted in an instant, complete even in its smallest details. He saw that this was his life; and that now it only remained to him to be patient and to live it out to the end. His eyes filled with tears; and an uncontrollable agitation ran through him. He started to cry aloud meaningless words, turning over and over in the bed and looking intently into the darkness, as though he longed to illuminate it and see the curtain of the future torn asunder. While he was at the height of this exaltation, he heard the door open.

It was the nurse. Below her fur-trimmed coat which she had thrown hurriedly over her shoulders appeared the crumpled edge of a long muslin nightgown. Luca saw her make a sign of silence with her finger on her lips. Her eyes were shining more brightly than ever, seeming to light up her whole face despite the darkness of the room. She closed the door cautiously and very slowly turned the key in the lock; then took a table napkin from the bed table and wrapped it round the lamp. She did all this without hurrying, like someone doing a thing he had done a thousand times in his life already; and Luca, lying back on his pillows, his arms spread out on the bed in front of him, watched her without excitement or embarrassment, with a curiosity that he felt to be innocent, as though she were not getting the place ready for a love scene but performing the preordained gestures of some unknown rite of her own. Having finished her preparations, she came over to the bed and, standing majestically erect, looking straight into his eyes with her own sparkling ones, she raised both her hands, took the coat from her shoulders and placed it on a chair. In this gesture she bent sideways, revealing the massive but unshapely character of her body—her hips not rounded but almost square, with broad surfaces of flesh pressing against the stuff of the nightgown; her back broad and thick; her arms gone flabby. She stood still for a moment, as if to allow Luca to admire her at leisure, then, with a vigorous, impatient gesture, she raised her arms and began slipping the nightgown over her head. Higher and higher the muslin rose, like the curtain of a theatre, but hesitant and awkward, jerkily disclosing the spectacle beneath it—her legs big but straight, like towers of brown, pink-flushed flesh; the hollow of her lap, the only retired, shadowy place among so much displayed profusion; her belly, overflowing vessel of desire; and finally her bosom, narrow between the two broad hollows below her raised arms, like a dark and hilly tract of ground between two white, deserted roads. With a final pull, at once slow and full of imperious resolution, she freed herself completely from her nightdress, throwing it to the floor, and stood facing Luca naked, with her customary air of munificence, of promise, of magnanimity. She behaved, thought Luca, as though she had been still young and beautiful and as though he looked upon her as such; and this pleased him because it seemed to him a lovable, generous illusion. When she considered that Luca had looked at her long enough, she turned back the bedclothes and slipped majestically into bed, lying down at his side. It was not so much an embrace he experienced as a sinking of the whole of himself in a limitless expanse of flesh. And when she passed her hand unhurriedly over his body, seeking his sex, and, having found it, took hold of it by the root as though she wished to tear it away, implanting it then in her own body, he had the precise feeling that she was taking him by the hand and introducing him, a reverent novice, into a mysterious cave dedicated to a religious rite. This, he thought, was the life he had formerly invoked, and little did it matter if it presented itself to him in the garb of autumn. Filled with gratitude, he found himself kissing the thin brown face with the closed eyes, motionless as an effigy. But was it the face of the nurse, or that of some deity risen up from the earth for his possession? Certainly between his hands and those limbs that lay beneath his own there passed a tremor of veneration. Meanwhile the sense of relief continued, and, with its freshness and buoyancy, redeemed the ardor and the gravity of the embrace.

The nurse went away next day, as she had announced; and Luca was left with a feeling neither of regret nor of disgust, but rather of gratitude for his final initiation not merely into physical love but also into that more general love for all things, the first glimmer of which had reached him when he awoke from his delirium. He felt he had at last found a new and quite personal way of looking at reality—a way that was composed of sympathy and patient expectation. This way of looking at things, he observed, permitted a rhythm of thought much calmer, much fuller, much more serene than before, and with it a vision that was no longer direct and aggressive but scrupulously, ineffably hesitant and cautious. Now, he thought, he would see things first with those new eyes which had opened that night inside him, and only afterward with the eyes which at his birth had been dazzled by the first light of day. Second and truer mother, the nurse had given him a second birth when, in his desire for death, he had been already dead. But he knew that this second birth could never have taken place if he had not first desired, so sincerely, so wholeheartedly, to die.

In the meantime there was more and more talk in the house of his departure for the mountains. Luca's parents had engaged a room for him in a sanatorium for convalescents and it only remained to fix the date of his journey. There was no mention of lessons now, except in reference to a distant day when Luca would be strong enough to face them again without harm to himself. While these preparations were going on, Luca, sitting wrapped in blankets in an armchair near the window, continued, half-asleep, to contemplate the sky which, as spring came on, grew steadily clearer and warmer. He enjoyed his own passive state now, ever since he had recognized, in things and in people, an order which was still unknown but capable of lifting him up and carrying him far away. Content to have become a part of this order, he found a new strength in accepting its mysterious, external nature.

At last the day of departure arrived. It was the end of March, and although the air was warm Luca's mother, who was going to accompany him to the sanatorium, muffled him up in several sweaters and a heavy overcoat. Luca, enveloped in this overcoat, remained quite inert, lying back in the armchair in the room which now seemed strange and filled with the light of departure—just as if he had been a suitcase or some other inanimate object. His passive state continued, persisted even at the moment when he ought to have at least taken a share in the arrangements made for him by others, rendered him inert just when inertia seemed impossible. He could hear his parents and the maids bustling about as they carried down the luggage; and he himself remained there motionless, just as though he were not going away. He felt very warm—perhaps too warm, and yet it was pleasant, also—and, without thinking of anything at all, he looked out at the pale morning sky. If he closed one eye, a flaw in the glass, tear-shaped, widened out in the sky, forming as it were a great white cleft. He heard his mother, entering the room breathlessly, cry out: "But what are you doing here? The taxi's down there, waiting"; and it was only then that he could make the effort to move. Formerly he would never have been able to resist the paltry infection of the fuss of departure, even if he showed it only by the display of a hostile phlegm. But this time, as he realized, he was truly indifferent as to whether he went or did not go, arrived or did not arrive. There were other trains, or—if it came to that—they could just stay. Later, while his mother was running nervously from one office to another, buying the tickets and getting them stamped, he let himself sink again into the depths of that satisfying inertia. Sitting on a suitcase, beneath the black and noisy dome of the station, among the rush and chatter of the crowd, he almost forgot that he was on the point of starting on a journey. Like a thread that is too weak, his participation in outside life snapped continually, and he did not trouble to refasten it.

But there was his mother, as there had been the taxi, as there would be the train and all those other means by which his inertia could be transported through space.—That same train, he could not help thinking as he obediently followed the luggage-laden porter, against which he had vomited months before, coming back from his holiday, in that crazy revolt of his whole body. Once in the train he closed his eyes drowsily as he sat holding the bundle of newspapers and reviews that his mother had bought for him. He heard the engine whistle and was conscious that beneath him the wheels were beginning to turn, and he continued to doze. When he opened his eyes again he was surprised to see the suburbs slipping past the window below the railway embankment. Through top-floor windows he could see people moving about in rooms among unmade beds they had just left. Whistling, the train steadily gathered speed, the houses became more and more rare, and then, after the train had crossed a bridge at full speed and with a tearing clatter, the country began.

The train rushed on, and he felt this rushing movement as a delicious contrast to his own inertia. What else was the train, in relation to him, but a thing with a purpose, a direction, a will—as, previously, the nurse's passion had been and his parents' solicitude? He thought that it would be fine to go on like this all one's life. The train, the nurse, his parents—these would be succeeded by larger, if not more mysterious, forces; and he would trust himself to them with equal confidence and equal delight. He saw himself as a ragged, wounded, hungry soldier, in an army of whose orders and objectives he knew nothing; as a beggar, in a misery for which he was not responsible and of which he was not even conscious; rich, with wealth of which he had not earned one halfpenny; exalted to a power which he had never sought; a priest in a church of which he did not know the rites; and finally dead—the last delight—through a catastrophe which he had neither foreseen nor wished to avoid. The rattling of the train as it crossed the switches, the swift, regular beat of the wheels, the whistle of the engine tearing to shreds the silence of the countryside, even the backward flight of that same countryside past the train windows—all these stimulated the flow of his thoughts. Yes, he was now in the midst of a broad, swirling, powerful stream in which he was but a straw that cannot help being carried along, scarcely hoping to keep afloat to the end. And closing his eyes, he abandoned himself to it trustfully, as he had abandoned himself a few days before in the arms of the nurse.

In fact, he closed his eyes to examine this thought more carefully; and his mother, anxious for his comfort and thinking he wished to sleep, put a cushion behind his head with gentle and loving hands. Until then he had not thought of the nurse except with vague reference to that initiation of which she had been the unconscious instrument. Now he sought to define in his own mind the true and deeper meaning of that initiation. He remembered that at the moment of the embrace he had felt a sudden, strong desire to enter completely, with the whole of his body, into the woman's belly, and to curl up there, in that warm, rich darkness, just as he had lain curled up before he was born. But now he understood that that womb was nothing else than the womb of life itself, hitherto repudiated by him but which the woman, imperiously, had compelled him to accept. Yes, he concluded, that is what life should be: not sky and earth and sea, not human beings and their organizations, but rather a dark, moist cavern of loving, maternal flesh into which he could enter confidently, sure that he would be protected there as he had been protected by his mother all the time she was carrying him in her womb. Life meant the sinking of oneself in this flesh and feeling its darkness, its engulfing power, its convulsion, to be beneficent, vital things. Suddenly he understood the significance of the sense of relief that had refreshed him while the nurse was crushing him in her embrace.

This thought kept him company during the whole afternoon, and after supper, when the sleeping berths were let down and his mother and he had gone to bed, for a good part of the night until he fell asleep. While he was asleep, the train crossed a long steel bridge over a very broad river, and he heard the resounding din of the girders beneath its weight. Much later, he was aware of a lively clatter of voices and of echoing footsteps in a sudden stillness, and realized that the train had come into a big station and stopped there. But this was still in the depths of the night, and turning over on his side he went off to sleep again and was not conscious either of the train shunting as it changed engines, nor of its leaving the station again. He went on sleeping, waking every now and again and becoming conscious of the movement of the train with the same pleasure each time. When he finally woke up the day was well advanced, and he knew by the slow and labored rhythm of the wheels that the train was going upgrade.

His mother helped him to wash and dress; then the porter put up the sleeping berths and he sat by the window and looked out at the landscape. The train was close by the side of a mountain and was turning and twisting round a narrow gorge at the bottom of which could be seen a rushing torrent. Another mountain slope rose steeply on the far side of the torrent, shutting out the sky. Luca gazed at the foaming waters of the torrent, at the uptorn masses of rock round which the waters dashed and broke, and at the thick pine forests which flowed down the mountainside till they bathed their roots in those tumultuous waves. In the pale light of the cloudy morning the water of the torrent looked dirty, grayish-white in color, the rocks a rusty red and the pines a dark, melancholy, dim green. An air of ancient and indifferent dullness inclosed this alpine solitude. It was the first time Luca had seen the mountains and thought they were not so beautiful as he had believed; and he felt disappointed.

But the train, as it wound around the side of the mountain, came out into an open place and Luca saw, at the far end of the gorge, towering above two smaller mountains entirely covered with forest, a snow-covered peak which looked to him immensely high. The clouds in the sky had parted and the sun, lighting up this distant snow, made it sparkle. And then, he did not know why, at the sight of that untouched whiteness, so majestic and so lonely, a sudden elation seized him. The idea of being carried along and of trustfully allowing himself to be carried toward an unknown goal came back to him; but this time it was to some extent modified by the entirely new feeling of being carried and of allowing himself to be carried toward those snows that were so lofty and so white. He kept his wide-open eyes fixed on the mountain peak; and the more he looked, the more he felt the trustful, drunken exultation growing within him. He knew there was no material reason for rejoicing just because he caught sight of the snowy top of a mountain; and yet he could not help realizing that it was that particular sight which started up the mechanism, so long dislocated, of his deepest hopes. Almost without meaning to, he turned toward his mother and asked: "What about the nurse?"

His mother, surprised, answered: "I suppose she's looking after some other invalid."

Yes, she looked after me well, thought Luca. And he said: "She was splendid . . . really, without her, I shouldn't have got well so quick."

"There's no need to exaggerate," said his mother, slightly offended at his forgetting the attentions that she herself had showered upon him, "but certainly she was excellent."

"Yes, she was splendid," repeated Luca.

"By the way," said his mother, "she must have got quite fond of you. She telephoned several times to know how you were."

"And what did you answer?"

"That you were quite well again."

Luca closed his eyes. At that same moment the train, with a long and mournful whistle, plunged into a tunnel. When he opened his eyes again he saw nothing but darkness, while a damp wind blew in his face from the dark walls of the tunnel, mixed with a faint drizzle of water and puffs of steam. Echoing from the vault of the tunnel, the beat of the wheels sounded to him like a monotonous, exultant voice repeating the same words over and over again. He seemed to be able to distinguish these words—the same words, full of hope, that had borne him company ever since his awakening from delirium, day by day during his slow recovery; and he knew that, from now onward, not only the clatter of a train in a tunnel or the whiteness of snow on a mountain peak, but all things would have a meaning for him and would speak to him in their own mute language. Then the train, with another whistle, came out into the light of day.

MORE ABOUT THIS STORY

The clinical psychologist is often called upon to prepare diagnostic and evaluative case histories for diverse purposes: school and guidance counseling, psychiatric and hospital referrals, and the like. Always the clinical psychologist seeks those pertinent details of social and interpersonal dynamics which affect total personality.

Since Luca Mansi in many ways resembles the middle-class adolescent who appears at the psychologist's desk, it may be of value to approximate here what a clinical psychologist would report factually about the experience Moravia records as fiction. While this "report" may not contribute directly to an esthetic appreciation of the story, it may help the reader—by adding a purely psychological dimension to his approach—to reach more substantial insights.

THE CASE HISTORY OF LUCA MANSI

General Description

Luca is a tall, thin, narrow-shouldered boy, delicate in body and health. He is extremely touchy and easily roused to anger. It is difficult to know, however, from the information provided, whether he was so when younger. Now Luca's reactions to people are usually quick and intense. The dominant impression of Luca is of his extraordinary—excessive—sensitivity.

Intellectual Evaluation

He appears to be intellectually superior. His past achievement in school tends to verify this assumption as, more significantly, does his comprehension of the crisis he is experiencing. He demonstrates acute insight into his own problems. At present, however, Luca is not constructively applying his intelligence in his school work.

Individual Differences

Apparently the product of a normal developmental pattern, he is, to some extent, unique within the framework of that pattern. Physically, he is normal for his age: despite his fifteen years, he is as tall as most adults. Normal also are his violent outbreaks of temper. Even his inadequate application of his intelligence at school is characteristic at this stage. But although his emerging awareness of self is perhaps the most conventional aspect of his behavior pattern, the intensity and the extremism of his reactions most decisively reveal Luca's individual differences. Few adolescent boys carry their battle for independence or their rebellion against family and authority figures to his lengths, namely, a near fulfillment of a drive toward death.

Self-Image

Luca's self-image—until his recent experience with his nurse—has been one of self-hate, unworthiness, shame, and guilt, all sufficiently strong to enforce his death wish. Although this image has taken a long while to evolve, Luca skillfully reconstructs its development: in the early stages he experiences sheer delight with his "collection"—marionettes, stamps, and "things"; later come feelings of disgust and shame about these possessions, followed by a greedy desire to hoard his money; finally, he manifests a need to destroy all—his collection, his money, and his life. Also, he traces his relations with his middle-class parents from an early, pure love for them to a revulsion induced by their worship of "things." Especially traumatic has been Luca's discovery that his parents have stored money behind a painting of the Madonna he loved to pray before. But however he justifies his current hostility toward parents and things, the central target of his hatred remains himself.

Conflicts

Adolescence always brings with it a number of vital problems involving adjustment to adult standards. Because the child is growing up too rapidly to allow either his family or himself a much-needed perspective that might enable tolerance and patience, major areas of conflict are likely to develop. Luca's extravagant determination to die (by "not eating") suggests that his strongest conflict is located in his rebellion against familial authority. As a child he had apparently obeyed his parents and teachers passively and unquestioningly. Now, at fifteen, he feels imposed upon and actively resents his parents' ignoring his desires, needs, and rights. He extends his battle for independence to school and rebels against his teachers through a withdrawal that precludes academic success. His uncontrollable resentment of authority compels actions motivated by inward rather than external necessity—actions, paradoxically, of self-destruction.

Another area of conflict develops out of the clash between his parents' wholly materialistic, impersonal values and Luca's inward, abstract, and intensely felt personal values. Hence his demand that they love him for what he is and respect his determination to be an individual. The third area of conflict is, of course, sex. Lust and love have become confused and undifferentiated in his mind, especially as his sexual feelings commingle with his sadistic impulses of hate and his masochistic urge to destroy anything that gives him pleasure. From a Freudian point of view, the sexual conflict at this time indicates an aggravation of the Oedipal complex: both of Luca's affairs involve mature women from whom Luca may seek the love his mother denied him.

Defenses

Luca's two strongest conscious defenses are intellectualization and withdrawal. Intellectualization—what Anna Freud calls the "thinking over" of strong affective impulses—helps the adolescent avoid the emotional impact of his heightened libidinal energies. With Luca, intellectualization operates ceaselessly. He *analyzes* his feelings, structures a system of rational motives to explain his apathy, and develops a defensive code of values along with a pattern of behavior compatible with those values. By trying to *define* rather than acknowledge or admit his deeply felt resentment of authority, Luca avoids the taboo of openly expressing anger and aggression. Instead, he posits a logical, developmental pattern—from joy of possession to disgust and shame and, at last, the impulse to destroy—as the reasonable basis for his loathing all things.

Luca adopts too a pattern of withdrawal from his greatest conflict, his rebellion against authority. Self-invoked daydreaming, sleeping, apathy, and passivity all serve to remove him from the areas of conflict and allow him some measure of self-satisfaction. Rationalization is also manifest in Luca's persistent justification of his behavior. His parents, for example, are deservedly unloved because they have behaved basely.

Strengths

Because Luca has been unnecessarily harsh and unkind to himself, his self-image (before the final act of initiation into manhood) does not accord with his real self. He is in fact a kind, loving, sensitive boy agonized by unendurable emotions of hatred. It is most important to recognize that when he believes he is dying, his luminous moment of awareness convinces him that his dying is not an act of hate but of love. The very love that has made him hate so fiercely happily redirects him away from his original goal of self-annihilation and also helps him to refocus his self-image.

The two sexual experiences in Luca's adolescence follow a normal developmental pattern for this stage of youth (though of course few adolescents have identical experiences with governesses). It is not surprising that he was sexually aroused by the governess, for she *was* there and she *was* intensely physical. Nor is it surprising that he was simultaneously repelled, for she was neither pretty nor young. Desire and nausea frequently mark the adolescent's ambivalent response to an initial sexual engagement. Luca, however, survived his traumatic experience with the governess. When the nurse arrived, he was ready—self-assured, unashamed, and free from revulsion or sex nausea.

Thus, despite Luca's overwhelming hate and his compulsive death wish, his greatest strengths remain his desire to love and his determination to live as an independent being. These goals—joined with his resolute search for order in his turbulent inner world of thought and emotion—have sustained the boy and helped prepare him for his ultimate and restorative assignation with the nurse.

FOR FURTHER READING

Baldanza, Frank. "The Classicism of Alberto Moravia," *Modern Fiction Studies*, III (1958), 309–320.

Freud, Anna. *The Ego and the Mechanisms of Defense.* New York: International Universities Press, 1946, pp. 172–189.

Johnson, Ben and Maria de Dominiciis. "Interview with Alberto Moravia," *The Paris Review,* No. 6 (1955), 17–37.

Lewis, R. W. B. "Eros and Existence," *The Picaresque Saint.* New York: J. B. Lippincott, 1959.

Pacifici, Sergio. *A Guide to Contemporary Italian Literature.* New York: Meridian Books, 1962, pp. 40–56.

Araby

BY JAMES JOYCE (1882–1941)

Like Chekhov's "After the Theater" and Hemingway's "The Three-Day Blow," James Joyce's "Araby" concerns first love. Like those authors too, Joyce ignores plot and episode, concentrating instead on the ironies of inner awareness. But although Joyce's narrator is younger than either Hemingway's Nick or Chekhov's Nadya, his experience is as intense as theirs and its significance more sharply and directly perceived. Whereas Chekhov and Hemingway maintain the distance afforded by omniscient narration, Joyce thrusts his narrator to the forefront. Yet it is not a boy who tells the story, but, as in Anderson's "The Man Who Became a Woman," a narrator grown beyond his youthful experience, recalling its exhilarating promise and its subsequent torment of disillusion. What endures for the narrator is an ineradicable memory of that moment of awareness or insight—Joyce called it an *epiphany*, "a showing forth"— which marked the end of innocence.

Everything in the story is relevant to a full understanding of Joyce's complex theme, and the tragic lure of the exotic for this sensitive, lonely boy is foreshadowed by innumerable details of landscape, object, and language. Despite the musty air and dingy litter of a dead house on a dead-end street in a dying city, the boy determines quixotically to bear his "chalice safely through a throng of foes." The Christian symbol of the chalice merges with the Oriental symbol of the bazaar to shape an illusory world of almost mystically ideal beauty. Moreover, each of these central symbols is supported by numerous romantically associated images of color as well as of light and shade.

Mangan's sister reigns as the mysterious princess of his confused fantasy, and it is to her that he secretly intones "strange prayers and

145

praises." But he has also heard other voices: "the shrill litanies of shop-boys who stood on guard by the barrels of pigs' cheeks, the nasal chanting of street singers . . . ," voices that echo the drab ugliness of reality. Trapped between these polarities of dream and reality, the boy bursts forth on his futile quest.

Further ironies appear in the characterization. Although the boy's uncle, for example, is crudely ordinary and insensitively unaware of his nephew, his allusion to "The Arab's Farewell to his Steed" stirs (and, ironically, corrupts) the boy's imagination. Far more interesting, however, is the role assigned to Mangan's sister. To what extent, the reader should ask, has Joyce consciously avoided filling in the dimensions of her personality? Is she worthy of the boy's adoration, or has she little more spiritual substance than the shopgirl at the dreary bazaar?

THE STORY

North Richmond Street, being blind, was a quiet street except at the hour when the Christian Brothers' School set the boys free. An uninhabited house of two stories stood at the blind end, detached from its neighbours in a square ground. The other houses of the street, conscious of decent lives within them, gazed at one another with brown imperturbable faces.

The former tenant of our house, a priest, had died in the back drawing-room. Air, musty from having been long enclosed, hung in all the rooms, and the waste room behind the kitchen was littered with old useless papers. Among these I found a few paper-covered books, the pages of which were curled and damp: *The Abbot,* by Walter Scott, *The Devout Communicant,* and *The Memoirs of Vidocq.* I liked the last best because its leaves were yellow. The wild garden behind the house contained a central apple tree and a few straggling bushes under one of which I found the late tenant's rusty bicycle pump. He had been a very charitable priest; in his will he had left all his money to institutions and the furniture of his house to his sister.

When the short days of winter came dusk fell before we had well eaten our dinners. When we met in the street the houses had grown sombre. The space of sky above us was the colour of ever-changing violet and towards it the lamps of the street lifted their feeble lanterns. The cold air stung us and we played till our bodies glowed. Our shouts echoed in the silent street. The career of our play brought us through the dark muddy lanes behind the houses where we ran the gauntlet of the rough tribes from the cottages, to the back doors of the dark dripping gardens where odours arose from the ash-pits, to the dark odorous stables where a coachman smoothed and combed the horse or shook

music from the buckled harness. When we returned to the street, light from
the kitchen windows had filled the areas. If my uncle was seen turning the
corner we hid in the shadow until we had seen him safely housed. Or if
Mangan's sister came out on the doorstep to call her brother in to his tea we
watched her from our shadow peer up and down the street. We waited to see
whether she would remain or go in and, if she remained, we left our shadow
and walked up to Mangan's steps resignedly. She was waiting for us, her figure
defined by the light from the half-opened door. Her brother always teased her
before he obeyed and I stood by the railings looking at her. Her dress swung
as she moved her body and the soft rope of her hair tossed from side to side.

Every morning I lay on the floor in the front parlour watching her door.
The blind was pulled down to within an inch of the sash so that I could not be
seen. When she came out on the doorstep my heart leaped. I ran to the hall,
seized my books and followed her. I kept her brown figure always in my eye
and, when we came near the point at which our ways diverged, I quickened
my pace and passed her. This happened morning after morning. I had never
spoken to her, except for a few casual words, and yet her name was like a
summons to all my foolish blood.

Her image accompanied me even in places the most hostile to romance.
On Saturday evenings when my aunt went marketing I had to go to carry some
of the parcels. We walked through the flaring streets, jostled by drunken men
and bargaining women, amind the curses of labourers, the shrill litanies of
shop-boys who stood on guard by the barrels of pigs' cheeks, the nasal chanting of street-singers, who sang a *come-all-you* about O'Donovan Rossa, or a
ballad about the troubles in our native land. These noises converged in a
single sensation of life for me: I imagined that I bore my chalice safely
through a throng of foes. Her name sprang to my lips at moments in strange
prayers and praises which I myself did not understand. My eyes were often
full of tears (I could not tell why) and at times a flood from my heart seemed
to pour itself out into my bosom. I thought little of the future. I did not know
whether I would ever speak to her or not or, if I spoke to her, how I could
tell her of my confused adoration. But my body was like a harp and her
words and gestures were like fingers running upon the wires.

One evening I went into the back drawing-room in which the priest had
died. It was a dark rainy evening and there was no sound in the house. Through
one of the broken panes I heard the rain impinge upon the earth, the fine in-
cessant needles of water playing in the sodden beds. Some distant lamp or
lighted window gleamed below me. I was thankful that I could see so little.
All my senses seemed to desire to veil themselves and, feeling that I was about
to slip from them, I pressed the palms of my hands together until they trembled,
murmuring: *"O love! O love!"* many times.

At last she spoke to me. When she addressed the first words to me I was so confused that I did not know what to answer. She asked me was I going to *Araby*. I forgot whether I answered yes or no. It would be a splendid bazaar, she said she would love to go.

"And why can't you?" I asked.

While she spoke she turned a silver bracelet round and round her wrist. She could not go, she said, because there would be a retreat that week in her convent. Her brother and two other boys were fighting for their caps and I was alone at the railings. She held one of the spikes, bowing her head towards me. The light from the lamp opposite our door caught the white curve of her neck, lit up her hair that rested there and, falling, lit up the hand upon the railing. It fell over one side of her dress and caught the white border of a petticoat, just visible as she stood at ease.

"It's well for you," she said.

"If I go," I said, "I will bring you something."

What innumerable follies laid waste my waking and sleeping thoughts after the evening! I wished to annihilate the tedious intervening days. I chafed against the work of school. At night in my bedoom and by day in the classroom her image came between me and the page I strove to read. The syllables of the word *Araby* were called to me through the silence in which my soul luxuriated and cast an Eastern enchantment over me. I asked for leave to go to the bazaar on Saturday night. My aunt was surprised and hoped it was not some Freemason affair. I answered few questions in class. I watched my master's face pass from amiability to sternness; he hoped I was not beginning to idle. I could not call my wandering thoughts together. I had hardly any patience with the serious work of life which, now that it stood between me and my desire, seemed to me child's play, ugly monotonous child's play.

On Saturday morning I reminded my uncle that I wished to go to the bazaar in the evening. He was fussing at the hall-stand, looking for the hat brush, and answered me curtly:

"Yes, boy, I know."

As he was in the hall I could not go into the front parlour and lie at the window. I left the house in bad humour and walked slowly towards the school. The air was pitilessly raw and already my heart misgave me.

When I came home to dinner my uncle had not yet been home. Still it was early. I sat staring at the clock for some time and, when its ticking began to irritate me, I left the room. I mounted the staircase and gained the upper part of the house. The high cold empty gloomy rooms liberated me and I went from room to room singing. From the front window I saw my companions playing below in the street. Their cries reached me weakened and indistinct and, leaning my forehead against the cool glass, I looked over at the dark house where she lived. I may have stood there for an hour, seeing nothing but the brown-clad figure cast by my imagination, touched discreetly by the lamplight at the curved neck, at the hand upon the railings and at the border below the dress.

When I came downstairs again I found Mrs. Mercer sitting at the fire. She was an old garrulous woman, a pawnbroker's widow, who collected used stamps for some pious purpose. I had to endure the gossip of the tea-table. The meal was prolonged beyond an hour and still my uncle did not come. Mrs. Mercer stood up to go: she was sorry she couldn't wait any longer, but it was after eight o'clock and she did not like to be out late, as the night air was bad for her. When she had gone I began to walk up and down the room, clenching my fists. My aunt said:

"I'm afraid you may put off your bazaar for this night of Our Lord."

At nine o'clock I heard my uncle's latchkey in the halldoor. I heard him talking to himself and heard the hallstand rocking when it had received the weight of his overcoat. I could interpret these signs. When he was midway through his dinner I asked him to give me the money to go to the bazaar. He had forgotten.

"The people are in bed and after their first sleep now," he said.

I did not smile. My aunt said to him energetically:

"Can't you give him the money and let him go? You've kept him late enough as it is."

My uncle said he was very sorry he had forgotten. He said he believed in the old saying: "All work and no play makes Jack a dull boy." He asked me where I was going and, when I had told him a second time, he asked me did I know *The Arab's Farewell to his Steed*. When I left the kitchen he was about to recite the opening lines of the piece to my aunt.

I held a florin tightly in my hand as I strode down Buckingham Street towards the station. The sight of the streets thronged with buyers and glaring with gas recalled to me the purpose of my journey. I took my seat in a third-class carriage of a deserted train. After an intolerable delay the train moved out of the station slowly. It crept onward among ruinous houses and over the twinkling river. At Westland Row Station a crowd of people pressed to the carriage doors; but the porters moved them back, saying that it was a special train for the bazaar. I remained alone in the bare carriage. In a few minutes the train drew up beside an improvised wooden platform. I passed out on to the road and saw by the lighted dial of a clock that it was ten minutes to ten. In front of me was a large building which displayed the magical name.

I could not find any sixpenny entrance and, fearing that the bazaar would be closed, I passed in quickly through a turnstile, handing a shilling to a weary-looking man. I found myself in a big hall girdled at half its height by a gallery. Nearly all the stalls were closed and the greater part of the hall was in darkness. I recognised a silence like that which pervades a church after a service. I walked into the center of the bazaar timidly. A few people were gathered about the stalls which were still open. Before a curtain, over which the words *Café Chantant* were written in coloured lamps, two men were counting money on a salver. I listened to the fall of the coins.

Remembering with difficulty why I had come I went over to one of the stalls and examined porcelain vases and flowered tea-sets. At the door of the stall a young lady was talking and laughing with two young gentlemen. I remarked their English accents and listened vaguely to their conversation.

"O, I never said such a thing!"

"O, but you did!"

"O, but I didn't!"

"Didn't she say that?"

"Yes. I heard her."

"O, there's a . . . fib!"

Observing me, the young lady came over and asked me did I wish to buy anything. The tone of her voice was not encouraging; she seemed to have spoken to me out of a sense of duty. I looked humbly at the great jars that stood like eastern guards at either side of the dark entrance to the stall and murmured:

"No, thank you."

The young lady changed the position of one of the vases and went back to the two young men. They began to talk of the same subject. Once or twice the young lady glanced at me over her shoulder.

I lingered before her stall, though I knew my stay was useless, to make my interest in her wares seem the more real. Then I turned away slowly and walked down the middle of the bazaar. I allowed the two pennies to fall against the sixpence in my pocket. I heard a voice call from one end of the gallery that the light was out. The upper part of the hall was now completely dark.

Gazing up into the darkness I saw myself as a creature driven and derided by vanity; and my eyes burned with anguish and anger.

MORE ABOUT THIS STORY

To his friend Louis Gillet, Joyce once observed that he was an autobiographical writer, that his "work and life make one . . . interwoven in the same fabric." For Joyce, work and life were a tide swollen by the tributaries of family and nation. Viewed psychologically, all his writing is an attempt to dam that tide and to convert latent but destructive power into constructive energy—to transform conflict into creativity. Joyce engineered his triumph, but he needed distance—from kin and country—to do so. Although his way was that of the exile (he spent his adult life on the Continent), the world of fiction he re-created was peopled by family and friends in Dublin.

"Araby," like the other stories in *Dubliners,* Joyce's earliest published fiction, provides an example of his initial efforts to adapt and integrate his ego through art, to make of work and life "the same fabric." Thus, many of the external details in "Araby" derive from direct experience. Late in 1894, con-fronted by economic disaster—a common circumstance in the Joyce family— John Joyce moved his family of eleven (James was almost thirteen years of age) to a grimy house on North Richmond Street. A priest had died there recently, and a cluttered, unweeded garden sprawled behind the house. A few doors away stood the Christian Brothers School where young James had earlier spent two unpleasant years.

Other less obvious details are even more suggestive. Only James among the Joyce children loved his father. "He was a bankrupt," Joyce said later of him, thinking perhaps of his moral as well as economic debts—many of them recorded elsewhere in *Dubliners.* But he loved his father nonetheless, espe-cially for his enormous vitality, and memorialized his ebullience in the portrait of Simon Dedalus in *A Portrait of the Artist as a Young Man.* In "Araby," written when Joyce was twenty-three, only the germ of that later character-ization appears, but Joyce's ambivalence is already marked in the sketch of the uncle who can conjure fantasy in the boy's mind even as he casually forgets to let him leave early enough for the bazaar.

The pervasive Christian imagery of "Araby" also finds its source in Joyce's boyhood experience. Reared by a devout mother and educated at a Jesuit school, he was fascinated and awed by Catholic ritual and practice. But he was also puzzled and troubled by the cruelty of many of his priestly teachers, by his father's blatant anti-clericalism, and, chiefly, by his own intellectual doubts about the Christian doctrines of sin and resurrection. Sexually, he was inexperienced (a lack he would supply at the age of fourteen) but the adora-tion of Mangan's sister in "Araby" suggests that her image has blended with that of the Virgin Mary.

By the time the now-adolescent Joyce had moved to North Richmond Street, not only the dwelling place of his body but also of his spirit seemed stifling and arid. He had gone, Richard Ellmann writes in his biography of Joyce, "through a series of violent changes and emerged from them sober and aloof, except with the few friends to whom he exhibited his joy, his candor, his bursting youth; even with these he was a little strange, never wholly companionable because each time he laid bare his soul he importuned greater loyalty, until friendship became for them almost an impossible burden of submission." [1]

Here then are some of the materials Joyce drew from his life and deployed

[1] *James Joyce* (New York: Oxford, 1959), p. 42.

as fiction. We present them here, however, not as data for a clinical case history about adolescence but as an illustration of how the artist distills and transmutes the particulars of actual experience. Although such data rarely open the door to a total comprehension of artistic purpose, they do enhance appreciation and support insight. They should certainly help the reader, for example, to recognize that "Araby" was written not so much to exorcise the demons of dream and disillusion as to embrace them. Those who dream, the narrator warns, are vain, and he recalls as the price of his own vanity that his eyes "burned with anguish and anger." Yet not to dream is to die, to suffocate, in that "special odour of corruption" which clouds Ireland, or, even worse, to remain immobilized in Dublin, "the center of paralysis." The tensions of life are reflected in art, and in "Araby" the now-grown narrator, by virtue of his creative act of fiction, continues his quest for the mirage beyond the wasteland.

FOR FURTHER READING

Brooks, Cleanth and Robert Penn Warren. " 'Araby': An Interpretation," in *Understanding Fiction*. Second Edition. New York: Appleton-Century-Crofts, 1959, pp. 189–192.

Joyce, Stanislaus. *Recollections of James Joyce by His Brother*. New York: The James Joyce Society, 1950.

Magalaner, Marvin and Richard Kain. *Joyce: The Man, the Work, the Reputation*. New York: New York University Press, 1956, pp. 53–102.

After the Theater

BY ANTON CHEKHOV (1860–1904)

As the dominant theme of the literature of adolescence is self-discovery, its dominant mood is high seriousness, usually communicated through a profound tragic irony. But if, as Anton Chekhov has written, "the aim of fiction is absolute truth," then the comic surely deserves its place in that literature as well. In "After the Theater" Chekhov explores the possibilities of comedy.

The great Russian writer who acknowledged medicine as his wife and literature as his mistress possessed enough of knowledge and insight, of tenderness and compassion, to satisfy both his loves. In this brief story no detail of Nadya's shifting moods eludes his clinical eye, neither the absurdity nor the ecstasy. And both are vividly real and moving.

Of plot action in "After the Theater" there is almost nothing; what little exists grows out of Nadya's memories and expectations. Nevertheless, her room serves as a stage where she acts out the full inward range of her emotions. The real-life props—a writing table and letter paper, tears and laughter, the smell of wormwood, and an icon above the bed —structure and direct the girl's moods from a comically affected grandiloquence to a warm, simple embrace of the sheer joy of living in God's world. Only once does Chekhov intrude his own consciousness of the girl's situation—in a poetic figure that simultaneously pinpoints her amusing childishness and transcendent lyricism: "At first the joy was small and rolled like a little rubber ball, then it became broader, bigger, and flowed like a wave."

153

THE STORY

TRANSLATED BY GEORGE GIBIAN

When Nadya Zelenina returned with her mother from the theatre, where they had seen *Eugene Onegin,* and came into her room, she threw off her dress and loosened her hair. Wearing only her slip and white blouse, she sat down quickly at the table in order to write a letter in the manner of Tatyana.

"I love you," she wrote, "but you do not love me, you do not love me!" When she had written this, she laughed.

She was only sixteen and had not yet loved anyone. She knew that the officer Gorny and the student Gruzdev both loved her, but now, after the opera, she felt like doubting their love. How interesting it is, to be unloved and unhappy! There is something affecting and poetic about it when one loves deeply and the other is indifferent. Onegin is interesting because he is not in love at all, while Tatyana is charming because she is very much in love. If they loved each other equally, and were happy, then they would probably seem boring.

"Stop protesting that you love me," Nadya wrote, thinking of the officer Gorny. "I cannot believe you. You are very clever, educated, serious. You have great talent, and a brilliant future may be in store for you. I am an uninteresting, insignificant girl, and you know yourself that I shall only be a burden in your life. Yes, you were attracted by me and thought that in me you had found your ideal, but that was a mistake, and now you are asking yourself in despair—why did I meet that girl? Only your kindness prevents you from admitting it."

Nadya began to feel sorry for herself. She wept a little, and went on:

"It is difficult for me to leave my mother and my brother, or else I should take the veil and go wherever my eyes lead me. You would then be free and would fall in love with another. I wish I were to die!"

Through her tears she could not make out what she had written. On the table, on the floor and on the ceiling, little rainbows quivered as if Nadya were looking through a prism. She could not write; she leaned on the back of the chair and began to think about Gorny.

Oh, how fascinating men are! Nadya remembered what a beautiful, appealing, guilty and tender expression the officer always had when people argued with him about music, and what efforts he made on such occasions to control himself so that his voice would not sound passionate. In society, where cool haughtiness and indifference are considered a sign of good breeding and noble manners, one must hide one's passion. He does try to hide it, but he does not succeed, and everybody can tell perfectly well that he loves music passionately. The endless arguments about music and the rash judgments of people who do not understand it keep him in a state of constant tension. He becomes frightened, timid, silent. He plays the piano superbly, like a real concert pianist, and if he were not an officer, he would certainly be a famous musician.

The tears dried in her eyes. Nadya recalled that Gorny had declared his love for her at a symphony concert and then again downstairs by the coat-stand where there was a draft coming from every direction.

"I am very glad that you have at last become acquainted with the student Gruzdev," she went on. "He is very intelligent, and you will certainly like him very much. Yesterday he came here for a visit and stayed till two o'clock in the morning. We were all enthusiastic about him, and I was sorry that you had not come to see us. He said a number of striking things."

Nadya laid her hands on the table and rested her head on them. Her hair covered the letter. She remembered that the student Gruzdev also loved her and that he had as much right to her letter as Gorny. As a matter of fact, would it not be better to write to Gruzdev? For no reason at all, joy stirred in her breast. At first the joy was small and rolled like a little rubber ball, then it became broader, bigger, and flowed like a wave. Nadya had already forgotten about Gorny and Gruzdev. Her thoughts became confused, and her joy grew and grew, went from her breast to her arms and legs, and it seemed as if a light cool breeze blew on her head and stirred her hair. Her shoulders trembled with quiet laughter, the table trembled, the glass on the lamp also, and tears from her eyes splashed on to the letter. She did not have the strength to stop this laughter. In order to show herself that she was not laughing without reason, she quickly tried to think of something funny.

"What a funny poodle!" she said, feeling that she would suffocate with laughter. "What a funny poodle!"

She remembered how Gruzdev had played with the poodle Maxim yesterday after tea-time, and then told a story about a very clever poodle who had chased a crow in the yard. The crow had looked around and said to him: "Oh, you scamp!" The poodle, who had not known that he was dealing with a learned crow, became terribly confused, and went away puzzled. Then he began to bark.

It will be better if I love Gruzdev, Nadya decided and tore up the letter.

She began to think about the student, his love, and her own love, but the thoughts in her head all ran together and she thought about everything: her mother, the street, the pencil, the piano. . . . She was joyful, as she thought, and found that everything was good and splendid. Her joy told her that this was not yet all, that if she waited a little, things would be still better. Soon spring, then summer, and she will go with her mother to stay at Gorbiki. Gorny will come there on his leave, go walking with her in the garden, and make love to her. Gruzdev, too, will come. He will play at croquet and skittles with her, and tell her funny, wonderful things. She began to long passionately for the garden, darkness, clear sky, stars. Again her shoulders trembled with laughter, and it seemed to her that there was a smell of wormwood in the room and that a little branch had struck against the window.

She went over to her bed, and sat down. Not knowing what to do with the immense joy which was wearying her, she looked up at the icon which hung at the head of her bed.

"Oh God, Oh God, Oh God," she said.

MORE ABOUT THIS STORY

First love, psychologists have long observed, sounds an open diapason of adolescent emotions. Intense and absorbing, lyrical and agonized, this short-lived period marks another normal stage in the process of substituting parental alternates. The next story in this book, Hemingway's "The Three-Day Blow," tells about the end of a first love as adroitly as Chekhov accounts for its beginning. Consider the following questions as they concern both the specific situations and the craft of the short story.

1. Nick Adams has been reading Meredith's *The Ordeal of Richard Feverel;* Nadya has just returned from a performance of Pushkin's *Eugene Onegin.* What relevance have these literary works to Nick's and Nadya's respective psychological situations?
2. Nick is probably a few years older than Nadya. How much more certain than Nadya's is Nick's control over the conflict between illusion and reality? Which of the two adolescents is better prepared to meet and master the next crisis?
3. What does Nadya's evaluation of the qualities of her lovers suggest about the maturity of her love?
4. What purposes in structure and characterization docs the poodle serve?
5. Does Nadya's apostrophe to the icon effectively conclude the story, or is the intrusion of a religious note strained and alien?
6. Writing about Chekhov in *A Moveable Feast,* Hemingway said that reading Katherine Mansfield, whose work strongly reveals Chekhov's influence, is "like hearing the carefully artificial tales of a young old-maid compared to those of an articulate and knowing physician who was a good and simple writer." What is it like to read Hemingway after Chekhov (or vice versa)? In what ways does Hemingway show his own appreciation and use of Chekhov's techniques of fiction?

FOR FURTHER READING

Josselyn, Irene. *The Happy Child.* New York: Random House, 1955.
Simmons, Ernest J. *Chekhov: A Biography.* Boston: Atlantic-Little, Brown, 1962.

The Three-Day Blow

BY ERNEST HEMINGWAY (1899–1961)

"If a man writes clearly enough, anyone can see if he fakes." Hemingway's sentence, from *Death in the Afternoon*, expresses his lifelong contempt for writers who mask fuzzy abstraction with rhetoric and verbiage. Until the tragic close of his career he clung to the code of stylistic discipline self-imposed forty years earlier. Recalling his struggles with his first short story, Hemingway writes in the posthumously published *A Moveable Feast*, "I found that I could cut that scrollwork or ornament out and throw it away and start with the first true declarative sentence I had written." In Hemingway's best fiction—and many discerning readers argue that his short stories demonstrate a more refined craft than his novels—the prose is spare, the diction simple, the dialogue terse, and the plot minimal. Together, however, they flesh out the skeleton of underlying themes. What seems at first flat and artless proves on inspection taut, supple, and expressive.

In "The Three-Day Blow," for example, the story may initially puzzle the reader as he tries to identify either the protagonist or the direction of the plot. Neither is clearly established at the outset. Nevertheless, as the youths sprawl before the fire drinking, rambling about baseball, weather, literature, and family, an alert reader senses a tension that heightens suspense and at once binds and separates the two young men. For example, Bill's remark early in their conversation, "Wouldn't it be hell to be in town?" seems innocuous and irrelevant until the reader comprehends its latent irony and discerns how subtly and inevitably it anticipates Bill's later observation, "You don't want to think about it."

The laconic dialogue and even the language also serve to show that the boys have assumed roles neither is honestly comfortable with. Af-

157

fecting a monosyllabic pseudo-sophistication—everything, for example, is "swell": Irish whisky and literature, fathers and logs—Nick tries to arrest or circumvent his progress toward a confrontation with a disgreeable reality. So long as thinking can be avoided, his pose implies, all will be well. Again, however, the reader feels that something more must emerge, some inwardness that adds dimension to the otherwise banal exchange. When Nick's submerged and suppressed feelings of loss do at last surface, the reader should understand what Hemingway means by a disciplined craft of fiction.

In more than twenty stories about Nick Adams' boyhood, adolescence, and manhood, Hemingway sketches the lineaments of his later "code" heroes, the men who, like Jake Barnes in *The Sun Also Rises* and Fred Henry in *A Farewell to Arms,* face down the terror of life with courage, poise, and an astonishing tolerance for psychic pain: they learn "to grin and bear it." Like style, life too must be disciplined, Hemingway believes, though his stories reveal that trying to order experience usually promises less success. Even that limited measure of control, his fiction proves, must be wrenched from the violent, intractable world of everyday living. Although the young Nick Adams of "The Three-Day Blow" has already been scarred by experience, he is still an acolyte sifting the data of life but not yet fully tutored in the refinements of the "code."

Earlier, in a story called "Indian Camp," Nick, still a child, accompanies his father, a doctor, into a forested Indian settlement where, as he watches his father perform a Caesarean operation on a squaw, her husband, frantic with her agonized screams, slits his throat. Unable to face the reality of death, Nick takes refuge in fantasy: "he felt quite sure that he would never die." In "The Three-Day Blow" Nick has not yet wholly emerged from the cocoon of illusion.

"The End of Something," a chronologically antecedent companion piece to "The Three-Day Blow," relates the end of an adolescent love affair between Nick and a girl named Marjorie. Rowing with her past a landscape dotted by sites romantically associated with their love, Nick responds unfeelingly. At their beach rendezvous, Nick rejects Marjorie's gentle but insistent affection. "It isn't fun anymore," he tells her, admitting also with remorse, "I feel as though everything was gone to hell inside of me." When Marjorie leaves, Nick feels neither joy nor release. Bill's arrival and his efforts to console Nick also fail to help. To Bill's "How do you feel?" Nick answers, "Oh, go away, Bill! Go away for a while."

"The Three-Day Blow" brings Bill back once more to compel Nick to contemplate the poignant reality of a shattered romance. Though Hemingway maintains detachment throughout the story, his attitude toward Nick implies that the young man has not yet achieved maturity. The reader must determine whether the ambivalence of the dénouement is appropriate to Nick's stage of development or whether Hemingway has merely failed to resolve the implications of his story.

THE STORY

The rain stopped as Nick turned into the road that went up through the orchard. The fruit had been picked and the fall wind blew through the bare trees. Nick stopped and picked up a Wagner apple from beside the road, shiny in the brown grass from the rain. He put the apple in the pocket of his Mackinaw coat.

The road came out of the orchard on to the top of the hill. There was the cottage, the porch bare, smoke coming from the chimney. In back was the garage, the chicken coop and the second-growth timber like a hedge against the woods behind. The big trees swayed far over in the wind as he watched. It was the first of the autumn storms.

As Nick crossed the open field above the orchard the door of the cottage opened and Bill came out. He stood on the porch looking out.

"Well, Wemedge," he said.

"Hey, Bill," Nick said, coming up the steps.

They stood together, looking out across the country, down over the orchard, beyond the road, across the lower fields and the woods of the point to the lake. The wind was blowing straight down the lake. They could see the surf along Ten Mile point.

"She's blowing," Nick said.

"She'll blow like that for three days," Bill said.

"Is your dad in?" Nick said.

"No. He's out with the gun. Come on in."

Nick went inside the cottage. There was a big fire in the fireplace. The wind made it roar. Bill shut the door.

"Have a drink?" he said.

He went out to the kitchen and came back with two glasses and a pitcher of water. Nick reached the whisky bottle from the shelf above the fireplace.

"All right?" he said.

"Good," said Bill.

They sat in front of the fire and drank the Irish whisky and water.

"It's got a swell, smoky taste," Nick said, and looked at the fire through the glass.

"That's the peat," Bill said.

"You can't get peat into liquor,' Nick said.

"That doesn't make any difference," Bill said.

"You ever seen any peat?" Nick asked.

"No," said Bill.

"Neither have I," Nick said.

His shoes, stretched out on the hearth, began to steam in front of the fire.

"Better take your shoes off," Bill said.

"I haven't got any socks on."

"Take them off and dry them and I'll get you some," Bill said. He went upstairs into the loft and Nick heard him walking about overhead. Upstairs was open under the roof and was where Bill and his father and he, Nick, sometimes slept. In back was a dressing room. They moved the cots back out of the rain and covered them with rubber blankets.

Bill came down with a pair of heavy wool socks.

"It's getting too late to go around without socks," he said.

"I hate to start them again," Nick said. He pulled the socks on and slumped back in the chair, putting his feet up on the screen in front of the fire.

"You'll dent in the screen," Bill said. Nick swung his feet over to the side of the fireplace.

"Got anything to read?" he asked.

"Only the paper."

"What did the Cards do?"

"Dropped a double header to the Giants."

"That ought to cinch it for them."

"It's a gift," Bill said. "As long as McGraw can buy every good ball player in the league there's nothing to it."

"He can't buy them all," Nick said.

"He buys all the ones he wants," Bill said. "Or he makes them discontented so they have to trade them to him."

"Like Heinie Zim," Nick agreed.

"That bonehead will do him a lot of good."

Bill stood up.

"He can hit," Nick offered. The heat from the fire was baking his legs.

"He's a sweet fielder, too," Bill said. "But he loses ball games."

"Maybe that's what McGraw wants him for," Nick suggested.

"Maybe," Bill agreed.

"There's always more to it than we know about," Nick said.

"Of course. But we've got pretty good dope for being so far away."

"Like how much better you can pick them if you don't see the horses."

"That's it."

Bill reached down the whisky bottle. His big hand went all the way around it. He poured the whisky into the glass Nick held out.

"How much water?"

"Just the same."

He sat down on the floor beside Nick's chair.

"It's good when the fall storms come, isn't it?" Nick said.

"It's swell."

"It's the best time of year," Nick said.

"Wouldn't it be hell to be in town?" Bill said.

"I'd like to see the World Series," Nick said.

"Well, they're always in New York or Philadelphia now," Bill said. "That doesn't do us any good."

"I wonder if the Cards will ever win a pennant?"

"Not in our lifetime," Bill said.

"Gee, they'd go crazy," Nick said.

"Do you remember when they got going that once before they had the train wreck?"

"Boy!" Nick said, remembering.

Bill reached over to the table under the window for the book that lay there, face down, where he had put it when he went to the door. He held his glass in one hand and the book in the other, leaning back against Nick's chair.

"What are you reading?"

"*Richard Feverel.*"

"I couldn't get into it."

"It's all right," Bill said. "It ain't a bad book, Wemedge."

"What else have you got I haven't read?" Nick asked.

"Did you read the *Forest Lovers?*"

"Yup. That's the one where they go to bed every night with the naked sword between them."

"That's a good book, Wemedge."

"It's a swell book. What I couldn't ever understand was what good the sword would do. It would have to stay edge up all the time because if it went over flat you could roll right over it and it wouldn't make any trouble."

"It's a symbol," Bill said.

"Sure," said Nick, "but it isn't practical."

"Did you ever read *Fortitude?*"

"It's fine," Nick said. "That's a real book. That's where his old man is after him all the time. Have you got any more by Walpole?"

"*The Dark Forest,*" Bill said. "It's about Russia."

"What does he know about Russia?" Nick asked.

"I don't know. You can't ever tell about those guys. Maybe he was there when he was a boy. He's got a lot of dope on it."

"I'd like to meet him," Nick said.

"I'd like to meet Chesterton," Bill said.

"I wish he was here now," Nick said. "We'd take him fishing to the 'Voix tomorrow."

"I wonder if he'd like to go fishing," Bill said.

"Sure," said Nick. "He must be about the best guy there is. Do you remember the *Flying Inn?*"

" 'If an angel out of heaven
Gives you something else to drink,

Thank him for his kind intentions;
Go and pour them down the sink.' "

"That's right," said Nick. "I guess he's a better guy than Walpole."

"Oh, he's a better guy, all right," Bill said.

"But Walpole's a better writer."

"I don't know," Nick said. "Chesterton's a classic."

"Walpole's a classic, too," Bill insisted.

"I wish we had them both here," Nick said. "We'd take them both fishing to the 'Voix tomorrow."

"Let's get drunk," Bill said.

"All right," Nick agreed.

"My old man won't care," Bill said.

"Are you sure?" said Nick.

"I know it," Bill said.

"I'm a little drunk now," Nick said.

"You aren't drunk," Bill said.

He got up from the floor and reached for the whisky bottle. Nick held out his glass. His eyes fixed on it while Bill poured.

Bill poured the glass half full of whisky.

"Put in your own water," he said. "There's just one more shot."

"Got any more?" Nick asked.

"There's plenty more but dad only likes me to drink what's open."

"Sure," said Nick.

"He says opening bottles is what makes drunkards," Bill explained.

"That's right," said Nick. He was impressed. He had never thought of that before. He had always thought it was solitary drinking that made drunkards.

"How is your dad?" he asked respectfully.

"He's all right," Bill said. "He gets a little wild sometimes."

"He's a swell guy," Nick said. He poured water into his glass out of the pitcher. It mixed slowly with the whisky. There was more whisky than water.

"You bet your life he is," Bill said.

"My old man's all right," Nick said.

"You're damn right he is," said Bill.

"He claims he's never taken a drink in his life," Nick said, as though announcing a scientific fact.

"Well, he's a doctor. My old man's a painter. That's different."

"He's missed a lot," Nick said sadly.

"You can't tell," Bill said. "Everything's got its compensations."

"He says he's missed a lot himself," Nick confessed.

"Well, dad's had a tough time," Bill said.

"It all evens up," Nick said.

They sat looking into the fire and thinking of this profound truth.

"I'll get a chunk from the back porch," Nick said. He had noticed while looking into the fire that the fire was dying down. Also he wished to show he could hold his liquor and be practical. Even if his father had never touched a drop Bill was not going to get him drunk before he himself was drunk.

"Bring one of the big beech chunks," Bill said. He was also being consciously practical.

Nick came in with the log through the kitchen and in passing knocked a pan off the kitchen table. He laid the log down and picked up the pan. It had contained dried apricots, soaking in water. He carefully picked up all the apricots off the floor, some of them had gone under the stove, and put them back in the pan. He dipped some more water onto them from the pail by the table. He felt quite proud of himself. He had been thoroughly practical.

He came in carrying the log and Bill got up from the chair and helped him put it on the fire.

"That's a swell log," Nick said.

"I'd been saving it for the bad weather," Bill said. "A log like that will burn all night."

"There'll be coals left to start the fire in the morning," Nick said.

"That's right," Bill agreed. They were conducting the conversation on a high plane.

"Let's have another drink," Nick said.

"I think there's another bottle open in the locker," Bill said.

He kneeled down in the corner in front of the locker and brought out a square-faced bottle.

"It's Scotch," he said.

"I'll get some more water," Nick said. He went out into the kitchen again. He filled the pitcher with the dipper dipping cold spring water from the pail. On his way back to the living room he passed a mirror in the dining room and looked in it. His face looked strange. He smiled at the face in the mirror and it grinned back at him. He winked at it and went on. It was not his face but it didn't make any difference.

Bill had poured out the drinks.

"That's an awfully big shot," Nick said.

"Not for us, Wemedge," Bill said.

"What'll we drink to?" Nick asked, holding up the glass.

"Let's drink to fishing," Bill said.

"All right," Nick said. "Gentlemen, I give you fishing."

"All fishing," Bill said. "Everywhere."

"Fishing," Nick said. "That's what we drink to."

"It's better than baseball," Bill said.

"There isn't any comparison," said Nick. "How did we ever get talking about baseball?"

"It was a mistake," Bill said. "Baseball is a game for louts."

They drank all that was in their glasses.

"Now let's drink to Chesterton."

"And Walpole," Nick interposed.

Nick poured out the liquor. Bill poured in the water. They looked at each other. They felt very fine.

"Gentlemen," Bill said, "I give you Chesterton and Walpole."

"Exactly, gentlemen," Nick said.

They drank. Bill filled up the glasses. They sat down in the big chairs in front of the fire.

"You were very wise, Wemedge," Bill said.

"What do you mean?" asked Nick.

"To bust off that Marge business," Bill said.

"I guess so," said Nick.

"It was the only thing to do. If you hadn't, by now you'd be back home working trying to get enough money to get married."

Nick said nothing.

"Once a man's married he's absolutely bitched," Bill went on. "He hasn't got anything more. Nothing. Not a damn thing. He's done for. You've seen the guys that got married."

Nick said nothing.

"You can tell them," Bill said. "They get this sort of fat married look. They're done for."

"Sure," said Nick.

"It was probably bad busting it off," Bill said. "But you always fall for somebody else and then it's all right. Fall for them but don't let them ruin you."

"Yes," said Nick.

"If you'd have married her you would have had to marry the whole family. Remember her mother and that guy she married."

Nick nodded.

"Imagine having them around the house all the time and going to Sunday dinners at their house, and having them over to dinner and her telling Marge all the time what to do and how to act."

Nick sat quiet.

"You came out of it damned well," Bill said. "Now she can marry somebody of her own sort and settle down and be happy. You can't mix oil and water and you can't mix that sort of thing any more than if I'd marry Ida that works for Strattons. She'd probably like it, too."

Nick said nothing. The liquor had all died out of him and left him alone. Bill wasn't there. He wasn't sitting in front of the fire or going fishing tomorrow with Bill and his dad or anything. He wasn't drunk. It was all gone. All he knew was that he had once had Majorie and that he had lost her. She was gone and he had sent her away. That was all that mattered. He might never see her again. Probably he never would. It was all gone, finished.

"Let's have another drink," Nick said.

Bill poured it out. Nick splashed in a little water.

"If you'd gone on that way we wouldn't be here now," Bill said.

That was true. His original plan had been to go down home and get a job. Then he had planned to stay in Charlevoix all winter so he could be near Marge. Now he did not know what he was going to do.

"Probably we wouldn't even be going fishing tomorrow," Bill said. "You had the right dope, all right."

"I couldn't help it," Nick said.

"I know. That's the way it works out," Bill said.

"All of a sudden everything was over," Nick said. "I don't know why it was. I couldn't help it. Just like when the three-day blows come now and rip all the leaves off the trees."

"Well, it's over. That's the point," Bill said.

"It was my fault," Nick said.

"It doesn't make any difference whose fault it was," Bill said.

"No, I suppose not," Nick said.

The big thing was that Marjorie was gone and that probably he would never see her again. He had talked to her about how they would go to Italy together and the fun they would have. Places they would be together. It was all gone now.

"So long as it's over that's all that matters," Bill said. "I tell you, Wemedge, I was worried while it was going on. You played it right. I understand her mother is sore as hell. She told a lot of people you were engaged."

"We weren't engaged," Nick said.

"It was all around that you were."

"I can't help it," Nick said. "We weren't."

"Weren't you going to get married?" Bill asked.

"Yes. But we weren't engaged," Nick said.

"What's the difference?" Bill asked judicially.

"I don't know. There's a difference."

"I don't see it," said Bill.

"All right," said Nick. "Let's get drunk."

"All right," Bill said. "Let's get really drunk."

"Let's get drunk and then go swimming," Nick said.

He drank off his glass.

"I'm sorry as hell about her but what could I do?" he said. "You know what her mother was like!"

"She was terrible," Bill said.

"All of a sudden it was over," Nick said. "I oughtn't to talk about it."

"You aren't," Bill said. "I talked about it and now I'm through. We won't ever speak about it again. You don't want to think about it. You might get back into it again."

Nick had not thought about that. It had seemed so absolute. That was a thought. That made him feel better.

"Sure," he said. "There's always that danger."

He felt happy now. There was not anything that was irrevocable. He might go into town Saturday night. Today was Thursday.

"There's always a chance," he said.

"You'll have to watch yourself," Bill said.

"I'll watch myself," he said.

He felt happy. Nothing was finished. Nothing was ever lost. He would go into town on Saturday. He felt lighter, as he had felt before Bill started to talk about it. There was always a way out.

"Let's take the guns and go down to the point and look for your dad," Nick said.

"All right."

Bill took down the two shotguns from the rack on the wall. He opened a box of shells. Nick put on his Mackinaw coat and his shoes. His shoes were stiff from the drying. He was still quite drunk but his head was clear.

"How do you feel?" Nick asked.

"Swell. I've just got a good edge on." Bill was buttoning up his sweater.

"There's no use getting drunk."

"No. We ought to get outdoors."

They stepped out the door. The wind was blowing a gale.

"The birds will lie right down in the grass with this," Nick said.

They struck down toward the orchard.

"I saw a woodcock this morning," Bill said.

"Maybe we'll jump him," Nick said.

"You can't shoot in this wind," Bill said.

Outside now the Marge business was no longer so tragic. It was not even very important. The wind blew everything like that away.

"It's coming right off the big lake," Nick said.

Against the wind they heard the thud of a shotgun.

"That's dad," Bill said. "He's down in the swamp."

"Let's cut down that way," Nick said.

"Let's cut across the lower meadow and see if we jump anything," Bill said.

"All right," Nick said.

None of it was important now. The wind blew it out of his head. Still he could always go into town Saturday night. It was a good thing to have in reserve.

MORE ABOUT THIS STORY

The excerpt reprinted below from Joseph DeFalco's *The Hero in Hemingway's Short Stories* represents a typical example of its author's technique. Admittedly indebted to Carl J. Jung's psychoanalytic method, Mr. DeFalco insists that his approach avoids rigid conformity to any thesis: "The story itself is always the determiner in the formulation of patterns and interpretation." Among the several themes he isolates as part of Nick's ritual journey toward manhood, Mr. DeFalco especially stresses "individuation, or the quest for self-illumination."

The subject matter directly complements "The End of Something." The events take place not long after those depicted in the earlier story and illustrate Nick's reactions. Essentially an adjustment story, it relates Nick's coming to Bill's cabin and talking of baseball, literature, and his affair with Marjorie. At the conclusion, having first decided to get drunk, then having decided not to get drunk, they go out to find Bill's father and to hunt. The surface line of action is obviously scant, but that is of little significance. What is important is the revelation of Nick's attitudes toward his experiences and toward life in general.

At the psychological level something quite different is expressed from what at first glance seems obvious at the literal level. Nick here engages in a fantasy of infantile regression and escape within that regression. This tendency is not unusual in any journey toward discovery of the self, for the implications of experience with the forces beyond the control of the individual are terrifying. No one would choose to destroy himself—an act which is what the discovery of the self implies—unless under the severest provocation. Thus it is that all heroes who set out on this journey have at some point faltered on the way. Nick Adams is no exception.

In the opening of the story Hemingway resorts to an expressionistic device in order to externalize the inner attitudes of his central character. It is autumn, the fruit has been picked, and the wind is blowing through bare trees. Nick picks up a fallen apple "shiny in the brown grass from the rain." Next he views the idyllic scene into which he is to retreat: "The road came out of the orchard on the top of the hill. There was the cottage, the porch bare, smoke coming from the chimney. In back was the garage, the chicken coop and the second growth timber like a hedge against the woods behind." Still, reflected against this idyll are signs and portents of nature which point to something other than retreat from inner disturbances over the Marjorie affair: "The big trees swayed far over in the wind as he watched. It was the first of the autumn storms". Nature itself indicates that severance, though it may be transient—as are the seasons of nature— is also cyclic. For Nick, if he could translate these omens, the implication would be clear: the episode with Marjorie is only one of many coming hurts that as a man and part of this cycle he will have to undergo.

Another factor of importance to the psychology of Nick's development is his turning to a number of escape mechanisms to compensate for the inner frustrations created by his severance from Marjorie. With Bill he indulges in "sophisticated" adult talk. Throughout this exchange it is apparent that Nick has progressed to a level of maturity beyond that of Bill. Nick has experienced an emotional hurt, and he exhibits the knowledge he has gained because of it. When they are discussing a book called *Forest Lovers,* an obviously romantic and sentimental piece, Bill suggests that it is a good book. Nick, on the other hand, in a passage reminiscent of Huck's attitude toward Tom Sawyer's pirate books in *The Adventures of Huckleberry Finn,* evinces a more realistic attitude:

"What else you got I haven't read?" Nick asked.

"Did you ever read the *Forest Lovers?*"

"Yup. That's the one where they go to bed every night with the naked sword between them."

"That's a good book, Wemedge."

"It's a swell book. What I couldn't ever understand was what good the sword would do. It would have to stay edge up all the time because if it went over flat you could roll right over it and it wouldn't make any trouble."

"It's a symbol," Bill said.

"Sure," said Nick, "but it isn't practical."

Bill's reference to Nick as "Wemedge" reflects the typical adolescent posture in its attempt to appear "sophisticated." Rather than depicting poise, however, it pointedly illustrates an adolescent habit of mind. Nick's "practical" bent, on the other hand, portrays an awakened mode of thought.

The pivotal point in the narrative comes when the conversation turns to Marjorie.

"All of a sudden it was over," Nick said. "I oughtn't to talk about it."

"You aren't," Bill said. "I talked about it and now I'm through. We won't ever speak about it again. You don't want to think about it. You might get back into it again."

Nick had not thought about that. It had seemed so absolute. That was a thought. That made him feel better.

"Sure," he said. "There's always that danger."

He felt happy now. There was not anything that was irrevocable. He might go into town Saturday night. Today was Thursday.

"There's always the chance," he said.

Here Hemingway concisely telescopes the optimism that a youthful hero may hold. To deny the positive insight that a vital experience has provided is in effect to regress. When Nick thinks that "nothing was finished" and that "nothing was ever lost," he reverts to the infantile and illusory attitudes expressed in "Indian Camp" where he felt he could "live forever." This is not adjustment to the experience— a necessary step toward development; it is a direct denial of the implications of that experience. Poised on the threshold of illumination, Nick takes a step backward. He is not capable of crossing the threshold into more vital experiences as yet.

Having sidestepped the too dangerous movement forward in his own development toward maturity, Nick further exhibits the regressive tendencies invoked at the moment of crisis. He and Bill feel "swell," and they decide to seek the comfort of adolescent excitement by going out to hunt. They are not to go alone, however, for they are going to seek Bill's father. Nick in effect seeks the security of a surrogate father-hero—Bill's father—and once again turns to the comfort and security of the protective parental mantle.

Hemingway supports this type of interpretation by so imposing details of external nature that it is obvious they are complementary to the central theme of the story. Nick's belief that something can be undone— "You *can* go home again," to distort Wolfe's phrase—is a denial of the lesson nature teaches. Although the changes of external nature are cyclic and seem to indicate that spring is not far behind winter, to not realize that these are small cycles in the midst of a greater cosmic cycle of things where change is the very essence is to misinterpret. Nick here, too, is guilty, and in the end of the story he is poised at the peak of his infantile optimism: "None of it was important now. The wind blew it out of his head. Still he could always go into town Saturday night. It was a good thing to have in reserve."

Hemingway apparently was keenly aware of and much interested in the inability of youth to accept the reality of a given situation. In all of these early stories, even though an external narrator relates the events, it is the youthful Nick's sensibility that is always the central focus. No doubt this was a conscious consideration on Hemingway's part in the construction of the stories, for the tone that dominates these narratives if not sympathetic at least is not one of condemnation. The stories deal with a segment of real-life experience. The hero's exposure to the variety of forces which operate in the world and over which he has no control point to Hemingway's concern with the relationship of all men to an external world not of their making. The fact that many of the stories are complementary to each other, as in the Nick sequence, illustrates not so much Hemingway's concern with one generic hero as his intense desire to explore the various psychological implications of the first, almost primal experiences with life.

FOR FURTHER READING

Baker, Carlos. *Hemingway: The Writer as Artist*. Princeton: Princeton University Press, 1956.

Cowley, Malcolm. "A Portrait of Mr. Papa," in *Ernest Hemingway: The Man and His Work,* ed. J. K. M. McCaffery. Cleveland: World, 1950.

Rovit, Earl. *Ernest Hemingway*. New York: Twayne, 1963.

Wilson, Edmund. *The Wound and the Bow*. New York: Houghton Mifflin, 1951.

Young, Philip. *Ernest Hemingway*. New York: Rinehart, 1952.

The Man Who Became a Woman

BY SHERWOOD ANDERSON (1876–1941)

Both Ernest Hemingway and William Faulkner wrote entertaining but cruel parodies of Sherwood Anderson's fiction.[1] Yet each of them admired and respected the best of Anderson's stories. "They were simply written and sometimes beautifully written," Hemingway says in *A Moveable Feast,* "and he knew the people he was writing about and cared deeply for them." Recalling those apprentice years in New Orleans when Anderson, already famous as the author of *Winesburg, Ohio,* helped him to find a publisher for his first novel, Faulkner cites Anderson's "fumbling for exactitude, the exact word and phrase within the limited scope of a vocabulary controlled and even repressed by what was in him almost a fetish of simplicity . . . to seek always to penetrate to thought's uttermost end." [2]

The finest of Anderson's stories beyond the many in *Winesburg* —"I Want to Know Why," "The Egg," "I'm a Fool," and "The Man Who Became a Woman"—share this deceptively artless simplicity, an awkward but insistent lyricism that refuses to be bound by the demands of narrative structure. All of these stories are narrated from an internal, first-person point of view by youths who are shy, sensitive, and desperate. What surges within them cannot be ordered and channeled. Herman Dudley, the narrator of "The Man Who Became a Woman," stumbles and digresses—occasionally he veers directly into the essay form—before he plunges toward the dénouement. Even though Herman narrates from the judicious distance of elapsed time, the events have a terrible

---

[1] See Hemingway's *Torrents of Spring,* a parody of *Dark Laughter;* and Faulkner's introduction to William Spratling's *Sherwood Anderson and Other Famous Creoles.*

[2] "Sherwood Anderson: An Appreciation," *Atlantic Monthly* (June, 1953).

immediacy that erases the time gap. A man tells the story, but the turbulent rhythms, colloquial language, Gothic nightmare images and symbols suggest the tangled emotions of adolescence lived rather than recalled.

"I am a child, a confused child in a confused world," Anderson wrote in his *Notebooks* in 1916. Herman's attempts to sort out his conflicting feelings about sex and society dramatically project Anderson's confusion. Like many American writers, Anderson deplored the destructive force of industrialism, chiefly because it diminished and isolated the individual and at last deprived him of even his sexual identity. Herman's story details the struggle against that reductive process.

The thematic unity of this unstructured story emerges cumulatively. As Anderson has observed, "life is a loose, flowing thing . . . but the whole . . . leaves a definite impression." The reader must therefore move cautiously and warily along many devious channels. The setting, for example, near a slaughterhouse and a mining town—has pointed social relevance as has the status of the Negro in both stable and town. Herman's problem of self-discovery thus links with an issue larger than himself. But the central problem is one of sexual identity, and about it Anderson twists several unlikely strands. Horses, women, and Negroes intertwine in Herman's imagination to symbolize not only his sexual conflict but also his moral and social strife. Among the questions a reader may therefore profitably ask himself are these: Why should the horse symbolize sex for Herman? What qualities beyond sex stir his love for horses? Why is he drawn to Burt and other Negroes even more strongly than to Tom Means?

The grotesque climax at the slaughterhouse ends Herman's initiation into manhood, but the process of living extends beyond that rite. As the story ends, a reader may wish to ask why Herman, now married, has felt so urgently compelled to rehearse this crucial episode of late adolescence.

THE STORY

My father was a retail druggist in our town, out in Nebraska, which was so much like a thousand other towns I've been in since that there's no use fooling around and taking up your time and mine trying to describe it.

Anyway I became a drug clerk and after Father's death the store was sold and Mother took the money and went West, to her sister in California, giving me four hundred dollars with which to make my start in the world. I was only nineteen years old then.

I came to Chicago, where I worked as a drug clerk for a time, and then, as my health suddenly went back on me, perhaps because I was so sick of my lonely life in the city and of the sight and smell of the drugstore, I decided to set out on what seemd to me then the great adventure and became for a time a tramp, working now and then, when I had no money, but spending all the time I could loafing around out of doors or riding up and down the land on freight trains and trying to see the world. I even did some stealing in lonely towns at night—once a pretty good suit of clothes that someone had left hanging out on a clothesline, and once some shoes out of a box in a freight car—but I was in constant terror of being caught and put into jail, so I realized that success as a thief was not for me.

The most delightful experience of that period of my life was when I once worked as a groom, or swipe, with race horses, and it was during that time I met a young fellow of about my own age who has since become a writer of some prominence.

The young man of whom I now speak had gone into race track work as a groom, to bring a kind of flourish, a high spot, he used to say, into his life.

He was then unmarried and had not been successful as a writer. What I mean is he was free and I guess, with him as with me, there was something he liked about the people who hang about a race track, the touts, swipes, drivers, niggers and gamblers. You know what a gaudy undependable lot they are—if you've ever been around the tracks much—about the best liars I've ever seen, and not saving money or thinking about morals, like most druggists, dry-goods merchants and the others who used to be my father's friends in our Nebraska town—and not bending the knee much either, or kowtowing to people they thought must be grander or richer or more powerful than themselves.

What I mean is, they were an independent, go-to-the-devil, come-have-a-drink-of-whisky, kind of a crew and when one of them won a bet, "knocked 'em off," we called it, his money was just dirt to him while it lasted. No king or president or soap manufacturer—gone on a trip with his family to Europe —could throw on more dog than one of them, with his big diamond rings and the diamond horseshoe stuck in his necktie and all.

I liked the whole blamed lot pretty well and he did too.

He was groom temporarily for a pacing gelding named Lumpy Joe owned by a tall black-mustached man named Alfred Kreymborg and trying the best he could to make the bluff to himself he was a real one. It happened that we were on the same circuit, doing the West Pennsylvania county fairs all that fall, and on fine evenings we spent a good deal of time walking and talking together.

Let us suppose it to be a Monday or Tuesday evening and our horses had been put away for the night. The racing didn't start until later in the week, maybe Wednesday, usually. There was always a little place called a dining hall, run mostly by the Woman's Christian Temperance Associations of the towns, and we would go there to eat where we could get a pretty good meal for twenty-five cents. At least then we thought it pretty good.

. I would manage it so that I sat beside this fellow, whose name was Tom Means, and when we had got through eating we would go look at our two horses again and when we got there Lumpy Joe would be eating his hay in his box stall and Alfred Kreymborg would be standing there, pulling his mustache and looking as sad as a sick crane.

But he wasn't really sad. "You two boys want to go downtown to see the girls. I'm an old duffer and way past that myself. You go on along. I'll be setting here anyway, and I'll keep an eye on both the horses for you," he would say.

So we would set off, going, not into the town to try to get in with some of the town girls, who might have taken up with us because we were strangers and race track fellows, but out into the country. Sometimes we got into a hilly country and there was a moon. The leaves were falling off the trees and lay in the road so that we kicked them up with the dust as we went along.

To tell the truth, I suppose I got to love Tom Means, who was five years older than me, although I wouldn't have dared say so, then. Americans are shy and timid about saying things like that and a man here don't dare own up he loves another man, I've found out, and they are afraid to admit such feelings to themselves even. I guess they're afraid it may be taken to mean something it don't need to at all.

Anyway we walked along and some of the trees were already bare and looked like people standing solemnly beside the road and listening to what we had to say. Only I didn't say much. Tom Means did most of the talking.

Sometimes we came back to the race track and it was late and the moon had gone down and it was dark. Then we often walked round and round the track, sometimes a dozen times, before we crawled into the hay to go to bed.

Tom talked always on two subjects, writing and race horses, but mostly about race horses. The quiet sounds about the race tracks and the smells of horses, and the things that go with horses, seemed to get him all excited. "Oh hell, Herman Dudley," he would burst out suddenly, "don't go talking to me. I know what I think. I've been around more than you have and I've seen a world of people. There isn't any man or woman, not even a fellow's own mother, as fine as a horse, that it to say a thoroughbred horse."

Sometimes he would go on like that a long time, speaking of people he had seen and their characteristics. He wanted to be a writer later, and what he said was that when he came to be one he wanted to write the way a well-bred horse runs or trots or paces. Whether he ever did it or not I can't say. He has written a lot, but I'm not too good a judge of such things. Anyway I don't think he has.

But when he got on the subject of horses he certainly was a darby. I would never have felt the way I finally got to feel about horses or enjoyed my stay among them half so much if it hadn't been for him. Often he would go on talking for an hour maybe, speaking of horses' bodies and of their minds and wills as though they were human beings. "Lord help us, Herman," he would say, grabbing hold of my arm, "don't it get you up in the throat? I say now, when a good one, like that Lumpy Joe I'm swiping, flattens himself at the head of the stretch and he's coming, and you know he's coming, and you know his heart's sound, and he's game, and you know he isn't going to let himself get licked—don't it get you Herman, don't it get you like the old Harry?"

That's the way he would talk, and then later, sometimes, he'd talk about writing and get himself all het up about that too. He had some notions about writing I've never got myself around to thinking much about but just the same maybe his talk, working in me, has led me to want to begin to write this story myself.

There was one experience of that time on the tracks that I am forced, by some feeling inside myself, to tell.

Well, I don't know why, but I've just got to. It will be kind of like confession is, I suppose, to a good Catholic, or maybe, better yet, like cleaning up the room you live in, if you are a bachelor, like I was for so long. The room gets pretty mussy and the bed not made some days and clothes and things thrown on the closet floor and maybe under the bed. And then you clean all up and put on new sheets, and then you take off all your clothes and get down on your hands and knees, and scrub the floor so clean you could eat bread off it, and then take a walk and come home after a while and your room smells sweet and you feel sweetened-up and better inside yourself too.

What I mean is, this story has been on my chest, and I've often dreamed about the happenings in it, even after I married Jessie and was happy. Sometimes I even screamed out at night and so I said to myself, "I'll write the dang story," and here goes.

Fall had come on and in the mornings now when we crept out of our blankets, spread out on the hay in the tiny lofts above the horse stalls, and put our heads out to look around, there was a white rime of frost on the ground. When we woke, the horses woke too. You know how it is at the tracks—the little barnlike stalls with the tiny lofts above are all set along in a row and there are two doors to each stall, one coming up to a horse's breast and then a top one, that is only closed at night and in bad weather.

In the mornings the upper door is swung open and fastened back and the horses put their heads out. There is the white rime on the grass over inside the gray oval the track makes. Usually there is some outfit that has six, ten or even twelve horses, and perhaps they have a Negro cook who does his cooking at an open fire in the clear space before the row of stalls and he is at work now, and the horses with their big fine eyes are looking about and whinnying, and a stallion looks out at the door of one of the stalls and sees a sweet-eyed mare looking at him and sends up his trumpet call, and a man's voice laughs, and there are no women anywhere in sight or no sign of one anywhere, and everyone feels like laughing and usually does.

It's pretty fine, but I didn't know how fine it was until I got to know Tom Means and heard him talk about it all.

At the time the thing happened of which I am trying to tell now, Tom was no longer with me. A week before, his owner, Alfred Kreymborg, had taken his horse Lumpy Joe over into the Ohio Fair Circuit and I saw no more of Tom at the tracks.

There was a story going about the stalls that Lumpy Joe, a big rangy brown gelding, wasn't really named Lumpy Joe at all, that he was a ringer who had made a fast record out in Iowa and up through the Northwest country the year before, and that Kreymborg had picked him up and had kept him under wraps all winter and had brought him over into the Pennsylvania country under this new name and made a cleanup in the books.

I know nothing about that and never talked to Tom about it, but anyway he, Lumpy Joe and Kreymborg were all gone now.

I suppose I'll always remember those days, and Tom's talk at night, and before that, in the early September evenings, how we sat around in front of the stalls, and Kreymborg sitting on an upturned feed box and pulling at his long black mustache and some times humming a little ditty one couldn't catch the words of. It was something about a deep well and a little gray squirrel crawling up the sides of it, and he never laughed or smiled much, but there was something in his solemn gray eyes, not quite a twinkle, something more delicate than that.

The others talked in low tones, and Tom and I sat in silence. He never did his best talking except when he and I were alone.

For his sake—if he ever sees my story—I should mention that at the only big track we ever visited, at Readville, Pennsylvania, we saw old Pop Geers, the great racing driver, himself. His horses were at a place far away across the tracks from where we were stabled. I suppose a man like him was likely to get the choice of all the good places for his horses.

We went over there one evening and stood about, and there was Geers himself, sitting before one of the stalls on a box, tapping the ground with a riding whip. They called him, around the tracks, "the silent man from Tennessee," and he was silent—that night anyway. All we did was to stand and look at him for maybe a half hour and then we went away, and that night Tom talked better than I had ever heard him. He said that the ambition of his life was to wait until Pop Geers died and then write a book about him, and to show in the book that there was at least one American who never went nutty about getting rich or owning a big factory or being any other kind of a hell of a fellow. "He's satisfied, I think, to sit around like that and wait until the big moments of his life come, when he heads a fast one into the stretch and then, darn his soul, he can give all of himself to the thing right in front of him," Tom said, and then he was so worked up he began to blubber. We were walking along the fence on the inside of the tracks and it was dusk and, in some trees nearby, some birds, just sparrows maybe, were making a chirping sound, and you could hear insects singing and, where there was a little light, off to the west between some trees, motes were dancing in the air. Tom said that about Pop Geers, although I think he was thinking most about something he wanted to be himself and wasn't, and then he went and stood by the fence and sort of blubbered and I began to blubber too, although I didn't know what about.

But perhaps I did know, after all. I suppose Tom wanted to feel, when he became a writer, like he thought old Pop must feel when his horse swung around the upper turn, and there lay the stretch before him, and if he was going to get his horse home in front he had to do it right then. What Tom said was that any man had something in him that understands about a thing like that but that no woman ever did except up in her brain. He often got off things like that about women, but I notice he later married one of them just the same.

But to get back to my knitting. After Tom had left, the stable I was with kept drifting along through nice little Pennsylvania county seat towns. My owner, a strange excitable kind of a man from over in Ohio, who had lost a lot of money on horses but was always thinking he would maybe get it all back in some big killing, had been playing in pretty good luck that year. The horse I had, a tough little gelding, a five-year-old, had been getting home in front pretty regular and so he took some of his winnings and bought a three-years-old black pacing stallion named O My Man. My gelding was called Pick-it-boy, because when he was in a race and had got into the stretch my owner always got half wild with excitement and shouted so you could hear him a mile and a half. "Go, pick it boy, pick it boy, pick it boy," he kept shouting and so when he had got hold of this good little gelding he had named him that.

The gelding was a fast one, all right. As the boys at the tracks used to say, he "picked 'em up sharp and set 'em down clean," and he was what we called a natural race horse, right up to all the speed he had, and didn't require much training. "All you got to do is to drop him down on the track and he'll go," was what my owner was always saying to other men, when he was bragging about his horse.

And so, you see, after Tom left, I hadn't much to do evenings and then the new stallion, the three-year-old, came on with a Negro swipe named Burt. I liked him fine and he liked me, but not the the same as Tom and me. We got to be friends all right, and I suppose Burt would have done things for me, and maybe me for him, that Tom and me wouldn't have done for each other.

But with a Negro you couldn't be close friends like you can with another white man. There's some reason you can't understand but it's true. There's been too much talk about the difference between whites and blacks and you're both shy, and anyway no use trying, and I suppose Burt and I both knew it and so I was pretty lonesome.

Something happened to me that happened several times, when I was a young fellow, that I have never exactly understood. Sometimes now I think it was all because I had got to be almost a man and had never been with a woman. I don't know what's the matter with me. I can't ask a woman. I've tried it a good many times in my life but every time I've tried the same thing happened.

Of course, with Jessie now, it's different, but at the time of which I'm speaking Jessie was a long ways off and a good many things were to happen to me before I got to her.

Around a race track, as you may suppose, the fellows who are swipes and drivers and strangers in the towns do not go without women. They don't have to. In any town there are always some fly girls will come around a place like that. I suppose they think they are fooling with men who lead romantic lives. Such girls will come along by the front of the stalls where the race horses are and, if you look all right to them, they will stop and make a fuss over your horse. They rub their little hands over the horse's nose and then is the time for you—if you aren't a fellow like me who can't get up the nerve—then is the time for you to smile and say, "Hello, kid," and make a date with one of them for that evening uptown after supper. I couldn't do that, although the Lord knows I tried hard enough, often enough. A girl would come along alone, and she would be a little thing and give me the eye, and I would try and try but couldn't say anything. Both Tom, and Burt afterward, used to laugh at me about it sometimes but what I think is that, had I been able to speak up to one of them and had managed to make a date with her, nothing would have come of it. We would probably have walked around the town and got off together in the dark somewhere, where the town came to an end, and then she would have had to knock me over with a club before it got any further.

And so there I was, having got used to Tom and our talks together, and Burt of course had his own friends among the black men. I got lazy and mopey and had a hard time doing my work.

It was like this. Sometimes I would be sitting, perhaps under a tree in the late afternoon when the races were over for the day and the crowds had gone away. There were always a lot of other men and boys who hadn't any horses in the races that day and they would be standing or sitting about in front of the stalls and talking.

I would listen for a time to their talk and then their voices would seem to go far away. The things I was looking at would go far away too. Perhaps there would be a tree, not more than a hundred yards away, and it would just come out of the ground and float away like a thistle. It would get smaller and smaller, away off there in the sky, and then suddenly—bang, it would be back where it belonged, in the ground, and I would begin hearing the voices of the men talking again.

When Tom was with me that summer the nights were splendid. We usually walked about and talked until pretty late and then I crawled up into my hole and went to sleep. Always out of Tom's talk I got something that stayed in my mind, after I was off by myself, curled up in my blanket. I suppose he had a way of making pictures as he talked and the pictures stayed by me as Burt was always saying pork chops did by him. "Give me the old pork chops, they stick to the ribs," Burt was always saying, and with the imagination it was always that way about Tom's talks. He started something inside you that went on and on, and your mind played with it like walking about in a strange town and seeing the sights, and you slipped off to sleep and had splendid dreams and woke up in the morning feeling fine.

And then he was gone and it wasn't that way any more and I got into the fix I have described. At night I kept seeing women's bodies and women's lips and things in my dreams, and woke up in the morning feeling like the old Harry.

Burt was pretty good to me. He always helped me cool Pick-it-boy out after a race and he did the things himself that take the most skill and quickness, like getting the bandages on a horse's leg smooth, and seeing that every strap is setting just right, and every buckle drawn up to just the right hole, before your horse goes out on the track for a heat.

Burt knew there was something wrong with me and put himself out not to let the boss know. When the boss was around he was always bragging about me. "The brightest kid I've ever worked with around the tracks," he would say and grin, and that at a time when I wasn't worth my salt.

When you go out with the horses there is one job that always takes a lot of time. In the late afternoon, after your horse has been in a race and after you have washed him and rubbed him out, he has to be walked slowly, sometimes for hours and hours, so he'll cool out slowly and won't get musclebound. I got so I did that job for both our horses and Burt did the more important things. It left him free to go talk or shoot dice with the other niggers and I didn't mind. I rather liked it and after a hard race even the stallion O My Man was tame enough, even when there were mares about.

You walk and walk and walk, around a little circle, and your horse's head is right by your shoulder, and all around you the life of the place you are in is going on, and in a queer way you get so you aren't really a part of it at all. Perhaps no one ever gets as I was then, except boys that aren't quite men yet and who, like me, have never been with girls or women—to really be with them, up to the hilt, I mean. I used to wonder if young girls got that way too before they married or did what we used to call "go on the town."

If I remember it right though, I didn't do much thinking then. Often I would have forgotten supper if Burt hadn't shouted at me and reminded me, and sometimes he forgot and went off to town with one of the other niggers and I did forget.

There I was with the horse, going slow slow slow, around a circle that way. The people were leaving the fairgrounds now, some afoot, some driving away to the farms in wagons and Fords. Clouds of dust floated in the air and over to the west, where the town was, maybe the sun was going down, a red ball of fire through the dust. Only a few hours before, the crowd had been all filled with excitement and everyone shouting. Let us suppose my horse had been in a race that afternoon and I had stood in front of the grandstand with my horse blanket over my shoulder, alongside of Burt perhaps, and when they came into the stretch my owner began to call, in that queer high voice of his that seemed to float over the top of all the shouting up in the grandstand. And his voice was saying over and over, "Go, pick it boy, pick it boy, pick it boy," the way he always did, and my heart was thumping so I could hardly breathe, and Burt was leaning over and snapping his fingers and muttering, "Come, little sweet. Come on home. Your mama wants you. Come get your 'lasses and bread, little Pick-it-boy."

Well, all that was over now and the voices of the people left around were all low. And Pick-it-boy—I was leading him slowly around the little ring, to cool him out slowly, as I've said—he was different too. Maybe he had pretty nearly broken his heart trying to get down to the wire in front, or getting down there in front, and now everything inside him was quiet and tired, as it was nearly all the time those days in me, except in me tired but not quiet.

You remember I've told you we always walked in a circle, round and round and round. I guess something inside me got to going round and round and round too. The sun did sometimes and the trees and the clouds of dust. I had to think sometimes about putting down my feet so they went down in the right place and I didn't get to staggering like a drunken man.

And a funny feeling came that it is going to be hard to describe. It had something to do with the life in the horse and in me. Sometimes, these late years, I've thought maybe Negroes would understand what I'm trying to talk about now better than any white man ever will. I mean something about men and animals, something between them, something that can perhaps only happen to a white man when he has slipped off his base a little, as I suppose I had then. I think maybe a lot of horsey people feel it sometimes though. It's something like this, maybe—do you suppose it could be that something we whites have got, and think such a lot of, and are so proud about, isn't much of any good after all?

It's something in us that wants to be big and grand and important maybe and won't let us just be, like a horse or a dog or a bird can. Let's say Pick-it-boy had won his race that day. He did that pretty often that summer. Well, he was neither proud, like I would have been in his place, or mean in one part of the inside of him either. He was just himself, doing something with a kind of simplicity. That's what Pick-it-boy was like and I got to feeling it in him as I walked with him slowly in the gathering darkness. I got inside him in some way I can't explain and he got inside me. Often we would stop walking for no cause and he would put his nose up against my face.

I wished he was a girl sometimes or that I was a girl and he was a man. It's an odd thing to say but it's a fact. Being with him that way, so long, and in such a quiet way, cured something in me a little. Often after an evening like that I slept all right and did not have the kind of dreams I've spoken about.

But I wasn't cured for very long and couldn't get cured. My body seemed all right and just as good as ever but there wasn't no pep in me.

Then the fall got later and later and we came to the last town we were going to make before my owner laid his horses up for the winter, in his home town over across the state line in Ohio, and the track was up on a hill, or rather in a kind of high plain above the town.

It wasn't much of a place and the sheds were rather rickety and the track bad, especially at the turns. As soon as we got to the place and got stabled, it began to rain and kept it up all week so the fair had to be put off.

As the purses weren't very large a lot of the owners shipped right out but our owner stayed. The fair owners guaranteed expenses, whether the races were held the next week or not.

And all week there wasn't much of anything for Burt and me to do but clean manure out of the stalls in the morning, watch for a chance when the rain let up a little to jog the horses around the track in the mud and then clean them off, blanket them and stick them back in their stalls.

It was the hardest time of all for me. Burt wasn't so bad off as there were a dozen or two blacks around and in the evening they went off to town, got liquored up a little and came home late, singing and talking, even in the cold rain.

And then one night I got mixed up in the thing I'm trying to tell you about.

It was a Saturday evening and when I look back at it now it seems to me everyone had left the tracks but just me. In the early evening swipe after swipe came over to my stall and asked me if I was going to stick around. When I said I was he would ask me to keep an eye out for him, that nothing happened to his horse. "Just take a stroll down that way now and then, eh, kid," one of them would say, "I just want to run up to town for an hour or two."

I would say "Yes" to be sure, and so pretty soon it was dark as pitch up there in that little ruined fairground and nothing living anywhere around but the horses and me.

I stood it as long as I could, walking here and there in the mud and rain, and thinking all the time I wished I was someone else and not myself. "If I were someone else," I thought, "I wouldn't be here but down there in town with the others." I saw myself going into saloons and having drinks and later going off to a house maybe and getting myself a woman.

I got to thinking so much that, as I went stumbling around up there in the darkness, it was as though what was in my mind was actually happening.

Only I wasn't with some cheap woman, such as I would have found had I had the nerve to do what I wanted but with such a woman as I thought then I should never find in this world. She was slender and like a flower and with something in her like a race horse too, something in her like Pick-it-boy in the stretch, I guess.

And I thought about her and thought about her until I couldn't stand thinking any more. "I'll do something anyway," I said to myself.

So, although I had told all the swipes I would stay and watch their horses, I went out of the fairgrounds and down the hill a ways. I went down until I came to a little low saloon, not in the main part of the town itself but halfway up the hillside. The saloon had once been a residence, a farmhouse perhaps, but if it was ever a farmhouse I'm sure the farmer who lived there and worked the land on that hillside hadn't made out very well. The country didn't look like a farming country, such as one sees all about the other county-seat towns we had been visiting all through the late summer and fall. Everywhere you looked there were stones sticking out of the ground and the trees mostly of the stubby, stunted kind. It looked wild and untidy and ragged, that's what I mean. On the flat plain, up above, where the fairground was, there were a few fields and pastures, and there were some sheep raised and in the field right next to the tracks, on the furtherest side from town, on the back-stretch side, there had once been a slaughterhouse, the ruins of which were still standing. It hadn't been used for quite some time but there were bones of animals lying all about in the field, and there was a smell coming out of the old building that would curl your hair.

The horses hated the place, just as we swipes did, and in the morning when we were jogging them around the track in the mud, to keep them in racing condition, Pick-it-boy and O My Man both raised old Ned every time we headed them up the back stretch and got near to where the old slaughterhouse stood. They would rear and fight at the bit, and go off their stride and run until they got clear of the rotten smells, and neither Burt nor I could make them stop it. "It's a hell of a town down there and this is a hell of a track for racing," Burt kept saying. "If they ever have their danged old fair someone's going to get spilled and maybe killed back here." Whether they did or not I don't know as I didn't stay for the fair, for reasons I'll tell you pretty soon, but Burt was speaking sense all right. A race horse isn't like a human being. He won't stand for it to have to do his work in any rotten ugly kind of a dump the way a man will, and he won't stand for the smells a man will either.

But to get back to my story again. There I was, going down the hillside in the darkness and the cold soaking rain and breaking my word to all the others about staying up above and watching the horses. When I got to the little saloon I decided to stop and have a drink or two. I'd found out long before that about two drinks upset me so I was two-thirds piped and couldn't walk straight, but on that night I didn't care a tinker's dam.

So I went up a kind of path, out of the road, toward the front door of the saloon. It was in what must have been the parlor of the place when it was a farmhouse and there was a little front porch.

I stopped before I opened the door and looked about a little. From where I stood I could look right down into the main street of the town, like being in a big city, like New York or Chicago, and looking down out of the fifteenth floor of an office building into the street.

The hillside was mighty steep and the road up had to wind and wind or no one could ever have come up out of the town to their plagued old fair at all.

It wasn't much of a town I saw—a main street with a lot of saloons and a few stores, one or two dinky moving-picture places, a few Fords, hardly any women or girls in sight and a raft of men. I tried to think of the girl I had been dreaming about, as I walked around in the mud and darkness up at the fairgrounds, living in the place but I couldn't make it. It was like trying to think of Pick-it-boy getting himself worked up to the state I was in then, and going into the ugly dump I was going into. It couldn't be done.

All the same I knew the town wasn't all right there in sight. There must have been a good many of the kinds of houses Pennsylvania miners live in back in the hills, or around a turn in the valley in which the main street stood.

What I suppose is that, it being Saturday night and raining, the women and kids had all stayed at home and only the men were out, intending to get themselves liquored up. I've been in some other mining towns since and if I was a miner and had to live in one of them, or in one of the houses they live in with their women and kids, I'd get out and liquor myself up too.

So there I stood looking, and as sick as a dog inside myself, and as wet and cold as a rat in a sewer pipe. I could see the mass of dark figures moving about down below, and beyond the main street there was a river that made a sound you could hear distinctly, even up where I was, and over beyond the river were some railroad tracks with switch engines going up and down. I suppose they had something to do with the mines in which the men of the town worked. Anyway, as I stood watching and listening there was, now and then, a sound like thunder rolling down the sky, and I suppose that was a lot of coal, maybe a whole carload, being let down plunk into a coal car.

And then besides there was, on the side of a hill far away, a long row of coke ovens. They had little doors, through which the light from the fire within leaked out, and as they were set closely, side by side, they looked like the teeth of some big man-eating giant lying and waiting over there in the hills.

The sight of it all, even the sight of the kind of hellholes men are satisfied to go on living in, gave me the fantods and the shivers right down in my liver, and on that night I guess I had in me a kind of contempt for all men, including myself, that I've never had so thoroughly since. Come right down to it, I suppose women aren't so much to blame as men. They aren't running the show.

Then I pushed open the door and went into the saloon. There were about a dozen men, miners I suppose, playing cards at tables in a little long dirty room, with a bar at one side of it, and with a big red-faced man with a mustache standing back of the bar.

The place smelled, as such places do where men hang around who have worked and sweated in their clothes and perhaps slept in them too, and have never had them washed but have just kept on wearing them. I guess you know what I mean if you've ever been in a city. You smell that smell in a city, in streetcars on rainy nights when a lot of factory hands get on. I got pretty used to that smell when I was a tramp and pretty sick of it too.

And so I was in the place now, with a glass of whisky in my hand, and I thought all the miners were staring at me, which they weren't at all, but I thought they were and so I felt just the same as though they had been. And then I looked up and saw my own face in the old cracked looking glass back of the bar. If the miners had been staring, or laughing at me, I wouldn't have wondered when I saw what I looked like.

It—I mean my own face—was white and pasty-looking, and for some reason, I can't tell exactly why, it wasn't my own face at all. It's a funny business I'm trying to tell you about and I know what you may be thinking of me as well as you do, so you needn't suppose I'm innocent or ashamed. I'm only wondering. I've thought about it a lot since and I can't make it out. I know I was never that way before that night and I know I've never been that way since. Maybe it was lonesomeness, just lonesomeness, gone on in me too long. I've often wondered if women generally are lonesomer than men.

The point is that the face I saw in the looking glass back of that bar, when I looked up from my glass of whisky that evening, wasn't my own face at all but the face of a woman. It was a girl's face, that's what I mean. That's what it was. It was a girl's face, and a lonesome and scared girl too. She was just a kid at that.

When I saw that the glass of whisky came pretty near falling out of my hand but I gulped it down, put a dollar on the bar, and called for another. "I've got to be careful here—I'm up against something new," I said to myself. "If any of these men in here get on to me there's going to be trouble." When

I had got the second drink in me I called for a third and I thought, "When I get this third drink down I'll get out of here and back up the hill to the fairgrounds before I make a fool of myself and begin to get drunk."

And then, while I was thinking and drinking my third glass of whisky, the men in the room began to laugh and of course I thought they were laughing at me. But they weren't. No one in the place had really paid any attention to me.

What they were laughing at was a man who had just come in at the door. I'd never seen such a fellow. He was a huge big man, with red hair that stuck straight up like bristles out of his head, and he had a red-haired kid in his arms. The kid was just like himself, big, I mean, for his age, and with the same kind of stiff red hair.

He came and set the kid up on the bar, close beside me, and called for a glass of whisky for himself, and all the men in the room began to shout and laugh at him and his kid. Only they didn't shout and laugh when he was looking so he could tell which ones did it, but did all their shouting and laughing when his head was turned the other way. They kept calling him "cracked." "The crack is getting wider in the old tin pan," someone sang and then they all laughed.

I'm puzzled you see, just how to make you feel as I felt that night. I suppose, having undertaken to write this story, that's what I'm up against, trying to do that. I'm not claiming to be able to inform you or to do you any good. I'm just trying to make you understand some things about me, as I would like to understand some things about you, or anyone, if I had the chance. Anyway the whole blamed thing, the thing that went on I mean in that little saloon on that rainy Saturday night, wasn't like anything quite real. I've already told you how I had looked into the glass back of the bar and had seen there, not my own face but the face of a scared young girl. Well, the men, the miners, sitting at the tables in the half-dark room, the red-faced bartender, the unholy-looking big man who had come in and his queer-looking kid, now sitting on the bar—all of them were like characters in some play, not like real people at all.

There was myself, that wasn't myself—and I'm not any fairy. Anyone who has ever known me knows better than that.

And then there was the man who had come in. There was a feeling came out of him that wasn't like the feeling you get from a man at all. It was more like the feeling you get maybe from a horse, only his eyes weren't like a horse's eyes. Horses' eyes have a kind of calm something in them and his hadn't. If you've ever carried a lantern through a wood at night, going along a path, and then suddenly you felt something funny in the air and stopped, and there ahead of you somewhere were the eyes of some little animal, gleaming out at you from a dead wall of darkness— The eyes shine big and quiet but there is a point right in the center of each, where there is something dancing and wavering. You aren't afraid the little animal will jump at you, you are afraid the little eyes will jump at you—that's what's the matter with you.

Only of course a horse, when you go into his stall at night, or a little animal you had disturbed in a wood that way, wouldn't be talking and the big man who had come in there with his kid was talking. He kept talking all the time, saying something under his breath, as they say, and I could only understand now and then a few words. It was his talking made him kind of terrible. His eyes said one thing and his lips another. They didn't seem to get together, as though they belonged to the same person.

For one thing, the man was too big. There was about him an unnatural bigness. It was in his hands, his arms, his shoulders, his body, his head, a bigness like you might see in trees and bushes in a tropical country perhaps. I've never been in a tropical country but I've seen pictures. Only his eyes were small. In his big head they looked like the eyes of a bird. And I remember that his lips were thick, like Negroes' lips.

He paid no attention to me or to the others in the room but kept on muttering to himself, or to the kid sitting on the bar—I couldn't tell to which. First he had one drink and then, quick, another. I stood staring at him and thinking—a jumble of thoughts, I suppose.

What I must have been thinking was something like this. "Well he's one of the kind you are always seeing about towns," I thought. I meant he was one of the cracked kind. In almost any small town you go to you will find one, and sometimes two or three cracked people, walking around. They go through the street, muttering to themselves and people generally are cruel to them. Their own folks make a bluff at being kind, but they aren't really, and the others in the town, men and boys, like to tease them. They send such a fellow, the mild silly kind, on some fool errand after a round square or a dozen postholes or tie cards on his back saying "Kick me," or something like that, and then carry on and laugh as though they had done something funny.

And so there was this cracked one in that saloon and I could see the men in there wanted to have some fun putting up some kind of horseplay on him, but they didn't quite dare. He wasn't one of the mild kind, that was a cinch. I kept looking at the man and at his kid, and then up at that strange unreal reflection of myself in the cracked looking glass back of the bar. "Rats, rats, digging in the ground—miners are rats, little jack rabbit," I heard him say to his solemn-faced kid. I guess, after all, maybe he wasn't so cracked.

The kid sitting on the bar kept blinking at his father, like an owl caught out in the daylight, and now the father was having another glass of whisky. He drank six glasses, one right after the other, and it was cheap ten-cent stuff. He must have had cast-iron insides all right.

Of the men in the room there were two or three (maybe they were really more scared than the others so had to put up a bluff of bravery by showing off) who kept laughing and making funny cracks about the big man and his kid and there was one fellow was the worst of the bunch. I'll never forget that fellow because of his looks and what happened to him afterward.

He was one of the showing-off kind all right, and he was the one that had started the song about the crack getting bigger in the old tin pan. He sang it two or three times, and then he grew bolder and got up and began walking up and down the room singing it over and over. He was a showy kind of man with a fancy vest, on which there were brown tobacco spots, and he wore glasses. Every time he made some crack he thought was funny, he winked at the others as though to say, "You see me. I'm not afraid of this big fellow," and then the others laughed.

The proprietor of the place must have known what was going on, and the danger in it, because he kept leaning over the bar and saying, "Shush, now quit it," to the showy-off man, but it didn't do any good. The fellow kept prancing like a turkey cock and he put his hat on one side of his head and stopped right back of the big man and sang that song about the crack in the old tin pan. He was one of the kind you can't shush until they get their blocks knocked off, and it didn't take him long to come to it that time anyhow.

Because the big fellow just kept on muttering to his kid and drinking his whisky, as though he hadn't heard anything, and then suddenly he turned and his big hand flashed out and he grabbed, not the fellow who had been showing off, but me. With just a sweep of his arm he brought me up against his big body. Then he shoved me over with my breast jammed against the bar and looking right into his kid's face and he said, "Now you watch him, and if you let him fall I'll kill you," in just quiet ordinary tones as though he was saying "good morning" to some neighbor.

Then the kid leaned over and threw his arms around my head, and in spite of that I did manage to screw my head around enough to see what happened.

It was a sight I'll never forget. The big fellow had whirled around, and he had the showy-off man by the shoulder now, and the fellow's face was a sight. The big man must have had some reputation as a bad man in the town, even though he was cracked, for the man with the fancy vest had his mouth open now, and his hat had fallen off his head, and he was silent and scared. Once, when I was a tramp, I saw a kid killed by a train. The kid was walking on the rail and showing off before some other kids, by letting them see how close he could let an engine come to him before he got out of the way. And the engine was whistling and a woman, over on the porch of a house nearby, was jumping up and down and screaming, and the kid let the engine get nearer and nearer, wanting more and more to show off, and then he stumbled and fell. God, I'll never forget the look on his face, in just the second before he got hit and killed, and now, there in that saloon, was the same terrible look on another face.

I closed my eyes for a moment and was sick all through me and then, when I opened my eyes, the big man's fist was just coming down in the other man's face. The one blow knocked him cold and he fell down like a beast hit with an axe.

And then the most terrible thing of all happened. The big man had on heavy boots, and he raised one of them and brought it down on the other man's shoulder, as he lay white and groaning on the floor. I could hear the bones crunch and it made me so sick I could hardly stand up, but I had to stand up and hold on to that kid or I knew it would be my turn next.

Because the big fellow didn't seem excited or anything, but kept on muttering to himself as he had been doing when he was standing peacefully by the bar drinking his whisky, and now he had raised his foot again, and maybe this time he would bring it down in the other man's face and, "just eliminate his map for keeps," as sports and prize fighters sometimes say. I trembled, like I was having a chill, but thank God at that moment the kid, who had his arms around me and one hand clinging to my nose, so that there were the marks of his fingernails on it the next morning, at that moment the kid, thank God, began to howl, and his father didn't bother any more with the man on the floor but turned around, knocked me aside, and taking the kid in his arms tramped out of that place, muttering to himself as he had been doing ever since he came in.

I went out too but I didn't prance out with any dignity, I'll tell you that. I slunk out like a thief or a coward, which perhaps I am, partly anyhow.

And so there I was, outside there in the darkness, and it was as cold and wet and black and Godforsaken a night as any man ever saw. I was so sick at the thought of human beings that night I could have vomited to think of them at all. For a while I just stumbled along in the mud of the road, going up the hill, back to the fairgrounds, and then, almost before I knew where I was, I found myself in the stall with Pick-it-boy.

That was one of the best and sweetest feelings I've ever had in my whole life, being in that warm stall alone with that horse that night. I had told the other swipes that I would go up and down the row of stalls now and then and have an eye on the other horses, but I had altogether forgotten my promise now. I went and stood with my back against the side of the stall, thinking how mean and low and all balled up and twisted up human beings can become, and how the best of them are likely to get that way any time, just because they are human beings and not simple and clear in their minds, and inside themselves, as animals are, maybe.

Perhaps you know how a person feels at such a moment. There are things you think of, odd little things you had thought you had forgotten. Once, when you were a kid, you were with your father, and he was all dressed up, as for a funeral or Fourth of July, and was walking along a street holding your hand. And you were going past a railroad station, and there was a woman standing.

She was a stranger in your town and was dressed as you had never seen a woman dressed before, and never thought you would see one looking so nice. Long afterward you knew that was because she had lovely taste in clothes, such as so few women have really, but then you thought she must be a queen. You had read about queens in fairy stories and the thoughts of them thrilled you. What lovely eyes the strange lady had and what beautiful rings she wore on her fingers.

Then your father came out, from being in the railroad station, maybe to set his watch by the station clock, and took you by the hand and he and the woman smiled at each other, in an embarrassed kind of way, and you kept looking longingly back at her, and when you were out of her hearing you asked your father if she really were a queen. And it may be that your father was one who wasn't so very hot on democracy and a free country and talked-up bunk about a free citizenry, and he said he hoped she was a queen, and maybe, for all he knew, she was.

Or maybe, when you get jammed up as I was that night, and can't get things clear about yourself or other people and why you are alive, or for that matter why anyone you can think about is alive, you think, not of people at all but of other things you have seen and felt—like walking along a road in the snow in the winter, perhaps out in Iowa, and hearing soft warm sounds in a barn close to the road, or of another time when you were on a hill and the sun was going down and the sky suddenly became a great soft-colored bowl, all glowing like a jewel-handled bowl, a great queen in some faraway mighty kingdom might have put on a vast table out under the tree, once a year, when she invited all her loyal and loving subjects to come and dine with her.

I can't, of course, figure out what you try to think about when you are as desolate as I was that night. Maybe you are like me and inclined to think of women, and maybe you are like a man I met once, on the road, who told me that when he was up against it he never thought of anything but grub and a big nice clean warm bed to sleep in. "I don't care about anything else and I don't ever let myself think of anything else," he said. "If I was like you and went to thinking about women sometime I'd find myself hooked up to some skirt, and she'd have the old double cross on me, and the rest of my life maybe I'd be working in some factory for her and her kids."

As I say, there I was anyway, up there alone with that horse in that warm stall in that dark lonesome fairground and I had that feeling about being sick at the thought of human beings and what they could be like.

Well, suddenly I got again the queer feeling I'd had about him once or twice before, I mean the feeling about our understanding each other in some way I can't explain.

So having it again I went over to where he stood and began running my hands all over his body, just because I loved the feel of him and as sometimes, to tell the plain truth, I've felt about touching with my hands the body of a woman I've seen and who I thought was lovely too. I ran my hands over his head and neck and then down over his hard firm round body and then over his flanks and down his legs. His flanks quivered a little I remember and once he turned his head and stuck his cold nose down along my neck and nipped my shoulder a little, in a soft playful way. It hurt a little but I didn't care.

So then I crawled up through a hole into the loft above thinking that night was over anyway and glad of it, but it wasn't, not by a long sight.

As my clothes were all soaking wet and as we race track swipes didn't own any such things as night-gowns or pajamas I had to go to bed naked, of course.

But we had plenty of horse blankets and so I tucked myself in between a pile of them and tried not to think any more that night. The being with Pick-it-boy and having him close right under me that way made me feel a little better.

Then I was sound asleep and dreaming and—bang, like being hit with a club by someone who has sneaked up behind you—I got another wallop.

What I suppose is that, being upset the way I was, I had forgotten to bolt the door to Pick-it-boy's stall down below and two Negro men had come in there, thinking they were in their own place, and had climbed up through the hole where I was. They were half lit up but not what you might call dead drunk, and I suppose they were up against something a couple of white swipes who had some money in their pockets wouldn't have been up against.

What I mean is that a couple of white swipes, having liquored themselves up and being down there in the town on a bat, if they wanted a woman or a couple of women, would have been able to find them. There is always a few women of that kind can be found around any town I've ever seen or heard of, and of course a bartender would have given them the tip where to go.

But a Negro, up there in that country, where there aren't any, or anyway mighty few Negro women, wouldn't know what to do when he felt that way and would be up against it.

It's so always. Burt and several other Negroes I've known pretty well have talked to me about it, lots of times. You take now a young Negro man—not a race track swipe or a tramp or any other lowdown kind of a fellow—but, let us say, one who has been to college, and has behaved himself and tried to be a good man, the best he could, and be clean, as they say. He isn't any better off, is he? If he has made himself some money and wants to go sit in a swell restaurant, or go to hear some good music, or see a good play at the theatre, he gets what we used to call on the tracks, "the messy end of the dung fork," doesn't he?

And even in such a low-down place as what people call a "bad house" it's the same way. The white swipes and others can go into a place where they have Negro women fast enough, and they do it too, but you let a Negro swipe try it the other way around and see how he comes out.

You see, I can think this whole thing out fairly now, sitting here in my own house and writing, and with my wife Jessie in the kitchen making a pie or something, and I can show just how the two Negro men who came into that loft, where I was asleep, were justified in what they did, and I can preach about how the Negroes are up against it in this country, like a daisy, but I tell you what, I didn't think things out that way that night.

For, you understand, what they thought, they being half liquored up, and when one of them had jerked the blankets off me, was that I was a woman. One of them carried a lantern but it was smoky and dirty and didn't give out much light. So they must have figured it out—my body being pretty white and slender then, like a young girl's body I suppose—that some white swipe had brought me up there. The kind of girls around a town that will come with a swipe to a race track on a rainy night aren't very fancy females but you'll find that kind in towns all right. I've seen many a one in my day.

And so, I figure, these two big buck niggers, being piped that way, just made up their minds they would snatch me away from the white swipe who had brought me out there, and who had left me lying carelessly around.

"Jes' you lie still honey. We ain't gwine hurt you none," one of them said, with a little chuckling laugh that had something in it besides a laugh, too. It was the kind of laugh that gives you the shivers.

The devil of it was I couldn't say anything, not even a word. Why I couldn't yell out and say "What the hell," and just kid them a little and shoo them out of there I don't know, but I couldn't. I tried and tried so that my throat hurt but I didn't say a word. I just lay there staring at them.

It was a mixed-up night. I've never gone through another night like it.

Was I scared? Lord Almighty, I'll tell you what, I was scared.

Because the two big black faces were leaning right over me now, and I could feel their liquored-up breaths on my cheeks, and their eyes were shining in the dim light from that smoky lantern, and right in the center of their eyes was that dancing flickering light I've told you about your seeing in the eyes of wild animals, when you were carrying a lantern through the woods at night.

It was a puzzler! All my life, you see—me never having had any sisters, and at that time never having had a sweetheart either—I had been dreaming and thinking about women, and I suppose I'd always been dreaming about a pure innocent one, for myself, made for me by God, maybe. Men are that way. No matter how big they talk about "let the women go hang," they've always got that notion tucked away inside themselves, somewhere. It's a kind of chesty man's notion, I suppose, but they've got it and the kind of up-and-coming women we have nowadays who are always saying, "I'm as good as a man and will do what the men do," are on the wrong trail if they really ever want to, what you might say "hog-tie" a fellow of their own.

So I had invented a kind of princess, with black hair and a slender willowy body to dream about. And I thought of her as being shy and afraid to ever tell anything she really felt to anyone but just me. I suppose I fancied that if I ever found such a woman in the flesh I would be the strong sure one and she the timid shrinking one.

And now I was that woman, or something like her, myself.

I gave a kind of wriggle, like a fish you have just taken off the hook. What I did next wasn't a thought-out thing. I was caught and I squirmed, that's all.

The two niggers both jumped at me but somehow—the lantern having been kicked over and having gone out the first move they made—well in some way, when they both lunged at me they missed.

As good luck would have it my feet found the hole, where you put hay down to the horse in the stall below, and through which we crawled up when it was time to go to bed in our blankets up in the hay, and down I slid, not bothering to try to find the ladder with my feet but just letting myself go.

In less than a second I was out of doors in the dark and the rain and the two blacks were down the hole and out the door of the stall after me.

How long or how far they really followed me I suppose I'll never know. It was black dark and raining hard now and a roaring wind had begun to blow. Of course, my body being white, it must have made some kind of a faint streak in the darkness as I ran, and anyway I thought they could see me and I knew I couldn't see them and that made my terror ten times worse. Every minute I thought they would grab me.

You know how it is when a person is all upset and full of terror as I was. I suppose maybe the two niggers followed me for a while, running across the muddy race track and into the grove of trees that grew in the oval inside the track, but likely enough, after just a few minutes, they gave up the chase and went back, found their own place and went to sleep. They were liquored up, as I've said, and maybe partly funning too.

But I didn't know that, if they were. As I ran I kept hearing sounds, sounds made by the rain coming down through the dead old leaves left on the trees and by the wind blowing, and it may be that the sound that scared me most of all was my own bare feet stepping on a dead branch and breaking it or something like that.

There was something strange and scary, a steady sound, like a heavy man running and breathing hard, right at my shoulder. It may have been my own breath, coming quick and fast, And I thought I heard that chuckling laugh I'd heard up in the loft, the laugh that sent the shivers right down through me. Of course every tree I came close to looked like a man standing there, ready to grab me, and I kept dodging and going—bang—into other trees. My shoulders kept knocking against trees in that way and the skin was all knocked off, and every time it happened I thought a big black hand had come down and clutched at me and was tearing my flesh.

How long it went on I don't know, maybe an hour, maybe five minutes. But anyway the darkness didn't let up, and the terror didn't let up, and I couldn't, to save my life, scream or make any sound.

Just why I couldn't I don't know. Could it be because at the time I was a woman, while at the same time I wasn't a woman? It may be that I was too ashamed of having turned into a girl and being afraid of a man to make any sound. I don't know about that. It's over my head.

But anyway I couldn't make a sound. I tried and tried and my throat hurt from trying and no sound came.

And then, after a long time, or what seemed like a long time, I got out from among the trees inside the track and was on the track itself again. I thought the two black men were still after me, you understand, and I ran like a madman.

Of course, running along the track that way, it must have been up the back stretch, I came after a time to where the old slaughterhouse stood, in that field, beside the track. I knew it by its ungodly smell, scared as I was. Then, in some way, I managed to get over the high old fairground fence and was in the field, where the slaughterhouse was.

All the time I was trying to yell or scream, or be sensible and tell those two black men that I was a man and not a woman, but I couldn't make it. And then I heard a sound like a board cracking or breaking in the fence and thought they were still after me.

So I kept on running like a crazy man, in the field, and just then I stumbled and fell over something. I've told you how the old slaughterhouse field was filled with bones, that had been lying there a long time and had all been washed white. There were heads of sheep and cows and all kinds of things.

And when I fell and pitched forward I fell right into the midst of something, still and cold and white.

It was probably the skeleton of a horse lying there. In small towns like that, they take an old worn-out horse, that has died, and haul him off to some field outside of town and skin him for the hide, that they can sell for a dollar or two. It doesn't make any difference what the horse has been, that's the way he usually ends up. Maybe even Pick-it-boy, or O My Man, or a lot of other good fast ones I've seen and known have ended that way by this time.

And so I think it was the bones of a horse lying there and he must have been lying on his back. The birds and wild animals had picked all his flesh away and the rain had washed his bones clean.

Anyway I fell and pitched forward and my side got cut pretty deep and my hands clutched at something. I had fallen right in between the ribs of the horse and they seemed to wrap themselves around me close. And my hands, clutching upwards, had got hold of the cheeks of that dead horse and the bones of his cheeks were cold as ice with the rain washing over them. White bones wrapped around me and white bones in my hands.

There was a new terror now that seemed to go down to the very bottom of me, to the bottom of the inside of me, I mean. It shook me like I have seen a rat in a barn shaken by a dog. It was a terror like a big wave that hits you when you are walking on a seashore, maybe. You see it coming and you try to run and get away but when you start to run inshore there is a stone cliff you can't climb. So the wave comes high as a mountain, and there it is, right in front of you and nothing in all this world can stop it. And now it had knocked you down and rolled and tumbled you over and over and washed you clean, clean, but dead maybe.

And that's the way I felt—I seemed to myself dead with blind terror. It was a feeling like the finger of God running down your back and burning you clean, I mean.

It burned all that silly nonsense about being a girl right out of me.

I screamed at last and the spell that was on me was broken. I'll bet the scream I let out of me could have been heard a mile and a half.

Right away I felt better and crawled out from among the pile of bones, and then I stood on my own feet again and I wasn't a woman, or a young girl any more but a man and my own self, and as far as I know I've been that way ever since. Even the black night seemed warm and alive now, like a mother might be to a kid in the dark.

Only I couldn't go back to the race track because I was blubbering and crying and was ashamed of myself and of what a fool I had made of myself. Someone might see me and I couldn't stand that, not at that moment.

So I went across the field, walking now, not running like a crazy man, and pretty soon I came to a fence and crawled over and got into another field, in which there was a straw stack, I just happened to find in the pitch darkness.

The straw stack had been there a long time and some sheep had nibbled away at it until they had made a pretty deep hole, like a cave, in the side of it. I found the hole and crawled in and there were some sheep in there, about a dozen of them.

When I came in, creeping on my hands and knees, they didn't make much fuss, just stirred around a little and then settled down.

So I settled down amongst them too. They were warm and gentle and kind, like Pick-it-boy, and being in there with them made me feel better than I would have felt being with any human person I knew at that time.

So I settled down and slept after a while, and when I woke up it was daylight and not very cold and the rain was over. The clouds were breaking away from the sky now and maybe there would be a fair the next week but if there was I knew I wouldn't be there to see it.

Because what I expected to happen did happen. I had to go back across the fields and the fairground to the place where my clothes were, right in the broad daylight, and me stark naked, and of course I knew someone would be up and would raise a shout, and every swipe and every driver would stick his head out and would whoop with laughter.

And there would be a thousand questions asked, and I would be too mad and too ashamed to answer, and would perhaps begin to blubber, and that would make me more ashamed than ever.

It all turned out just as I expected, except that when the noise and the shouts of laughter were going it the loudest, Burt came out of the stall where O My Man was kept, and when he saw me he didn't know what was the matter but he knew something was up that wasn't on the square and for which I wasn't to blame.

So he got so all-fired mad he couldn't speak for a minute, and then he grabbed a pitchfork and began prancing up and down before the other stalls, giving that gang of swipes and drivers such a royal old dressing-down as you never heard. You should have heard him sling language. It was grand to hear.

And while he was doing it I sneaked up into the loft, blubbering because I was so pleased and happy to hear him swear that way, and I got my wet clothes on quick and got down, and gave Pick-it-boy a good-bye kiss on the cheek and lit out.

The last I saw of all that part of my life was Burt, still going it, and yelling out for the man who had put up a trick on me to come out and get what was coming to him. He had the pitchfork in his hand and was swinging it around, and every now and then he would make a kind of lunge at a tree or something, he was so mad through, and there was no one else in sight at all. And Burt didn't even see me cutting out along the fence through a gate and down the hill and out of the race-horse and the tramp life for the rest of my days.

MORE ABOUT THIS STORY

In *The Challenge of Youth,* Erik Erikson observes about adolescence: "In no other stage of the life cycle . . . are the promise of finding oneself and the threat of losing oneself so closely allied." [1] Elsewhere he writes that "Like a trapeze artist, the young person in the middle of vigorous motion must let go of his safe hold on childhood and reach out for a firm grasp on adulthood depending for a breathless interval on a relatedness between the past and the future." [2] As an adult Herman Dudley, the narrator of "The Man Who Became a Woman," has swung at last to the safety of marriage. But his persistent reminders that all is now well and his compulsive need to rehearse his adolescent crisis token an inward insecurity, perhaps even a continuing restlessness, and at least a vague doubt about the firmness of his "grasp on adulthood." Nevertheless, the focus of Anderson's story is upon that crucial adolescent experience, and there the psychological implications may best be explored.

---

[1] (New York: Anchor Books, 1965), p. 11.
[2] *Insight and Responsibility* (New York: Norton, 1964), p. 90.

Above all, this is less a story about homosexuality than about the bisexual conflict (often referred to as "gender identity" to discriminate the psychosocial from the sexual aspects of the problem)[3] integral with the adolescent identity struggle. At puberty almost no boy has achieved the capacity to love in a way that sustains marriage and parenthood, nor can he until he has unqualifiedly accepted his physical maleness. Between the advent of genital maturity and the assumption of responsible adulthood occurs what Erikson calls a "psychosocial moratorium"—a period of experimentation with a variety of roles which ultimately shape a pattern of inner identity. Preadolescent experience has already, of course, equipped some more adequately than others to encounter these difficult years. Herman Dudley, for example, leaves us with a negative impression of his parents: his father a philistine and puritan, his mother a cipher (the idealized "queen" of his childhood is a stranger glimpsed at a station). Thus, Herman enters the critical stage of his adolescence almost wholly uprooted, his ego controls erratic, his sense of self shifting. Inevitably, his anxieties about accepting and integrating his sexual impulses and fixing them upon a satisfactory love object have become shatteringly intense.

Alone, poised between fantasy and reality, Herman grapples with his inward self, wondering at times whether he is even "part of it at all," rationalizing that "boys who aren't quite men and have never been with girls . . . slip off base that way." His friend Tom Means, similarly dislocated, verbalizes for Herman the symbolic analogy between horse and sex, preparing the path for Herman's subsequent fantasies. Burt and the Negro swipes, with their earthy sexual primitivism further motivate the psychic blending of man, animal, and woman. When Herman enters the saloon, he has almost determined to act out his aggressive male role: to get drunk and to find a woman. But the cumulative impact of social and moral contradictions has unmanned him. What he confronts in the mirror is the image of a "white and pasty-looking face," his own face seen as that of a "lonesome and scared girl."

The events in the saloon confirm his new female identity. The men in the bar are gross and violent; so too is the strange intruder—all embody the male principle Herman suddenly finds revolting. Moreover, holding the child in his arms almost literally assigns him a woman's role. As he flees to the stable, both sexes have inextricably twisted in his mind. To complicate further his near hysteria, he feels nausea at the very idea of being human: how "mean and low and all balled-up and twisted up" humanity can become. In the stall with the gelding, Pick-it-boy, things have always been simple and clear: "I got inside him and he got inside me . . . I wanted to deny the difference be-

[3] About the problem of bisexuality and gender identity, see Sandor Rado, "A Critical Examination of the Concept of Bisexuality," and R. J. Stoller, "Passing and the Continuum of Gender Identity," in *Sexual Inversion*, ed. Judd Marmor (New York: Basic Books, 1965).

tween man and animal . . . I wished he was a girl sometimes or that I was a girl and he was a man." Stroking the horse is a male sexual act but it is also—given the asexuality of the gelding—an ambivalent one. Later, lying naked in the loft, conscious of his soft, white flesh, Herman acknowledges his ambivalence during the attempted assault by the two Negro boys.

But the ritual of Herman's sexual initiation is not, fortunately, at that point consummated. The rite occurs after his maddened flight to the animal grave-yard. There, enclosed in the rib cage of a dead horse, Herman becomes simul-taneously passive female and embryonic male. However icy the white bones and the black, driving rain, Herman feels the night to be "warm and alive, like a mother might be to a kid in the dark." Thus transformed by cold and warmth, joy and terror, Herman rises and returns as an adult, "a man and my own self."

Herman's "great adventure" reaches its grotesque climax, then, in a grave-yard for horses, reminding us again that his most tender and rewarding adolescent relationships have been with animals rather than with humans. More important than this, however, is that Herman's experience enables him to renounce his pattern of flight (symbolized by the racetrack and the tramp-ing life) and to assert his sexual identity with enough authority to return to life as a man. Although he may continue, as the story hints, to suffer doubt, he will no longer feel "like a dog inside." Herman's frantic need for stability— evident in his craving for its obverse—speed and locomotion—has diminished. Only an echo of his agony occasionally rebounds, an echo that finds imagina-tive and compassionate voice in Anderson's art.

FOR FURTHER READING

Erikson, Erik. *Identity and the Life Cycle.* Chs. II, III. *Psychological Issues,* Monograph 1. New York: International Universities Press, 1959.

Fraiberg, Selma H. "Homosexual Conflicts," *Adolescents,* ed. S. Lorand and H. I. Schneer. New York: Delta Books, 1965.

Freud, Sigmund (J. Strachey, trans.). *Three Essays on the Theory of Sex-uality* (1905). New York: Basic Books, 1962.

Howe, Irving. *Sherwood Anderson.* New York: William Sloane, 1951, pp. 160–164.

Lesser, Simon. "Conscious and Unconscious Perception," *Fiction and the Unconscious.* Boston: Beacon Press, 1957, pp. 224–234.

Spiegel, Leo A. "Identity and Adolescence," *Adolescents,* ed. S. Lorand and H. I. Schneer. New York: Delta Books, 1965.

Trilling, Lionel. "Sherwood Anderson," *The Liberal Imagination.* New York: Doubleday, 1950.

When I Was Thirteen

BY DENTON WELCH (1915–1948)

At the age of twenty, while bicycling in suburban London, Denton Welch was knocked down by a motorist. For the rest of his brief life Welch was more often in physical agony than not and was frequently bedridden by spinal, pelvic, and kidney damage from his accident as well as by tubercular complications (he tells of his pain in his final, posthumous work, *A Voice Through a Cloud*, 1950). All of his writing followed the accident, though only a few scattered stories and a single novel, *Maiden Voyage* (1945), were published during his lifetime.

Within this short and blighted span, Welch fastened on the narrow spectrum of experience he knew best and felt most deeply—the range of adolescent sensibility. Except as the world impinged upon that sensitive core, he cared little for its values or its problems. "I will tell you what your danger is," Edith Sitwell told him (he recorded it in his *Journal*): "It is your ingrowing toe-nails. Everything is in, in, in." Welch insulated himself from the world yet perceived it sharply and wrote of it lucidly, surveying and appraising, sometimes wittily, more often bitterly. With brittle, comic clarity, the narrator of "When I Was Thirteen" fixes "a nice absurd Belgian woman, dressed from head to foot in a babyish suit of fluffy orange knitted wool." But the real force derives from the equally clear but more poignant impact of the adolescent's uncomprehending innocence and his desperate need to "connect."

In one sense at least "When I Was Thirteen" tells of the narrator's coming of age. Isolated, neglected, and ignored by his elder brother, the narrator exuberantly walks and skis toward manhood with the more responsive Archer: "It was wonderful to be really smoking with Archer.

197

He treated me just like a man. . . . He took me as I was and yet seemed to like me." From the psychic and sensual indulgences of a child—hot chocolate, creamy cake, and candy—the youth strides into a man's awareness of cigarettes, wine, and drunkenness. Never does the youth consciously understand (though he reports feelingly) the homoerotic nuances implicit in his rapport with Archer. Nor, the story implies, was there any reason that he should have tried to analyze or doubt Archer's motives. But because innocence rarely survives maturity, the narrator, in order to end as a man, must forego his pastoral idyll for domestic tragedy.

His brother's epithets—*bastard, harlot, sod*—seem to him the gibberish of a lunatic, words wholly new and alien. Only one word does he recognize—*devil*—and that single word marks him an immoralist, violates and taints his innocence, and, at least temporarily, ruptures his link with the adult world. Thus, Welch seems ironically to suggest, does the world make a man.

THE STORY

When I was thirteen, I went to Switzerland for the Christmas holidays in the charge of my eldest brother, who was at that time still up at Oxford.

In the hotel we found another undergraduate whom my brother knew. His name was Archer. They were not at the same college, but they had met and evidently had not agreed with each other. At first my brother William would say nothing about Archer; then one day, in answer to a question of mine, he said, "He's not very much liked; although he's a very good swimmer." As he spoke, William held his lips in a very firm, almost pursed, line which was most damaging to Archer.

After this I began to look at Archer with a certain amount of interest. He had broad shoulders but was not tall. He had a look of strength and solidity which I admired and envied. He had rather a nice pug face with insignficant nose and broad cheeks. Sometimes, when he was animated, a tassel of fair, almost colorless, hair would fall across his forehead, half covering one eye. He had a thick beautiful neck, rather meaty barbarian hands, and a skin as smooth and evenly colored as a pink fondant.

His whole body appeared to be suffused with this gentle pink color. He never wore proper skiing clothes of waterproof material like the rest of us. Usually he came out in nothing but a pair of gray flannels and a white cotton shirt with all the buttons left undone. When the sun grew very hot, he would even discard this thin shirt and ski up and down the slopes behind the hotel in nothing but his trousers. I had often seen him fall down in this half-naked state and get buried in snow. The next moment he would jerk himself to his feet again, laughing and swearing.

After William's curt nod to him on our first evening at the hotel, we had hardly exchanged any remarks. We sometimes passed one another on the way to the basement to get our skis in the morning, and often we found ourselves sitting near Archer on the glassed-in terrace; but some Oxford snobbery I knew nothing of, or some more profound reason, always made William throw off waves of hostility. Archer never showed any signs of wishing to approach. He was content to look at me sometimes with a mild inoffensive curiosity, but he seemed to ignore William completely. This pleased me more than I would have admitted at that time. I was so used to being passed over myself by all William's friends that it was pleasant when someone who knew him seemed to take a sort of interest, however slight and amused, in me.

William was often away from the hotel for days and nights together, going for expeditions with guides and other friends. He would never take me, because he said I was too young and had not enough stamina. He said that I would fall down a crevasse or get my nose frost bitten, or hang up the party by lagging behind.

In consequence, I was often alone at the hotel; but I did not mind this; I enjoyed it. I was slightly afraid of my brother William and found life very much easier and less exacting when he was not there. I think other people in the hotel thought that I looked lonely. Strangers would often come up and talk to me and smile, and once a nice absurd Belgian woman, dressed from head to foot in a babyish suit of fluffy orange knitted wool, held out a bright five-franc piece to me and told me to go and buy chocolate caramels with it. I think she must have taken me for a much younger child.

On one of these afternoons when I had come in from the Nursery Slopes and was sitting alone over my tea on the sun terrace, I noticed that Archer was sitting in the corner huddled over a book and munching greedily and absent-mindedly.

I, too, was reading a book, while I ate delicious rhum babas and little tarts filled with worm-castles of chestnut purée topped with caps of whipped cream. I have called the meal tea, but what I was drinking was not tea but chocolate. When I poured out, I held the pot high in the air, so that my cup, when filled should be covered in a rich froth of bubbles.

The book I was reading was Tolstoy's *Resurrection*. Although I did not quite understand some parts of it, it give me intense pleasure to read it while I ate the rich cakes and drank the frothy chocolate. I thought it a noble and terrible story, but I was worried and mystified by the words "illegitimate child" which had occurred several times lately. What sort of child could this be? Clearly a child that brought trouble and difficulty. Could it have some terrible disease, or was it a special sort of imbecile? I looked up from my book, still wondering about this phrase "illegitimate child," and saw that Archer had turned in his creaking wicker chair and was gazing blankly in my direction. The orchestra was playing "The Birth of the Blues" in a rather remarkable Swiss arrangement, and it was clear that Archer had been distracted from his book by the music, only to be lulled into a daydream, as he gazed into space.

Suddenly his eyes lost their blank look and focused on my face. "Your brother off up to the Jungfrau Joch again, or somewhere?" he called out.

I nodded my head, saying nothing, becoming slightly confused.

Archer grinned. He seemed to find me amusing.

"What are you reading?" he asked.

"This," I said, taking my book over to him. I did not want to call out either the word "Resurrection" or "Tolstoy." But Archer did not make fun of me for reading a "classic," as most of William's friends would have done. He only said, "I should think it's rather good. Mine's frightful; it's called *The Story of My Life,* by Queen Marie of Roumania." He held up the book and I saw an extraordinary photograph of a lady who looked like a snake charmer in full regalia. The headdress seemed to be made of white satin, embroidered with beads, stretched over cardboard. There were tassels and trailing things hanging down everywhere.

I laughed at the amusing picture and Archer went on, "I always read books like this when I can get them. Last week I had Lady Oxford's autobiography, and before that I found a perfectly wonderful book called *Flaming Sex.* It was by a French woman who married an English knight and then went back to France to shoot a French doctor. She didn't kill him, of course, but she was sent to prison, where she had a very interesting time with the nuns who looked after her in the hospital. I also lately found an old book by a Crown Princess of Saxony who ended up picnicking on a haystack with a simple Italian gentleman in a straw hat. I love these 'real life' stories, don't you?"

I again nodded my head, not altogether daring to venture on a spoken answer. I wondered whether to go back to my own table or whether to pluck up courage and ask Archer what an "illegitimate child' was. He solved the problem by saying "Sit down" rather abruptly.

I subsided next to him with "Tolstoy" on my knee. I waited for a moment and then plunged.

"What exactly does 'illegitimate child' mean?" I asked rather breathlessly.

"Outside the law—when two people have a child although they're not married."

"Oh." I went bright pink. I thought Archer must be wrong. I still believed that it was quite impossible to have a child unless one was married. The very fact of being married produced the child. I had a vague idea that some particularly reckless people attempted, without being married, to have children in places called "night clubs," but they were always unsuccessful, and this made them drink and plunge into the most hectic gaiety.

I did not tell Archer that I thought he had made a mistake, for I did not want to hurt his feelings. I went on sitting at his table and, although he turned his eyes back to his book and went on reading, I knew that he was friendly.

After some time he looked up again and said, "Would you like to come out with me tomorrow? We could take our lunch, go up the mountain, and then ski down in the afternoon."

I was delighted at the suggestion, but also a little alarmed at my own shortcomings. I thought it my duty to explain that I was not a very good skier, only a moderate one, and that I could only do stem turns. I hated the thought of being a drag on Archer.

"I expect you're much better than I am. I'm always falling down or crashing into something," I answered.

It was all arranged. We were to meet early, soon after six, as Archer wanted to go to the highest station on the mountain railway and then climb on skis to a nearby peak which had a small resthouse of logs.

I went to bed very excited, thankful that William was away on a long expedition. I lay under my enormous feather bed eiderdown, felt the freezing mountain air on my face, and saw the stars sparkling through the open window.

I got up very early in the morning and put on my most sober ski socks and woollen shirt, for I felt that Archer disliked any suspicion of bright colors or dressing up. I made my appearance as workmanlike as possible and then went down to breakfast.

I ate several crackly rolls, which I spread thickly with dewy slivers of butter and gobbets of rich black cherry jam; then I drank my last cup of coffee and went to wax my skis. As I passed through the hall I picked up my picnic lunch in its neat greaseproof paper packet.

The nails in my boots slid and then caught on the snow, trodden hard down to the basement door. I found my skis in their racks, took them down, and then heated the iron and the wax. I loved spreading the hot black wax smoothly on the white wood. Soon they were both done beautifully.

I will go like a bird, I thought.

I looked up and saw Archer standing in the doorway.

"I hope you haven't put too much on, else you'll be sitting on your arse all day," he said gaily.

How fresh and pink he looked! I was excited.

He started to wax his own skis. When they were finished, we went outside and strapped them on. Archer carried a rucksack and he told me to put my lunch and my spare sweater into it.

We started off down the gentle slopes to the station. The sun was shining prickingly. The lovely snow had rainbow colors in it. I was so happy I swung my sticks with their steel points and basket ends. I even tried to show off and jumped a little terrace which I knew well. Nevertheless it nearly brought me down. I just regained my balance in time. I would have hated at that moment to have fallen down in front of Archer.

When we got to the station we found a compartment to ourselves. It was still early. Gently we were pulled up the mountain, past the water station stop and the other three halts.

We got out at the very top where the railway ended. A huge unused snow-plow stood by the side of the track, with its vicious shark's nose pointed at me. We ran to the van to get out our skis. Archer found mine as well as his own and slung both pairs across his shoulders. He looked like a very tough Jesus carrying two crosses, I thought.

We stood by the old snowplow and slipped on our skis; then we began to climb laboriously up the ridge to the wooden resthouse. He hardly talked at all, for we needed all our breath, and, also, I was still shy of Archer. Sometimes he helped me, telling me where to place my skis, and, if I slipped backward, hauling on the rope which he had half playfully tied round my waist.

In spite of growing tired, I enjoyed the grim plodding. It gave me a sense of work and purpose. When Archer looked round to smile at me, his pink face was slippery with sweat. His white shirt above the small rucksack was plastered to his shoulder blades. On my own face I could feel the drops of sweat just being held back by my eyebrows. I would wipe my hand across my upper lip and break all the tiny beads that had formed there.

Every now and then Archer would stop. We would put our skis sideways on the track and rest, leaning forward on our sticks. The sun struck down on our necks with a steady seeping heat and the light striking up from the snow was as bright as the fiery dazzle of a mirror. From the ridge we could see down into two valleys; and standing all round us were the other peaks, black rock and white snow, tangling and mixing until the mountains looked like vast teeth which had begun to decay.

I was so tired when we reached the long gentle incline to the resthouse that I was afraid of falling down. The rope was still round my waist, and so the slightest lagging would have been perceptible to Archer. I think he must have slackened his pace for my benefit, for I somehow managed to reach the iron seats in front of the hut. I sank down, still with my skis on. I half shut my eyes. From walking so long with my feet turned out, my ankles felt almost broken.

The next thing I knew was that Archer had disappeared into the resthouse. He came out carrying a steaming cup.

"You must drink this," he said, holding out black coffee to me, which I hated. He unwrapped four lumps of sugar and dropped them in the cup.

"I don't like it black," I said.

"Never mind," he answered sharply, "drink it."

Rather surprised, I began to drink the syrupy coffee. "The sugar and the strong coffee will be good for you," said Archer. He went back into the rest-house and brought out a glass of what looked like hot water with a piece of lemon floating in it. The mountain of sugar at the bottom was melting into thin Arabian Nights wreaths and spirals, smoke rings of syrup.

"What else has it got in it?" I asked with an attempt at worldliness.

"Rum!" said Archer.

We sat there on the terrace and unwrapped our picnic lunches. We both had two rolls, one with tongue in it and one with ham, a hard-boiled egg, sweet biscuits, and a bar of delicious bitter chocolate; tangerine oranges were our dessert.

We began to take huge bites out of our rolls. We could not talk for some time. The food brought out a thousand times more clearly the beauty of the mountain peaks and sun. My tiredness made me thrillingly conscious of delight and satisfaction. I wanted to sit there with Archer for a long time.

At the end of the meal Archer gave me a piece of his own bar of chocolate, and then began to skin pigs of tangerine very skillfully and hand them to me on his outstretched palm, as one offers a lump of sugar to a horse. I thought for one moment of bending down my head and licking the pigs up in imitation of a horse; then I saw how mad it would look.

We threw the brilliant tangerine peel into the snow, which immediately seemed to dim and darken its color.

Archer felt in his hip pocket and brought out black, cheap Swiss cigarettes, wrapped in leaf. They were out of a slot machine. He put one between my lips and lighted it. I felt extremely conscious of the thing jutting out from my lips. I wondered if I would betray my ignorance by not breathing the smoke in and out correctly. I turned my head a little away from Archer and experimented. It seemed easy if one did not breathe too deeply. It was wonderful to be really smoking with Archer. He treated me just like a man.

"Come on, let's get cracking," he said, "or, if anything happens, we'll be out all night."

I scrambled to my feet at once and snapped the clips of the skis round my boot heels. Archer was in high spirits from the rum. He ran on his skis along the flat ridge in front of the resthouse and then fell down.

"Serves me right," he said. He shook off the snow, and we started properly. In five minutes we had swooped down the ridge we had climbed so painfully all morning. The snow was perfect; new and dry, with no crust. We followed a new way that Archer had discovered. The ground was uneven with dips and curves. Often we were out of sight of each other. When we came to the icy path through a wood, my courage failed me.

"Stem like hell and don't get out of control," Archer yelled back at me. I pointed my skis together, praying that they would not cross. I leaned on my sticks, digging their metal points into the compressed snow. Twice I fell, though not badly.

"Well done, well done!" shouted Archer, as I shot past him and out of the wood into a thick snowdrift. He hauled me out of the snow and stood me on my feet, beating me all over hastily to get off the snow; then we began the descent of a field called the "Bumps." Little hillocks, if maneuvered successfully, gave one that thrilling sinking and rising feeling experienced on a scenic railway at a fun fair.

Archer went before me, dipping and rising, shouting and yelling in his exuberance. I followed more sedately. We both fell several times, but in that not unpleasant, bouncing way which brings you to your feet again almost at once.

Archer was roaring now and trying to yodel in an absurd, rich contralto. I had never enjoyed myself quite so much before. I thought him the most wonderful companion, not a bit intimidating, in spite of being rather a hero.

When at last we swooped down to the village street, it was nearly evening. Early orange lights were shining in the shop windows. We planked our skis down on the hard, iced road, trying not to slip.

I looked in at the *patisserie, confiserie* window, where all the electric bulbs had fluffy pink shades like powder puffs. Archer saw my look.

"Let's go in," he said. He ordered me hot chocolate with whipped cream, and *croissant* rolls. Afterward we both went up to the little counter and chose cakes. I had one shaped like a little log. It was made of soft chocolate, and had green moss trimmings made in pistachio nut. When Archer went to pay the bill be bought me some chocolate caramels, in a little birdseye maple box, and a bar labeled *"Chocolat Polychrome."* Each finger was a different colored cream: mauve, pink, green, yellow, orange, brown, white, even blue.

We went out into the village street and began to climb up the path to the hotel. About halfway up Archer stopped outside a little wooden chalet and said, "This is where I hang out."

"But you're staying at the hotel," I said incredulously.

"Oh, yes, I have all my meals there, but I sleep here. It's a sort of little annex when there aren't any rooms left in the hotel. It's only got two rooms; I've paid just a bit more and got it all to myself. Someone comes every morning and makes the bed and stokes the boiler and the stove. Come in and see it."

I followed Archer up the outside wooden staircase and stood with him on the little landing outside the two rooms. The place seemed wonderfully warm and dry. The walls were unpainted wood; there were double windows. There was a gentle creaking in all the joints of the wood when one moved. Archer pushed open one of the doors and ushered me in. I saw in one corner a huge white porcelain stove, the sort I had only before seen in pictures. Some of Archer's skiing gloves and socks were drying round it on a ledge. Against another wall were two beds, like wooden troughs built into the wall. The balloon-like quilts bulged up above the wood.

"I hardly use the other room," said Archer. "I just throw my muck into it and leave my trunks there." He opened the connecting door and I saw a smaller room with dirty clothes strewn on the floor; white shirts, hard evening collars, some very short pants, and many pairs of thick gray socks. The room smelled mildly of Archer's old sweat. I didn't mind at all.

Archer shut the door and said, "I'm going to run the bath."

"Have you a bathroom, too—all your own?" I exclaimed enviously. "Every time anyone has a bath at the hotel, he has to pay two francs fifty to the fräulein before she unlocks the door. I've only had two proper baths since I've been here. I don't think it matters though. It seems almost impossible to get really dirty in Switzerland, and you can always wash all over in your bedroom basin."

"Why don't you have a bath here after me? The water's lovely and hot, although there's not much of it. If you went back first and got your evening clothes, you could change straight into them."

I looked at Archer a little uncertainly. I longed to soak in hot water after my wonderful but grueling day.

"Could I really bathe here?" I asked.

"If you don't mind using my water. I'll promise not to pee in it. I'm not really filthy, you know."

Archer laughed and chuckled, because he saw me turning red at his coarseness. He lit another of his peasant cigarettes and began to unlace his boots. He got me to pull them off. I knelt down, bowed my head, and pulled. When the ski boot suddenly flew off, my nose dipped forward and I smelt Archer's foot in its woolly, hairy, humid casing of sock.

"Would you just rub my foot and leg?" Archer said urgently, a look of pain suddenly shooting across his face. "I've got cramp. It often comes on at the end of the day."

He shot his leg out rigidly and told me where to rub and massage. I felt each of his curled toes separately and the hard tendons in his leg. His calf was like a firm sponge ball. His thigh, swelling out, amazed me. I likened it in my mind to the trumpet of some musical instrument. I went on rubbing methodically. I was able to feel his pain melting away.

When the tense look had quite left his face, he said, "Thanks," and stood up. He unbuttoned his trousers, let them fall to the ground, and pulled his shirt up. Speaking to me with his head imprisoned in it, he said, "You go and get your clothes and I'll begin bathing."

I left him and hurried up to the hotel, carrying my skis on my shoulder. I ran up to my room and pulled my evening clothes out of the wardrobe. The dinner jacket and trousers had belonged to my brother William six years before, when he was my age. I was secretly ashamed of this fact, and had taken my brother's name from the inside of the breast pocket and had written my own in elaborate lettering.

I took my comb, face flannel and soap, and getting out my toboggan slid back to Archer's chalet in a few minutes. I let myself in and heard Archer splashing. The little hall was full of steam and I saw Archer's shoulders and arms like a pink smudge through the open bathroom door.

"Come and scrub my back," he yelled; "it gives me a lovely feeling." He thrust a large stiff nailbrush into my hands and told me to scrub as hard as I could.

I ran it up and down his back until I'd made harsh red tramlines. Delicious tremors seemed to be passing through Archer.

"Ah! go on!" said Archer in a dream, like a purring cat. "When I'm rich I'll have a special back-scratcher slave." I went on industriously scrubbing his back till I was afraid that I would rub the skin off. I liked to give him pleasure.

At last he stood up all dripping and said, "Now it's your turn."

I undressed and got into Archer's opaque, soapy water. I lay back and wallowed. Archer poured some very smelly salts on to my stomach. One crystal stuck in my navel and tickled and grated against me.

"This whiff ought to cover up all remaining traces of me!" Archer laughed.

"What's the smell supposed to be?" I asked, brushing the crystals off my stomach into the water and playing with the one that lodged so snugly in my navel.

"Russian pine," said Archer, shutting his eyes ecstatically and making in-breathing dreamy noises. He rubbed himself roughly with the towel and made his hair stand up on end.

I wanted to soak in the bath for hours, but it was already getting late, and so I had to hurry.

Archer saw what difficulty I had in tying my tie. He came up to me and said, "Let me do it." I turned around relieved, but slightly ashamed of being incompetent.

I kept very still, and he tied it tightly and rapidly with his ham-like hands. He gave the bows a little expert jerk and pat. His eyes had a very concentrated, almost crossed, look, and I felt him breathing down on my face. All down the front our bodies touched featherily; little points of warmth came together. The hard-boiled shirts were like slightly warmed dinner plates.

When I had brushed my hair, we left the chalet and began to walk up the path to the hotel. The beaten snow was so slippery, now that we were shod only in patent-leather slippers, that we kept sliding backward. I threw out my arms, laughing, and shouting to Archer to rescue me; then, when he grabbed me and started to haul me to him, he, too, would begin to slip. It was a still, Prussian-blue night with rather weak stars. Our laughter seemed to ring across the valley, to hit the mountains, and then to travel on and on and on.

We reached the hotel a little the worse for wear. The soles of my patent-leather shoes had become soaked, and there was snow on my trousers. Through bending forward, the studs in Archer's shirt had burst undone, and the slab of hair hung over one of his eyes as I had noticed before. We went into the cloakroom to readjust ourselves; then we entered the dining room.

"Come and sit at my table," Archer said; then he added:

"No, we'll sit at yours, as there are two places there already."

We sat down and began to eat Roman *gnocchi*. (The proprietor of the hotel was Italian-Swiss.) I did not like mine very much and was glad when I could go on to *œufs au beurre noir*. Now that my brother was away I could pick and choose in this way, leaving out the meat course, if I chose to, without causing any comment.

Archer drank Pilsner and suggested that I should, too. Not wanting to disagree with him, I nodded my head, although I hated the pale, yellow, bitter water.

After the meal Archer ordered me *créme de menthe* with my coffee; I had seen a near-by lady drinking this pretty liquid and asked him about it. To be ordered a liqueur in all seriousness was a thrilling moment for me. I sipped the fumy peppermint, which left such an artificial heat in my throat and chest, and thought that apart from my mother who was dead, I had never liked anyone so much as I liked Archer. He didn't try to interfere with me at all. He just took me as I was and yet seemed to like me.

Archer was now smoking a proper cigar, not the leaf-rolled cigarettes we had had at lunchtime. He offered me one, too, but I had the sense to realize that he did not mean me to take one and smoke it there before the eyes of all the hotel. I knew also that it would have made me sick, for my father had given me a cigar when I was eleven, in an attempt to put me off smoking forever.

I always associated cigars with middle-aged men, and I watched Archer interestedly, thinking how funny the stiff fat thing looked sticking out of his young mouth.

We were sitting on the uncurtained sun terrace, looking out on to the snow in the night; the moon was just beginning to rise. It made the snow glitter suddenly, like fish scales. Behind us people were dancing in the salon and adjoining rooms. The music came to us in angry snatches, some notes distorted, others quite obliterated. Archer did not seem to want to dance. He seemed content to sit with me in silence.

Near me on a what-not stand stood a high-heeled slipper made of china. I took it down and slipped my hand into it. How hideously ugly the china pompons were down the front! The painted centipede climbing up the red heel wore a knowing, human expression. I moved my fingers in the china shoe, pretending they were toes.

"I love monstrosities, too," said Archer, as I put the shoe back beside the fern in its crinkly paper-covered pot.

Later we wandered to the buffet bar and stood there drinking many glasses of the *limonade,* which was made with white wine. I took the tinkly pieces of ice into my mouth and sucked them, trying to cool myself a little. Blood seemed to rise in my face; my head buzzed.

Suddenly I felt full of *limonade* and lager. I left Archer to go to the cloakroom, but he followed and stood beside me in the next china niche, while the water flushed and gushed importantly in the polished copper tubes, and an interesting, curious smell came from the wire basket which held some strange disinfectant crystals. Archer stood so quietly and guardingly beside me there that I had to say:

"Do I look queer?"

"No, you don't look queer; you look nice," he said simply.

A rush of surprise and pleasure made me hotter still. We clanked over the tiles and left the cloakroom.

In the hall, I remembered that I had left all my skiing clothes at the chalet. "I shall need them in the morning," I said to Archer.

"Let's go down there now, then I can make cocoa on my spirit lamp, and you can bring the clothes back with you."

We set out in the moonlight; Archer soon took my arm, for he saw that I was drunk, and the path was more slippery than ever. Archer sang *Stille Nacht* in German, and I began to cry. I could not stop myself. It was such a delight to cry in the moonlight with Archer singing my favorite song; and William far away up the mountain.

Suddenly we both sat down on our behinds with a thump. There was a jarring pain at the bottom of my spine, but I began to laugh wildly; so did Archer. We lay there laughing, the snow melting under us and soaking through the seats of our trousers and the shoulders of our jackets.

Archer pulled me to my feet and dusted me off with hard slaps. My teeth grated together each time he slapped me. He saw that I was becoming more and more drunk in the freezing air. He propelled me along to the chalet, more or less frog-marching me in an expert fashion. I was quite content to leave myself in his hands.

When he got me upstairs, he put me into one of the bunks and told me to rest. The feathers ballooned out round me. I sank down deliciously. I felt as if I were floating down some magic staircase forever.

Archer got his little meta stove out and made coffee—not cocoa as he had said. He brought me over a strong cup and held it to my lips. I drank it unthinkingly and not tasting it, doing it only because he told me to.

When he took the cup away, my head fell back on the pillow, and I felt myself sinking and floating away again. I was on skis this time, but they were liquid skis, made of melted glass, and the snow was glass, too, but a sort of glass that was springy, like gelatine, and flowing like water.

I felt a change in the light, and knew that Archer was bending over me. Very quietly he took off my shoes, undid my tie, loosened the collar and unbuttoned my braces in front. I remembered thinking, before I finally fell asleep, how clever he was to know about undoing the braces; they had begun to feel so tight pulling down on my shoulders and dragging the trousers up between my legs. Archer covered me with several blankets and another quilt.

When I woke in the morning, Archer was already up. He had made me some tea and had put it on the stove to keep warm. He brought it over to me and I sat up. I felt ill, rather sick. I remembered what a glorious day yesterday had been, and thought how extraordinary it was that I had not slept in my own bed at the hotel, but in Archer's room, in my clothes.

I looked at him shamefacedly. "What happened last night? I felt peculiar," I said.

"The lager and the lemonade and the *créme de menthe* made you a bit tight, I'm afraid," Archer said, laughing.

"Do you feel better now? We'll go up to the hotel and have breakfast soon."

I got up and washed and changed into my skiing clothes. I still felt rather sick. I made my evening clothes into a neat bundle and tied them on to my toboggan. I had the sweets Archer had given me in my pocket.

We went up to the hotel, dragging the toboggan behind us.

And there on the doorstep we met William with one of the guides. They had had to return early, because someone in the party had broken a ski.

William was in a temper. He looked at us and then said to me, "What have you been doing?"

I was at a loss to know what to answer. The very sight of William had so troubled me that this added difficulty of explaining my actions was too much for me.

I looked at him miserably and mouthed something about going in to have breakfast.

William turned to Archer fiercely, but said nothing.

Archer explained, "Your brother's just been down to my place. We went skiing together yesterday and he left some clothes at the chalet."

"It's very early," was all William said; then he swept me on into the hotel before him, without another word to the guide or to Archer.

He went up to my room with me and saw that the bed had not been slept in.

I said clumsily, "The maid must have been in and done my room early." I could not bear to explain to William about my wonderful day, or why I had slept at the chalet.

William was so furious that he took no more notice of my weak explanations and lies.

When I suddenly said in desperation, "I feel sick," he seized me, took me to the basin, forced his fingers down my throat and struck me on the back till a yellow cascade of vomit gushed out of my mouth. My eyes were filled with stinging water; I was trembling. I ran the water in the basin madly, to wash away this sign of shame.

Gradually I grew a little more composed. I felt better, after being sick, and William had stopped swearing at me. I filled the basin with freezing water and dipped my face into it. The icy feel seemed to bite round my eye sockets and make the flesh round my nose firm again. I waited, holding my breath for as long as possible.

Suddenly my head was pushed down and held. I felt William's hard fingers digging into my neck. He was hitting me now with a slipper, beating my buttocks and my back with slashing strokes, hitting a different place each time, as he had been taught as a prefect at school, so that the flesh should not be numbed from a previous blow.

I felt that I was going to choke. I could not breathe under the water, and realized that I would die. I was seized with such a panic that I wrenched myself free from William and darted round the room, with him after me. Water dripped on the bed, the carpet, the chest of drawers. Splashes of it spat against the mirror in the wardrobe door. William aimed vicious blows at me until he had driven me into a corner. There he beat against my up-lifted arms, yelling in a hoarse, mad, religious voice, "Bastard, Devil, Harlot, Sod!"

As I cowered under his blows, I remember thinking that my brother had suddenly become a lunatic and was talking gibberish in his madness, for, of the words he was using, I had not heard any before, except "Devil."

MORE ABOUT THIS STORY

In his studies of adolescence, Harry Stack Sullivan persistently argues that the most profound attachments of earliest adolescence are between "chums" (as he calls them) of the same sex. Often their feelings may be erotic and their play overtly sexual, but unless an outsider insists upon labelling their shared experience aberrant, their homophilic love should ultimately enrich rather than impoverish their heterosexual love adjustments of the future. The trap, of course, lies just below the surface: *unless* the outsider marks them "queer." In a culture anxious and guilt-ridden about sexuality, *unless* frequently becomes *when*—with disastrous results.

Since "When I Was Thirteen" presents such a problem, the reader should consider the following questions:

1. To what extent do you share William's antagonism toward Archer and sympathize with his violent reaction to his younger brother's contact with him?
2. How do you think the narrator will ultimately recall his experience with Archer—with delight, shame, gratitude, anger? Why?
3. How specific are the physical suggestions of homosexuality in the relation-

ship between the narrator and Archer? What do the narrator's responses to various sensory and sexual stimuli lead you to predict about his chances for heterosexual adjustment? Can such a prediction be based solely on such response? If not, what other influences must be considered?

4. What relevance do you find in the narrator's reading Tolstoi's *Resurrection,* in his interest in the words "illegitimate child," and in the orchestra's playing "The Birth of the Blues"?

5. What parallels do you find between the roles assigned to Tom Means in Anderson's "The Man Who Became a Woman" and Archer?

6. As in Anderson's story, the narrative point of view is that of the hero, apparently now a mature man. What is gained or lost by this perspective in time? Does it, for example, intensify or diminish the immediacy of the experience?

FOR FURTHER READING

Friedenberg, Edgar Z. *The Vanishing Adolescent.* New York: Dell and Co., 1962, pp. 39–70.

Sullivan, Harry Stack. *The Interpersonal Theory of Psychiatry.* New York: W. W. Norton, 1953, pp. 245–262.

See also the bibliography listed for Sherwood Anderson's "The Man Who Became a Woman."

The Conversion of the Jews

BY PHILIP ROTH (1933-   )

For the past fifteen years Jewish writers have nearly dominated the American literary scene. A roster of American Jewish critics, for example, includes some of the most discriminating and provocative minds of our time: Lionel Trilling, Alfred Kazin, Irving Howe, Leslie Fiedler, and Norman Podhoretz, to name but a few. Among the novelists, Saul Bellow, Norman Mailer, J. D. Salinger, Bernard Malamud, and Philip Roth head a long and distinguished list. Although no simple explanation of this literary renaissance deserves credence, certain facts cannot be ignored. Historically a "chosen" as well as a persecuted people, Jews have mingled a stubborn pride and faith with an equally stubborn determination to survive. For centuries, the acute demands of survival took precedence over artistic creativity. But more recently—especially in America, where opportunities, despite undeniable obstacles, have been economically, socially, and educationally richer than abroad—the Jewish writer has encountered an audience increasingly receptive to his voice. More important, he has become increasingly eager to communicate with the Gentile world.

In the broadest sense, these writers are American, not Jewish writers. As Stanley Kauffman has observed, "there are certain root congruencies between Jewish and American ideas: the Chosen Land or People, the concern with social justice, and the fundamental belief . . . that the son must be 'better' than the father—in education and status." What usually makes these writers recognizably and definably Jewish as well, however, is their indestructible link with a unique heritage of pathos and humor, suffering and compassion, and a restless, penetrating moral awareness. Whether they affirm or deny their heritage, they seem inevitably to

212

react to it more vigorously than non-Jews. In this heritage, Irving Howe writes, they have shaped the great themes of Yiddish literature: "The virtue of powerlessness, the power of helplessness, the company of the dispossessed, the sanctity of the insulted and injured."

To these themes Philip Roth, a New Jersey-born graduate of Bucknell and the University of Chicago, brings a skeptical intelligence, a shrewd wit, a keen eye for episode, and an alert ear for dialogue. Roth won the National Book Award in 1960 for *Goodbye, Columbus,* a collection of stories which contains "The Conversion of the Jews," and in 1962, his long first novel, *Letting Go,* roused considerable discussion. In "Jewishness and the Younger Intellectuals," written for a symposium in *Commentary* (April, 1961), Roth disassociated himself from belief in the binding force of Jewish tradition: ". . . where the Jewish past has informed my spirit and imagination, so too has the political and cultural past of America, and the literary past of England. Neither reverence toward the tradition, nor reverent feeling about the Jewish past seem to me sufficient to bind American Jews together today."

Because the historical past that united Jews against a common enemy is *past,* Roth argues, proclaiming one's identity as a Jew today in America serves little purpose. Nor can Roth settle comfortably into a religious compact with his ancestors, for though he shares their rejection of the Christian notion of a Savior, he cannot yet accept the God of Abraham, Isaac, and Jacob. The query to other Jews with which Roth ends his statement may serve any reader as he begins "The Conversion of the Jews": "How are you connected to me as another man is not?"

Technically, "The Conversion of the Jews" is scrupulously wrought, the structural pattern clear and logical, the language accurate and evocative. But though the conflicts are sharply and precisely etched, the reader should carefully consider whether the characters who present them are fleshed out to reality or serve merely as bloodlessly embodied communicants of ideas.

THE STORY

"You're a real one for opening your mouth in the first place," Itzie said. "What do you open your mouth all the time for?"

"I didn't bring it up, Itz, I didn't," Ozzie said.

"What do you care about Jesus Christ for anyway?"

"I didn't bring up Jesus Christ. He did. I didn't even know what he was talking about. Jesus is historical, he kept saying. Jesus is historical." Ozzie mimicked the monumental voice of Rabbi Binder.

"Jesus was a person that lived like you and me," Ozzie continued. "That's what Binder said—"

"Yeah? . . . So what! What do I give two cents whether he lived or not.

And what do you gotta open your mouth!" Itzie Lieberman favored closed-mouthedness, especially when it came to Ozzie Freedman's questions. Mrs. Freedman had to see Rabbi Binder twice before about Ozzie's questions and this Wednesday at four-thirty would be the third time. Itzie preferred to keep *his* mother in the kitchen; he settled for behind-the-back subtleties such as gestures, faces, snarls and other less delicate barnyard noises.

"He was a real person, Jesus, but he wasn't like God, and we don't believe he is God." Slowly, Ozzie was explaining Rabbi Binder's position to Itzie, who had been absent from Hebrew School the previous afternoon.

"The Catholics," Itzie said helpfully, "they believe in Jesus Christ, that he's God." Itzie Lieberman used "the Catholics" in its broadest sense—to include the Protestants.

Ozzie received Itzie's remark with a tiny head bob, as though it were a footnote, and went on. "His mother was Mary, and his father probably was Joseph," Ozzie said. "But the New Testament says his real father was God."

"His *real* father?"

"Yeah," Ozzie said, "that's the big thing, his father's supposed to be God."

"Bull."

"That's what Rabbi Binder says, that it's impossible—"

"Sure it's impossible. That stuff's all bull. To have a baby you gotta get laid," Itzie theologized. "Mary hadda get laid."

"That's what Binder says: 'The only way a woman can have a baby is to have intercourse with a man.'"

"He said *that*, Ozz?" For a moment it appeared that Itzie had put the theological question aside. "He said that, intercourse?" A little curled smile shaped itself in the lower half of Itzie's face like a pink mustache. "What you guys do, Ozz, you laugh or something?"

"I raised my hand."

"Yeah? Whatja say?"

"That's when I asked the question."

Itzie's face lit up. "Whatja ask about—intercourse?"

"No, I asked the question about God, how if He could create the heaven and earth in six days, and make all the animals and the fish and the light in six days—the light especially, that's what always gets me, that He could make the light. Making fish and animals, that's pretty good—"

"That's damn good." Itzie's appreciation was honest but unimaginative: it was as though God had just pitched a one-hitter.

"But making light . . . I mean when you think about it, it's really something," Ozzie said. "Anyway, I asked Binder if He could make all that in six days, and He could *pick* the six days he wanted right out of nowhere, why couldn't He let a woman have a baby without having intercourse."

"You said intercourse, Ozz, to Binder?"

"Yeah."

"Right in class?"

"Yeah."

Itzie smacked the side of his head.

"I mean, no kidding around," Ozzie said, "that'd really be nothing. After all that other stuff, that'd practically be nothing."

Itzie considered a moment. "What'd Binder say?"

"He started all over again explaining how Jesus was historical and how he lived like you and me but he wasn't God. So I said I under*stood* that. What I wanted to know was different."

What Ozzie wanted to know was always different. The first time he had wanted to know how Rabbi Binder could call the Jews "The Chosen People" if the Declaration of Independence claimed all men to be created equal. Rabbi Binder tried to distinguish for him between political equality and spiritual legitimacy, but what Ozzie wanted to know, he insisted vehemently, was different. That was the first time his mother had to come.

Then there was the plane crash. Fifty-eight people had been killed in a plane crash at La Guardia. In studying a casualty list in the newspaper his mother had discovered among the list of those dead eight Jewish names (his grandmother had nine but she counted Miller as a Jewish name); because of the eight she said the plane crash was "a tragedy." During free-discussion time on Wednesday Ozzie had brought to Rabbi Binder's attention this matter of "some of his relations" always picking out the Jewish names. Rabbi Binder had begun to explain cultural unity and some other things when Ozzie stood up at his seat and said that what he wanted to know was different. Rabbi Binder insisted that he sit down and it was then that Ozzie shouted that he wished all fifty-eight were Jews. That was the second time his mother came.

"And he kept explaining about Jesus being historical, and so I kept asking him. No kidding, Itz, he was trying to make me look stupid."

"So what he finally do?"

"Finally he starts screaming that I was deliberately simple-minded and a wise guy, and that my mother had to come, and this was the last time. And that I'd never get bar-mitzvahed if he could help it. Then, Itz, then he starts talking in that voice like a statue, real slow and deep, and he says that I better think over what I said about the Lord. He told me to go to his office and think it over." Ozzie leaned his body towards Itzie. "Itz, I thought it over for a solid hour, and now I'm convinced God could do it."

Ozzie had planned to confess his latest transgression to his mother as soon as she came home from work. But it was a Friday night in November and already dark, and when Mrs. Freedman came through the door she tossed off her coat, kissed Ozzie quickly on the face, and went to the kitchen table to light the three yellow candles, two for the Sabbath and one for Ozzie's father.

When his mother lit the candles she would move her two arms slowly towards her, dragging them through the air, as though persuading people whose minds were half made up. And her eyes would get glassy with tears. Even when his father was alive Ozzie remembered that her eyes had gotten glassy, so it didn't have anything to do with his dying. It had something to do with lighting the candles.

As she touched the flaming match to the unlit wick of a Sabbath candle, the phone rang, and Ozzie, standing only a foot from it, plucked off the receiver and held it muffled to his chest. When his mother lit candles Ozzie felt there should be no noise; even breathing, if you could manage it, should be softened. Ozzie pressed the phone to his breast and watched his mother dragging whatever she was dragging, and he felt his own eyes get glassy. His mother was a round, tired, gray-haired penguin of a woman whose gray skin had begun to feel the tug of gravity and the weight of her own history. Even when she was dressed up she didn't look like a chosen person. But when she lit candles she looked like something better; like a woman who knew momentarily that God could do anything.

After a few mysterious minutes she was finished. Ozzie hung up the phone and walked to the kitchen table where she was beginning to lay the two places for the four-course Sabbath meal. He told her that she would have to see Rabbi Binder next Wednesday at four-thirty, and then he told her why. For the first time in their life together she hit Ozzie across the face with her hand.

All through the chopped liver and chicken soup part of the dinner Ozzie cried; he didn't have any appetite for the rest.

On Wednesday, in the largest of the three basement classrooms of the synagogue, Rabbi Marvin Binder, a tall, handsome, broad-shouldered man of thirty with thick strong-fibered black hair, removed his watch from his pocket and saw that it was four o'clock. At the rear of the room Yakov Blotnik; the seventy-one-year-old custodian, slowly polished the large window, mumbling to himself, unaware that it was four o'clock or six o'clock, Monday or Wednesday. To most of the students Yakov Blotnik's mumbling, along with his brown curly beard, scythe nose, and two heel-trailing black cats, made of him an object of wonder, a foreigner, a relic, towards whom they were alternately fearful and disrespectful. To Ozzie the mumbling had always seemed a monotonous, curious prayer; what made it curious was that old Blotnik had been mumbling so steadily for so many years, Ozzie suspected he had memorized the prayers and forgotten all about God.

"It is now free-discussion time," Rabbi Binder said. "Feel free to talk about any Jewish matter at all—religion, family, politics, sports—"

There was silence. It was a gusty, clouded November afternoon and it did not seem as though there ever was or could be a thing called baseball. So nobody this week said a word about that hero from the past, Hank Greenberg—which limited free discussion considerably.

And the soul-battering Ozzie Freedman had just received from Rabbi Binder had imposed its limitation. When it was Ozzie's turn to read aloud from the Hebrew book the rabbi had asked him petulantly why he didn't read more rapidly. He was showing no progress. Ozzie said he could read faster but that if he did he was sure not to understand what he was reading. Nevertheless, at the rabbi's repeated suggestion Ozzie tried, and showed a great talent, but in the midst of a long passage he stopped short and said he didn't understand a word he was reading, and started in again at a drag-footed pace. Then came the soul-battering.

Consequently when free-discussion time rolled around none of the students felt too free. The rabbi's invitation was answered only by the mumbling of feeble old Blotnik.

"Isn't there anything at all you would like to discuss?" Rabbi Binder asked again, looking at his watch. "No questions or comments?"

There was a small grumble from the third row. The rabbi requested that Ozzie rise and give the rest of the class the advantage of his thought.

Ozzie rose. "I forget it now," he said, and sat down in his place.

Rabbi Binder advanced a seat towards Ozzie and poised himself on the edge of the desk. It was Itzie's desk and the rabbi's frame only a dagger's-length away from his face snapped him to sitting attention.

"Stand up again, Oscar," Rabbi Binder said calmly, "and try to assemble your thoughts."

Ozzie stood up. All his classmates turned in their seats and watched as he gave an unconvincing scratch to his forehead.

"I can't assemble any," he announced, and plunked himself down.

"Stand up!" Rabbi Binder advanced from Itzie's desk to the one directly in front of Ozzie; when the rabbinical back was turned Itzie gave it five-fingers off the tip of his nose, causing a small titter in the room. Rabbi Binder was too absorbed in squelching Ozzie's nonsense once and for all to bother with titters. "Stand up, Oscar. What's your question about?"

Ozzie pulled a word out of the air. It was the handiest word. "Religion."

"Oh, now you remember?"

"Yes."

"What is it?"

Trapped, Ozzie blurted the first thing that came to him. "Why can't He make anything He wants to make!"

As Rabbi Binder prepared an answer, a final answer, Itzie, ten feet behind him, raised one finger on his left hand, gestured it meaningfully towards the rabbi's back, and brought the house down.

Binder twisted quickly to see what had happened and in the midst of the commotion Ozzie shouted into the rabbi's back what he couldn't have shouted to his face. It was a loud, toneless sound that had the timbre of something stored inside for about six days.

"You don't know! You don't know anything about God!"

The rabbi spun back towards Ozzie. "What?"

"You don't know—you don't—"

"Apologize, Oscar, apologize!" It was a threat.

"You don't—"

Rabbi Binder's hand flicked out at Ozzie's cheek. Perhaps it had only been meant to clamp the boy's mouth shut, but Ozzie ducked and the palm caught him squarely on the nose.

The blood came in a short, red spurt on to Ozzie's shirt front.

The next moment was all confusion. Ozzie screamed, "You bastard, you bastard!" and broke for the classroom door. Rabbi Binder lurched a step backwards, as though his own blood had started flowing violently in the opposite direction, then gave a clumsy lurch forward and bolted out the door after Ozzie. The class followed after the rabbi's huge blue-suited back, and before old Blotnik could turn from his window, the room was empty and everyone was headed full speed up the three flights leading to the roof.

If one should compare the light of day to the life of man: sunrise to birth; sunset—the dropping down over the edge—to death; then as Ozzie Freedman wiggled through the trapdoor of the synagogue roof, his feet kicking backwards bronco-style at Rabbi Binder's outstretched arms—at that moment the day was fifty years old. As a rule, fifty or fifty-five reflects accurately the age of late afternoons in November, for it is in that month, during those hours, that one's awareness of light seems no longer a matter of seeing, but of hearing: light begins clicking away. In fact, as Ozzie locked shut the trapdoor in the rabbi's face, the sharp click of the bolt into the lock might momentarily have been mistaken for the sound of the heavier gray that had just throbbed through the sky.

With all his weight Ozzie kneeled on the locked door; any instant he was certain that Rabbi Binder's shoulder would fling it open, splintering the wood into shrapnel and catapulting his body into the sky. But the door did not move and below him he heard only the rumble of feet, first loud then dim, like thunder rolling away.

A question shot through his brain. "Can this be me?" For a thirteen-year-old who had just labeled his religious leader a bastard, twice, it was not an improper question. Louder and louder the question came to him—"Is it me? Is it me?"—until he discovered himself no longer kneeling, but racing crazily toward the edge of the roof, his eyes crying, his throat screaming, and his arms flying everywhichway as though not his own.

"Is it me? Is it me ME ME ME ME! It has to be me—but is it!"

It is the question a thief must ask himself the night he jimmies open his first window, and it is said to be the question with which bridegrooms quiz themselves before the altar.

In the few wild seconds it took Ozzie's body to propel him to the edge of the roof, his self-examination began to grow fuzzy. Gazing down at the street he became confused as to the problem beneath the question: was it, is-it-me-who-called-Binder-a-Bastard? or, is-it-me-prancing-around-on-the-roof? However, the scene below settled all, for there is an instant in any action when whether it is you or somebody else is academic. The thief crams the money in his pockets and scoots out the window. The bridegroom signs the hotel register for two. And the boy on the roof finds a streetful of people gaping at him, necks stretched backwards, faces up, as though he were the ceiling of the Hayden Planetarium. Suddenly you know it's you.

"Oscar! Oscar Freedman!" A voice rose from the center of the crowd, a voice that, could it have been seen, would have looked like the writing on a scroll. "Oscar Freedman, get down from there. Immediately!" Rabbi Binder was pointing one arm stiffly up at him; and at the end of that arm, one finger aimed menacingly. It was the attitude of a dictator, but one—the eyes confessed all—whose personal valet had spit neatly in his face.

Ozzie didn't answer. Only for a blink's length did he look towards Rabbi Binder. Instead his eyes began to fit together the world beneath him, to sort out people from places, friends from enemies, participants from spectators. In little jagged starlike clusters his friends stood around Rabbi Binder, who was still pointing. The topmost point on a star compounded not of angels but of five adolescent boys was Itzie. What a world it was, with those stars below, Rabbi Binder below . . . Ozzie, who a moment earlier hadn't been able to control his own body, started to feel the meaning of the word control: he felt Peace and he felt Power.

"Oscar Freedman, I'll give you three to come down."

Few dictators give their subjects three to do anything; but as always, Rabbi Binder only looked dictatorial.

"Are you ready, Oscar?"

Ozzie nodded his head yes, although he had no intention in the world—the lower one of the celestial one he'd just entered—of coming down even if Rabbi Binder should give him a million.

"All right then," said Rabbi Binder. He ran a hand through his black Samson hair as though it were the gesture prescribed for uttering the first digit. Then, with his other hand cutting a circle out of the small piece of sky around him, he spoke. "One!"

There was no thunder. On the contrary, at that moment, as though "one" was the cue for which he had been waiting, the world's least thunderous person appeared on the synagogue steps. He did not so much come out the synagogue door as lean out, onto the darkening air. He clutched at the door-knob with one hand and looked up at the roof.

"Oy!"

Yakov Blotnik's old mind hobbled slowly, as if on crutches, and though he couldn't decide precisely what the boy was doing on the roof, he knew it wasn't good—that is, it wasn't-good-for-the-Jews. For Yakov Blotnik life had fractionated itself simply: things were either good-for-the-Jews or no-good-for-the-Jews.

He smacked his free hand to his in-sucked cheek, gently. "Oy, Gut!" And then quickly as he was able, he jacked down his head and surveyed the street. There was Rabbi Binder (like a man at an auction with only three dollars in his pocket, he had just delivered a shaky "Two!"); there were the students, and that was all. So far it-wasn't-so-bad-for-the-Jews. But the boy had to come down immediately, before anybody saw. The problem: how to get the boy off the roof?

Anybody who has ever had a cat on the roof knows how to get him down. You call the fire department. Or first you call the operator and you ask her for the fire department. And the next thing there is great jamming of brakes and clanging of bells and shouting of instructions. And then the cat is off the roof. You do the same thing to get a boy off the roof.

That is, you do the same thing if you are Yakov.Blotnik and you once had a cat on the roof.

When the engines, all four of them, arrived, Rabbi Binder had four times given Ozzie the count of three. The big hook-and-ladder swung around the corner and one of the firemen leaped from it, plunging headlong towards the yellow fire hydrant in front of the synagogue. With a huge wrench he began to unscrew the top nozzle. Rabbi Binder raced over to him and pulled at his shoulder.

"There's no fire . . ."

The fireman mumbled back over his shoulder and, heatedly, continued working at the nozzle.

"But there's no fire, there's no fire . . ." Binder shouted. When the fireman mumbled again, the rabbi grasped his face with both his hands and pointed it up at the roof.

To Ozzie it looked as though Rabbi Binder was trying to tug the fireman's head out of his body, like a cork from a bottle. He had to giggle at the picture they made: it was a family portrait—rabbi in black skullcap, fireman in red fire hat, and the little yellow hydrant squatting beside like a kid brother, bare-headed. From the edge of the roof Ozzie waved at the portrait, a one-handed, flapping, mocking wave; in doing it his right foot slipped from under him. Rabbi Binder covered his eyes with his hands.

Firemen work fast. Before Ozzie had even regained his balance, a big, round, yellowed net was being held on the synagogue lawn. The firemen who held it looked up at Ozzie with stern, feelingless faces.

One of the firemen turned his head towards Rabbi Binder. "What, is the kid nuts or something?"

Rabbi Binder unpeeled his hands from his eyes, slowly, painfully, as if they were tape. Then he checked: nothing on the sidewalk, no dents in the net.

"Is he gonna jump, or what?" the fireman shouted.

In a voice not at all like a statue, Rabbi Binder finally answered. "Yes, Yes, I think so . . . He's been threatening to . . ."

Threatening to? Why, the reason he was on the roof, Ozzie remembered, was to get away; he hadn't even thought about jumping. He had just run to get away, and the truth was that he hadn't really headed for the roof as much as he'd been chased there.

"What's his name, the kid?"

"Freedman," Rabbi Binder answered. "Oscar Freedman."

The fireman looked up at Ozzie. "What is it with you, Oscar? You gonna jump, or what?"

Ozzie did not answer. Frankly, the question had just arisen.

"Look, Oscar, if you're gonna jump, jump—and if you're not gonna jump, don't jump. But don't waste our time, willya?"

Ozzie looked at the fireman and then at Rabbi Binder. He wanted to see Rabbi Binder cover his eyes one more time.

"I'm going to jump."

And then he scampered around the edge of the roof to the corner, where there was no net below, and he flapped his arms at his sides, swishing the air and smacking his palms to his trousers on the downbeat. He began screaming like some kind of engine, "Wheeeee . . . wheeeee," and leaning way out over the edge with the upper half of his body. The firemen whipped around to cover the ground with the net. Rabbi Binder mumbled a few words to Somebody and covered his eyes. Everything happened quickly, jerkily, as in a silent movie. The crowd, which had arrived with the fire engines, gave out a long, Fourth-of-July fireworks oooh-aahhh. In the excitement no one had paid the crowd much heed, except, of course, Yakov Blotnik, who swung from the doorknob counting heads. "Fier und tsvantsik . . . finf und tsvantsik . . . Oy, Gut!" It wasn't like this with the cat.

Rabbi Binder peeked through his fingers, checked the sidewalk and net. Empty. But there was Ozzie racing to the other corner. The firemen raced with him but were unable to keep up. Whenever Oscar wanted to he might jump and splatter himself upon the sidewalk, and by the time the firemen scooted to the spot all they could do with their net would be to cover the mess.

"Wheeeee . . . wheeeee . . ."

"Hey, Oscar," the winded fireman yelled, "What the hell is this, a game or something?"

"Wheeeee . . . wheeeee . . ."

"Hey, Oscar—"

But he was off now to the other corner, flapping his wings fiercely. Rabbi Binder couldn't take it any longer—the fire engines from nowhere, the screaming suicidal boy, the net. He fell to his knees, exhausted, and with his hands curled together in front of his chest like a little dome, he pleaded, "Oscar, stop it, Oscar. Don't jump, Oscar. Please come down . . . Please don't jump."

And further back in the crowd a single voice, a single young voice, shouted a lone word to the boy on the roof.

"Jump!"

It was Itzie. Ozzie momentarily stopped flapping.

"Go ahead, Ozz—jump!" Itzie broke off his point of the star and courageously, with the inspiration not of a wise-guy but of a disciple, stood alone. "Jump, Ozz, jump!"

Still on his knees, his hands still curled, Rabbi Binder twisted his body back. He looked at Itzie, then, agonizingly, back to Ozzie.

"OSCAR, DON'T JUMP! PLEASE, DON'T JUMP . . . please please . . ."

"Jump!" This time it wasn't Itzie but another point of the star. By the time Mrs. Freedman arrived to keep her four-thirty appointment with Rabbi Binder, the whole little upside down heaven was shouting and pleading for Ozzie to jump, and Rabbi Binder no longer was pleading with him not to jump, but was crying into the dome of his hands.

Understandably Mrs. Freedman couldn't figure out what her son was doing on the roof. So she asked.

"Ozzie, my Ozzie, what are you doing? My Ozzie, what is it?"

Ozzie stopped wheeeeeing and slowed his arms down to a cruising flap, the kind birds use in soft winds, but he did not answer. He stood against the low, clouded, darkening sky—light clicked down swiftly now, as on a small gear—flapping softly and gazing down at the small bundle of a woman who was his mother.

"What are you doing, Ozzie?" She turned towards the kneeling Rabbi Binder and rushed so close that only a paper-thickness of dusk lay between her stomach and his shoulders.

"What is my baby doing?"

Rabbi Binder gaped up at her but he too was mute. All that moved was the dome of his hands; it shook back and forth like a weak pulse.

"Rabbi, get him down! He'll kill himself. Get him down, my only baby . . ."

"I can't," Rabbi Binder said, "I can't . . ." and he turned his handsome head towards the crowd of boys behind him. "It's them. Listen to them."

And for the first time Mrs. Freedman saw the crowd of boys, and she heard what they were yelling.

"He's doing it for them. He won't listen to me. It's them." Rabbi Binder spoke like one in a trance.

"For them?"

"Yes."

"Why for them?"

"They want him to . . ."

Mrs. Freedman raised her two arms upward as though she were conducting the sky. "For them he's doing it!" And then in a gesture older than pyramids, older than prophets and floods, her arms came slapping down to her sides. "A martyr I have. Look!" She tilted her head to the roof. Ozzie was still flapping softly. "My martyr."

"Oscar, come down, *please*," Rabbi Binder groaned.

In a startlingly even voice Mrs. Freedman called to the boy on the roof. "Ozzie, come down, Ozzie. Don't be a martyr, my baby."

As though it were a litany, Rabbi Binder repeated her words. "Don't be a martyr, my baby. Don't be a martyr."

"Gawhead, Ozz—*be* a Martin!" It was Itzie. "Be a Martin, be a Martin," and all the voices joined in singing for Martindom, whatever *it* was. "Be a Martin, be a Martin . . ."

Somehow when you're on a roof the darker it gets the less you can hear. All Ozzie knew was that two groups wanted two new things: his friends were spirited and musical about what they wanted; his mother and the rabbi were even-toned, chanting, about what they didn't want. The rabbi's voice was without tears now and so was his mother's.

The big net stared up at Ozzie like a sightless eye. The big, clouded sky pushed down. From beneath it looked like a gray corrugated board. Suddenly, looking up into that unsympathetic sky, Ozzie realized all the strangeness of what these people, his friends, were asking: they wanted him to jump, to kill himself; they were singing about it now—it made them that happy. And there was an even greater strangeness: Rabbi Binder was on his knees, trembling. If there was a question to be asked now it was not "Is it me?" but rather "Is it us? . . . Is it us?"

Being on the roof, it turned out, was a serious thing. If he jumped would the singing become dancing? Would it? What would jumping stop? Yearningly, Ozzie wished he could rip open the sky, plunge his hands through, and pull out the sun; and on the sun, like a coin, would be stamped JUMP or DON'T JUMP.

Ozzie's knees rocked and sagged a little under him as though they were setting him for a dive. His arms tightened, stiffened, froze, from shoulders to fingernails. He felt as if each part of his body were going to vote as to whether he should kill himself or not—and each part as though it were independent of *him*.

The light took an unexpected click down and the new darkness, like a gag, hushed the friends singing for this and the mother and rabbi chanting for that.

Ozzie stopped counting votes, and in a curiously high voice, like one who wasn't prepared for speech, he spoke.

"Mamma?"

"Yes, Oscar."

"Mamma, get down on your knees, like Rabbi Binder."

"Oscar—"

"Get down on your knees," he said, "or I'll jump."

Ozzie heard a whimper, then a quick rustling, and when he looked down where his mother had stood he saw the top of a head and beneath that a circle of dress. She was kneeling beside Rabbi Binder.

He spoke again. "Everybody kneel." There was the sound of everybody kneeling.

Ozzie looked around. With one hand he pointed towards the synagogue entrance. "Make *him* kneel."

There was a noise, not of kneeling, but of body-and-cloth stretching. Ozzie could hear Rabbi Binder saying in a gruff whisper, ". . . or he'll *kill* himself," and when next he looked there was Yakov Blotnik off the doornob and for the first time in his life upon his knees in the Gentile posture of prayer.

As for the firemen—it is not as difficult as one might imagine to hold a net taut while you are kneeling.

Ozzie looked around again; and then he called to Rabbi Binder.

"Rabbi?"

"Yes, Oscar."

"Rabbi Binder, do you believe in God."

"Yes."

"Do you believe God can do Anything?" Ozzie leaned his head out into the darkness. "Anything?"

"Oscar, I think—"

"Tell me you believe God can do Anything."

There was a second's hesitation. Then: "God can do Anything."

"Tell me you believe God can make a child without intercourse."

"He can."

"Tell me!"

"God," Rabbi Binder admitted, "can make a child without intercourse."

"Mamma, you tell me."

"God can make a child without intercourse," his mother said.

"Make *him* tell me." There was not doubt who *him* was.

In a few moments Ozzie heard an old comical voice say something to the increasing darkness about God.

Next, Ozzie made everybody say it. And then he made them all say they believed in Jesus Christ—first one at a time, then all together.

When the catechizing was through it was the beginning of evening. From the street it sounded as if the boy on the roof might have sighed.

"Ozzie?" A woman's voice dared to speak. "You'll come down now?"

There was no answer, but the woman waited, and when a voice finally did speak it was thin and crying, and exhausted as that of an old man who has just finished pulling the bells.

"Mamma, don't you see—you shouldn't hit me. He shouldn't hit me. You shouldn't hit me about God, Mamma. You should never hit anybody about God—"

"Ozzie, please come down now."

"Promise me, promise me you'll never hit anybody about God."

He had asked only his mother, but for some reason everyone kneeling in the street promised he would never hit anybody about God.

Once again there was silence.

"I can come down now Mamma," the boy on the roof finally said. He turned his head both ways as though checking the traffic lights. "Now I can come down . . ."

And he did, right into the center of the yellow net that glowed in the evening's edge like an overgrown halo.

MORE ABOUT THIS STORY

In *The Future of an Illusion,* Sigmund Freud argues that men invest God with the traits of the father: omnipotence, awesomeness, and protectiveness. Man's desire for God is at once identical with his "longing-for-the-father" and with his "need for protection against the consequences of human weakness." In an essay about Leonardo da Vinci, Freud makes explicit the Oedipal implications of religious belief: "Psychoanalysis has made us aware of the intimate connections between the father complex and the belief in God, and has taught us that the personal God is psychologically nothing other than a magnified father; it shows us every day how young people can lose their religious faith as soon as the father's authority collapses. We thus recognize the root of religious need as lying in the parental complex." [1]

Read in these terms, "The Conversion of the Jews" might be understood as the story of Ozzie's effort to retain faith in God as a symbol of his dead father's authority. Almost too neatly, the story fits the classical pattern that re-enacts the Oedipal syndrome. Helpless, emotionally yet too immature to stand alone, Ozzie nevertheless rebels—the family name is *Freed*man— against the tyranny of his surrogate father, Rabbi Binder (also appropriately named). Not only is the Rabbi dictatorial but he threatens Ozzie's love relationship with his mother, for Binder's complaints about the boy cause her to

[1] "Leonardo da Vinci and a Memory of His Childhood," in *Works* (Standard Edition) (London: Hogarth Press), p. 133. More readily available is the Modern Library paperback, where the translation of this passage by A. A. Brill (p. 98) differs slightly from that given above.

strike him for the first time. To overcome his trauma and to realize his aspiration of rapport with his mother and love for his father, Ozzie must transcend (destroy?) Rabbi Binder and create a new God-father possessed at once of Old Testament grandeur and New Testament love. The Christian thesis of the Virgin Birth enables him to defeat Rabbi Binder, restore faith in the omnipotent but also protective father, and assure his mother's virginity.

Freud's premise about religious experience has not, however, gone unchallenged. Gordon W. Allport, for example, in *Becoming*, writes that the "error of the psychoanalytic theory of religion . . . lies in locating religious belief in the defensive functions of the ego rather than in the core and center and substance of the developing ego itself." [2] Without denying the validity of the defensive function, Allport insists that religion affords too a "forward intention," enabling the individual to relate at each stage of his development to the totality of being. In *Insight and Responsibility*, Erik Erikson also acknowledges that while religion "exploits, for the sake of its own political establishment, the most infantile strivings of man," it serves a more rewarding purpose, "namely that of giving concerted expression to adult man's need to provide the young and the weak with a world-image sustaining hope." [3] But as Erikson observes in *The Challenge of Youth*, an understanding of psychosocial evolution is ill served by reducing motivation to clinical statement. *Fidelity*—Erikson's word for the "strength of disciplined devotion—emerges only after the adolescent has tested the validity of his inherited tradition: ". . . it is the young who carry in them the power to confirm those who confirm them, and joining the issues, to renew and to regenerate, or to reform and to rebel." [4]

Even more directly apposite to "The Conversion of the Jews" is Erich Fromm's distinction between authoritarian and humanistic religion. In *Psychoanalysis and Religion*, Fromm characterizes authoritarian religious experience as the "surrender to a power transcending man," a surrender embodying obedience as the cardinal virtue, disobedience as the cardinal sin. By acknowledging God's omnipotence and his own impotence, man "escapes from his feeling of aloneness and limitation," sacrificing his individuality in the process. Humanistic religion, on the other hand, centers upon man's awareness of his own powers of reason, and upon his potential for discovering through love his relationship to himself and to the world about him. "The prevailing mood is that of joy," Fromm writes of humanistic religion, "while the prevailing mood in authoritarian religion is that of sorrow and guilt. . . ." Both the humanistic and authoritarian struggle ceaselessly for supremacy in the traditional Judeo-Christian framework, and it is against this paralyzing impasse that Ozzie Freedman shouts his protest from the rooftop.

[2] (New Haven: Yale University Press, 1955), p. 96.
[3] (New York: W. W. Norton, 1964), p. 153.
[4] (New York: Anchor Books, 1965), pp. 22–23.

It is not God's creative omnipotence that Ozzie challenges. On the contrary, he demands an even greater outpouring of faith not only from Rabbi Binder, but also from Itzie Lieberman, Mrs. Freedman, Yakov Blotnik, and the firemen—each of them caught and trapped by an unquestioning "orthodoxy" that prevents them from truly knowing anything about God. Ozzie resents those who violate the "spiritual legitimacy" of the religious ideal, hate in the name of love, and tear man asunder from himself and his fellow man in the name of unity. Whereas the Freudian thesis derives from the premise of man's weakness and irrationality, Fromm's approach, like Erikson's, enables an interpretation that points to man's latent psychic strength through the power of reason. Thus, when Ozzie rebels against Binder's authoritarianism, he protests a brutish, irrational evasion of the profoundly "different" questions. Ozzie's purpose seems neither to undermine authority nor humanism, but rather to resolve the conflict between them through a willed gesture, an action sponsored by reason as well as by feeling.

Not yet thirteen, Ozzie has thrust upon him the responsibility of a far older person, that of a prophet charged with the conversion of the Jews. His leap into the symbolic yellow net that "glowed in the evening's edge like a halo" silently celebrates the manifold implications of that conversion. Not least among them is that Ozzie has become a man—before his *bar mitzvah*.

FOR FURTHER READING

Fiedler, Leslie. "Jewish Americans, Go Home!" *Waiting for the End*. New York: Stein and Day, 1964.

Malin, Irving. *Jews and Americans*. Carbondale: Southern Illinois University Press, 1965.

See also the textual references in the footnotes to Allport, Erikson, Freud, and Fromm.

In Dreams Begin Responsibilities

BY DELMORE SCHWARTZ (1913–   )

A man of diverse and exceptional talent, Delmore Schwartz is poet, critic, editor, and teacher as well as writer of fiction. Despite his gifts, however, Schwartz reveals in his creative work a tormented consciousness haunted by a pervasive—though unlocated—guilt and mocked by an ironic tone of personal inadequacy. In his poetry, for example, Schwartz ridicules himself in the image of a "heavy bear," clumsy, lumbering, and too fond of "candy, anger, and sleep." This is a bear who—like the dreamer of "In Dreams Begin Responsibilities"—howls when he dreams of the darkness beneath his trembling tightrope, and who "Trembles to think that his quivering meat/Must finally wince to nothing at all."

Vividly poetic imagery abounds in Schwartz's fiction as well. Thus, in our story, "an automobile, looking like an enormous upholstered sofa, puffs and passes"; the waves "arch their backs . . . showing green and white veins amid the black." But the technical genius of the story rests in its central narrative device, the silent film. "Dots and rays" of flickering light blur action and diffuse time. A flat, impersonal "silent" scenario counterpoints loud, dramatic interruptions by both dreamer and audience. The narrative halts and leaps surrealistically, a screened image of the dreamer's efforts both to discover and to avoid his identity.

In a poem dedicated to Delmore Schwartz,[1] Robert Lowell, Schwartz's colleague at Harvard after World War II, recalls Schwartz's saying one evening: "We poets in our youth begin sadness;/Thereof in the end

---

[1] "To Delmore Schwartz," *Life Studies* (New York: Farrar, Straus and Giroux, 1959), pp. 53–54.

come despondency and madness." Each of these emotions surges through "In Dreams Begin Responsibilities" as the dreamer is half unwillingly dragged "into the bleak winter morning" of his twenty-first birthday. Terrified by the prospect of manhood and responsibility, he tries to fend them off, to recreate a past he can control, a past assuring no present. But he fails to stop the eerie rhythm of the jumpy, almost absurd film as it silently, inexorably unreels the process of his birth. His shouts of protest avail nothing: "Don't you know," the usher says as he drags the dreamer out to the lobby, "that you can't do whatever you want to do?"

Schwartz's dreamer—like most of his protagonists—has suffered what Schwartz calls "the wound of consciousness." Whether the reader believes that the protagonist can be healed depends perhaps upon how much stress he wishes to place on the closing images of snow "shining" on the windowsill and "the morning already begun."

THE STORY

I think it is the year 1909. I feel as if I were in a motion picture theatre, the long arm of light crossing the darkness and spinning, my eyes fixed on the screen. This is a silent picture as if an old Biograph one, in which the actors are dressed in ridiculously old-fashioned clothes, and one flash succeeds another with sudden jumps. The actors too seem to jump about and walk too fast. The shots themselves are full of dots and rays, as if it were raining when the picture was photographed. The light is bad.

It is Sunday afternoon, June 12th, 1909, and my father is walking down the quiet streets of Brooklyn on his way to visit my mother. His clothes are newly pressed and his tie is too tight in his high collar. He jingles the coins in his pockets, thinking of the witty things he will say. I feel as if I had by now relaxed entirely in the soft darkness of the theatre; the organist peals out the obvious and approximate emotions on which the audience rocks unknowingly. I am anonymous, and I have forgotten myself. It is always so when one goes to the movies, it is, as they say, a drug.

My father walks from street to street of trees, lawns and houses, once in a while coming to an avenue on which a street-car skates and gnaws, slowly progressing. The conductor, who has a handle-bar mustache, helps a young lady wearing a hat like a bowl with feathers on to the car. She lifts her long skirts slightly as she mounts the steps. He leisurely makes change and rings his bell. It is obviously Sunday, for everyone is wearing Sunday clothes, and the street-car's noises emphasize the quiet of the holiday. Is not Brooklyn the City of Churches? The shops are closed and their shades drawn, but for an occasional stationery store or drug-store with great green balls in the window.

My father has chosen to take this long walk because he likes to walk and think. He thinks about himself in the future and so arrives at the place he is to visit in a state of mild exaltation. He pays no attention to the houses he is passing, in which the Sunday dinner is being eaten, nor to the many trees which patrol each street, now coming to their full leafage and the time when they will room the whole street in cool shadow. An occasional carriage passes, the horse's hooves falling like stones in the quiet afternoon, and once in a while an automobile, looking like an enormous upholstered sofa, puffs and passes.

My father thinks of my mother, of how nice it will be to introduce her to his family. But he is not yet sure that he wants to marry her, and once in a while he becomes panicky about the bond already established. He reassures himself by thinking of the big men he admires who are married: William Randolph Hearst, and William Howard Taft, who has just become President of the United States.

My father arrives at my mother's house. He has come too early and so is suddenly embarrassed. My aunt, my mother's sister, answers the loud bell with her napkin in her hand, for the family is still at dinner. As my father enters, my grandfather rises from the table and shakes hands with him. My mother has run upstairs to tidy herself. My grandmother asks my father if he has had dinner, and tells him that Rose will be downstairs soon. My grandfather opens the conversation by remarking on the mild June weather. My father sits uncomfortably near the table, holding his hat in his hand. My grandmother tells my aunt to take my father's hat. My uncle, twelve years old, runs into the house, his hair touseled. He shouts a greeting to my father, who has often given him a nickel, and then runs upstairs. It is evident that the respect in which my father is held in this household is tempered by a good deal of mirth. He is impressive, yet he is very awkward.

Finally my mother comes downstairs, all dressed up, and my father being engaged in conversation with my grandfather becomes uneasy, not knowing whether to greet my mother or continue the conversation. He gets up from the chair clumsily and says "hello" gruffly. My grandfather watches, examining their congruence, such as it is, with a critical eye, and meanwhile rubbing his bearded cheek roughly, as he always does when he reflects. He is worried; he is afraid that my father will not make a good husband for his oldest daughter. At this point something happens to the film, just as my father is saying something funny to my mother; I am awakened to myself and my unhappiness just as my interest was rising. The audience begins to clap impatiently. Then the trouble is cared for but the film has been returned to a portion just shown, and once more I see my grandfather rubbing his bearded cheek and pondering my father's character. It is difficult to get back into the picture once more and forget myself, but as my mother giggles at my father's words, the darkness drowns me.

My father and mother depart from the house, my father shaking hands with my mother once more, out of some unknown uneasiness. I stir uneasily also, slouched in the hard chair of the theatre. Where is the older uncle, my mother's older brother? He is studying in his bedroom upstairs, studying for his final examination at the College of the City of New York, having been dead of rapid pneumonia for the last twenty-one years. My mother and father walk down the same quiet streets once more. My mother is holding my father's arm and telling him of the novel which she has been reading; and my father utters judgments of the characters as the plot is made clear to him. This is a habit which he very much enjoys, for he feels the utmost superiority and confidence when he approves and condemns the behavior of other people. At times he feels moved to utter a brief "Ugh,"—whenever the story becomes what he would call sugary. This tribute is paid to his manliness. My mother feels satisfied by the interest which she has awakened; she is showing my father how intelligent she is, and how interesting.

They reach the avenue, and the street-car leisurely arrives. They are going to Coney Island this afternoon, although my mother considers that such pleasures are inferior. She has made up her mind to indulge only in a walk on the boardwalk and a pleasant dinner, avoiding the riotous amusements as being beneath the dignity of so dignified a couple.

My father tells my mother how much money he has made in the past week, exaggerating an amount which need not have been exaggerated. But my father has always felt that actualities somehow fall short. Suddenly I begin to weep. The determined old lady who sits next to me in the theatre is annoyed and looks at me with an angry face, and being intimidated, I stop. I drag out my handkerchief and dry my face, licking the drop which has fallen near my lips. Meanwhile I have missed something, for here are my mother and father alighting at the last stop, Coney Island.

They walk toward the boardwalk, and my father commands my mother to inhale the pungent air from the sea. They both breathe in deeply, both of them laughing as they do so. They have in common a great interest in health, although my father is strong and husky, my mother frail. Their minds are full of theories of what is good to eat and not good to eat, and sometimes they engage in heated discussions of the subject, the whole matter ending in my father's announcement, made with a scornful bluster, that you have to die sooner or later anyway. On the boardwalk's flagpole, the American flag is pulsing in an intermittent wind from the sea.

My father and mother go to the rail of the boardwalk and look down on the beach where a good many bathers are casually walking about. A few are in the surf. A peanut whistle pierces the air with its pleasant and active whine, and my father goes to buy peanuts. My mother remains at the rail and stares at the ocean. The ocean seems merry to her; it pointedly sparkles and again and again the pony waves are released. She notices the children digging in the wet sand, and the bathing costumes of the girls who are her own age. My father returns with the peanuts. Overhead the sun's lightning strikes and strikes, but neither of them are at all aware of it. The boardwalk is full of people dressed in their Sunday clothes and idly strolling. The tide does not reach as far as the boardwalk, and the strollers would feel no danger if it did. My mother and father lean on the rail of the boardwalk and absently stare at the ocean. The ocean is becoming rough; the waves come in slowly, tugging strength from far back. The moment before they somersault, the moment when they arch their backs so beautifully, showing green and white veins amid the black, that moment is intolerable. They finally crack, dashing fiercely upon the sand, actually driving, full force downward, against the sand, bouncing upward and forward, and at last petering out into a small stream which races up the beach and then is recalled. My parents gaze absentmindedly at the ocean, scarcely interested in its harshness. The sun overhead does not disturb them. But I stare at the terrible sun which breaks up sight, and the fatal, merciless, passionate ocean, I forget my parents. I stare fascinated and finally, shocked by the indifference of my father and mother, I burst out weeping once more. The old lady next to me pats me on the shoulder and says "There, there, all of this is only a movie, young man, only a movie," but I look up once more at the terrifying sun and the terrifying ocean, and being unable to control my tears, I get up and go to the men's room, stumbling over the feet of the other people seated in my row.

When I return, feeling as if I had awakened in the morning sick for lack of sleep, several hours have apparently passed and my parents are riding on the merry-go-round. My father is on a black horse, my mother on a white one, and they seem to be making an eternal circuit for the single purpose of snatching the nickel rings which are attached to the arm of one of the posts. A hand-organ is playing; it is one with the ceaseless circling of the merry-go-round.

For a moment it seems that they will never get off the merry-go-round because it will never stop. I feel like one who looks down on the avenue from the 50th story of a building. But at length they do get off; even the music of the hand-organ has ceased for a moment. My father has acquired ten rings, my mother only two, although it was my mother who really wanted them.

They walk on along the boardwalk as the afternoon descends by imperceptible degrees into the incredible violet of dusk. Everything fades into a relaxed glow, even the ceaseless murmuring from the beach, and the revolutions of the merry-go-round. They look for a place to have dinner. My father suggests the best one on the boardwalk and my mother demurs, in accordance with her principles.

However they do go to the best place, asking for a table near the window, so that they can look out on the boardwalk and the mobile ocean. My father feels omnipotent as he places a quarter in the waiter's hand as he asks for a table. The place is crowded and here too there is music, this time from a kind of string trio. My father orders dinner with a fine confidence.

As the dinner is eaten, my father tells of his plans for the future, and my mother shows with expressive face how interested she is, and how impressed. My father becomes exultant. He is lifted up by the waltz that is being played, and his own future begins to intoxicate him. My father tells my mother that he is going to expand his business, for there is a great deal of money to be made. He wants to settle down. After all, he is twenty-nine, he has lived by himself since he was thirteen, he is making more and more money, and he is envious of his married friends when he visits them in the cozy security of their homes, surrounded, it seems, by the calm domestic pleasures, and by delightful children, and then, as the waltz reaches the moment when all the dancers swing madly, then, then with awful daring, then he asks my mother to marry him, although awkwardly enough and puzzled, even in his excitement, at how he had arrived at the proposal, and she, to make the whole business worse, begins to cry, and my father looks nervously about, not knowing at all what to do now, and my mother says: "It's all I've wanted from the moment I saw you," sobbing, and he finds all of this very difficult, scarcely to his taste, scarcely as he had thought it would be, on his long walks over Brooklyn Bridge in the revery of a fine cigar, and it was then that I stood up in the theatre and shouted: "Don't do it. It's not too late to change your minds, both of you. Nothing good will come of it, only remorse, hatred, scandal, and two children whose characters are monstrous." The whole audience turned to look at me, annoyed, the usher came hurrying down the aisle flashing his searchlight, and the old lady next to me tugged me down into my seat, saying: "Be quiet. You'll be put out, and you paid thirty-five cents to come in." And so I shut my eyes because I could not bear to see what was happening. I sat there quietly.

But after awhile I begin to take brief glimpses, and at length I watch again with thirsty interest, like a child who wants to maintain his sulk although offered the bribe of candy. My parents are now having their picture taken in a photographer's booth along the boardwalk. The place is shadowed in the mauve light which is apparently necessary. The camera is set to the side on its tripod and looks like a Martian man. The photographer is instructing my parents in how to pose. My father has his arm over my mother's shoulder, and both of them smile emphatically. The photographer brings my mother a bouquet of flowers to hold in her hand but she holds it at the wrong angle. Then the photographer covers himself with the black cloth which drapes the camera and all that one sees of him is one protruding arm and his hand which clutches the rubber ball which he will squeeze when the picture is finally taken. But he is not satisfied with their appearance. He feels with certainty that somehow there is something wrong in their pose. Again and again he issues from his hidden place with new directions. Each suggestion merely makes matters worse. My father is becoming impatient. They try a seated pose. The photographer explains that he has pride, he is not interested in all of this for the money, he wants to make beautiful pictures. My father says: "Hurry up, will you? We haven't got all night." But the photographer only scurries about apologetically, and issues new directions. The photographer charms me. I approve of him with all my heart, for I know just how he feels, and as he criticizes each revised pose according to some unknown idea of rightness, I become quite hopeful. But then my father says angrily: "Come on, you've had enough time, we're not going to wait any longer." And the photographer, sighing unhappily, goes back under his black covering, holds out his hand, says: "One, two, three, Now!", and the picture is taken, with my father's smile turned to a grimace and my mother's bright and false. It takes a few minutes for the picture to be developed and as my parents sit in the curious light they become quite depressed.

They have passed a fortune-teller's booth, and my mother wishes to go in, but my father does not. They begin to argue about it. My mother becomes stubborn, my father once more impatient, and then they begin to quarrel, and what my father would like to do is walk off and leave my mother there, but he knows that that would never do. My mother refuses to budge. She is near to tears, but she feels an uncontrollable desire to hear what the palm-reader will say. My father consents angrily, and they both go into a booth which is in a way like the photographer's, since it is draped in black cloth and its light is shadowed. The place is too warm, and my father keeps saying this is all nonsense, pointing to the crystal ball on the table. The fortune-teller, a fat, short woman, garbed in what is supposed to be Oriental robes, comes into the room from the back and greets them, speaking with an accent. But suddenly my father feels that the whole thing is intolerable; he tugs at my mother's arm, but my mother refuses to budge. And then, in terrible anger, my father lets go of my mother's arm and strides out, leaving my mother stunned. She moves to go after my father, but the fortune-teller holds her arm tightly and begs her not to do so, and I in my seat am shocked more than can ever be said, for I feel as if I were walking a tight-rope a hundred feet over a circus-audience and suddenly the rope is showing signs of breaking, and I get up from my seat and begin to shout once more the first words I can think of to communicate my terrible fear and once more the usher comes hurrying down the aisle flashing his searchlight, and the old lady pleads with me, and the shocked audience has turned to stare at me, and I keep shouting: "What are they doing? Don't they know what they are doing? Why doesn't my mother go after my father? If she does not do that, what will she do? Doesn't my father know what he is doing?"—But the usher has seized my arm and is dragging me away, and as he does so, he says: "What are *you* doing? Don't you know that you can't do whatever you want to do? Why should a young man like you, with your whole life before you, get hysterical like this? Why don't you *think* of what you're doing? You can't act like this even if other people aren't around! You will be sorry if you do not do what you should do, you can't carry on like this, it is not right, you will find that out soon enough, everything you do matters too much," and he said that dragging me through the lobby of the theatre into the cold light, and I woke up into the bleak winter morning of my 21st birthday, the windowsill shining with its lip of snow, and the morning already begun.

MORE ABOUT THIS STORY

Most psychologists agree that dreams symbolize unacknowledged but none-theless real problems. Beyond this point, however, theoretical divergences splay out in several directions. Freud, for example, argues that dreams express and fulfil hidden wishes, especially sexual cravings otherwise repressed as taboo. Jung vigorously disputed Freud's assumption that dream analysis discovers the cause of neurosis. Admitting that dreams might well embody suppressed wishes or fears, Jung pointed out that dreams might also embody countless other things: "ineluctable truths, philosophical pronouncements, illusions . . . memories, plans, anticipations. . . ." Many later theorists have pursued Jung's line of thought, challenging not only Freud's rigid sexual causality but also his premise that dreams distort or censor reality. Karen Horney writes that "in dreams we are closer to the reality of ourselves; they represent attempts to solve our conflicts; . . . in them constructive forces can be at work, even at a time when they are hardly visible otherwise." [1]

Our notes toward an analysis of Delmore Schwartz's "dream" follow the direction of interpersonal rather than Freudian psychology. They assume that the dreamer's personality derives from social and interpersonal influences— not primarily, as Freud insists—from sexual experience.[2]

Apparently unable while awake to acknowledge his latent terror, the youth encounters in his dream, events, characters, images, and settings that compel him feelingly to confront the sources of his anguish. Thus, the dream exposes his ambivalence toward himself, his parents, and, chiefly, toward the most harrowing prospect of all—the imminence of manhood and responsibility.

At the outset, he perceives both time and space fuzzily but pleasurably. In the womblike "soft darkness of the theater" all is at first vague, imprecise,

---

[1] "The Road of Psychoanalytic Therapy," *Collected Works* (New York: W. W. Norton, 1942), II, 349.

[2] See *Postscript*.

relaxing. He *thinks* but cannot be certain that the year is 1909, and only *feels as if* he were in a movie theater. In brief, he begins with oblivion, one of the polarities he desires: "I am anonymous, and I have forgotten myself."

The ensuing succession of fantasied events and images destroys his illusion of detached non-existence, though his wish to restore himself to non-identity persists. As his parents leave for their outing, however, he observes, "I am awakened to myself and my unhappiness just as my interest was rising." Thereafter, swept into the turbulent reality of his conflict, the dreamer struggles with his fate—birth, or, by extension—manhood.

His feelings of anxiety increase and his emotional control diminishes as his parents' image assumes full and ominous shape upon the screen of his consciousness. When, for example, his father exaggerates his income ("my father has always felt that actualities somehow fall short"), the dreamer weeps for the first time. In part his tears deplore and protest his father's empty materialism. More important, his tears reflect his traumatic fear that his own "actuality" will never satisfy his father. Thus, his infantile regression to weeping suggests his awareness that his father will forever reject him. He weeps again when his parents vapidly stare out from the boardwalk, their thoughts preoccupied with food, indifferent to their profound obligations and responsibilities as father (symbolized on one level by the sun) and mother (symbolically represented by the ocean). They are unaware too of the awesome, "intolerable" moment of birth that obsesses the dreamer and is imaged in the ocean's rolling tide.

Schwartz' symbolism here is multiple and shifting rather than fixed. Thus, apart from its possible association with the father, the sun may represent, as its "lightning strikes and strikes" his unknowing, unfeeling parents, the dreamer's willed act of aggression against them. Even more fascinating to him is the ocean, a symbolic life force so enthralling with its promise and threat that the dreamer momentarily forgets his parents. But the shock of their indifference to the ocean and their immunity to the sun (son?) swiftly reverberates, and his tears—though still inadequate as an outward manifestation of his repressed hostility—assert once more his feelings of rejection.

To this point, the dreamer's two episodes of weeping indicate that his overt acts of hostility and aggression have been at least partially repressed. On the first occasion, the irritated glance of the "determined old lady" (who may symbolize parental discipline) is enough to "intimidate" him and stop his tears. Later, however, even the old lady's maternal forbearance cannot assuage his anger and hurt; he must leave to control his feelings.

Soon afterwards, his anxieties shatter his weakened emotional control and, no longer weeping, he shouts his protest against his parents' marriage and, by corollary, against his own existence. Nothing good can come of such a union, he howls, only "remorse, hatred, scandal, and two children whose characters are monstrous." The merry-go-round incident and the clumsy, casual, almost accidental marriage proposal in the restaurant motivate this outburst. Astride their carousel horses, his parents shadow forth the image and attributes of the steeds in Plato's *Phaedrus*—black for sensuality, white for spirit. Ironically, the dreamer who, as charioteer, should guide and restrain the horses, feels hopelessly distant from the scene, incapable of controlling anything, much less these vain, insensate riders on a circular journey to nowhere. Appalled by the prospect of not being able to fashion his own image and, worse, of having it stamped in imitation of these insensitive ring snatchers, he shrieks against that act that makes his life inevitable. Once more, however, the threat of parental discipline (the old lady and the usher) silences the dreamer, though he flees the reality of his dream by closing his eyes.

Because his feeling for life still pulsates, the film soon recaptures his attention. In the final episodes, until the usher (parent) drags him from the lobby (womb) out into "the cold light" (life), the dreamer's feelings toward his approaching birth somewhat alter. His hopes rise for a fleeting instant as he identifies with the sensitive, artistic photographer (a self-image as well as a desired father-image) who tries to alter the frozen reality of the parental image "according to some unknown idea of rightness." But the father's impatience sends the photographer scurrying beneath the death-like cowl of his black cloth. What briefly seemed a chance to refocus his self-image through a fresh and vibrant portrait of his parents ends with the depressingly sharp image of their smiles—his father's a "grimace," his mother's "bright and false."

Again, at the fortune-teller's booth, the dreamer anticipates a prophetic vision of the future (though the oracle is disappointingly short and fat, her booth forebodingly draped in black) that may resolve his conflict about himself and his parents. The prophecy, significantly, is never made, for the dreamer usurps the prophet's role, not to predict but to demand his right to birth and to manhood. This time his shout releases all of his repressed hostility—against his death wish, his parents, and his society. He will not be placated or warned or ignored; he will let all know of his "terrible fear," namely, that unless he is born, he cannot exist.

The dream has revealed the youth to himself by heightening his awareness of reality, not by censoring it. However reluctantly, he does at last embrace the real world. Ironically, despite the dreamer's willed return to life, a strangely pessimistic note lingers. For, after all, the usher ignobly drags him into the light regardless of his own intention. To what purpose has he then suffered his dream of life and death if no choice were there from the outset? What responsibilities have begun as a result of his dream? As he wakes on the morn of his twenty-first birthday, the dreamer, unhappily, cannot be certain that he has shattered the mold into which he had long ago been poured.

Perhaps this dour view of experience explains Robert Lowell's recollection of Delmore Schwartz's wry but grim comment at a party: "Let Joyce and Freud, the Masters of Joy, be our guest here."

POSTSCRIPT

We have found especially suggestive in preparing this afterword Walter Bonime's description of the elements of dreams in his book *The Clinical Use of Dreams* (New York: Basic Books, 1962). The description of those elements given below should prove useful to the student. Our own essay indicates how we have bent his necessarily clinical approach to our broader purpose.

Dr. Bonime describes four elements of dreams:

Action: What the dreamer does, thinks, and feels in the "action" of his dream, and how he behaves toward others and is affected by their behavior toward him—these help us to understand what the dreamer is doing or trying to do in his waking life.

Feeling: "Feelings . . . are perhaps the most subtle, accurate, and comprehensive indicators of the total personality." [p. 49] What feelings the symbolic actions, individuals, or surroundings may imply, and what feelings the dreamer actually experiences while dreaming—these help us to understand the dreamer's values and ideas in his waking life.

Individuals: The characters in a dream often identify specific traits rather than specific people, or a variety of characters may represent various traits of the dreamer.

Surroundings: ". . . not only the places in which the action occurs and where individuals are but also all the components of nature and all the products of civilization and any realistic or unrealistic synthesis or abstraction or fragment of them not identifiable in the dream as any of the other elements." [p. 8] The surroundings, then, help to identify action, feeling, and individual.

FOR FURTHER READING

Freud, Sigmund. *The Interpretation of Dreams.* New York: Basic Books, 1959, pp. 7–11, 550–572, 588–609.

Howe, Irving. Review of "In Dreams Begin Responsibilities," *Sewanee Review,* LVII (1949), 147–148.

Jung, Carl G. *Psychological Reflections.* New York: Harper and Row, 1961, pp. 46–70.

Malin, Irving. *Jews and Americans.* Carbondale: Southern Illinois University Press, 1965, pp. 37–39, 62–65.

Of This Time, Of That Place

BY LIONEL TRILLING (1905–   )

Since 1931 Lionel Trilling has been a professor of English at Columbia University. Distinguished as a scholar for his studies of Matthew Arnold and E. M. Forster, and as an essayist for *The Liberal Imagination* and *The Opposing Self,* he has only occasionally written fiction. Nevertheless, his works of fiction—a single novel, *The Middle of the Journey,* and a few short stories—have, like his other writing, won much praise and stirred considerable discussion.

All of Trilling's work resolutely insists upon what he calls "moral realism," a demand that men of good will recognize the hazards and the complexity of their good intentions. It is not enough, he suggests in "Manners, Morals, and the Novel," to adopt a comprehensively liberal stance. The inward motives inspiring that liberalism must first be honestly and ruthlessly scrutinized. Too often, Trilling reveals, the motive may prove an ironic mockery, even a corruption of an avowedly noble purpose. Men must then know themselves—they must become "moral realists"—before they can achieve a significant relationship with their culture. What that knowledge amounts to is the substance of Trilling's critical and creative work.

In "Of This Time, Of That Place" it is an adult rather than an adolescent who attains that knowledge. Although the focus upon an adult mind violates our convention of choosing only those tales that explore the mind of an adolescent, it compensates, we believe, by extending the range of irony and complexity apparent in human relations. For the young, however insular they may seem to be, inhabit and affect an adult world. Thus, Ferdinand R. Tertan and Theodore Blackburn, in sharply different ways, wrench and distort Professor Howe's sense of himself. The impact and implication of the encounter gain force and clarity because the narrative point of view—the recording consciousness of character and incident—is located in Howe's intelligence and sensibility.

Unobtrusively but with masterly control, Trilling draws taut the lines of Howe's ambivalence. Structurally bounded by the limits of an academic year, the narrative uses irony, ambiguity, and symbol to enrich the curriculum of Howe's self-education. Note, for example, how the suggestive names of the students and the equally suggestive anonymity of the Dean, the presence of a camera at the outset and at the close of the story, and the classroom discussion of Ibsen's *Ghosts* all serve to lead Howe to his ultimate confrontation with himself.

THE STORY

It was a fine September day. By noon it would be summer again but now it was true autumn with a touch of chill in the air. As Joseph Howe stood on the porch of the house in which he lodged, ready to leave for his first class of the year, he thought with pleasure of the long indoor days that were coming. It was a moment when he could feel glad of his profession.

On the lawn the peach tree was still in fruit and young Hilda Aiken was taking a picture of it. She held the camera tight against her chest. She wanted the sun behind her but she did not want her own long morning shadow in the foreground. She raised the camera but that did not help, and she lowered it but that made things worse. She twisted her body to the left, then to the right. In the end she had to step out of the direct line of the sun. At last she snapped the shutter and wound the film with intense care.

Howe, watching her from the porch, waited for her to finish and called good morning. She turned, startled, and almost sullenly lowered her glance. In the year Howe had lived at the Aikens', Hilda had accepted him as one of her family, but since his absence of the summer she had grown shy. Then suddenly she lifted her head and smiled at him, and the humorous smile confirmed his pleasure in the day. She picked up her bookbag and set off for school.

The handsome houses on the streets to the college were not yet fully awake but they looked very friendly. Howe went by the Bradby house where he would be a guest this evening at the first dinner-party of the year. When he had gone the length of the picket fence, the whitest in town, he turned back. Along the path there was a fine row of asters and he went through the gate and picked one for his buttonhole. The Bradbys would be pleased if they happened to see him invading their lawn and the knowledge of this made him even more comfortable.

He reached the campus as the hour was striking. The students were hurrying to their classes. He himself was in no hurry. He stopped at his dim cubicle of an office and lit a cigarette. The prospect of facing his class had suddenly presented itself to him and his hands were cold, the lawful seizure of power he was about to make seemed momentous. Waiting did not help. He put out his cigarette, picked up a pad of theme paper and went to his classroom.

As he entered, the rattle of voices ceased and the twenty-odd freshmen settled themselves and looked at him appraisingly. Their faces seemed gross, his heart sank at their massed impassivity, but he spoke briskly.

"My name is Howe," he said and turned and wrote it on the blackboard. The carelessness of the scrawl confirmed his authority. He went on: "My office is 412 Slemp Hall and my office hours are Monday, Wednesday, and Friday from eleven-thirty to twelve-thirty."

He wrote: "M., W., F., 11.30–12.30." He said: "I'll be very glad to see any of you at that time. Or if you can't come then, you can arrange with me for some other time."

He turned again to the blackboard and spoke over his shoulder. "The text for the course is Jarman's *Modern Plays,* revised edition. The Co-op has it in stock." He wrote the name, underlined "revised edition" and waited for it to be taken down in the new note-books.

When the bent heads were raised again, he began his speech of prospectus. "It is hard to explain—" he said, and paused as they composed themselves. "It is hard to explain what a course like this is intended to do. We are going to try to learn something about modern literature and something about prose composition."

As he spoke, his hands warmed and he was able to look directly at the class. Last year on the first day the faces had seemed just as cloddish, but as the term wore on they became gradually alive and quite likeable. It did not seem possible that the same thing could happen again.

"I shall not lecture in this course," he continued. "Our work will be carried on by discussion and we will try to learn by an exchange of opinion. But you will soon recognize that my opinion is worth more than anyone else's here."

He remained grave as he said it, but two boys understood and laughed. The rest took permission from them and laughed too. All Howe's private ironies protested the vulgarity of the joke but the laughter made him feel benign and powerful.

When the little speech was finished, Howe picked up the pad of paper he had brought. He announced that they would write an extemporaneous theme. Its subject was traditional: "Who I am and why I came to Dwight College." By now the class was more at ease and it gave a ritualistic groan of protest.

Then there was a stir as fountain-pens were brought out and the writing arms of the chairs were cleared and the paper was passed about. At last all the heads bent to work and the room became still. Howe sat idly at his desk. The sun shone through the tall clumsy windows. The cool of the morning was already passing. There was a scent of autumn and of varnish, and the stillness of the room was deep and oddly touching. Now and then a student's head was raised and scratched in the old elaborate students' pantomime that calls the teacher to witness honest intellectual effort.

Suddenly a tall boy stood within the frame of the open door. "Is this," he said, and thrust a large nose into a college catalogue, "is this the meeting place of English 1A? The section instructed by Dr. Joseph Howe?"

He stood on the very sill of the door, as if refusing to enter until he was perfectly sure of all his rights. The class looked up from work, found him absurd and gave a low mocking cheer.

The teacher and the new student, with equal pointedness, ignored the disturbance. Howe nodded to the boy, who pushed his head forward and then jerked it back in a wide elaborate arc to clear his brow of a heavy lock of hair. He advanced into the room and halted before Howe, almost at attention. In a loud clear voice he announced: "I am Tertan, Ferdinand R., reporting at the direction of Head of Department Vincent."

The heraldic formality of this statement brought forth another cheer. Howe looked at the class with a sternness he could not really feel, for there was indeed something ridiculous about this boy. Under his displeased regard the rows of heads dropped to work again. Then he touched Tertan's elbow, led him up to the desk and stood so as to shield their conversation from the class.

"We are writing an extemporaneous theme," he said. "The subject is: 'Who I am and why I came to Dwight College.'"

He stripped a few sheets from the pad and offered them to the boy. Tertan hesitated and then took the paper, but he held it only tentatively. As if with the effort of making something clear, he gulped, and a slow smile fixed itself on his face. It was at once knowing and shy.

"Professor," he said, "to be perfectly fair to my classmates"—he made a large gesture over the room—"and to you"—he inclined his head to Howe— "this would not be for me an extemporaneous subject."

Howe tried to understand. "You mean you've already thought about it— you've heard we always give the same subject? That doesn't matter."

Again the boy ducked his head and gulped. It was the gesture of one who wishes to make a difficult explanation with perfect candor. "Sir," he said, and made the distinction with great care, "the topic I did not expect but I have given much ratiocination to the subject."

Howe smiled and said: "I don't think that's an unfair advantage. Just go ahead and write."

Tertan narrowed his eyes and glanced sidewise at Howe. His strange mouth smiled. Then in quizzical acceptance, he ducked his head, threw back the heavy dank lock, dropped into a seat with a great loose noise and began to write rapidly.

The room fell silent again and Howe resumed his idleness. When the bell rang, the students who had groaned when the task had been set now groaned again because they had not finished. Howe took up the papers and held the class while he made the first assignment. When he dismissed it, Tertan bore down on him, his slack mouth held ready for speech.

"Some professors," he said, "are pedants. They are Dryasdusts. However, some professors are free souls and creative spirits. Kant, Hegel, and Nietzsche were all professors." With this pronouncement he paused. "It is my opinion." he continued, "that you occupy the second category."

Howe looked at the boy in surprise and said with good-natured irony: "With Kant, Hegel, and Nietzsche?"

Not only Tertan's hand and head but his whole awkward body waved away the stupidity. "It is the kind and not the quantity of the kind," he said sternly.

Rebuked, Howe said as simply and seriously as he could: "It would be nice to think so." He added: "Of course, I am not a professor."

This was clearly a disappointment but Tertan met it. "In the French sense," he said with composure. "Generically, a teacher."

Suddenly he bowed. It was such a bow, Howe fancied, as a stage-director might teach an actor playing a medieval student who takes leave of Abelard— stiff, solemn, with elbows close to the body and feet together. Then, quite as suddenly, he turned and left.

A queer fish, and as soon as Howe reached his office he sifted through the batch of themes and drew out Tertan's. The boy had filled many sheets with his unformed headlong scrawl. "Who am I?" he had begun. "Here, in a mundane, not to say commercialized academe, is asked the question which from time long immemorably out of mind has accreted doubts and thoughts in the psyche of man to pester him as a nuisance. Whether in St. Augustine (or Austin as sometimes called) or Miss Bashkirtsieff or Frederic Amiel or Empedocles, or in less lights of the intellect than these, this posed question has been ineluctable."

Howe took out his pencil. He circled "academe" and wrote "vocab." in the margin. He underlined "time long immemorably out of mind" and wrote "Diction!" But this seemed inadequate for what was wrong. He put down his pencil and read ahead to discover the principle of error in the theme. "To-day as ever, in spite of gloomy prophets of the dismal science (economics) the question is uninvalidated. Out of the starry depths of heaven hurtles this spear of query demanding to be caught on the shield of the mind ere it pierces the skull and the limbs be unstrung."

Baffled but quite caught, Howe read on. "Materialism, by which is meant the philosophic concept and not the moral idea, provides no aegis against the question which lies beyond the tangible (metaphysics). Existence without alloy is the question presented. Environment and heredity relegated aside, the rags and old clothes of practical life discarded, the name and the instrumentality of livelihood do not, as the prophets of the dismal science insist on in this connection, give solution to the interrogation which not from the professor merely but veritably from the cosmos is given. I think, therefore I am (cogito etc.) but who am I? Tertan I am, but what is Tertan? Of this time, of that place, of some parentage, what does it matter?"

Existence without alloy: the phrase established itself. Howe put aside Tertan's paper and at random picked up another. "I am Arthur J. Casebeer, Jr.," he read. "My father is Arthur J. Casebeer and my grandfather was Arthur J. Casebeer before him. My mother is Nina Wimble Casebeer. Both of them are college graduates and my father is in insurance. I was born in St. Louis eighteen years ago and we still make our residence there."

Arthur J. Casebeer, who knew who he was, was less interesting than Tertan, but more coherent. Howe picked up Tertan's paper again. It was clear that none of the routine marginal comments, no "sent. str." or "punct." or "vocab." could cope with its torrential rhetoric. He read ahead, contenting himself with underscoring the errors against the time when he should have the necessary "conference" with Tertan.

It was a busy and official day of cards and sheets, arrangements and small decisions, and it gave Howe pleasure. Even when it was time to attend the first of the weekly Convocations he felt the charm of the beginning of things when intention is still innocent and uncorrupted by effort. He sat among the young instructors on the platform and joined in their humorous complaints at having to assist at the ceremony, but actually he got a clear satisfaction from the ritual of prayer and prosy speech and even from wearing his academic gown. And when the Convocation was over the pleasure continued as he crossed the campus, exchanging greetings with men he had not seen since the spring. They were people who did not yet, and perhaps never would, mean much to him, but in a year they had grown amiably to be part of his life. They were his fellow-townsmen.

The day had cooled again at sunset and there was a bright chill in the September twilight. Howe carried his voluminous gown over his arm, he swung his doctoral hood by its purple neckpiece and on his head he wore his mortarboard with its heavy gold tassel bobbing just over his eye. These were the weighty and absurd symbols of his new profession and they pleased him. At twenty-six Joseph Howe had discovered that he was neither so well off nor so bohemian as he had once thought. A small income, adequate when supplemented by a sizable cash legacy, was genteel poverty when the cash was all spent. And the literary life—the room at the Lafayette or the small apartment without a lease, the long summers on the Cape, the long afternoons and the social evenings—began to weary him. His writing filled his mornings and should perhaps have filled his life, yet it did not. To the amusement of his friends and with a certain sense that he was betraying his own freedom, he had used the last of his legacy for a year at Harvard. The small but respectable reputation of his two volumes of verse had proved useful—he continued at Harvard on a fellowship and when he emerged as Dr. Howe he received an excellent appointment, with prospects, at Dwight.

He had his moments of fear when all that had ever been said of the dangers of the academic life had occurred to him. But after a year in which he had tested every possibility of corruption and seduction he was ready to rest easy. His third volume of verse, most of it written in his first year of teaching, was not only ampler but, he thought, better than its predecessors.

There was a clear hour before the Bradby dinner-party and Howe looked forward to it. But he was not to enjoy it, for lying with his mail on the hall table was a copy of this quarter's issue of *Life and Letters,* to which his landlord subscribed. Its severe cover announced that its editor, Frederic Woolley, had this month contributed an essay called "Two Poets," and Howe, picking it up, curious to see who the two poets might be, felt his own name start out at him with cabalistic power—Joseph Howe. As he continued to turn the pages his hand trembled.

Standing in the dark hall, holding the neat little magazine, Howe knew that his literary contempt for Frederic Woolley meant nothing, for he suddenly understood how he respected Woolley in the way of the world. He knew this by the trembling of his hand. And of the little world as well as the great, for although the literary groups of New York might dismiss Woolley, his name carried high authority in the academic world. At Dwight it was even a revered name, for it had been here at the college that Frederic Woolley had made the distinguished scholarly career from which he had gone on to literary journalism. In middle life he had been induced to take the editorship of *Life and Letters,* a literary monthly not widely read but heavily endowed and in its pages he had carried on the defence of what he sometimes called the older values. He was not without wit, he had great knowledge and considerable taste and even in the full movement of the "new" literature he had won a certain respect for his refusal to accept it. In France, even in England, he would have been connected with a more robust tradition of conservatism, but America gave him an audience not much better than genteel. It was known in the college that to the subsidy of *Life and Letters* the Bradbys contributed a great part.

As Howe read, he saw that he was involved in nothing less than an event. When the Fifth Series of *Studies in Order and Value* came to be collected, this latest of Frederic Woolley's essays would not be merely another step in the old direction. Clearly and unmistakably, it was a turning-point. All his literary life Woolley had been concerned with the relation of literature to morality, religion, and the private and delicate pieties, and he had been unalterably opposed to all that he had called "inhuman humanitarianism." But here, suddenly, dramatically late, he had made an about-face, turning to the public life and to the humanitarian politics he had so long despised. This was the kind of incident the histories of literature make much of. Frederic Woolley was opening for himself a new career and winning a kind of new youth. He contrasted the two poets, Thomas Wormser who was admirable, Joseph Howe who was almost dangerous. He spoke of the "precious subjectivism" of Howe's verse. "In times like ours," he wrote, "with millions facing penury and want, one feels that the qualities of the *tour d'ivoire* are well-nigh inhuman, nearly insulting. The *tour d'ivoire* becomes the *tour d'ivresse* and it is not self-intoxicated poets that our people need." The essay said more: "The problem is one of meaning. I am not ignorant that the creed of the esoteric poets declares that a poem does not and should not *mean* anything, that it *is* something. But poetry is what the poet makes it, and if he is a true poet he makes what his society needs. And what is needed now is the tradition in which Mr. Wormser writes, the true tradition of poetry. The Howes do no harm, but they do no good when positive good is demanded of all responsible men. Or do the Howes indeed do no harm? Perhaps Plato would have said they do, that in some ways theirs is the Phrygian music that turns men's minds from the struggle. Certainly it is true that Thomas Wormser writes in the lucid Dorian mode which sends men into battle with evil."

It was easy to understand why Woolley had chosen to praise Thomas Wormser. The long, lilting lines of *Corn Under Willows* hymned, as Woolley put it, the struggle for wheat in the Iowa fields and expressed the real lives of real people. But why out of the dozen more notable examples he had chosen Howe's little volume as the example of "precious subjectivism" was hard to guess. In a way it was funny, this multiplication of himself into "the Howes." And yet this becoming the multiform political symbol by whose creation Frederic Woolley gave the sign of a sudden new life, this use of him as a sacrifice whose blood was necessary for the rites of rejuvenation, made him feel oddly unclean.

Nor could Howe get rid of a certain practical resentment. As a poet he had a special and respectable place in the college life. But it might be another thing to be marked as the poet of a wilful and selfish obscurity.

As he walked to the Bradbys Howe was a little tense and defensive. It seemed to him that all the world knew of the "attack" and agreed with it. And indeed the Bradbys had read the essay, but Professor Bradby, a kind and pretentious man, said, "I see my old friend knocked you about a bit, my boy," and his wife Eugenia looked at Howe with her child-like blue eyes and said: "I shall *scold* Frederic for the untrue things he wrote about you. You aren't the least obscure." They beamed at him. In their genial snobbery they seemed to feel that he had distinguished himself. He was the leader of Howe-ism. He enjoyed the dinner-party as much as he had thought he would.

And in the following days, as he was more preoccupied with his duties, the incident was forgotten. His classes had ceased to be mere groups. Student after student detached himself from the mass and required or claimed a place in Howe's awareness. Of them all it was Tertan who first and most violently signalled his separate existence. A week after classes had begun Howe saw his silhouette on the frosted glass of his office door. It was motionless for a long time, perhaps stopped by the problem of whether or not to knock before entering. Howe called, "Come in!" and Tertan entered with his shambling stride.

He stood beside the desk, silent and at attention. When Howe asked him to sit down, he responded with a gesture of head and hand as if to say that such amenities were beside the point. Nevertheless he did take the chair. He put his ragged crammed brief-case between his legs. His face, which Howe now observed fully for the first time, was confusing, for it was made up of florid curves, the nose arched in the bone and voluted in the nostril, the mouth loose and soft and rather moist. Yet the face was so thin and narrow as to seem the very type of asceticism. Lashes of unusual length veiled the eyes and, indeed, it seemed as if there were a veil over the whole countenance. Before the words actually came, the face screwed itself into an attitude of preparation for them.

"You can confer with me now?" Tertan said.

"Yes, I'd be glad to. There are several things in your two themes I want to talk to you about." Howe reached for the packet of themes on his desk and sought for Tertan's. But the boy was waving them away.

"These are done perforce," he said. "Under the pressure of your requirement. They are not significant, mere duties." Again his great hand flapped vaguely to dismiss his themes. He leaned forward and gazed at his teacher.

"You are," he said, "a man of letters? You are a poet?" It was more declaration than question.

"I should like to think so," Howe said.

At first Tertan accepted the answer with a show of appreciation, as though the understatement made a secret between himself and Howe. Then he chose to misunderstand. With his shrewd and disconcerting control of expression, he presented to Howe a puzzled grimace. "What does that mean?" he said.

Howe retracted the irony. "Yes. I am a poet." It sounded strange to say.

"That," Tertan said, "is a wonder." He corrected himself with his ducking head. "I mean that is wonderful."

Suddenly he dived at the miserable brief-case between his legs, put it on his knees and began to fumble with the catch, all intent on the difficulty it presented. Howe noted that his suit was worn thin, his shirt almost unclean. He became aware, even, of a vague and musty odor of garments worn too long in unaired rooms. Tertan conquered the lock and began to concentrate upon a search into the interior. At last he held in his hand what he was after, a torn and crumpled copy of *Life and Letters*.

"I learned it from here," he said, holding it out.

Howe looked at him sharply, his hackles a little up. But the boy's face was not only perfectly innocent, it even shone with a conscious admiration. Apparently nothing of the import of the essay had touched him except the wonderful fact that his teacher was a "man of letters." Yet this seemed too stupid and Howe, to test it, said: "The man who wrote that doesn't think it's wonderful."

Tertan made a moist hissing sound as he cleared his mouth of saliva. His head, oddly loose on his neck, wove a pattern of contempt in the air. "A critic," he said, "who admits *prima facie* that he does not understand." Then he said grandly: "It is the inevitable fate."

It was absurd, yet Howe was not only aware of the absurdity but of a tension suddenly and wonderfully relaxed. Now that the "attack" was on the table between himself and this strange boy and subject to the boy's funny and absolutely certain contempt, the hidden force of his feeling was revealed to him in the very moment that it vanished. All unsuspected, there had been a film over the world, a transparent but discoloring haze of danger. But he had no time to stop over the brightened aspect of things. Tertan was going on. "I also am a man of letters. Putative."

"You have written a good deal?" Howe meant to be no more than polite and he was surprised at the tenderness he heard in his words.

Solemnly the boy nodded, threw back the dank lock and sucked in a deep anticipatory breath. "First, a work of homiletics, which is a defence of the principles of religious optimism against the pessimism of Schopenhauer and the humanism of Nietzsche."

"Humanism? Why do you call it humanism?"

"It is my nomenclature for making a deity of man," Tertan replied negligently. "Then three fictional works, novels. And numerous essays in science, combating materialism. Is it your duty to read these if I bring them to you?"

Howe answered simply: "No, it isn't exactly my duty, but I shall be happy to read them."

Tertan stood up and remained silent. He rested his bag on the chair. With a certain compunction—for it did not seem entirely proper that, of two men of letters, one should have the right to blue-pencil the other, to grade him or to question the quality of his "sentence structure"—Howe reached for Tertan's papers. But before he could take them up, the boy suddenly made his bow-to-Abelard, the stiff inclination of the body with the hands seeming to emerge from the scholar's gown. Then he was gone.

But after his departure something was still left of him. The timbre of his curious sentences, the downright finality of so quaint a phrase as "It is the inevitable fate" still rang in the air. Howe gave the warmth of his feeling to the new visitor who stood at the door announcing himself with a genteel clearing of the throat.

"Dr. Howe, I believe?" the student said. A large hand advanced into the room and grasped Howe's hand. "Blackburn, sir, Theodore Blackburn, vice-president of the Student Council. A great pleasure, sir."

Out of a pair of ruddy cheeks a pair of small eyes twinkled good-naturedly. The large face, the large body were not so much fat as beefy and suggested something "typical," monk, politician, or innkeeper.

Blackburn took the seat beside Howe's desk. "I may have seemed to introduce myself in my public capacity, sir," he said. "But it is really as an individual that I came to to see you. That is to say, as one of your students to be."

He spoke with an "English" intonation and he went on: "I was once an English major, sir."

For a moment Howe was startled, for the roast-beef look of the boy and the manner of his speech gave a second's credibility to one sense of his statement. Then the collegiate meaning of the phrase asserted itself, but some perversity made Howe say what was not really in good taste even with so forward a student: "Indeed? What regiment?"

Blackburn stared and then gave a little pouf-pouf of laughter. He waved the misapprehension away. *"Very* good, sir. It certainly is an ambiguous term." He chuckled in appreciation of Howe's joke, then cleared his throat to put it aside. "I look forward to taking your course in the romantic poets, sir," he said earnestly. "To me the romantic poets are the very crown of English literature."

Howe made a dry sound, and the boy, catching some meaning in it, said: "Little as I know them, of course. But even Shakespeare who is so dear to us of the Anglo-Saxon tradition is in a sense but the preparation for Shelley, Keats and Byron. And Wadsworth."

Almost sorry for him, Howe dropped his eyes. With some embarrassment, for the boy was not actually his student, he said softly: "Wordsworth."

"Sir?"

"Wordsworth, not Wadsworth. You said Wadsworth."

"Did I, sir?" Gravely he shook his head to rebuke himself for the error. "Wordsworth, of course—slip of the tongue." Then, quite in command again, he went on. "I have a favor to ask of you, Dr. Howe. You see, I began my college course as an English major"—he smiled—"as I said."

"Yes?"

"But after my first year I shifted. I shifted to the social sciences. Sociology and government—I find them stimulating and very *real."* He paused, out of respect for reality. "But now I find that perhaps I have neglected the other side."

"The other side?" Howe said.

"Imagination, fancy, culture. A well-rounded man." He trailed off as if there were perfect understanding between them. "And so, sir, I have decided to end my senior year with your course in the romantic poets."

His voice was filled with an indulgence which Howe ignored as he said flatly and gravely: "But that course isn't given until the spring term."

"Yes, sir, and that is where the favor comes in. Would you let me take your romantic prose course? I can't take it for credit, sir, my program is full, but just for background it seems to me that I ought to take it. I do hope," he concluded in a manly way, "that you will consent."

"Well, it's no great favor, Mr. Blackburn. You can come if you wish, though there's not much point in it if you don't do the reading."

The bell rang for the hour and Howe got up.

"May I begin with this class, sir?" Blackburn's smile was candid and boyish.

Howe nodded carelessly and together, silently, they walked to the classroom down the hall. When they reached the door Howe stood back to let his student enter, but Blackburn moved adroitly behind him and grasped him by the arm to urge him over the threshold. They entered together with Blackburn's hand firmly on Howe's biceps, the student inducting the teacher into his own room. Howe felt a surge of temper rise in him and almost violently he disengaged his arm and walked to the desk, while Blackburn found a seat in the front row and smiled at him.

II

The question was: At whose door must the tragedy be laid?

All night the snow had fallen heavily and only now was abating in sparse little flurries. The windows were valanced high with white. It was very quiet, something of the quiet of the world had reached the class and Howe found that everyone was glad to talk or listen. In the room there was a comfortable sense of pleasure in being human.

Casebeer believed that the blame for the tragedy rested with heredity. Picking up the book he read: "The sins of the fathers are visited on their children." This opinion was received with general favor. Nevertheless Johnson ventured to say that the fault was all Pastor Manders' because the Pastor had made Mrs. Alving go back to her husband and was always hiding the truth. To this Hibbard objected with logic enough: "Well, then, it was really all her husband's fault. He *did* all the bad things." De Witt, his face bright with an impatient idea, said that the fault was all society's. "By society I don't mean upper-crust society," he said. He looked around a little defiantly, taking in any members of the class who might be members of upper-crust society. "Not in that sense. I mean the social unit."

Howe nodded and said: "Yes, of course."

"If the society of the time had progressed far enough in science," De Witt went on, "then there would be no problem for Mr. Ibsen to write about.

Captain Alving plays around a little, gives way to perfectly natural biological urges, and he gets a social disease, a venereal disease. If the disease is cured, no problem. Invent salvarsan and the disease is cured. The problem of heredity disappears and li'l Oswald just doesn't get paresis. No paresis, no problem —no problem, no play."

This was carrying the ark into battle and the class looked at De Witt with respectful curiosity. It was his usual way and on the whole they were sympathetic with his struggle to prove to Howe that science was better than literature. Still, there was something in his reckless manner that alienated them a little.

"Or take birth-control, for instance," De Witt went on. "If Mrs. Alving had had some knowledge of contraception, she wouldn't have had to have li'l Oswald at all. No li'l Oswald, no play."

The class was suddenly quieter. In the back row Stettenhover swung his great football shoulders in a righteous sulking gesture, first to the right, then to the left. He puckered his mouth ostentatiously. Intellect was always ending up by talking dirty.

Tertan's hand went up and Howe said: "Mr. Tertan." The boy shambled to his feet and began his long characteristic gulp. Howe made a motion with his fingers, as small as possible, and Tertan ducked his head and smiled in apology. He sat down. The class laughed. With more than half the term gone, Tertan had not been able to remember that one did not rise to speak. He seemed unable to carry on the life of the intellect without this mark of respect for it. To Howe the boy's habit of rising seemed to accord with the formal shabbiness of his dress. He never wore the casual sweaters and jackets of his classmates. Into the free and comfortable air of the college classroom he brought the stuffy sordid strictness of some crowded metropolitan high school.

"Speaking from one sense," Tertan began slowly, "there is no blame ascribable. From the sense of determinism, who can say where the blame lies? The preordained is the preordained and it cannot be said without rebellion against the universe, a palpable absurdity."

. In the back row Stettenhover slumped suddenly in his seat, his heels held out before him, making a loud dry disgusted sound. His body sank until his neck rested on the back of his chair. He folded his hands across his belly and look significantly out of the window, exasperated not only with Tertan but with Howe, with the class, with the whole system designed to encourage this kind of thing. There was a certain insolence in the movement and Howe flushed. As Tertan continued to speak, Howe walked casually towards the window and placed himself in the line of Stettenhover's vision. He stared at the great fellow, who pretended not to see him. There was so much power in the big body, so much contempt in the Greek-athlete face under the crisp Greek-athlete curls, that Howe felt almost physical fear. But at last Stettenhover admitted him to focus and under his disapproving gaze sat up with slow indifference. His eyebrows raised high in resignation, he began to examine his hands. Howe relaxed and turned his attention back to Tertan.

"Flux of existence," Tertan was saying, "produces all things, so that judgment wavers. Beyond the phenomena, what? But phenomena are adumbrated and to them we are limited."

Howe saw it for a moment as perhaps it existed in the boy's mind—the world of shadows which are cast by a great light upon a hidden reality as in the old myth of the Cave. But the little brush with Stettenhover had tired him and he said irritably: "But come to the point, Mr. Tertan."

He said it so sharply that some of the class looked at him curiously. For three months he had gently carried Tertan through his verbosities, to the vaguely respectful surprise of the other students, who seemed to conceive that there existed between this strange classmate and their teacher some special understanding from which they were content to be excluded. Tertan looked at him mildly and at once came brilliantly to the point. "This is the summation of the play," he said and took up his book and read: " 'Your poor father never found any outlet for the overmastering joy of life that was in him. And I brought no holiday into his home, either. Everything seemed to turn upon duty and I am afraid I made your poor father's home unbearable to him, Oswald.' Spoken by Mrs. Alving."

Yes, that was surely the "summation" of the play and Tertan had hit it, as he hit, deviously and eventually, the literary point of almost everything. But now, as always, he was wrapping it away from sight. "For most mortals," he said, "there are only joys of biological urgings, gross and crass, such as the sensuous Captain Alving. For certain few there are the transmutations beyond these to a contemplation of the utter whole."

Oh, the boy was mad. And suddenly the word, used in hyperbole, intended almost for the expression of exasperated admiration, became literal. Now that the word was used, it became simply apparent to Howe that Tertan was mad.

It was a monstrous word and stood like a bestial thing in the room. Yet it so completely comprehended everything that had puzzled Howe, it so arranged and explained what for three months had been perplexing him that almost at once its horror became domesticated. With this word Howe was able to understand why he had never been able to communicate to Tertan the value of a single criticism or correction of his wild, verbose themes. Their conferences had been frequent and long but had done nothing to reduce to order the splendid confusion of the boy's ideas. Yet, impossible though its expression was, Tertan's incandescent mind could always strike for a moment into some dark corner of thought.

And now it was suddenly apparent that it was not a faulty rhetoric that

Howe had to contend with. With his new knowledge he looked at Tertan's face and wondered how he could have so long deceived himself. Tertan was still talking and the class had lapsed into a kind of patient unconsciousness, a coma of respect for words which, for all that most of them knew, might be profound. Almost with a suffusion of shame, Howe believed that in some dim way the class had long ago had some intimation of Tertan's madness. He reached out as decisively as he could to seize the thread of Tertan's discourse before it should be entangled further.

"Mr. Tertan says that the blame must be put upon whoever kills the joy of living in another. We have been assuming that Captain Alving was a wholly bad man, but what if we assume that he became bad only because Mrs. Alving, when they were first married, acted towards him in the prudish way she says she did?"

It was a ticklish idea to advance to freshmen and perhaps not profitable. Not all of them were following.

"That would put the blame on Mrs. Alving herself, whom most of you admire. And she herself seems to think so." He glanced at his watch. The hour was nearly over. "What do you think, Mr. De Witt?"

De Witt rose to the idea, wanted to know if society couldn't be blamed for educating Mrs. Alving's temperament in the wrong way. Casebeer was puzzled, Stettenhover continued to look at his hands until the bell rang.

Tertan, his brows louring in thought, was making as always for a private word. Howe gathered his books and papers to leave quickly. At this moment of his discovery and with the knowledge still raw, he could not engage himself with Tertan. Tertan sucked in his breath to prepare for speech and Howe made ready for the pain and confusion. But at that moment Casebeer detached himself from the group with which he had been conferring and which he seemed to represent. His constituency remained at a tactful distance. The mission involved the time of an assigned essay. Casebeer's presentation of the plea— it was based on the freshmen's heavy duties at the fraternities during Carnival Week—cut across Tertan's preparations for speech. "And so some of us fellows thought," Casebeer concluded with heavy solemnity, "that we could do a better job, give our minds to it more, if we had more time."

Tertan regarded Casebeer with mingled curiosity and revulsion. Howe not only said that he would postpone the assignment but went on to talk about the Carnival and even drew the waiting constituency into the conversation. He was conscious of Tertan's stern and astonished stare, then of his sudden departure.

Now that the fact was clear, Howe knew that he must act on it. His course was simple enough. He must lay the case before the Dean. Yet he hesitated. His feeling for Tertan must now, certainly, be in some way invalidated. Yet could he, because of a word, hurry to assign to official and reasonable solicitude what had been, until this moment, so various and warm? He could at least delay and, by moving slowly, lend a poor grace to the necessary, ugly act of making his report.

It was with some notion of keeping the matter in his own hands that he went to the Dean's-office to look up Tertan's records. In the outer office the Dean's secretary greeted him brightly and at his request brought him the manila folder with the small identifying photograph pasted in the corner. She laughed. "He was looking for the birdie in the wrong place," she said.

Howe leaned over her shoulder to look at the picture. It was as bad as all the Dean's office photographs were, but it differed from all that Howe had ever seen. Tertan, instead of looking into the camera, as no doubt he had been bidden, had, at the moment of exposure, turned his eyes upward. His mouth, as though conscious of the trick played on the photographer, had the sly superior look that Howe knew.

The secretary was fascinated by the picture. "What a funny boy," she said. "He looks like Tartuffe!"

And so he did, with the absurd piety of the eyes and the conscious slyness of the mouth and the whole face bloated by the bad lens.

"Is he *like* that?" the secretary said.

"Like Tartuffe? No."

From the photograph there was little enough comfort to be had. The records themselves gave no clue to madness, though they suggested sadness enough. Howe read of a father, Stanislaus Tertan, born in Budapest and trained in engineering in Berlin, once employed by the Hercules Chemical Corporation—this was one of the factories that dominated the south end of the town—but now without employment. He read of a mother Erminie (Youngfellow) Tertan, born in Manchester, educated at a Normal School at Leeds, now housewife by profession. The family lived on Greenbriar Street, which Howe knew as a row of once elegant homes near what was now the factory district. The old mansions had long ago been divided into small and primitive apartments. Of Ferdinand himself there was little to learn. He lived with his parents, had attended a Detroit high school and had transferred to the local school in his last year. His rating for intelligence, as expressed in numbers, was high, his scholastic record was remarkable, he held a college scholarship for his tuition.

Howe laid the folder on the secretary's desk. "Did you find what you wanted to know?" she asked.

The phrases from Tertan's momentous first theme came back to him. "Tertan I am, but what is Tertan? Of this time, of that place, of some parentage, what does it matter?"

"No, I didn't find it," he said.

Now that he had consulted the sad half-meaningless record he knew all the more firmly that he must not give the matter out of his own hands. He must not release Tertan to authority. Not that he anticipated from the Dean anything but the greatest kindness for Tertan. The Dean would have the experience and skill which he himself could not have. One way or another the Dean could answer the question: "What is Tertan?" Yet this was precisely what he feared. He alone could keep alive—not for ever but for a somehow important time—the question: "What is Tertan?" He alone could keep it still a question. Some sure instinct told him that he must not surrender the question to a clean official desk in a clear official light to be dealt with, settled and closed.

He heard himself saying: "Is the Dean busy at the moment? I'd like to see him."

His request came thus unbidden, even forbidden, and it was one of the surprising and startling incidents of his life. Later, when he reviewed the events, so disconnected in themselves or so merely odd, of the story that unfolded for him that year, it was over this moment, on its face the least notable, that he paused longest. It was frequently to be with fear and never without a certainty of its meaning in his own knowledge of himself that he would recall this simple, routine request and the feeling of shame and freedom it gave him as he sent everything down the official chute. In the end, of course, no matter what he did to "protect" Tertan, he would have had to make the same request and lay the matter on the Dean's clean desk. But it would always be a landmark of his life that, at the very moment when he was rejecting the official way, he had been, without will or intention, so gladly drawn to it.

After the storm's last delicate flurry, the sun had come out. Reflected by the new snow, it filled the office with a golden light which was almost musical in the way it made all the commonplace objects of efficiency shine with a sudden sad and noble significance. And the light, now that he noticed it, made the utterance of his perverse and unwanted request even more momentous.

The secretary consulted the engagement pad. "He'll be free any minute. Don't you want to wait in the parlor?"

She threw open the door of the large and pleasant room in which the Dean held his Committee meetings and in which his visitors waited. It was designed with a homely elegance on the masculine side of the eighteenth-century manner. There was a small coal fire in the grate and the handsome mahogany table was strewn with books and magazines. The large windows gave on the snowy lawn and there was such a fine width of window that the white casements and walls seemed at this moment but a continuation of the snow, the snow but an extension of casement and walls. The outdoors seemed taken in and made safe, the indoors seemed luxuriously freshened and expanded.

Howe sat down by the fire and lighted a cigarette. The room had its intended effect upon him. He felt comfortable and relaxed, yet nicely organized, some young diplomatic agent of the eighteenth century, the newly fledged Swift carrying out Sir William Temple's business. The rawness of Tertan's case quite vanished. He crossed his legs and reached for a magazine.

It was that famous issue of *Life and Letters* that his idle hand had found and his blood raced as he sifted through it and the shape of his own name, Joseph Howe, sprang out at him, still cabalistic in its power. He tossed the magazine back on the table as the door of the Dean's office opened and the Dean ushered out Theodore Blackburn.

"Ah, Joseph!" the Dean said.

Blackburn said: "Good morning, Doctor." Howe winced at the title and caught the flicker of amusement over the Dean's face. The Dean stood with his hand high on the door-jamb and Blackburn, still in the doorway, remained standing almost under his long arm.

Howe nodded briefly to Blackburn, snubbing his eager deference. "Can you give me a few minutes?" he said to the Dean.

"All the time you want. Come in." Before the two men could enter the office, Blackburn claimed their attention with a long full "Er." As they turned to him, Blackburn said: "Can *you give me* a few minutes, Dr. Howe?" His eyes sparkled at the little audacity he had committed, the slightly impudent play with hierarchy. Of the three of them Blackburn kept himself the lowest, but he reminded Howe of his subaltern relation to the Dean.

"I mean, of course," Blackburn went on easily, "when you've finished with the Dean."

"I'll be in my office shortly," Howe said, turned his back on the ready "Thank you, sir," and followed the Dean into the inner room.

"Energetic boy," said the Dean. "A bit beyond himself but very energetic. Sit down."

The Dean lighted a cigarette, leaned back in his chair, sat easy and silent for a moment, giving Howe no signal to go ahead with business. He was a young Dean, not much beyond forty, a tall handsome man with sad, ambitious eyes. He had been a Rhodes scholar. His friends looked for great things from him and it was generally said that he had notions of education which he was not yet ready to try to put into practice.

His relaxed silence was meant as a compliment to Howe. He smiled and said: "What's the business, Joseph?"

"Do you know Tertan—Ferdinand Tertan, a freshman?"

The Dean's cigarette was in his mouth and his hands were clasped behind his head. He did not seem to search his memory for the name. He said: "What about him?"

Clearly the Dean knew something and he was waiting for Howe to tell him more. Howe moved only tentatively. Now that he was doing what he had resolved not to do, he felt more guilty at having been so long deceived by Tertan and more need to be loyal to his error.

"He's a strange fellow," he ventured. He said stubbornly: "In a strange way he's very brilliant." He concluded: "But very strange."

The springs of the Dean's swivel chair creaked as he came out of his sprawl and leaned forward to Howe. "Do you mean he's so strange that it's something you could give a name to?"

Howe looked at him stupidly. "What do you mean?" he said.

"What's his trouble?" the Dean said more neutrally.

"He's very brilliant, in a way. I looked him up and he has a top intelligence rating. But somehow, and it's hard to explain just how, what he says is always on the edge of sense and doesn't quite make it."

The Dean looked at him and Howe flushed up. The Dean had surely read Woolley on the subject of "the Howes" and the *tour d'ivresse*. Was that quick glance ironical?

The Dean picked up some papers from his desk and Howe could see that they were in Tertan's impatient scrawl. Perhaps the little gleam in the Dean's glance had come only from putting facts together.

"He sent me this yesterday," the Dean said. "After an interview I had with him. I haven't been able to do more than glance at it. When you said what you did, I realized there was something wrong."

Twisting his mouth, the Dean looked over the letter. "You seem to be involved," he said without looking up. "By the way, what did you give him at mid-term?"

Flushing, setting his shoulders, Howe said firmly: "I gave him A-minus."

The Dean chuckled. "Might be a good idea if some of our nicer boys went crazy—just a little." He said, "Well," to conclude the matter and handed the papers to Howe. "See if this is the same thing you've been finding. Then we can go into the matter again."

Before the fire in the parlor, in the chair that Howe had been occupying, sat Blackburn. He sprang to his feet as Howe entered.

"I said my office, Mr. Blackburn." Howe's voice was sharp. Then he was almost sorry for the rebuke, so clearly and naïvely did Blackburn seem to relish his stay in the parlor, close to authority.

"I'm in a bit of a hurry, sir," he said, "and I did want to be sure to speak to you, sir."

He was really absurd, yet fifteen years from now he would have grown up to himself, to the assurance and mature beefiness. In banks, in consular offices, in brokerage firms, on the bench, more seriously affable, a little sterner, he would make use of his ability to be administered by his job. It was almost reassuring. Now he was exercising his too-great skill on Howe. "I owe you an apology, sir," he said.

Howe knew that he did but he showed surprise.

"I mean, Doctor, after your having been so kind about letting me attend your class, I stopped coming." He smiled in deprecation. "Extra-curricular activities take up so much of my time. I'm afraid I undertook more than I could perform."

Howe had noticed the absence and had been a little irritated by it after Blackburn's elaborate plea. It was an absence that might be interpreted as a comment on the teacher. But there was only one way for him to answer. "You've no need to apologize," he said. "It's wholly your affair."

Blackburn beamed. "I'm so glad you feel that way about it, sir. I was worried you might think I had stayed away because I was influenced by—" He stopped and lowered his eyes.

Astonished, Howe said: "Influenced by what?"

"Well, by—" Blackburn hesitated and for answer pointed to the table on which lay the copy of *Life and Letters*. Without looking at it, he knew where to direct his hand. "By the unfavorable publicity, sir." He hurried on. "And that brings me to another point, sir. I am secretary of Quill and Scroll, sir, the student literary society, and I wonder if you would address us. You could read your own poetry, sir, and defend your own point of view. It would be very interesting."

It was truly amazing. Howe looked long and cruelly into Blackburn's face, trying to catch the secret of the mind that could have conceived this way of manipulating him, this way so daring and inept—but not entirely inept—with its malice so without malignity. The face did not yield its secret. Howe smiled broadly and said: "Of course I don't think you were influenced by the unfavorable publicity."

"I'm still going to take—regularly, for credit—your romantic poets course next term," Blackburn said.

"Don't worry, my dear fellow, don't worry about it."

Howe started to leave and Blackburn stopped him with: "But about Quill, sir?"

"Suppose we wait until next term? I'll be less busy then."

And Blackburn said: "Very good, sir, and thank you."

In his office the little encounter seemed less funny to Howe, was even in some indeterminate way disturbing. He made an effort to put it from his mind by turning to what was sure to disturb him more, the Tertan letter read in the new interpretation. He found what he had always found, the same florid leaps beyond fact and meaning, the same headlong certainty. But as his eye passed over the familiar scrawl it caught his own name and for the second time that hour he felt the race of his blood.

"The paraclete," Tertan had written to the Dean, "from a Greek word meaning to stand in place of, but going beyond the primitive idea to mean traditionally the helper, the one who comforts and assists, cannot without fundamental loss be jettisoned. Even if taken no longer in the supernatural sense, the concept remains deeply in the human consciousness inevitably. Humanitarianism is no reply, for not every man stands in the place of every other man for this other's comrade comfort. But certain are chosen out of the human race to be the consoler of some other. Of these, for example, is Joseph Barker Howe, Ph.D. Of intellects not the first yet of true intellect and lambent instructions, given to that which is intuitive and irrational, not to what is logical in the strict word, what is judged by him is of the heart and not the head. Here is one chosen, in that he chooses himself to stand in the place of another for comfort and consolation. To him more than another I give my gratitude, with all respect to our Dean who reads this, a noble man, but merely dedicated, not consecrated. But not in the aspect of the Paraclete only is Dr. Joseph Barker Howe established, for he must be the Paraclete to another aspect of himself, that which is driven and persecuted by the lack of understanding in the world at large, so that he in himself embodies the full history of man's tribulations and, overflowing upon others, notably the present writer, is the ultimate end."

This was love. There was no escape from it. Try as Howe might to remember that Tertan was mad and all his emotions invalidated, he could not destroy the effect upon him of his student's stern, affectionate regard. He had betrayed not only a power of mind but a power of love. And however firmly he held before his attention the fact of Tertan's madness, he could do nothing to banish the physical sensation of gratitude he felt. He had never thought of himself as "driven and persecuted" and he did not now. But still he could not make meaningless his sensation of gratitude. The pitiable Tertan sternly pitied him, and comfort came from Tertan's never-to-be-comforted mind.

III

In an academic community, even an efficient one, official matters move slowly. The term drew to a close with no action in the case of Tertan, and Joseph Howe had to confront a curious problem. How should he grade his strange student, Tertan?

Tertan's final examination had been no different from all his other writing, and what did one "give" such a student? De Witt must have his A, that was clear. Johnson would get a B. With Casebeer it was a question of a B-minus or a C-plus, and Stettenhover, who had been crammed by the team tutor to fill half a blue-book with his thin feminine scrawl, would have his C-minus which he would accept with mingled indifference and resentment. But with Tertan it was not so easy.

The boy was still in the college process and his name could not be omitted from the grade sheet. Yet what should a mind under suspicion of madness be graded? Until the medical verdict was given, it was for Howe to continue as Tertan's teacher and to keep his judgment pedagogical. Impossible to give him an F: he had not failed. B was for Johnson's stolid mediocrity. He could not be put on the edge of passing with Stettenhover, for he exactly did not pass. In energy and richness of intellect he was perhaps even De Witt's superior, and Howe toyed grimly with the notion of giving him an A, but that would lower the value of the A De Witt had won with his beautiful and clear, if still arrogant, mind. There was a notation which the Registrar recognized—Inc. for Incomplete and in the horrible comedy of the situation, Howe considered that. But really only a mark of M for Mad would serve.

In his perplexity, Howe sought the Dean, but the Dean was out of town. In the end, he decided to maintain the A-minus he had given Tertan at mid-term. After all, there had been no falling away from that quality. He entered it on the grade sheet with something like bravado.

Academic time moves quickly. A college year is not really a year, lacking as it does three months. And it is endlessly divided into units which, at their beginning, appear larger than they are—terms, half-terms, months, weeks. And the ultimate unit, the hour, is not really an hour, lacking as it does ten minutes. And so the new term advanced rapidly and one day the fields about the town were all brown, cleared of even the few thin patches of snow which had lingered so long.

Howe, as he lectured on the romantic poets, became conscious of Black-burn emanating wrath. Blackburn did it well, did it with enormous dignity. He did not stir in his seat, he kept his eyes fixed on Howe in perfect attention, but he abstained from using his notebook, there was no mistaking what he proposed to himself as an attitude. His elbow on the writing-wing of the chair, his chin on the curled fingers of his hand, he was the embodiment of intel-lectual indignation. He was thinking his own thoughts, would give no public offence, yet would claim his due, was not to be intimidated. Howe knew that he would present himself at the end of the hour.

Blackburn entered the office without invitation. He did not smile, there was no cajolery about him. Without invitation he sat down beside Howe's desk. He did not speak until he had taken the blue-book from his pocket. He said: "What does this mean, sir?"

It was a sound and conservative student tactic. Said in the usual way it meant: "How could you have so misunderstood me?" or "What does this mean for my future in the course?" But there were none of the humbler tones in Blackburn's way of saying it.

Howe made the established reply: "I think that's for you to tell me."

Blackburn continued icy. "I'm sure I can't, sir."

There was a silence between them. Both dropped their eyes to the blue-book on the desk. On its cover Howe had penciled: "F. This is very poor work."

Howe picked up the blue-book. There was always the possibility of injustice. The teacher may be bored by the mass of papers and not wholly attentive. A phrase, even the student's handwriting, may irritate him unreasonably. "Well," said Howe, "let's go through it."

He opened the first page. "Now here: you write: 'In *The Ancient Mariner,* Coleridge lives in and transports us to a honey-sweet world where all is rich and strange, a world of charm to which we can escape from the humdrum existence of our daily lives, the world of romance. Here, in this warm and honey-sweet land of charming dreams we can relax and enjoy ourselves.' "

Howe lowered the paper and waited with a neutral look for Blackburn to speak. Blackburn returned the look boldly, did not speak, sat stolid and lofty. At last Howe said, speaking gently: "Did you mean that, or were you just at a loss for something to say?"

"You imply that I was just 'bluffing'?" The quotation marks hung palpable in the air about the word.

"I'd like to know. I'd prefer believing that you were bluffing to believing that you really thought this."

Blackburn's eyebrows went up. From the height of a great and firm-based idea he looked at his teacher. He clasped the crags for a moment and then pounced, craftily, suavely. "Do you mean, Dr. Howe, that there aren't two opinions possible?"

It was superbly done in its air of putting all of Howe's intellectual life into the balance. Howe remained patient and simple. "Yes, many opinions are possible, but not this one. Whatever anyone believes of *The Ancient Mariner,* no one can in reason believe that it represents a—a honey-sweet world in which we can relax."

"But that is what I *feel,* sir."

This was well done too. Howe said: "Look, Mr. Blackburn. Do you really relax with hunger and thirst, the heat and the sea-serpents, the dead men with staring eyes, Life in Death and the skeletons? Come now, Mr. Blackburn."

Blackburn made no answer and Howe pressed forward. "Now you say of Wordsworth: 'Of peasant stock himself, he turned from the effete life of the salons and found in the peasant the hope of a flaming revolution which would sweep away all the old ideas. This is the subject of his best poems.' "

Beaming at his teacher with youthful eagerness, Blackburn said: "Yes, sir, a rebel, a bringer of light to suffering mankind. I see him as a kind of Prothemeus."

"A kind of what?"

"Prothemeus, sir."

"Think, Mr. Blackburn. We were talking about him only today and I men-

tioned his name a dozen times. You don't mean Prothemeus. You mean—"
Howe waited but there was no response.

"You mean Prometheus."

Blackburn gave no assent and Howe took the reins. "You've done a bad
job here, Mr. Blackburn, about as bad as could be done." He saw Blackburn stiffen and his genial face harden again. "It shows either a lack of preparation or a complete lack of understanding." He saw Blackburn's face begin
to go to pieces and he stopped.

"Oh, sir," Blackburn burst out, "I've never had a mark like this before,
never anything below a B, never. A thing like this has never happened to me
before."

It must be true, it was a statement too easily verified. Could it be that other
instructors accepted such flaunting nonsense? Howe wanted to end the interview. "I'll set it down to lack of preparation," he said. "I know you're busy.
That's not an excuse but it's an explanation. Now suppose you really prepare
and then take another quiz in two weeks. We'll forget this one and count the
other."

Blackburn squirmed with pleasure and gratitude. "Thank you, sir. You're
really very kind, very kind."

Howe rose to conclude the visit. "All right then—in two weeks."

It was that day that the Dean imparted to Howe the conclusion of the case
of Tertan. It was simple and a little anticlimactic. A physician had been called
in, and had said the word, given the name.

"A classic case, he called it," the Dean said. "Not a doubt in the world," he
said. His eyes were full of miserable pity and he clutched at a word. "A classic
case, a classic case." To his aid and to Howe's there came the Parthenon and
the form of the Greek drama, the Aristotelian logic, Racine and the Well-
Tempered Clavichord, the blueness of the Aegean and its clear sky. Classic—
that is to say, without a doubt, perfect in its way, a veritable model, and, as
the Dean had been told, sure to take a perfectly predictable and inevitable
course to a foreknown conclusion.

It was not only pity that stood in the Dean's eyes. For a moment there was
fear too. "Terrible," he said, "it is simply terrible."

Then he went on briskly. "Naturally we've told the boy nothing. And
naturally we won't. His tuition's paid by his scholarship and we'll continue
him on the rolls until the end of the year. That will be kindest. After that
the matter will be out of our control. We'll see, of course, that he gets into
the proper hands. I'm told there will be no change, he'll go on like this, be
as good as this, for four to six months. And so we'll just go along as usual."

So Tertan continued to sit in Section 5 of English 1A, to his classmates
still a figure of curiously dignified fun, symbol to most of them of the respectable but absurd intellectual life. But to his teacher he was now very
different. He had not changed—he was still the greyhound casting for the

scent of ideas and Howe could see that he was still the same Tertan, but he could not feel it. What he felt as he looked at the boy sitting in his accustomed place was the hard blank of a fact. The fact itself was formidable and depressing. But what Howe was chiefly aware of was that he had permitted the metamorphosis of Tertan from person to fact.

As much as possible he avoided seeing Tertan's upraised hand and eager eye. But the fact did not know of its mere factuality, it continued its existence as if it were Tertan, hand up and eye questioning, and one day it appeared in Howe's office with a document.

"Even the spirit who lives egregiously, above the herd, must have its relations with the fellow-man," Tertan declared. He laid the document on Howe's desk. It was headed "Quill and Scroll Society of Dwight College. Application for Membership."

"In most ways these are crass minds," Tertan said, touching the paper. "Yet as a whole, bound together in their common love of letters, they transcend their intellectual lacks, since it is not a paradox that the whole is greater than the sum of its parts."

"When are the elections?" Howe asked.

"They take place to-morrow."

"I certainly hope you will be successful."

"Thank you. Would you wish to implement that hope?" A rather dirty finger pointed to the bottom of the sheet. "A faculty recommender is necessary," Tertan said stiffly, and waited.

"And you wish me to recommend you?"

"It would be an honor."

"You may use my name."

Tertan's finger pointed again. "It must be a written sponsorship, signed by the sponsor." There was a large blank space on the form under the heading: "Opinion of Faculty Sponsor."

This was almost another thing and Howe hesitated. Yet there was nothing else to do and he took out his fountain-pen. He wrote: "Mr. Ferdinand Tertan is marked by his intense devotion to letters and by his exceptional love of all things of the mind." To this he signed his name which looked bold and assertive on the white page. It disturbed him, the strange affirming power of a name. With a business-like air, Tertan whipped up the paper, folded it with decision and put it into his pocket. He bowed and took his departure, leaving Howe with the sense of having done something oddly momentous.

And so much now seemed odd and momentous to Howe that should not have seemed so. It was odd and momentous, he felt, when he sat with Blackburn's second quiz before him and wrote in an excessively firm hand the grade of C-minus. The paper was a clear, an indisputable failure. He was carefully and consciously committing a cowardice. Blackburn had told the truth when he had pleaded his past record. Howe had consulted it in the

Dean's office. It showed no grade lower than a B-minus. A canvass of some of Blackburn's previous instructors had brought vague attestations to the adequate powers of a student imperfectly remembered and sometimes surprise that his abilities could be questioned at all.

As he wrote the grade, Howe told himself that this cowardice sprang from an unwillingness to have more dealings with a student he disliked. He knew it was simpler than that. He knew he feared Blackburn: that was the absurd truth. And cowardice did not solve the matter after all. Blackburn, flushed with a first success, attacked at once. The minimal passing grade had not assuaged his feelings, and he sat at Howe's desk and again the blue-book lay between them. Blackburn said nothing. With an enormous impudence, he was waiting for Howe to speak and explain himself.

At last Howe said sharply and rudely: "Well?" His throat was tense and the blood was hammering in his head. His mouth was tight with anger at himself for his disturbance.

Blackburn's glance was almost baleful. "This is impossible, sir."

"But there it is," Howe answered.

"Sir?" Blackburn had not caught the meaning but his tone was still haughty.

Impatiently Howe said: "There it is, plain as day. Are you here to complain again?"

"Indeed I am, sir." There was surprise in Blackburn's voice that Howe should ask the question.

"I shouldn't complain if I were you. You did a thoroughly bad job on your first quiz. This one is a little, only a very little, better." This was not true. If anything, it was worse.

"That might be a matter of opinion, sir."

"It is a matter of opinion. Of my opinion."

"Another opinion might be different, sir."

"You really believe that?" Howe said.

"Yes." The omission of the "sir" was monumental.

"Whose, for example?"

"The Dean's, for example." Then the fleshy jaw came forward a little. "Or a certain literary critic's, for example."

It was colossal and almost too much for Blackburn himself to handle. The solidity of his face almost crumpled under it. But he withstood his own audacity and went on. "And the Dean's opinion might be guided by the knowledge that the person who gave me this mark is the man whom a famous critic, the most eminent judge of literature in this country, called a drunken man. The Dean might think twice about whether such a man is fit to teach Dwight students."

Howe said in quiet admonition, "Blackburn, you're mad," meaning no more than to check the boy's extravagance.

But Blackburn paid no heed. He had another shot in the locker. "And the

Dean might be guided by the information, of which I have evidence, documentary evidence"—he slapped his breast-pocket twice—"that this same person personally recommended to the college literary society, the oldest in the country, that he personally recommended a student who is crazy, who threw the meeting into an uproar, a psychiatric case. The Dean might take that into account."

Howe was never to learn the details of that "uproar." He had always to content himself with the dim but passionate picture which at that moment sprang into his mind, of Tertan standing on some abstract height and madly denouncing the multitude of Quill and Scroll who howled him down.

He sat quiet a moment and looked at Blackburn. The ferocity had entirely gone from the student's face. He sat regarding his teacher almost benevolently. He had played a good card and now, scarcely at all unfriendly, he was waiting to see the effect. Howe took up the blue-book and negligently sifted through it. He read a page, closed the book, struck out the C-minus and wrote an F.

"Now you may take the paper to the Dean," he said. "You may tell him that after reconsidering it, I lowered the grade."

The gasp was audible. "Oh, sir!" Blackburn cried. "Please!" His face was agonized. "It means my graduation, my livelihood, my future. Don't do this to me."

"It's done already."

Blackburn stood up. "I spoke rashly, sir, hastily. I had no intention, no real intention, of seeing the Dean. It rests with you—entirely, entirely. I *hope* you will restore the first mark."

"Take the matter to the Dean or not, just as you choose. The grade is what you deserve and it stands."

Blackburn's head dropped. "And will I be failed at mid-term, sir?"

"Of course."

From deep out of Blackburn's great chest rose a cry of anguish. "Oh, sir, if you want me to go down on my knees to you, I will, I will."

Howe looked at him in amazement.

"I will, I will. On my knees, sir. This mustn't, mustn't happen."

He spoke so literally, meaning so very truly that his knees and exactly his knees were involved and seeming to think that he was offering something of tangible value to his teacher, that Howe, whose head had become icy clear in the nonsensical drama, thought, "The boy is mad," and began to speculate fantastically whether something in himself attracted or developed aberration. He could see himself standing absurdly before the Dean and saying: "I've found another. This time it's the vice-president of the Council, the manager of the debating team, and secretary of Quill and Scroll." One more such discovery, he thought, and he himself would be discovered! And there, suddenly, Blackburn was on his knees with a thump, his huge thighs straining his trousers, his hands outstretched in a great gesture of supplication.

With a cry, Howe shoved back his swivel chair and it rolled away on its casters half across the little room. Blackburn knelt for a moment to nothing at all, then got to his feet.

Howe rose abruptly. He said: "Blackburn, you will stop acting like an idiot. Dust your knees off, take your paper and get out. You've behaved like a fool and a malicious person. You have half a term to do a decent job. Keep your silly mouth shut and try to do it. Now get out."

Blackburn's head was low. He raised it and there was a pious light in his eyes. "Will you shake hands, sir?" he said. He thrust out his hand.

"I will not," Howe said.

Head and hand sank together. Blackburn picked up his blue-book and walked to the door. He turned and said: "Thank you, sir." His back, as he departed, was heavy with tragedy and stateliness.

IV

After years of bad luck with the weather, the College had a perfect day for Commencement. It was wonderfully bright, the air so transparent, the wind so brisk that no one could resist talking about it.

As Howe set out for the campus he heard Hilda calling from the back yard. She called, "Professor, professor," and came running to him.

Howe said: "What's this 'professor' business?"

"Mother told me," Hilda said. "You've been promoted. And I want to take your picture."

"Next year," said Howe. "I won't be a professor until next year. And you know better than to call anybody 'professor.' "

"It was just in fun," Hilda said. She seemed disappointed.

"But you can take my picture if you want. I won't look much different next year." Still, it was frightening. It might mean that he was to stay in this town all his life.

Hilda brightened. "Can I take it in this?" she said, and touched the gown he carried over his arm.

Howe laughed. "Yes, you can take it in this."

"I'll get my things and meet you in front of Otis," Hilda said. "I have the background all picked out."

On the campus the Commencement crowd was already large. It stood about in eager, nervous little family groups. As he crossed, Howe was greeted by a student, capped and gowned, glad of the chance to make an event for his parents by introducing one of his teachers. It was while Howe stood there chatting that he saw Tertan.

He had never seen anyone quite so alone, as though a circle had been woven about him to separate him from the gay crowd on the campus. Not that Tertan was not gay—he was the gayest of all. Three weeks had passed since Howe had last seen him, the weeks of examination, the lazy week before Commencement, and this was now a different Tertan. On his head he wore a panama hat, broad-brimmed and fine, of the shape associated with South American planters. He wore a suit of raw silk, luxurious but yellowed with age and much too tight, and he sported a whangee cane. He walked sedately, the hat tilted at a devastating angle, the stick coming up and down in time to his measured tread. He had, Howe guessed, outfitted himself to greet the day in the clothes of that ruined father whose existence was on record in the Dean's office. Gravely and arrogantly he surveyed the scene—in it, his whole bearing seemed to say, but not of it. With his haughty step, with his flashing eye, Tertan was coming nearer. Howe did not wish to be seen. He shifted his position slightly. When he looked again, Tertan was not in sight.

The chapel clock struck the quarter hour. Howe detached himself from his chat and hurried to Otis Hall at the far end of the campus. Hilda had not yet come. He went up into the high portico and, using the glass of the door for a mirror, put on his gown, adjusted the hood on his shoulders and set the mortar-board on his head. When he came down the steps Hilda had arrived.

Nothing could have told him more forcibly that a year had passed than the development of Hilda's photographic possessions from the box camera of the previous fall. By a strap about her neck was hung a leather case, so thick and strong, so carefully stitched and so moulded to its contents that it could only hold a costly camera. The appearance was deceptive, Howe knew, for he had been present at the Aikens' pre-Christmas conference about its purchase. It was only a fairly good domestic camera. Still, it looked very impressive. Hilda carried another leather case from which she drew a collapsible tripod. Decisively she extended each of its gleaming legs and set it up on the path. She removed the camera from its case and fixed it to the tripod. In its compact efficiency the camera almost had a life of its own, but Hilda treated it with easy familiarity, looked into its eye, glanced casually at its gauges. Then from a pocket she took still another leather case and drew from it a small instrument through which she looked first at Howe, who began to feel inanimate and lost, and then at the sky. She made some adjustment on the instrument, then some adjustment on the camera. She swept the scene with her eye, found a spot and pointed the camera in its direction. She walked to the spot, stood on it and beckoned to Howe. With each new leather case, with each new instrument and with each new adjustment she had grown in ease and now she said: "Joe, will you stand here?"

Obediently Howe stood where he was bidden. She had yet another instrument. She took out a tape-measure on a mechanical spool. Kneeling down before Howe, she put the little metal ring of the tape under the tip of his shoe. At her request, Howe pressed it with his toe. When she had measured her distance, she nodded to Howe who released the tape. At a touch, it sprang back into the spool. "You have to be careful if you're going to get what you want," Hilda said. "I don't believe in all this snap-snap-snapping," she remarked loftily. Howe nodded in agreement, although he was beginning to think Hilda's care excessive.

Now at last the moment had come. Hilda squinted into the camera, moved the tripod slightly. She stood to the side, holding the plunger of the shutter-cable. "Ready," she said. "Will you relax, Joseph, please?" Howe realized that he was standing frozen. Hilda stood poised and precise as a setter, one hand holding the little cable, the other extended with curled dainty fingers like a dancer's, as if expressing to her subject the precarious delicacy of the moment. She pressed the plunger and there was the click. At once she stirred to action, got behind the camera, turned a new exposure. "Thank you," she said. "Would you stand under that tree and let me do a character study with light and shade?"

The childish absurdity of the remark restored Howe's ease. He went to the little tree. The pattern the leaves made on his gown was what Hilda was after. He had just taken a satisfactory position when he heard in the unmistakable voice: "Ah, Doctor! Having your picture taken?"

Howe gave up the pose and turned to Blackburn who stood on the walk, his hands behind his back, a little too large for his bachelor's gown. Annoyed that Blackburn should see him posing for a character study in light and shade, Howe said irritably: "Yes, having my picture taken."

Blackburn beamed at Hilda. "And the little photographer," he said. Hilda fixed her eyes on the ground and stood closer to her brilliant and aggressive camera. Blackburn, teetering on his heels, his hands behind his back, wholly prelatical and benignly patient, was not abashed at the silence. At last Howe said: "If you'll excuse us, Mr. Blackburn, we'll go on with the picture."

"Go right ahead, sir. I'm running along." But he only came closer. "Dr. Howe," he said fervently, "I want to tell you how glad I am that I was able to satisfy your standards at last."

Howe was surprised at the hard insulting brightness of his own voice and even Hilda looked up curiously as he said: "Nothing you have ever done has satisfied me and nothing you could ever do would satisfy me, Blackburn."

With a glance at Hilda, Blackburn made a gesture as if to hush Howe—as though all his former bold malice had taken for granted a kind of understanding between himself and his teacher, a secret which must not be betrayed to a third person. "I only meant, sir," he said, "that I was able to pass your course after all."

Howe said: "You didn't pass my course. I passed you out of my course. I passed you without even reading your paper. I wanted to be sure the college would be rid of you. And when all the grades were in and I did read your paper, I saw I was right not to have read it first."

Blackburn presented a stricken face. "It was very bad, sir?"

But Howe had turned away. The paper had been fantastic. The paper had been, if he wished to see it so, mad. It was at this moment that the Dean came up behind Howe and caught his arm. "Hello, Joseph," he said. "We'd better be getting along, it's almost late."

He was not a familiar man, but when he saw Blackburn, who approached to greet him, he took Blackburn's arm too. "Hello, Theodore," he said. Leaning forward on Howe's arm and on Blackburn's, he said: "Hello, Hilda dear." Hilda replied quietly: "Hello, Uncle George."

Still clinging to their arms, still linking Howe and Blackburn, the Dean said: "Another year gone, Joe, and we've turned out another crop. After you've been here a few years, you'll find it reasonably upsetting—you wonder how there can be so many graduating classes while you stay the same. But, of course, you don't stay the same." Then he said, "Well," sharply to dismiss the thought. He pulled Blackburn's arm and swung him around to Howe. "Have you heard about Teddy Blackburn?" he asked. "He has a job already, before graduation, the first man of his class to be placed." Expectant of congratulations, Blackburn beamed at Howe. Howe remained silent.

"Isn't that good?" the Dean said. Still Howe did not answer and the Dean, puzzled and put out, turned to Hilda. "That's a very fine-looking camera, Hilda." She touched it with affectionate pride.

"Instruments of precision," said a voice. "Instruments of precision." Of the three with joined arms, Howe was the nearest to Tertan, whose gaze took in all the scene except the smile and the nod which Howe gave him. The boy leaned on his cane. The broad-brimmed hat, canting jauntily over his eye, confused the image of his face that Howe had established, suppressed the rigid lines of the ascetic and brought out the baroque curves. It made an effect of perverse majesty.

"Instruments of precision," said Tertan for the last time, addressing no one, making a casual comment to the universe. And it occurred to Howe that Tertan might not be referring to Hilda's equipment. The sense of the thrice-woven circle of the boy's loneliness smote him fiercely. Tertan stood in majestic jauntiness, superior to all the scene, but his isolation made Howe ache with a pity of which Tertan was more the cause than the object, so general and indiscriminate was it.

Whether in his sorrow he made some unintended movement towards Tertan which the Dean checked or whether the suddenly tightened grip on his arm was the Dean's own sorrow and fear, he did not know. Tertan watched them in the incurious way people watch a photograph being taken and suddenly the thought that, to the boy, it must seem that the three were posing for a picture together made Howe detach himself almost rudely from the Dean's grasp.

"I promised Hilda another picture," he announced—needlessly, for Tertan was no longer there, he had vanished in the last sudden flux of visitors who, now that the band had struck up, were rushing nervously to find seats.

"You'd better hurry," the Dean said. "I'll go along, it's getting late for me." He departed and Blackburn walked stately by his side.

Howe again took his position under the little tree which cast its shadow over his face and gown. "Just hurry, Hilda, won't you?" he said. Hilda held the cable at arm-length, her other arm crooked and her fingers crisped. She rose on her toes and said "Ready," and pressed the release. "Thank you," she said gravely and began to dismantle her camera as he hurried off to join the procession.

MORE ABOUT THIS STORY

The most valid literary as well as psychological ground for a study of Trilling's story lies in an analysis of Howe's dilemma, the dilemma of a professor confronted by a student whose mind is disconcertingly different—as brilliant as it is distressingly incoherent—and whose very presence threatens to upset the tidy balance of the professor's orderly life.

As the central figure, Howe presents an image of conflict. Poet, conscientious and compassionate teacher, man of good will, Joseph Barker Howe is also a man comfortably aware that his academic status enables him to be "benign and powerful." His scrawl on the blackboard was careless, but it "confirmed his authority." Howe enjoys the neatness, decorum, and regimen of academic bureaucracy. The hostile critic who deplored in Howe's poetry a "precious subjectivism" that ignored tradition might have learned with considerable surprise of Howe's "pleasure" in the official routine "of cards and sheets, arrangements and small decisions," or of his "clear satisfaction from the ritual of prayer and prosy speech" at the opening convocation.

Facing the "massed impassivity" of "gross," "cloddish" freshmen, Howe is as grateful for Tertan's creative independence and splendid—if sometimes absurd and ridiculous—isolation from the rest of the class as he is strangely uncomfortable. The poet in Howe responds to the poet in Tertan. Without fully understanding all that Tertan writes or says, Howe is stirred by the young man's profound and innocent idealism. At first, Tertan's deification of Howe as poet, humanist, and man of letters, his awkward attempts to identify with him merely amuse the teacher. What fascinates and grips Howe at last, however, is neither Tertan's quaintness nor absurdity but the intricacy of his mind and his unwavering reverence for knowledge. Tertan's explosive virtuosity, however elusive, sprawling, abstract, or even incoherent, piques Howe's curiosity, especially when contrasted with the achievement of his peers: "stolid mediocrity," "the edge of passing," and even DeWitt's "beautiful and clear" mind. Above all, Tertan's "energy and richness of intellect," however dislocated, shines beside Blackburn's brassy "Wadsworthian" chicanery. Para-

LIONEL TRILLING : 271

doxically, though Howe feels compassion for Tertan and contempt for Blackburn, he denies his own impulse, rewards the blackmailer, and condemns the innocent Tertan to eternal isolation in his timeless, placeless mind-capsule. Why?

A clue lies in Howe's carelessly uttering the same phrase—"the boy is mad"—about both Tertan and Blackburn. Would Howe have been shocked to hear a psychiatrist confute his judgment about Blackburn? Assuredly not. Moreover, Howe would surely have withdrawn his comment about Blackburn; but he sustains—with the approval of the psychiatrist and the Dean—the charge against Tertan. The dividing line between mental institution and institute of higher learning thins here to a razor's edge, an edge that cuts deep into Howe's psyche.

Howe's own identity conflict—whether to be idealist or opportunist, rebel or conformist—lies close to the surface of his experience with these two boys. Ironically, Blackburn's behavior proves socially more acceptable. Yet, just as ironically, no sound evidence exists for Howe's initiating the process which reduces Tertan from "person to fact." Tertan did not seriously disrupt Howe's classroom or foul his teacher's dignity. His "madness" lay in failing to conceal his difference from others and in his inability to spare or protect others from that difference. Where he differs, of course, from others is in exposing the raw nerve ends of his sensibility and projecting his concern about identity, truth, and knowledge. However conscious he may be of these same concerns, Howe cannot face them directly and so sweeps them—along with Tertan—into a dusty corner. But the dust rises and stifles Howe. What Howe finally learns reverberates from Tertan's "casual comment to the universe" at the end of the story. "Instruments of precision," Tertan remarks as young Hilda Aiken proudly exhibits her new camera to Howe, Blackburn, and the Dean as they stand by, their arms intertwined. Howe recoils from the multiple implications of Tertan's observation, aware that Tertan may justly have lumped men and machines, or, more, have united Howe with the Dean, symbol of paternal authority, and with Blackburn, symbol of callous, vulgar opportunism.

Pulling away from the Dean's tightening grasp fails to loosen Howe's bondage. Unlike Tertan, whose very freedom from the confines of time and place suggests madness, Howe remains caught, fixed, paralyzed within the limits of the conventional. Hilda tries to capture in the dappled pattern of the leaves shadowing Howe's academic gown "a character study with light and shade." A darker study has already been etched on the sensitive plate of Howe's own consciousness, for he knows now that he is not, as Tertan says of himself, an "existence without alloy." In an essay entitled "Freud and Literature," Lionel Trilling writes about mankind what might well apply to Professor Howe: "Everything that he gains he pays for in more than equal coin; compromise in the compounding with defeat constitutes his best way of getting through the

world. His best qualities are the result of a struggle whose outcome is tragic."
One more point may be made. The Dean reports to Howe that the psychiatrist has analyzed Tertan's as a "classic case . . . sure to take its perfectly predictable and inevitable course to a foregone conclusion." Not all psychiatrists would agree, especially since many persons with behavior patterns more bizarre than Tertan's have benefited from proper care. *Schizophrenia* is a frightening word to those who take fright easily. Howe, whose inner conflict had been triggered by Tertan's presence, flees after a pitifully brief struggle against his fear. When he hurries off "to join the procession," Howe denies more than an integral part of himself. He denies another human being whom he might have helped. The extent of Howe's responsibility to help Tertan discover his identity may, of course, be argued, but it cannot be ignored or, worse, evaded, by a glib phrase—"The boy is mad." As the eminent psychiatrist Harry Stack Sullivan has written, "We are all much more simply human than otherwise, be we happy and successful, contented and detached, miserable and mentally disordered, or whatever."

To be human, however, does not prove always to imply the humane, even in the enlightened world of the academy. A real-life footnote to Tertan's experience may illustrate the point. Diana Trilling, wife of the author of "Of This Time, Of That Place," tells in her *Claremont Essays* (1965) how the "beat" poet Allen Ginsberg, once a brilliant but difficult and rebellious student of her husband's at Columbia, was expelled for scribbling an obscene phrase on the dust of a dormitory window. Years later he returned to the campus hoping to repay a two-hundred-dollar debt to the university with a poetry reading. College officials sanctioned the occasion but refused to pay for it. The reader may here recall the opening line of the second section of Trilling's story: "The question was: At whose door must the tragedy be laid?"

FOR FURTHER READING

Arieti, Silvano. "Schizophrenia: The Manifest Symptomatology, the Psychodynamic and Formal Mechanisms," *American Handbook of Psychiatry,* ed. S. Arieti. New York: Basic Books, 1959. I, 455–484.

Eisinger, Chester. *Fiction of the Forties.* Chicago: University of Chicago, 1963, pp. 135–145.

Lewis, R. W. B. "Lionel Trilling and the New Stoicism," *Hudson Review,* III (Summer, 1950), 313–317.

Sullivan, Harry Stack, *Clinical Studies in Psychiatry.* New York: W. W. Norton, 1956, pp. 304–360.

Rip Van Winkle

BY WASHINGTON IRVING (1783–1859)

The last of our stories is the earliest in date of composition (1819–1820) and has as its hero the oldest adolescent of all. Chronologically, of course, Rip Van Winkle far exceeds the age limit of adolescence. But wherever Washington Irving's tale is read and enjoyed (which is to say, everywhere) Rip lingers in memory as one who refused the rite of becoming, who tried to stop the passage of time and to stave off the responsibilities of manhood. A fuller discussion of the psychological implications of this good-natured Dutch loafer's slumbrous flight from maturity has been left for the afterword. Meanwhile, as the reader shares Rip's strange vision, he might ponder one critic's observation that "The Rip Van Winkle complex may mean as much as the Oedipus complex in the modern American world."

Apart from these broader meanings, "Rip Van Winkle" appeals through its rare narrative skill. Grace, geniality, and intimacy infuse Irving's style, lending an apparent simplicity that disguises a subtle craft. Like "The Legend of Sleepy Hollow," its companion piece in *The Sketch Book,* "Rip Van Winkle" drew heavily upon German sources. But what Irving borrowed he made his own. The playful device of a fictitious historian, the delicate balance between the reality of the Hudson River and the "fairy mountains" of the Kaatskills, and the suggestive counterpoint of nature's tranquility and silence against the harsh sounds of home and village—all of these hallmark not only Irving's urbanity and romantic imagination but also his originality.

America's first internationally acclaimed man of letters, Irving admitted that Europe's "accumulated treasures of age" held more for him than America's "youthful promise." He longed, as he said, to "escape

273

from the commonplace realities of the present," to lose himself "among the shadowy grandeurs of the past." In a very real sense, then, Rip's dream parallels his creator's. Both men resist change and both rhapsodize about the past. Among the reasons that "Rip Van Winkle" commands interest after one hundred and fifty years is that Rip's dream remains as fresh, appealing, and tragic as our own last and perhaps similar reverie.

THE STORY
A POSTHUMOUS WRITING OF DIEDRICH KNICKERBOCKER

By Woden, God of Saxons,
From whence comes Wensday, that is Wodensday.
Truth is a thing that ever I will keep
Unto thylke day in which I creep into
My sepulchre—

CARTWRIGHT

The following tale was found among the papers of the late Diedrich Knickerbocker, an old gentleman of New York, who was very curious in the Dutch history of the province, and the manners of the descendants from its primitive settlers. His historical reserches, however, did not lie so much among books as among men; for the former are lamentably scanty on his favorite topics; whereas he found the old burghers, and still more their wives, rich in that legendary lore so invaluable to true history. Whenever, therefore, he happened upon a genuine Dutch family, snugly shut up in its low-roofed farmhouse under a spreading sycamore, he looked upon it as a little clasped volume of black-letter, and studied it with the zeal of a book worm.

The result of all these researches was a history of the province during the reign of the Dutch governors, which he published some years since. There have been various opinions as to the literary character of his work, and, to tell the truth, it is not a whit better than it should be. Its chief merit is its scrupulous accuracy, which indeed was a little questioned on its first appearance, but has since been completely established; and it is now admitted into all historical collections, as a book of unquestionable authority.

The old gentleman died shortly after the publication of his work, and now that he is dead and gone, it cannot do much harm to his memory to say that his time might have been much better employed in weightier labors. He, however, was apt to ride his hobby his own way; and though it did now and then kick up the dust a little in the eyes of his neighbors, and grieve the spirit of some friends, for whom he felt the truest deference and affection; yet his errors and follies are remembered "more in sorrow than in anger," and it begins to be suspected that he never intended to injure or offend. But however his memory may be appreciated by critics, it is still held dear by many folk, whose good opinion is well worth having; particularly by certain biscuit bakers, who have gone so far as to imprint his likeness on their New-Year cakes; and have thus given him a chance for immortality, almost equal to the being stamped on a Waterloo Medal, or a Queen Anne's Farthing.

Whoever has made a voyage up the Hudson must remember the Kaatskill Mountains. They are a dismembered branch of the great Appalachian family, and are seen away to the west of the river, swelling up to a noble height, and lording it over the surrounding country. Every change of season, every change of weather, indeed every hour of the day, produces some change in the magical hues and shapes of these mountains, and they are regarded by all the good wives, far and near, as perfect barometers. When the weather is fair and settled, they are clothed in blue and purple, and print their bold outlines on the clear evening sky; but sometimes, when the rest of the landscape is cloudless, they will gather a hood of gray vapors about their summits, which, in the last rays of the setting sun, will glow and light up like a crown of glory.

At the foot of these fairy mountains, the voyager may have descried the light smoke curling up from a village, whose shingle-roofs gleam among the trees, just where the blue tints of the upland melt away into the fresh green of the nearer landscape. It is a little village of great antiquity, having been founded by some of the Dutch colonists in the early times of the province, just about the beginning of the government of the good Peter Stuyvesant, (may he rest in peace!) and there were some of the houses of the original settlers standing within a few years, built of small yellow bricks brought from Holland, having latticed windows and gable fronts, surmounted with weathercocks.

In that same village, and in one of these very houses (which, to tell the precise truth, was sadly time-worn and weather-beaten), there lived, many years since, while the country was yet a province of Great Britain, a simple, good-natured fellow, of the name of Rip Van Winkle. He was a descendant of the Van Winkles who figured so gallantly in the chivalrous days of Peter Stuyvesant, and accompanied him to the siege of Fort Christina. He inherited, however, but little of the martial character of his ancestors. I have observed that he was a simple, good-natured man; he was, moreover, a kind neighbor, and an obedient hen-pecked husband. Indeed, to the latter circumstance might be owing that meekness of spirit which gained him such universal popularity; for those men are most apt to be obsequious and conciliating abroad, who are under the discipline of shrews at home. Their tempers, doubtless, are rendered pliant and malleable in the fiery furnace of domestic tribulation; and a curtain-lecture is worth all the sermons in the world for teaching the virtues of patience and long-suffering. A termagant wife may, therefore, in some respects be considered a tolerable blessing; and if so, Rip Van Winkle was thrice blessed.

Certain it is, that he was a great favorite among all the good wives of the village, who, as usual with the amiable sex, took his part in all family squabbles; and never failed, whenever they talked those matters over in their evening gossipings, to lay all the blame on Dame Van Winkle. The children of the village, too, would shout with joy whenever he approached. He assisted at their sports, made their playthings, taught them to fly kites and shoot marbles, and told them long stories of ghosts, witches, and Indians. Whenever he went dodging about the village, he was surrounded by a troop of them, hanging on his skirts, clambering on his back, and playing a thousand tricks on him with impunity; and not a dog would bark at him throughout the neighborhood.

The great error in Rip's composition was an insuperable aversion to all kinds of profitable labor. It could not be from the want of assiduity or perseverance; for he would sit on a wet rock, with a rod as long and heavy as a Tartar's lance, and fish all day without a murmur, even though he should not be encouraged by a single nibble. He would carry a fowling-piece on his shoulder for hours together, trudging through woods and swamps, and up hill and down dale, to shoot a few squirrels or wild pigeons. He would never refuse to assist a neighbor, even in the roughest toil, and was a foremost man at all country frolics for husking Indian corn, or building stone-fences; the women of the village, too, used to employ him to run their errands, and to do such little odd jobs as their less obliging husbands would not do for them. In a word, Rip was ready to attend to anybody's business but his own; but as to doing family duty, and keeping his farm in order, he found it impossible.

In fact, he declared it was of no use to work on his farm; it was the most pestilent little piece of ground in the whole country; everything about it went wrong, and would go wrong, in spite of him. His fences were continually falling to pieces; his cow would either go astray or get among the cabbages; weeds were sure to grow quicker in his fields than anywhere else; the rain always made a point of setting in just as he had some outdoor work to do; so that though his patrimonial estate had dwindled away under his management, acre by acre, until there was little more left than a mere patch of Indian corn and potatoes, yet it was the worst-conditioned farm in the neighborhood.

His children, too, were as ragged and wild as if they belonged to nobody. His son Rip, an urchin begotten in his own likeness, promised to inherit the habits, with the old clothes of his father. He was generally seen trooping like a colt at his mother's heels, equipped in a pair of his father's cast-off galligaskins, which he had much ado to hold up with one hand, as a fine lady does her train in bad weather.

Rip Van Winkle, however, was one of those happy mortals, of foolish, well-oiled dispositions, who take the world easy, eat white bread or brown, whichever can be got with least thought or trouble, and would rather starve on a penny than work for a pound. If left to himself, he would have whistled life away in perfect contentment; but his wife kept continually dinning in his ears about his idleness, his carelessness, and the ruin he was bringing on his family. Morning, noon, and night, her tongue was incessantly going, and everything he said or did was sure to produce a torrent of household eloquence. Rip had but one way of replying to all lectures of the kind, and that, by frequent use, had grown into a habit. He shrugged his shoulders, shook his head, cast up his eyes, but said nothing. This, however, always provoked a fresh volley from his wife; so that he was fain to draw off his forces, and take to the outside of the house—the only side which, in truth, belongs to a hen-pecked husband.

Rip's sole domestic adherent was his dog Wolf, who was as much hen-pecked as his master; for Dame Van Winkle regarded them as companions in idleness, and even looked upon Wolf with an evil eye, as the cause of his master's going so often astray. True it is, in all points of spirit befitting an honorable dog, he was as courageous an animal as ever scoured the woods—but what courage can withstand the ever-during and all-besetting terrors of a woman's tongue? The moment Wolf entered the house his crest fell, his tail drooped to the ground, or curled between his legs, he sneaked about with a gallows air, casting many a sidelong glance at Dame Van Winkle, and at the least flourish of a broomstick or ladle he would fly to the door with yelping precipitation.

Times grew worse and worse with Rip Van Winkle as years of matrimony rolled on; a tart temper never mellows with age, and a sharp tongue is the only edged tool that grows keener with constant use. For a long while he used to console himself, when driven from home, by frequenting a kind of perpetual club of the sages, philosophers, and other idle personages of the village, which held its sessions on a bench before a small inn, designated by a rubicund portrait of His Majesty George the Third. Here they used to sit in the shade through a long, lazy summer's day, talking listlessly over village gossip, or telling endless sleepy stories about nothing. But it would have been worth any statesman's money to have heard the profound discussions that sometimes took place, when by chance an old newspaper fell into their hand from some passing traveller. How solemnly they would listen to the contents, as drawled out by Derrick Van Bummel, the schoolmaster, a dapper learned little man, who was not to be daunted by the most gigantic word in the dictionary; and how sagely they would deliberate upon public events some months after they had taken place.

The opinions of this junto were completely controlled by Nicholas Vedder, a patriarch of the village, and landlord of the inn, at the door of which he took his seat from morning till night, just moving sufficiently to avoid the sun and keep in the shade of a large tree; so that the neighbors could tell the hour by his movements as accurately as by a sundial. It is true he was rarely heard to speak, but smoked his pipe incessantly. His adherents, however (for every great man has his adherents), perfectly understood him, and knew how to gather his opinions. When anything that was read or related displeased him, he was observed to smoke his pipe vehemently, and to send forth short, frequent, and angry puffs; but when pleased, he would inhale the smoke slowly

278 : THE RITE OF BECOMING

and tranquilly, and emit it in light and placid clouds; and sometimes, taking the pipe from his mouth, and letting the fragrant vapor curl about his nose, would gravely nod his head in token of perfect approbation.

From even this stronghold the unlucky Rip was at length routed by his termagant wife, who would suddenly break in upon the tranquillity of the assemblage and call the members all to naught; nor was that august personage, Nicholas Vedder himself, sacred from the daring tongue of this terrible virago, who charged him outright with encouraging her husband in habits of idleness.

Poor Rip was at last reduced almost to despair; and his only alternative, to escape from the labor of the farm and clamor of his wife, was to take gun in hand and stroll away into the woods. Here he would sometimes seat himself at the foot of a tree, and share the contents of his wallet with Wolf, with whom he sympathized as a fellow-sufferer in persecution. "Poor Wolf," he would say, "thy mistress leads thee a dog's life of it; but never mind, my lad, whilst I live thou shalt never want a friend to stand by thee!" Wolf would wag his tail, look wistfully in his mater's face; and if dogs can feel pity I verily believe he reciprocated the sentiment with all his heart.

In a long ramble of the kind on a fine autumnal day, Rip had unconsciously scrambled to one of the highest parts of the Kaatskill mountains. He was after his favorite sport of squirrel shooting, and the still solitudes had echoed and reëchoed with the reports of his gun. Panting and fatigued, he threw himself, late in the afternoon, on a green knoll, covered with mountain herbage, that crowned the brow of a precipice. From an opening between the trees he could overlook all the lower country for many a mile of rich woodland. He saw at a distance the lordly Hudson, far, far below him, moving on its silent but majestic course, with the reflection of a purple cloud, or the sail of a lagging bark, here and there sleeping on its glassy bosom, and at last losing itself in the blue highlands.

On the other side he looked down into a deep mountain glen, wild, lonely, and shagged, the bottom filled with fragments from the impending cliffs, and scarcely lighted by the reflected rays of the setting sun. For some time Rip lay musing on this scene; evening was gradually advancing; the mountains began to throw their long blue shadows over the valleys; he saw that it would be dark long before he could reach the village, and he heaved a heavy sigh when he thought of encountering the terrors of Dame Van Winkle.

As he was about to descend, he heard a voice from a distance, hallooing, "Rip Van Winkle, Rip Van Winkle!" He looked round, but could see nothing but a crow winging its solitary flight across the mountain. He thought his fancy must have deceived him, and turned again to descend, when he heard the same cry ring through the still evening air: "Rip Van Winkle! Rip Van Winkle!"— at the same time Wolf bristled up his back, and giving a low growl, skulked to his master's side, looking fearfully down into the glen. Rip now felt a vague apprehension stealing over him; he looked anxiously in the same direction, and perceived a strange figure slowly toiling up the rocks, and bending under the weight of something he carried on his back. He was surprised to see any human being in this lonely and unfrequented place; but supposing it to be some one of the neighborhood in need of his assistance, he hastened down to yield it.

On nearer approach he was still more surprised at the singularity of the stranger's appearance. He was a short, square-built old fellow, with thick bushy hair, and a grizzled beard. His dress was of the antique Dutch fashion,—a cloth jerkin strapped round the waist—several pair of breeches, the outer one of ample volume, decorated with rows of buttons down the sides, and bunches at the knees. He bore on his shoulder a stout keg, that seemed full of liquor, and made signs for Rip to approach and assist him with the load. Though rather shy and distrustful of this new acquaintance, Rip complied with his usual alacrity; and mutually relieving one another, they clambered up a narrow gully, apparently the dry bed of a mountain torrent. As they ascended, Rip every now and then heard long, rolling peals, like distant thunder, that seemed to issue out of a deep ravine, or rather cleft, between lofty rocks, toward which their rugged path conducted. He paused for an instant, but supposing it to be the muttering of one of those transient thunder-showers which often take place in mountain heights, he proceeded. Passing through the ravine, they came to a hollow, like a small amphitheatre, surrounded by perpendicular precipices, over the brinks of which impending trees shot their branches, so that you only caught glimpses of the azure sky and the bright evening cloud. During the whole time Rip and his companion had labored on in silence; for though the former marvelled greatly what could be the object of carrying a keg of liquor up this wild mountain, yet there was something strange and incomprehensible about the unknown, that inspired awe and checked familiarity.

On entering the amphitheatre, new objects of wonder presented themselves. On a level spot in the center was a company of odd-looking personages playing at ninepins. They were dressed in a quaint, outlandish fashion; some wore short doublets, others jerkins, with long knives in their belts, and most of them had enormous breeches, of similar style with that of the guide's. Their visages, too, were peculiar: one had a large beard, broad face, and small piggish eyes; the face of another seemed to consist entirely of nose, and was surmounted by a white sugar-loaf hat, set off with a little red cock's tail. They all had beards, of various shapes and colors. There was one who seemed to be the commander. He was a stout old gentleman, with a weather-beaten countenance; he wore a laced doublet, broad belt and hanger, high-crowned hat and feather, red stockings, and high-heeled shoes, with roses in them. The whole group reminded Rip of the figures in an old Flemish painting in the parlor of Dominie Van Shaick, the village parson, and which had been brought over from Holland at the time of the settlement.

What seemed particularly odd to Rip was, that though these folks were evidently amusing themselves, yet they maintained the gravest faces, the most mysterious silence, and were, withal, the most melancholy party of pleasure he had ever witnessed. Nothing interrupted the stillness of the scene but the noise of the balls, which, whenever they were rolled, echoed along the mountains like rumbling peals of thunder.

As Rip and his companion approached them, they suddenly desisted from their play, and stared at him with such fixed, statue-like gaze, and such strange, uncouth, lack-lustre countenances, that his heart turned within him, and his knees smote together. His companion now emptied the contents of the keg into large flagons, and made signs to him to wait upon the company. He obeyed with fear and trembling; they quaffed the liquor in profound silence, and then returned to their game.

By degrees Rip's awe and apprehension subsided. He even ventured, when no eye was fixed upon him, to taste the beverage, which he found had much of the flavor of excellent Hollands. He was naturally a thirsty soul, and was soon tempted to repeat the draught. One taste provoked another; and he reiterated his visits to the flagon so often that at length his senses were overpowered, his eyes swam in his head, his head gradually declined, and he fell into a deep sleep.

On waking, he found himself on the green knoll whence he had first seen the old man of the glen. He rubbed his eyes—it was a bright, sunny morning. The birds were hopping and twittering among the bushes, and the eagle was wheeling aloft, and breasting the pure mountain breeze. "Surely," thought Rip, "I have not slept here all night." He recalled the occurrences before he fell asleep. The strange man with a keg of liquor—the mountain ravine—the wild retreat among the rocks—the woe-begone party at ninepins—the flagon— "Oh! that flagon! that wicked flagon!" thought Rip—"what excuse shall I make to Dame Van Winkle?"

He looked round for his gun, but in place of the clean, well-oiled fowlingpiece, he found an old firelock lying by him, the barrel incrusted with rust, the lock falling off, and the stock worm-eaten. He now suspected that the grave roisters of the mountain had put a trick upon him, and, having dosed him with liquor, had robbed him of his gun. Wolf, too, had disappeared, but he might have strayed away after a squirrel or partridge. He whistled after him, and shouted his name, but all in vain; the echoes repeated his whistle and shout, but no dog was to be seen.

He determined to revisit the scene of the last evening's gambol, and if he met with any of the party, to demand his dog and gun. As he rose to walk, he found himself stiff in the joints, and wanting in his usual activity. "These mountain beds do not agree with me," thought Rip, "and if this frolic should lay me up with a fit of the rheumatism, I shall have a blessed time with Dame Van Winkle." With some difficulty he got down into the glen: he found the gully up which he and his companion had ascended the preceding evening;

but to his astonishment a mountain stream was now foaming down it, leaping from rock to rock, and filling the glen with babbling murmurs. He, however, made shift to scramble up its sides, working his toilsome way through thickets of birch, sassafras, and witch-hazel, and sometimes tripped up or entangled by the wild grapevines that twisted their coils or tendrils from tree to tree, and spread a kind of network in his path.

At length he reached to where the ravine had opened through the cliffs to the amphitheatre; but no traces of such opening remained. The rocks presented a high, impenetrable wall, over which the torrent came tumbling in a sheet of feathery foam, and fell into a broad, deep basin, black from the shadows of the surrounding forest. Here, then, poor Rip was brought to a stand. He again called and whistled after his dog; he was only answered by the cawing of a flock of idle crows, sporting high in air about a dry tree that overhung a sunny precipice; and who, secure in their elevation, seemed to look down and scoff at the poor man's perplexities. What was to be done? the morning was passing away, and Rip felt famished for want of his breakfast. He grieved to give up his dog and gun; he dreaded to meet his wife; but it would not do to starve among the mountains. He shook his head, shouldered the rusty firelock, and, with a heart full of trouble and anxiety, turned his steps homeward.

As he approached the village he met a number of people, but none whom he knew, which somewhat surprised him, for he had thought himself acquainted with every one in the country round. Their dress, too, was of a different fashion from that to which he was accustomed. They all stared at him with equal marks of surprise, and whenever they cast their eyes upon him, invariably stroked their chins. The constant recurrence of this gesture induced Rip, involuntarily, to do the same, when, to his astonishment, he found his beard had grown a foot long!

He had now entered the skirts of the village. A troop of strange children ran at his heels, hooting after him, and pointing at his gray beard. The dogs, too, not one of which he recognized for an old acquaintance, barked at him as he passed. The very village was altered; it was larger and more populous. There were rows of houses which he had never seen before, and those which had been his familiar haunts had disappeared. Strange names were over the doors—strange faces at the windows—everything was strange. His mind now misgave him; he began to doubt whether both he and the world around him were not bewitched. Surely this was his native village, which he had left but the day before. There stood the Kaatskill mountains—there ran the silver Hudson at a distance—there was every hill and dale precisely as it had always been. Rip was sorely perplexed. "That flagon last night," thought he, "has addled my poor head sadly!"

It was with some difficulty that he found the way to his own house, which he approached with silent awe, expecting every moment to hear the shrill voice of Dame Van Winkle. He found the house gone to decay—the roof fallen in, the windows shattered, and the doors off the hinges. A half-starved dog that looked like Wolf was skulking about it. Rip called him by name, but the cur snarled, showed his teeth, and passed on. This was an unkind cut indeed— "My very dog," sighed poor Rip, "has forgotten me!" He entered the house, which, to tell the truth, Dame Van Winkle had always kept in neat order. It was empty, forlorn, and apparently abandoned. This desolateness overcame all his connubial fears—he called loudly for his wife and children—the lonely chambers rang for a moment with his voice, and then again all was silence.

He now hurried forth, and hastened to his old resort, the village inn—but it, too, was gone. A large, rickety wooden building stood in its place, with great gaping windows, some of them broken and mended with old hats and petticoats, and over the door was painted, "The Union Hotel, by Jonathan Doolittle." Instead of the great tree that used to shelter the quiet little Dutch inn of yore, there now was reared a tall naked pole, with something on the top that looked like a red night-cap, and from it was fluttering a flag, on which was a singular assemblage of stars and stripes—all this was strange and incomprehensible. He recognized on the sign, however, the ruby face of King George, under which he had smoked so many a peaceful pipe; but even this was singularly metamorphosed. The red coat was changed for one of blue and buff, a sword was held in the hand instead of a sceptre, the head was decorated with a cocked hat, and underneath was painted in large characters, GENERAL WASHINGTON.

There was, as usual, a crowd of folk about the door, but none that Rip recollected. The very character of the people seemed changed. There was a busy, bustling, disputatious tone about it, instead of the accustomed phlegm and drowsy tranquillity. He looked in vain for the sage Nicholas Vedder, with his broad face, double chin, and fair long pipe, uttering clouds of tobacco-smoke instead of idle speeches; or Van Bummel, the schoolmaster, doling forth the contents of an ancient newspaper. In place of these, a lean, bilious-looking fellow, with his pockets full of handbills, was haranguing vehemently about rights of citizens—elections—members of Congress—liberty—Bunker's Hill— heroes of seventy-six—and other words, which were a perfect Babylonish jargon to the bewildered Van Winkle.

The appearance of Rip, with his long grizzled beard, his rusty fowling-piece, his uncouth dress, and an army of women and children at his heels, soon attracted the attention of the tavern-politicians. They crowded round him, eyeing him from head to foot with great curiosity. The orator bustled up to him, and, drawing him partly aside, inquired "on which side he voted?" Rip stared in vacant stupidity. Another short but busy little fellow pulled him by the arm, and, rising on tiptoe, inquired in his ear, "Whether he was Federal or Democrat?" Rip was equally at a loss to comprehend the question; when a knowing, self-important old gentleman, in a sharp cocked hat, made his way through the crowd, putting them to the right and left with his elbows as he passed, and planting himself before Van Winkle, with one arm akimbo, the other resting on his cane, his keen eyes and sharp hat penetrating, as it were, into his very soul, demanded in an austere tone, "what brought him to the election with a gun on his shoulder, and a mob at his heels, and whether he meant to breed a riot in the village?"—"Alas! gentlemen," cried Rip, somewhat dismayed, "I am a poor quiet man, a native of the place, and a loyal subject of the king, God bless him!"

Here a general shout burst from the bystanders—"A tory! a tory! a spy! a refugee! hustle him! away with him!" It was with great difficulty that the self-important man in the cocked hat restored order; and, having assumed a tenfold austerity of brow, demanded again of the unknown culprit what he came there for, and whom he was seeking? The poor man humbly assured him that he meant no harm, but merely came there in search of some of his neighbors, who used to keep about the tavern.

"Well—who are they?—name them."

Rip bethought himself a moment, and inquired, "Where's Nicholas Vedder?"

There was a silence for a little while, when an old man replied, in a thin, piping voice: "Nicholas Vedder! why, he is dead and gone these eighteen years! There was a wooden tombstone in the churchyard that used to tell all about him, but that's rotten and gone too."

"Where's Brom Dutcher?"

"Oh, he went off to the army in the beginning of the war; some say he was killed at the storming of Stony Point—others say he was drowned in a squall at the foot of Antony's Nose. I don't know—he never came back again."

"Where's Van Bummel, the schoolmaster?"

"He went off to the wars too, was a great militia general, and is now in Congress."

Rip's heart died away at hearing of these sad changes in his home and friends, and finding himself thus alone in the world. Every answer puzzled him too, by treating of such enormous lapses of time, and of matters which he could not understand: war—Congress—Stony Point; he had no courage to ask after any more friends, but cried out in despair, "Does nobody here know Rip Van Winkle?"

"Oh, Rip Van Winkle!" exclaimed two or three, "Oh, to be sure! that's Rip Van Winkle yonder, leaning against the tree."

Rip looked, and beheld a precise counterpart of himself, as he went up the mountain: apparently as lazy, and certainly as ragged. The poor fellow was now completely confounded. He doubted his own identity, and whether he was himself or another man. In the midst of his bewilderment, the man in the cocked hat demanded who he was, and what was his name?

"God knows," exclaimed he, at his wit's end; "I'm not myself—I'm some-

body else—that's me yonder—no—that's somebody else got into my shoes—
I was myself, last night, but I fell asleep on the mountain and they've changed
my gun, and everything's changed, and I'm changed, and I can't tell what's my
name, or who I am!"

The bystanders began now to look at each other, nod, wink significantly,
and tap their fingers against their foreheads. There was a whisper, also, about
securing the gun, and keeping the old fellow from doing mischief, at the
very suggestion of which the self-important man in the cocked hat retired
with some precipitation. At this critical moment a fresh, comely woman
pressed through the throng to get a peep at the gray-bearded man. She had
a chubby child in her arms, which, frightened at his looks, began to cry. "Hush,
Rip," cried she, "hush, you little fool; the old man won't hurt you." The name
of the child, the air of the mother, the tone of her voice, all awakened a
train of recollections in his mind. "What is your name, my good woman?"
asked he.

"Judith Gardenier."

"And your father's name?"

"Ah, poor man, Rip Van Winkle was his name, but it's twenty years since
he went away from home with his gun, and never has been heard of since,—
his dog came home without him, but whether he shot himself, or was carried
away by the Indians, nobody can tell. I was then but a little girl."

Rip had but one question more to ask; and he put it with a faltering voice:
"Where's your mother?"

"Oh, she too had died but a short time since; she broke a blood-vessel in a
fit of passion at a New England peddler."

There was a drop of comfort, at least, in this intelligence. The honest man
could contain himself no longer. He caught his daughter and her child in his
arms. "I am your father!" cried he—"Young Rip Van Wankle once—old Rip
Van Winkle now! Does nobody know poor Rip Van Winkle?"

All stood amazed, until an old woman, tottering out from among the
crowd, put her hand to her brow, and peering under it in his face for a
moment, exclaimed, "Sure enough it is Rip Van Winkle—it is himself! Welcome home again, old neighbor—Why, where have you been these twenty
long years?"

Rip's story was soon told, for the whole twenty years had been to him but
as one night. The neighbors stared when they heard it; some were seen to
wink at each other, and put their tongues in their cheeks; and the self-
important man in the cocked hat, who, when the alarm was over, had returned to the field, screwed down the corners of his mouth, and shook his
head—upon which there was a general shaking of the head throughout the
assemblage.

It was determined, however, to take the opinion of old Peter Vanderdonk,
who was seen slowly advancing up the road. He was a descendant of the

historian of that name, who wrote one of the earliest accounts of the province. Peter was the most ancient inhabitant of the village, and well versed in all the wonderful events and traditions of the neighborhood. He recollected Rip at once, and corroborated his story in the most satisfactory manner. He assured the company that it was a fact, handed down from his ancestor the historian, that the Kaatskill mountains had always been haunted by strange beings. That it was affirmed that the great Hendrick Hudson, the first discoverer of the river and country, kept a kind of vigil there every twenty years, with his crew of the Half-moon; being permitted in this way to revisit the scenes of his enterprise, and keep a guardian eye upon the river and the great city called by his name. That his father had once seen them in their old Dutch dresses playing at ninepins in a hollow of the mountain; and that he himself had heard, one summer afternoon, the sound of their balls, like distant peals of thunder.

To make a long story short, the company broke up, and returned to the more important concerns of the election. Rip's daughter took him home to live with her; she had a snug well-furnished house, and a stout cheery farmer for a husband, whom Rip recollected for one of the urchins that used to climb upon his back. As to Rip's son and heirs, who was the ditto of himself, seen leaning against the tree, he was employed to work on the farm, but evinced an hereditary disposition to attend to anything else but his business.

Rip now resumed his old walks and habits; he soon found many of his former cronies, though all rather the worse for the wear and tear of time, and preferred making friends among the rising generation, with whom he soon grew into great favor.

Having nothing to do at home, and being arrived at that happy age when a man can be idle with impunity, he took his place once more on the bench at the inn door, and was reverenced as one of the patriarchs of the village, and a chronicle of the old times "before the war." It was some time before he could get into the regular track of gossip, or could be made to comprehend the strange events that had taken place during his torpor. How that there had been a revolutionary war—that the country had thrown off the yoke of old England—and that, instead of being a subject of His Majesty George the Third, he was now a free citizen of the United States. Rip, in fact, was no politician; the changes of states and empires made but little impression on him; but there was one species of despotism under which he had long groaned, and that was—petticoat government. Happily that was at an end; he had got his neck out of the yoke of matrimony, and could go in and out whenever he pleased, without dreading the tyranny of Dame Van Winkle. Whenever her name was mentioned, however, he shook his head, shrugged his shoulders, and cast up his eyes, which might pass either for an expression of resignation to his fate, or joy at his deliverance.

He used to tell his story to every stranger that arrived at Mr. Doolittle's hotel. He was observed, at first, to vary on some points every time he told it, which was, doubtless, owing to his having so recently awaked. It at last settled down precisely to the tale I have related, and not a man, woman, or child in the neighborhood but knew it by heart. Some always pretended to doubt the reality of it, and insisted that Rip had been out of his head, and that this was one point on which he always remained flighty. The old Dutch inhabitants, however, almost universally gave it full credit. Even to this day they never hear a thunder-storm of a summer afternoon about the Kaatskill, but they say Hendrick Hudson and his crew are at their game of ninepins; and it is a common wish of all henpecked husbands in the neighborhood, when life hangs heavy on their hands, that they might have a quieting draught out of Rip Van Winkle's flagon.

NOTE

The foregoing Tale, one would suspect, had been suggested to Mr. Knickerbocker by a little German superstition about the Emperor Frederick *der Rothbart,* and the Kypphäuser mountain; the subjoined note, however, which he had appended to the tale, shows that it is an absolute fact, narrated with his usual fidelity.

"The story of Rip Van Winkle may seem incredible to many, but nevertheless I give it my full belief, for I know the vicinity of our old Dutch settlements to have been very subject to marvellous events and appearances. Indeed, I have heard many stranger stories than this, in the villages along the Hudson; all of which were too well authenticated to admit of a doubt. I have even talked with Rip Van Winkle myself, who, when last I saw him, was a very old venerable man, and so perfectly rational and consistent on every other point, that I think no conscientious person could refuse to take this into the bargain; nay, I have seen a certificate on the subject taken before a country justice and signed with a cross, in the justice's own handwriting. The story, therefore, is beyond the possibility of doubt.

"D. K."

POSTSCRIPT

The following are travelling notes from a memorandum-book of Mr. Knicker-bocker.

The Kaatsberg, or Catskill Mountains, have always been a region full of fable. The Indians considered them the abode of spirits, who influenced the weather, spreading sunshine or clouds over the landscape, and sending good or bad hunting-seasons. They were ruled by an old squaw spirit, said to be their mother. She dwelt on the highest peak of the Catskills, and had charge of the doors of day and night to open and shut them at the proper hour. She hung up the new moons in the skies, and cut up the old ones into stars. In times of drought, if properly propitiated, she would spin light summer clouds out of cobwebs and morning dew, and send them off from the crest of the mountain, flake after flake, like flakes of carded cotton, to float in the air; until, dissolved by the heat of the sun, they would fall in gentle showers, causing the grass to spring, the fruits to ripen, and the corn to grow an inch an hour. If displeased, however, she would brew up clouds black as ink, sitting in the midst of them like a bottle-bellied spider in the midst of its web; and when these clouds broke, woe betide the valleys!

In old times, say the Indian traditions, there was a kind of Manitou or Spirit, who kept about the wildest recesses of the Catskill Mountains, and took a mischievous pleasure in wreaking all kinds of evils and vexations upon the red men. Sometimes he would assume the form of a bear, a panther, or a deer, lead the bewildered hunter a weary chase through tangled forests and among ragged rocks; and then spring off with a loud ho! ho! leaving him aghast on the brink of a beetling precipice or raging torrent.

The favorite abode of this Manitou is still shown. It is a great rock or cliff on the loneliest part of the mountains, and, from the flowering vines which clamber about it, and the wild flowers which abound in its neighborhood, is known by the name of the Garden Rock. Near the foot of it is a small lake, the haunt of the solitary bittern, with water-snakes basking in the sun on the leaves of the pond-lilies which lie on the surface. This place was held in great awe by the Indians, insomuch that the boldest hunter would not pursue his game within its precincts. Once upon a time, however, a hunter who had lost his way, penetrated to the Garden Rock, where he beheld a number of gourds placed in the crotches of trees. One of these he seized and made off with it, but in the hurry of his retreat he let it fall among the rocks, when a great stream gushed forth which washed him away and swept him down precipices, where he was dashed to pieces, and the stream made its way to the Hudson, and continues to flow to the present day; being the identical stream known by the name of the Kaaters-kill.

MORE ABOUT THIS STORY

The latter portion of Philip Young's essay "Fallen From Time: The Mythic Rip Van Winkle," reprinted here, considers both the mythic and psychological implications of the tale. In the earlier stages of his argument, Mr. Young presents several analogues to "Rip Van Winkle" (Greek, Welsh, Chinese, Japanese, and German) and points to similarities linking them to one another: the hero sleeps for a long period of time; he enters a mysterious mountain and encounters strange-looking men; he watches a game—commonly bowling—and hears thunder; he quaffs a draught that both invigorates and over-powers him; he returns at last—much altered—to the real world.

All of these stories, Mr. Young suggests, seem to share a ritualistic origin, that is, they dramatize an event in the life of some divinity, usually the god who founded the rite. After considerable time, as Mr. Young indicates, "the rite may be performed more out of piety than from any belief in its efficacy, and finally may be forgotten while the myth endures."

"Rip Van Winkle," then, is our version of a myth that survives as a description of a nearly forgotten ceremony in the worship of Thor for the production of rain. It proceeds by a symbolic imitation of how rain is made. The ritual is of the magical sort, and is intended to influence nature through the physical sympathy, or resemblance, between the ceremony and the effect it is supposd to produce.[1] Indeed, the story is an example of what Robert Graves has called "true myth": it is an instance of "the reduction to narrative shorthand of ritual mime."

Exactly *why* Rip was allowed to witness this mystery is a secret which, since he was ignorant of the reason himself, he has been able to keep for many generations. So, in all likelihood, was Irving unaware of the original reason for the outsider's presence at the ceremony: even by Peter Klaus's [2] time the myth had so badly deteriorated into folklore that only the fragments we are deciphering remained. But the secret is out by now: Rip and Peter were initiates. Rip goes right through the steps: while he sits dreamily and alone on the green knoll the period of preliminary isolation passes; then he is summoned by name. Helping to carry the heavy keg up the side of the ravine, which he may have had to volunteer to do, is a sort of test. There followed a kind of procession, and something like a vigil, and finally the experience of communication with the divinity and his disciples. Rip is even given a magic drink, which as a novice he is first required to serve, and after this he is plunged into the magic sleep. When he wakes he is in a new phase of life, and on this level the great changes he finds about him are symbols of the changes in him, and of the differences in his situation, now he is initiate.

Rip has also been reborn in another, reinforcing way, for the imagery of his emergence into a new life inevitably and unavoidably suggests an issue "from the womb." This concept, which is often thrown about gratuitously, really urges itself here, for Irving's description of the entrance to the mountain, taken from "Peter Klaus," is extremely arresting—almost as pointed, say, as accounts anthropologists have given of pits dug in the ground by primitive tribesmen, and trimmed about the edges with overhanging shrubbery (which ditches the men dance about in the spring, while brandishing their spears and chanting that these are no ditches, but what they were built to represent). The imagery is the same when Rip is led eerily through the ravine till he comes to the bottom of a hollow, surrounded by perpendicular precipices, over the brinks of which hang the branches of trees.

From this setting he is delivered into his old age. Ripe for escape before, he has experienced an escape only one step short of death. Apparently well into middle age, and saddled with a wife who had completely lost her desirability, he laid down his gun and entered the mountain. Here he witnessed some symbolical activity—which, in the severely censored form of the pin and bowling balls,

---

[1] The thunder that Thor made came ordinarily from the roar of his chariot, of course, but the method described in the myth Irving drew on is by no means unknown. Grimm reported that on hearing thunder North Germans were likely to remark, "The angels are playing at bowls"; and in our own country there is a close parallel in the mythology of the Zuñi Indians of New Mexico, whose warriors when they die go off to make lightning in the sky, where rainmakers cause thunder with great "gaming stones." [P. Y.]

[2] Irving acknowledged familiarity with the German folk tale of Peter Klaus. [Ed.]

has overtones of human, as well as vegetable, fertility—and he saw it all as joyless and melancholy. Magically confirmed in his own feeling about the matter, he drank, slept like a baby, and was released into the world he had longed for—into an all-male society, the perpetual men's club that used to meet at the inn, which his wife can no longer violate as, unforgivably, she had done before. His gun is ruined and useless, and his wife is gone. But it makes no difference now; he has slept painlessly through his "change of life."

The trouble with this story as some kind of "male-menopause myth" is that the reading is partly based on a misinterpretation attributed, perhaps unfairly, to Rip. Lacking the information we have, he made a mistake: the men were lifeless and unhappy at their bowling because they were dead. More than that, they were still the followers of Thor, whose sign was lightning and whose emblem was a hammer. Thor was god of power, and of human fertility as well as vegetable. He was god of the vital moistures in general, an ithyphallic, not a detumescent, god. Even dead, his worshippers made a great deal of noise in his service. In short, the bowling which sends thunder across the Catskills is violently masculine symbolic activity in a very feminine mountain. And in this last vague but massive symbol is a final irony, for the mystery revealed to Rip had thus two aspects, animal or human, and vegetable—one for each of Thor's two fertility powers.

Of what pertinence were all these revelations to Rip? What does it mean to him that the strange men he saw have come down to us from the men of Thor, or that he was initiated into an ancient mystery and shown the sacred secrets of all life? No relevance at all to him and no meaning whatever. And that is the ironical point. Befuddled, unwitting, and likeable old Rip: no man in the valley, luxuriantly green already, thought less or as little about the crops, and no man he knew could have been chosen to witness the secrets of human fertility and found them more sleep-provoking.

What would have interested him, and what did he want? Concentrating somewhat anthropologically on the story's central scene in an attempt to get at the bottom of it, we have not got to the bottom of the character. But if for a moment we will think more as psychologists, and consider the story as a sort of dream— as a product of the unconscious, itself a kind of anthropologist—we open a whole new and remarkable area of meaning. Suddenly everything seems illusive, unreal; time goes into abeyance and the sense of history is lost; the very identity of the central figure is shaken, and reason dissolves.

The easiest entry to the dream level of "Rip Van Winkle" passes through that inn where Rip once sat with his friends—the inn which was "gone," and replaced by a hotel straight out of nightmare: "a large rickety wooden building . . . with great gaping windows . . . mended with old hats and petticoats"—and in front a sign with a familiar face all out of place in its setting. Soon, however, "idle with impunity" and "reverenced as one of the patriarchs of the village," Rip "took his place once more on the bench at the inn door." A conflict in Irving explains the confusion. He wanted to show the great changes a revolution had brought, but wished more deeply to feel, and wanted us to feel, that aside from the happy loss of his wife nothing had really happened to Rip. Toynbee, responding fully to this absence of time and change, made what amounts to the same mistake. But it is a meaningful slip, and on one level they are both right. For Rip, time and history *have* ceased operation. Nothing *has* happened, and the inn is there to signal the fact. What, then, are we to think when we come to the start of the very next paragraph and are told (in a kind of preliminary postscript at the end of the tale proper) that Rip is now telling his story "to every stranger that arrived at Mr. Doolittle's hotel"? The inn is there, is gone and replaced, is there again, is gone again. Reality is slithering away; and so it must eventually do, for this is not ultimately its world. Nor is this truly the world of fiction, unless of Kafka's. It is the world of the unconscious, where time and history are not suspended, exactly, but do not exist—where everything exists at once. It is the region where people and things are always appearing in unreasonable places, and everything is passing strange: but distorted toward some hard-to-recognize truth. The recurring transformation of Irving's hostelry belongs in this night world. It represents a "willful accident," and as such makes its own kind of sense. Irving was groping very darkly in a world of symbol, myth, and dream for meanings beyond awareness.

In this strange new world Rip's identity is harder to establish than the identity of that shifting meeting place. Removed as he is from time, the confusion of generations is appalling, and he is hard pressed to know in which of at least three generations he really "belongs." It will be next to impossible to know for sure, for the truth is he had almost as little part in his own generation as the one he slept through. This was entirely clear, had we the wit to see it, when we first met him. He was not an adult, but a child playing with children, a kid with a dog. He lived with his wife, to be sure, but only in a manner of speaking, for he accepted instead his "only alternative": "to take gun in hand and stroll away into the wood." Or, more striking, he would escape her by sitting on a wet rock with a rod in his hand "as long and heavy as a Tartar's lance, and fish all day . . . even though he should not be encouraged by a single nibble." "A great favorite among all the good wives of the village," he ran their errands and did "such little jobs as their less obliging husbands would not do for them"—not, by pointed implication, what their husbands would do: "as to doing family duty . . . he found it impossible."

At the inn with the menfolk, Rip shows that he wants to be a father. But at home he is a son, and not up to it: he is the son who wants to be the father, but his mother won't let him. He represents, to be technical for a moment, the ego arrested at the infantile level in an Oedipal situation; under pressure he reverts all the way back to the sleep of the womb.

The scene in the mountain now takes on a new and different suggestiveness. It is at once the dream of a child and an adult dream reflecting Rip's own predicament. The great noses of the mountain men give the next phallic clue, as they must likewise have done in the ancient Teutonic mythology (the psychoanalytic and the anthropological mix well: they are both—the first personally, the second culturally—"regressive"). From this viewpoint the dwarfs are really disguised little boys with pins and balls practicing, in highly activated silence, a forbidden rite; Rip is not invited to play too, and they make him work, so he sneaks their drink and goes off to sleep. On the other hand the dwarfs are also many mirrors to the "adult" Rip, held up as revelations which his conciousness is not likely to read: they are aged little men playing games, who have grown old but not up. Our protagonist, then, is both gerontion and child—or is neither, precisely. He has nor youth nor age, but as it were an after-dinner's sleep, dreaming on both.

On his return to the village, the sense of the decomposition of his "self" becomes even more awesome. His wife-mother is gone, but he is still a child as much as he is anything, and as such he must find his role in a relationship to someone else. But now it is completely bewildering. He is soon confronted with the very "ditto of himself," a negligent loafer named Rip—actually his son. Worse, he faces a woman who seems both strange and, as his poor mind struggles into recollection, hauntingly familiar. She had, she says, a father named Rip, and she carries in her arms a child of that name. Who, then, is our protagonist? His own unaccepted and "impossible" self, or the son of his wife that he used to be and emotionally remains? Or his own son, the loafer leaning there against the tree and, after the ravages of twenty years that passed as a night, looking more like the man Rip impersonated than he suddenly does himself? Or perhaps another Rip, the child of his daughter, now surrogate for his departed wife, and the sign of his true emotional state? Or even, conceivably, the husband, of this replacement-wife-mother, and the father of this son—or that one, or of himself? The sense of generation is shattered; his daughter's house, in which he lives, is a whole house of mirrors, and everywhere he looks he sees a different distortion. He has one moment of panicked insight: "God knows . . . I'm not myself— I'm somebody else—that's me yonder—no—that's somebody else got into my shoes. . . ." Small wonder he departs all the sons Rip and the rejuvenated mother for the security of the role he can play at Mr. Doolittle's.

It is clear now that Rip escaped no change of life, but his very manhood—went from childhood to second childhood with next to nothing in between. It is not just his wife he has dodged, either, but all the obligations of maturity: occupation, domestic and financial responsibility, a political position, duty to society in a time of war. His relation to history is so ambiguous that—ridiculous suspicion—he is thought a spy. Charming and infantile, he narcissistically prefers himself; he will tell his tale of twenty years' sleep at Mr. Doolittle's, where Irving leaves him for the last time. It has become a symbol for the sleep that has been his life.

Considering the universality of his fame, it is a wonder that no European, say, has pointed gleefully to this figure as a symbol of America, for he presents a near perfect image of the way a large part of the world looks at us: likeable enough, up to a point and at times, but essentially immature, self-centered, careless, and above all—and perhaps dangerously—innocent. Even more pointedly Rip is a stereotype of the American male as seen from abroad, or in some jaundiced quarters at home: he is perfectly the jolly overgrown child, abysmally ignorant of his own wife and the whole world of adult men—perpetually "one of the boys," hanging around what they are pleased to think of as a "perpetual men's club"; a disguised Rotarian who simply will not and cannot grow up. In moments of candor we will probably admit that a stereotype with no germ of truth in it could not exist: some such mythic America, some such mythic American, exist both actually and in the consciousness of the world. Rip will do very well as their prototype.

"Rip Van Winkle" is then, and, finally, a wonderfully rich tale—the richest in our lifetime—and an astonishingly complex experience arising from a struggle among many kinds of meaning. On the "prehistoric" level we are dimly aware of immemorial ritual significance, on the psychological of an extraordinary picture of the self arrested in a timeless infancy—rich appeals, both, to the child and primitive in everyone that never grow up and never die in anyone. These awarenesses conflict in the story, as they do in life, with the adult and rational perception that we do indeed grow old, that time and history never stop. In much the same way our affection for Rip himself must oppose our reluctant discovery that as a man we cannot fully respect him.

But in addition to all his other sides, this remarkable Van Winkle also, of course, projects and personifies our sense of the flight—and more: the ravages—of time. And this is what wins us ultimately to his side. We know perfectly well that as an adult this darling of generations of Americans will not entirely do. But if he does seem, finally, meek, blessed, pure in heart, and if we mock him for what he has missed we do it tenderly—partly because it is something hidden in ourselves we mock. And this is not just our own hidden childishness. It is all our own lost lives and roles, the lives and roles that once seemed possible and are possible no more. In twenty years all springs are over; without mockery it might be too sad to bear. Today would grieve, and tomorrow would grieve; best cover it over lightly.

And so here is Rip at the end: Lazarus come from the dead, come back to tell us all. He will tell us all, and, badgering any who will listen, he tries: Well now! —have you heard what happened to *me?* But it won't do; he doesn't know. And that is a pity, truly. Here is a man in whom rest complexities and deficiencies a lifetime might contemplate, as the world has done; a man who has peered toward the dawn of civilization, witnessed ancient mysteries, and stared at his essential nature; a man who now in town is looking at the future and realizing a dream of the ages. And he cannot communicate his visions.

But supposing that he could, that he could tell us all: Would it have been worthwhile? Visions, revelations like these are private. To translate what the thunder meant, to confront the meaning of life and the future of all our childish selves, we all have to go up into our own mountains.

FOR FURTHER READING

Campbell, Joseph. *The Hero with a Thousand Faces.* New York: Meridian Books, 1956, pp. 218–221, 226.

Heiman, Marcel. "Rip Van Winkle: A Psychoanalytic Note on the Story and Its Author," *American Imago,* XVI (1959), 3–47.

LeFevre, Louis, "Paul Bunyan and Rip Van Winkle," *Yale Review,* XXXVI (1946), 66–76.

Williams, Stanley T. "Washington Irving," in *The Literary History of the United States,* ed. R. E. Spiller *et al.* New York: Macmillan, 1948, pp. 242–252.

13-402